What the
Negro Wants

The African American Intellectual Heritage Series

What the Negro Wants

with A New Introduction
and Bibliography
by Kenneth Robert Janken

Edited by
Rayford W. Logan

UNIVERSITY OF NOTRE DAME PRESS
Notre Dame, Indiana

Library of Congress Cataloging-in-Publication Data
What the Negro wants / edited by Rayford W. Logan.
p.   cm. — (African American intellectual heritage series)
Originally published: Chapel Hill, N.C. : University of North Carolina Press,
1944. With new introd. and bibliographic update by Kenneth Robert
Janken, and pref. written by Logan for 1969 reprint.
Includes bibliographical references.
ISBN 0-268-01966-5 (alk. paper) —
ISBN 13: 978-0-268-01964-8 (pbk.: alk. paper)—
ISBN 10: 0-268-01964-9 (pbk.: alk. paper)
1. Afro-Americans—Civil rights. 2. Afro-Americans—Social conditions—
To 1964. 3. United States—Race relations. I. Logan, Rayford
Whittingham, 1897– II. Series.

E185.61.W57   2001
305'.96'073—dc21   00-049101

CONTENTS

WHAT THE NEGRO WANTS

INTRODUCTION TO RAYFORD W. LOGAN'S

WHAT THE NEGRO WANTS

BY KENNETH ROBERT JANKEN

The appearance in 1944 of *What the Negro Wants* by the University of North Carolina Press was a programmatic milestone in the history of the Civil Rights Movement. The controversy surrounding its publication is an outstanding example of racial paternalism and a startling instance of Southern liberal hypocrisy. Entering the World War II era, many African American leaders had preserved a measure of faith in the good will of white Southern liberals; the papers of Walter White, Secretary of the National Association for the Advancement of Colored People, are littered with items dating from the 1920s, 1930s, and 1940s expressing eternal hope that they could become active partners in the fight for black equality. But by the time *What the Negro Wants* was issued, this hope was all but gone, dispatched by the liberals' own mendacity.[1]

What the Negro Wants, a collection of essays by fourteen African American leaders, was edited by Rayford Logan, the prominent African American historian at Howard University. It went beyond other well-known books by African Americans on the race question published over the previous fifteen years. Robert Russa Moton, in *What the Negro Thinks* (1929), catalogued the grievances of "thinking Negroes" in such spheres of life as public transportation, housing, suffrage, and public policy;

---

1. The operating definition of a white Southern liberal comes from Morton Sosna, *In Search of the Silent South* (New York: Columbia University Press, 1977), viii: "The ultimate test of the white Southern liberal was his willingness or unwillingness to criticize racial mores."

and while he decried the debilitating effects of segregation—
and punctured the white Southerners' dogma that they "know
the Negro"—he accepted its existence and did not challenge
it as a system. James Weldon Johnson based his arguments
in *Negro Americans, What Now?* (1934) directly on the belief that
all Americans should enjoy equal rights, but his book was concerned principally with strategy and only secondarily with political demands. The contributors to *What the Negro Wants* elaborated upon these works; prominent African Americans of all
political persuasions and from the South as well as the North
declared that segregation must end. The debate in the post–
World War II era would no longer be about reforming the old
system but about constructing a new one.

The University of North Carolina Press appeared near mid-
century to be the logical publisher for a manuscript about the
African American freedom struggle by an ambitious and established black scholar. The Press's director, William Terry Couch,
styled himself a progressive Southerner. Under his leadership,
the Press issued volumes on the most sensitive issues of the day,
including two outstanding works on lynching: Arthur Raper's
The Tragedy of Lynching (1933) and J. H. Chadbourne's *Lynching
and the Law* (1939). In a region known for its racism and cen-
sorship, it published works by African Americans, like Horace
Cayton's and George Mitchell's *Black Workers and the New Unions*
(1939). But as the publishing record of *What the Negro Wants*
would show, Couch's and the UNC Press's tolerance for dissent
from white Southern mores was severely stunted. Couch never
hesitated to present controversial works by white Southerners to
the white South. But like the vast majority of his liberal confed-
erates, he was affronted by African Americans' direct challenges
to American apartheid. It was one matter for whites like Arthur
Raper to expose lynching; it was quite another, however, to have
blacks themselves condemn lynching and demand an end to
segregation.

In November 1941 Rayford Logan submitted a manuscript
to the UNC Press on "the Negro and the post-war society,"
which he hoped would fulfill a few purposes. As yet untitled, this
manuscript surveyed the conditions imposed on black people

around the world by colonialism, offered specific anti-imperialist and democratic solutions, and warned of dire consequences for the colonial powers should they ignore the issues he raised. A 1917 graduate of Williams College, Logan was W. E. B. Du Bois's close assistant and one of the principal organizers of the post–World War I Pan-African Congress movement. During the 1930s, while he earned his doctorate from Harvard, Logan taught at Virginia Union University in Richmond and Atlanta University, and in both cities helped to launch highly visible voting rights campaigns. In 1939, Logan joined the faculty at Howard University, taking a place next to such leading black intellectuals as Alain Locke, E. Franklin Frazier, and Ralph Bunche. By the time he completed work on "the Negro and the post-war society," Logan was established in black America as a thinker of considerable merit and a capable organizer.

In the 1940s, Howard University, because of the racism of academia, was about as far as any African American intellectual could hope to reach in his or her career. By submitting his monograph to the UNC Press, Logan hoped to expand his influence beyond Afro-America and establish himself among white American opinion makers. Couch was at first enthusiastic and agreed to publish the book, "provided certain minor revisions can be made." But after consulting with fellow racial liberal Guy B. Johnson, a sociologist at the University of North Carolina, who thought the manuscript irreparably defective, Couch backtracked.[2] More than a year later, in March 1943, Couch contacted Logan and presented as his own idea

2. Rayford W. Logan to Dr. W. T. Couch, July 24, 1941, Couch to Logan, July 28, 1941, Logan to Couch, November 28, 1941, Couch to Logan, January 15, 1942, Couch to Logan, February 5, 1942, University of North Carolina Press Records, Sub-Group 4, Series 1, "Logan, R.W. (ed.) What the Negro Wants," Southern Historical Collection, Library of the University of North Carolina at Chapel Hill. A copy of the original manuscript that Logan submitted to the UNC Press is in the Rayford W. Logan Papers, installation two, doc. box 16, unprocessed manuscript, Moorland-Spingarn Research Center, Howard University, Washington, D.C. Hereinafter cited as RL(H)-II, followed by a box number and, where appropriate, a folder; the first installation of the Logan Papers will be cited as RL(H)-I. A considerably altered version of this manuscript appeared as Rayford W. Logan, *The Negro and the Post-War World: A Primer* (Washington: Minorities Publishers, 1945).

a suggestion by Johnson that Logan "edit a book which represents the personal creed of 10 or 15 prominent Negroes."[3] Logan could not know it then, but this "on again, off again" pattern would be a significant characteristic of their partnership in *What the Negro Wants.*

At the end of March Logan readily agreed to edit such a volume. Unaware of Couch's intentions to give him carte blanche to shape the project, Logan asked Couch to help him define the book's character. "Should we," he inquired, "deliberately exclude such men as Richard Wright, Paul Robeson, Langston Hughes, and Max Yergan, whose affiliations are said to be euphemistically extreme left?"[4] Why would Logan suggest that a significant strand of African American thought be excluded from the proposed symposium? As a Pan-Africanist Logan disagreed with the Marxist-oriented left, but that never prevented him from working with African Americans or whites of that persuasion, even when distancing himself from them was the safe course of action. Logan's eagerness to cooperate with Couch likely stemmed from a desire to see that the symposium would be palatable to the Southern liberals and the white mainstream generally, who were the target audience.

Early progress on the volume was smooth. Couch counseled Logan to *include* left-wing blacks. "[I]t seems to me the book will be most interesting if it represents all the more important views now current among negroes, whether these views are radical or conservative or in between," he wrote Logan. This involved politically delicate decisions, but such was the editor's job, Couch wrote. He said he wanted to limit his role to that of an advisor while leaving all final choices entirely to Logan. He consistently qualified his suggestions with statements like "this is a matter on which you can use your own judgment," "do what you think is best," and "I mean this merely as a suggestion."[5]

For his part, Logan was busy lining up contributors. In early April he received acceptances from Willard Townsend of the

3. Johnson to Couch, January 22, 1942, Couch to Logan, March 26, 1943, UNC Press Records.

4. Logan to Couch, March 29, 1943, UNC Press Records.

5. Couch to Logan, March 31, 1943, UNC Press Records.

United Transport Service Employees–CIO, A. Philip Randolph, W. E. B. Du Bois, Sterling Brown, Walter White, the journalist George Schuyler, F. D. Patterson of Tuskegee, and Langston Hughes. By late June Logan had heard favorably from the remainder of the contributors: Gordon B. Hancock, Mary McLeod Bethune, Charles H. Wesley, Leslie Pinckney Hill, Doxey Wilkerson of the Communist Party, and Charles S. Johnson. (Johnson later withdrew after being unable to meet several deadlines. Walter White submitted a draft but was unable to revise it, due to an especially heavy schedule; he withdrew in favor of Roy Wilkins, whose submission was substantially similar to White's.)[6]

Meanwhile, Couch had been corresponding with Guy Johnson, who was concerned about the representativeness of the list of contributors. While Logan thought the roster was well-balanced, Johnson thought the list too radical.[7] The list, he told Couch, "needs a better balancing toward the *Right*—i.e., (1) conservative 'inter-racial cooperation' type, and if possible someone (2) who is really extreme right." He thought the addition of one or two presidents of Deep South state colleges for Negroes would dilute the list sufficiently.[8] Couch, who had previously been content to let Logan take charge of the volume, now questioned the wisdom of his initial decision. He worried that the book would not represent all views, and in particular that the left-wing point of view would dominate. "[Y]ou should not have two extreme left-wingers unless to balance

6. Logan to Couch, April 12, 26, 1943; Logan to contributors, July 5, 1943, UNC Press Records.

7. Logan's list cut across the political spectrum: five conservatives (Bethune, Patterson, Hancock, Hill, and Charles S. Johnson); five radicals (Wilkerson, Du Bois, Schuyler, Randolph, and Hughes); and five centrists (Logan, Wesley, Townsend, White, and Brown). This particular refraction of the political spectrum is Logan's, refers to the state of affairs in 1943, and is pegged to the willingness of the authors to speak out publicly and disturb the equanimity of the white power structure. Thus, Bethune et al. rarely did this, Logan and his cohorts did it only when they thought it expedient, while Du Bois and the radicals usually spoke out loudly and insistently. Political alignments were quite fluid then; within a matter of a few years, for example, George Schuyler moved to the extreme right.

8. Guy B. Johnson to Couch, [May 1943], Couch to Johnson, May 18, 1943, UNC Press Records.

them you have two extreme right-wingers," he now wrote to the editor. Logan resisted adding more conservatives.[9]

Logan delivered the assembled manuscript to Couch on September 8, and Couch was taken aback at its contents. He and Johnson half-expected the radicals to overshadow the moderates and conservatives, but they had no idea that the conservative African American leaders would join the left in demanding an end to segregation. One contributor after another, from Gordon Hancock to Doxey Wilkerson, called for complete equality and the discontinuance of Jim Crow. Couch complained that this made the articles redundant, but Logan had earlier anticipated this agreement and wrote to the contributors that "some repetition will inevitably result, but that repetition and perhaps unanimity on certain points will be all the more impressive."[10]

Logan was pleasantly surprised by the shape the book was taking. Du Bois's piece was excellent—"of course." He was amused by Doxey Wilkerson's article because, as a Communist, Wilkerson was "all-out for the war and . . . more enthusiastic about the progress the Negro has made during the war" than any of the other authors. Among the conservative contributions, Logan thought that Leslie Pinckney Hill's article was "beautifully written" and rated Patterson's essay "surprisingly courageous."[11]

He was most surprised, however, with the contribution of Gordon B. Hancock, a prominent racial gradualist. He had not expected to like it. The two men had been political enemies since the mid-1920s when both taught at Virginia Union University. They had engaged in several intense debates about the strategy and tactics of the incipient civil rights movement.

Logan invited Hancock to write his article from the perspective of the 1942 Durham Conference, a gathering of leading Southern African Americans. The idea for the conference originated with the white Texan Jessie Daniel Ames, the prominent

9. Couch to Logan, April 29, May 10, 1943, Logan to Couch, May 22, 1943, UNC Press Records.

10. Logan to contributors, July 5, 1943, UNC Press Records.

11. Rayford W. Logan Diary, August 17, 1943, Rayford W. Logan Papers, unprocessed manuscript, Manuscript Division, Library of Congress, Washington, D.C.

feminist, suffragist, and leader of the Commission on Interracial Cooperation. She wrote Hancock and urged him to organize a leadership meeting that would address major problems of race relations short of segregation. The conference's statement, known as the Durham Manifesto, called for equality in pay in industry, a federal anti-lynching law, hiring of African American police, and the abolition of the poll tax and the white primary. But it also chose to downplay the fight against segregation and reserved the adjustment of race relations for action by Southerners.[12] Logan had "especially asked him to present the point of view of this conference which I 'deplored' in my own contribution."[13] But when he read the article, Logan was impressed. It was, he said, "by no means bad," a comment on a political enemy that from Logan's pen was tantamount to a compliment.[14]

It was significant that Logan thought Hancock was modifying his position. For more than two decades, Hancock, an admirer of Booker T. Washington, had guarded the right wing of the African American people's movement for equality. During the 1930s Hancock advocated a "Hold-Your-Job" campaign that counseled blacks to go to any length to keep from being laid off, including accepting wage cuts, taking more abuse, and avoiding unions.[15] In this essay for Logan, he moved slightly yet significantly to the left. While he did not abandon his interracial cooperationist stance, he cast a jaundiced eye at its present worth. White Southern liberals took half-measures only and consistently capitulated to those whites who favored the continued subjection of the African American. Further, he was less

---

12. Sosna, *In Search of the Silent South*, 117–19; Raymond Gavins, *The Perils and Prospects of Southern Black Leadership: Gordon Blaine Hancock, 1884–1970* (Durham: Duke University Press, 1977), 120–28; Jacqueline Dowd Hall, *Revolt Against Chivalry: Jessie Daniel Ames and the Women's Campaign Against Lynching* (New York: Columbia University Press, 1979), 258–61; "The Durham Statement of 1942," in *A Documentary History of the Negro People in the United States*, vol. 4, *From the New Deal to the End of World War II*, ed. Herbert Aptheker (New York: Citadel Press, 1992), 421–22.

13. Logan Diary, August 14, 1943.

14. Logan Diary, August 17, 1943.

15. Gavins, *Perils and Prospects*, 59–71, 86.

insistent that the South be left alone to adjust racial tensions
and he cautioned that continued segregation meant "the extermination of the Negro."

Though conservative African American leaders moved to the
left, they certainly had not embraced the radicals or even the
centrists. Logan's essay, a wide-ranging piece, "The Negro Wants
First-Class Citizenship," discussed the outstanding differences.
His central argument was that race was a national issue, which
fact afforded a solution. As far as Logan was concerned, many of
the specific demands of the Durham Manifesto were proper, but
the conservative assumption that they could be achieved only
within a Southern framework was a step backward.

Logan also argued with the left. Nationwide protests, like the
threatened 1941 March on Washington, of which Logan was a
leader, were powerful only within definite limits. Logan believed
that the African American leadership could mobilize the masses
in numbers large enough to avoid being considered a bluff only
on rare occasions. "I definitely favor the March-on-Washington
or on other cities only as a rare, dramatic, powerful weapon
that should be used only when all other methods have failed,"
he wrote, thus demarcating himself from those like Randolph
who considered the march a staple tactic.[16] Similarly, he had
no principled objection to the nonviolent resistance advocated
by militant interracial groups like the Fellowship of Reconciliation; his concern was that the protracted process would sap
the movement of energy and would not yield a commensurate
return.

Logan's method for achieving first-class citizenship resem-
bled the NAACP's in substance: coordinated lobbying activities
to pass federal legislation guaranteeing equitable expenditures
of federal education funds; unity between the movement for
equality and the CIO, with built-in safeguards against discrimination by the labor movement; abolition of the poll tax and the
white primary; strict enforcement of the Fourteenth Amendment to reduce the South's strength in Congress in proportion

16. On Logan's role in the March on Washington Movement, see Logan Diary,
June 24, 1941.

to the number of disfranchised African Americans.[17] What distinguished Logan from the NAACP (aside from factional rivalry) was the tone with which he put forward his program. Logan saw no pressing need to be diplomatic or "responsible"; he often cast his statements in prophetic tones. This became especially clear once *What the Negro Wants* moved beyond the dismantling of legal Jim Crow.

If the contributors' unanimity on the issue of segregation dismayed Couch, their treatment of interracial marriage caused him much consternation. Fear of interracial unions was perhaps the most frequent reason whites gave for the maintenance of segregation and the denial of social equality. Couch was no exception. In a letter to the black sociologist Oliver C. Cox, whose manuscript the UNC Press was considering, Couch confessed, "If I am faced with choosing between mob violence and [biological integration], I have to choose violence."[18] With the completion of the manuscript of *What the Negro Wants*, Couch now had "proof" that the real agenda of the African American leaders was miscegenation.

Of the four authors who addressed the question of interracial liaisons, only Gordon Hancock tried to quiet white fears. Charles H. Wesley, the historian and President of Wilberforce University, devoted all of one sentence to the issue, demanding the right of every American to marry the person of his or her choice. Even so, Wesley offered no comfort to fearful whites.

The other two contributors who wrote about intermarriage were not in the business of reassuring the white world. Unwilling to sacrifice the personal rights of African Americans in the quest for political rights, Logan and Du Bois flouted convention and twitted white sensibilities. Logan conceded that "Most white Americans remain . . . opposed to intermarriage and many of them to the abolition of public segregation as a possible first step toward it." But white hysteria about the mongrelization

17. On Logan's considerable lobbying activities, see Logan Diary, April 30, 1941, April 7, 1943; for a more comprehensive statement of his position on organized labor, see Logan Diary, July 26, 1941.
18. Couch to Oliver C. Cox, April 5, 1944, UNC Press Records.

of the race flew in the face of all scientific fact as well as the social preferences of most African Americans and whites. Logan refused to coddle white opinion. If, after African Americans achieved economic, political, and cultural equality as a result of the abolition of public segregation, custom still opposed intermarriage, there would be few mixed marriages. But in a typically cavalier fashion Logan continued: "If, on the other hand, laws and public opinion should change and there should be more mixed marriages—why, we shall all be dead in 2044 and the people will do what they wish."

W. E. B. Du Bois was, from the standpoint of the white Southerner, most impertinent of all. In his autobiographical essay on his evolving program for racial equality, Du Bois recalled his time as a student in Germany. The Germans in the early 1900s, he noted, were not color conscious at all; in fact he fit in quite well with the other students, both male and female. The few tense moments occurred when visiting white Americans took offense at his familiar relations with European women; they tried, he said, to introduce Jim Crow in the student circles, but they did not succeed. A German woman, a colleague of Du Bois, wanted to marry him—immediately, he said. He regretted that he had to turn her down; but it would have been unfair to subject her to certain ostracism or worse in America. In his introduction to the 1969 edition of *What the Negro Wants*, Logan opined that Du Bois's remarks, which frankly and unapologetically discussed interracial marriage, touched the rawest part of Couch's psychological makeup. The white South's fear of miscegenation, especially when the white partner was a consenting woman, was pathological and prompted Couch to determine that the manuscript was not publishable.

Couch's negative appraisal received support from the Press's manuscript reviewers. O. J. Coffin was a liberal Southerner and a journalism professor at UNC, and he was disturbed that the book advocated "overnight the re-ordering of His world." Like Couch, Coffin disbelieved that the authors were speaking for the majority of African Americans. The contributors were "self-elected leaders," whose demands would "come as a distinct shock to the vast majority of whites, South, North, East and

West." The Southern way of life was threatened by the contributors, who "talk of intermarriage and world congresses of Negroes as nonchalantly as Walrus and Carpenter might discuss cabbages and kings." The Press was unwise even to consider publishing the manuscript, for the public would receive it poorly. Coffin returned his ten-dollar reviewer's fee, instructing Couch to give it to some "Negro charity."[19]

Other reviewers were equally negative, but they encouraged Couch to publish *What the Negro Wants*. Foremost among this group of reviewers was Howard Odum. Since 1920 this eminent sociologist had been at the University of North Carolina, where he founded and led the Institution for Research in Social Science and edited the *Journal of Social Forces*. His constant refrain was that race relations policy be based on knowledge procured through objective, dispassionate observation, yet he derided both the Ku Klux Klan and Walter White and the NAACP for their extremism. The one was just as bad as the other, he believed, as he staked the so-called rational middle ground in the race relations debate for the Southern liberals. Odum thought publication of the book would be a good way to expose the damage he thought the African American leaders were doing.

> The weakest chapter is Walter White's, which is too weak to publish in any book, but I would like to have it go in that way so that the public can get a real appraisal of Walter White's abilities. I am convinced that he is doing great harm and is likely to do more, but the only way to approach this problem is to let the public make its own appraisal.

Odum was quite pleased with what he gauged were the essays' weaknesses and cautioned Couch against changing them. "Extreme statements, cynical references, misstatement of fact—all of those are a part of the value inherent in the book," he wrote.[20]

N. C. Newbold, the North Carolina Superintendent of Public Instruction and a local leader in the interracial cooperation movement, was equally negative. He felt that *What the Negro*

19. O. J. Coffin to Couch, October 10, 1943, UNC Press Records.
20. Howard Odum to Couch, September 17, 1943, UNC Press Records.

Wants was bound to upset the racial status quo that he had helped form and maintain. Publication in its present form, he believed, would harden Southern attitudes toward African Americans. Further, Newbold thought that Northern African Americans were overrepresented among the contributors; he worried that this might create an impression among "Southern Negroes that their local leadership is not competent or cannot be trusted to treat the problems involved on a national scale." The book did not reflect a widespread militancy, but it could generate such opinion. Newbold wanted major changes in orientation in the articles, but in the event the authors were unwilling to comply, he suggested several specific alterations, including the deletion of all references to intermarriage.[21] Finally, he suggested that Couch write an introduction to the volume detailing the Press's, the university's, and the Southern majority's position on the contributors' positions.[22]

Couch digested the criticisms of the manuscript and packaged them up for Logan. A significant weakness of the work was that none of the contributors addressed African Americans' own complicity in their condition.

> I had been hoping that at least two or three of the fifteen authors would raise the question of how far the Negro is responsible for his condition, and deal with the problem of what Negroes themselves can do, regardless of what white people may do.

Even if they were only one-half of one percent responsible for their condition and whites were nearly 50 percent responsible—with fate accounting for the balance—this minuscule responsibility indicated culpability on the part of the African American population. "I cannot," he wrote, "escape the view that failure to give any attention to this question is a serious weakness and may lead to failure to achieve an enlarged responsibility."[23] Despite

---

21. N. C. Newbold to Couch, October 20, 1943, UNC Press Records.
22. Newbold to Couch, October 21, 1943, UNC Press Records.
23. Couch to Logan, October 8, 1943, UNC Press Records.

these weaknesses, Couch recommended publication, even if the authors declined to make the requested changes.[24]

But Couch was running out of patience with the project and rued ever having proposed it to Logan. In early November he penned an exasperated letter to Logan etched with a hard line on publication. "It never occurred to me during our negotiations that in response to our request a work of this nature would be written and submitted to us for publication." Publication of the book would have "extremely unfortunate" consequences on Southern race relations. He then put his position to Logan in the bluntest terms possible:

> The things Negroes are represented as wanting seem to me far removed from those they ought to want. Most of the things they are represented as wanting can be summarized in the phrase: complete abolition of segregation. If this is what the Negro wants, nothing could be clearer than that what he needs, and needs most urgently, is to revise his wants.

It was useless, he wrote, to cite the Declaration of Independence and the concept of equality as arguments for desegregation. Equality, as used in the Declaration of Independence, had a special meaning: a person was entitled to the resources and training necessary for him or her to realize his or her full potential. Couch implied here, and stated explicitly elsewhere, that since African Americans were culturally and racially inferior to whites, they were entitled to fewer resources than whites.[25]

In a letter to Langston Hughes around this time, Couch elaborated on his concept of equality. Individual African Americans may possess great talent—Couch named Joe Louis and Marian Anderson—and he could certainly not consider himself their equal. Their greater talent entitled them to certain claims on society—presumably the right to keep Couch out of the boxing ring and off the concert stage—to "segregate" him. Couch's presence in these arenas would dilute the caliber of talent. (He

---

24. Couch to Logan, October 21, 1943, UNC Press Records.
25. Couch to Logan, November 9, 1943, UNC Press Records.

did not take note of the fact, as Hughes did, that even people of great talent like Louis and Anderson were forced to bear the indignities of segregation despite their claims on society.) Because African Americans as a race were of inferior caliber to whites, Couch wrote to Hughes, "There seem to me to be areas in which a mechanically applied . . . discrimination is essential."[26]

In mid-November, Couch again pressed his objections on Logan. After attacking the theories of racial equality of social scientists like Gunnar Myrdal and Melville Herskovits, Couch expressed feelings of betrayal: "For years I have been . . . telling people the Negro . . . is not interested in social equality." Of more immediate importance to the publishing fate of *What the Negro Wants* was what bordered on an ultimatum. "I look forward to hearing what you and the contributors think of the criticisms and whether you think the articles can be revised so as to make them publishable."[27] Simultaneously, he got the Press's board of directors to approve a resolution to publish the book only if it was revised to meet the criticisms made by N. C. Newbold, the interracial cooperation leader.[28]

For the moment Logan noticeably softened. When the barrage began in the middle of October, Logan resisted making changes in the manuscript.[29] But by the middle of November Logan began to bend. He was not convinced by the intellectual force of Couch's arguments, as Couch may have thought, but by other circumstances. Logan had earlier received encouraging words from the Book-of-the-Month Club. The club's editors told Logan that they were contemplating giving the book a favorable review in their monthly newsletter and even making *What the Negro Wants* a selection of the month. But this was impossible, they related to Logan, so long as the book remained in its original form. His chance to make an impact on the white public depended upon his altering the manuscript to conform to white sensibilities.

26. Couch to Langston Hughes, December 27, 1943, Hughes to Couch, February 5, 1944, UNC Press Records.
27. Couch to Logan, November 17, 1943, UNC Press Records.
28. Couch to Newbold, November 12, 1943, UNC Press Records.
29. Logan to Couch, October 18, 1943, UNC Press Records.

But harmony shortly turned to dissonance. Although Logan agreed to alter the manuscript, he could not convince the contributors to do so. He met with W. E. B. Du Bois and Sterling Brown, who refused to budge. Du Bois had told Logan that the UNC Press would not "have the guts to publish it," and that he refused to make "anything but verbal changes here and there" in his piece.[30] Brown called Couch "muddleheaded" and "slightly 'crazy.'" The three of them resolved that Couch should come to Washington to confer with all the contributors. Willard Townsend felt that Couch had "not acted in good faith."[31]

At first Couch agreed to meet sometime in mid-December, but, suddenly hardening his position, declined to meet, suggesting consultation by mail. This was enough to end Logan's vacillations. He no longer considered Couch's suggestions an improvement; they would, in fact, "create a great deal of perplexity in their [the contributors'] mind in view of the fact that they were specifically requested to present their ideas of '*What the Negro Wants.*'"[32]

In mid-December matters came to a head. On December 14, Couch informed Logan that the UNC Press would not publish *What the Negro Wants* without drastic revisions along previously suggested lines. Logan should, he said, search for a new publisher, and then he added this parting insult: "Perhaps I ought to add I have no doubt a book worth publishing could be written opposing all the views I have expressed; but this would require more skill and imagination than are apparent in the present manuscript."[33]

Logan was incensed. "I went along with him," he wrote, "until he told me to find another publisher."[34] So four days after Couch's rejection, Logan fired off a one-sentence letter that

30. W. E. B. Du Bois to Logan, December 9, 1943, RL(H)-I, box 15, "W. T. Couch."

31. Logan Diary, December 24, 1943; Logan to Couch, November 27, 1943, UNC Press Records.

32. Couch to Logan, November 29, 1943, Couch to Logan, telegram, November 30, 1943, Logan to Couch, December 6, 1943, UNC Press Records.

33. Couch to Logan, December 14, 1943, UNC Press Records.

34. Logan Diary, December 24, 1943.

stated, "In reply to your letter of December 14 I have to say that I am consulting my attorneys."[35]

In the face of Logan's unexpected resistance, Couch panicked. To N. C. Newbold, Couch wrote that he could not fathom Logan's change in attitude. He could only wonder why Logan did not respond to more of the hard sell. Someone with evil intentions, he concluded, had Logan's ear: "I am afraid he is asking and accepting advice from someone who would prefer to see trouble rather than to see a good job done."[36]

Couch also sought the counsel of three other leading Southern liberals: Jackson Davis, Mark Ethridge, and Virginius Dabney. Davis, an official of the Rockefeller-funded General Education Board, and Ethridge, the publisher of the Louisville *Courier-Journal* and best known for his 1942 statement that "there is no power in the world . . . which could now force the Southern white people to the abandonment of the principle of social segregation,"[37] took note of what Davis termed the dynamite in the book, but neither believed it threatened the segregationist order. They urged publication.[38]

Virginius Dabney was the most perceptive as to the cause of the new militancy among African Americans. He was not surprised by the manuscript, although he thought some of the writing especially bad. But he expected such articles when a man like Logan was given free rein to solicit them.

> Logan is what I should term a radical. . . . Certainly nothing but extremism and denunciation of the whites, especially in the South, could have been anticipated from such contributors as Randolph, White and Schuyler. . . .
>
> [Y]ou were under the delusion, when you arranged for this book, that the Negro does not want the abolition of segregation, establishment of complete social equality etc.

35. Logan to Couch, December 18, 1943, UNC Press Records.

36. Couch to Newbold, December 22, 1943, UNC Press Records. See also Couch to Virginius Dabney, December 20, 1943, UNC Press Records, for more on Couch's surprise at Logan's actions.

37. Quoted in Gavins, *Perils and Prospects*, 133–34.

38. Jackson Davis to Couch, February 11, 1944, Mark Ethridge to Couch, April 11, 1944, UNC Press Records.

Back in 1941 he believed as Couch did, he wrote, but intervening events forced him to reevaluate his position. World War II was the underlying cause of Negroes' radicalization, Dabney wrote. "[T]he war and its slogans have roused in the breasts of our colored friends hopes, aspirations and desires which they formerly did not entertain, except in the rarest instances." The fourteen contributors did indeed speak for the African American people on the issue of segregation. The conservative Southern leaders had to play catch-up and criticize segregation, "lest they be considered 'Uncle Toms' or 'Handkerchief Heads.'"[39]

Dabney's insight into the causes of the radicalization of African American opinion did not mean that he thought that opinion ought to be publicized. Publication of the book, he warned, would do great harm in the South, causing a reaction against "reasonable concessions." Walter White and the NAACP were making extreme demands on white America and causing a great deal of tension. Their inflammatory rhetoric provoked the white Southern demagogues and would certainly cause racial violence. Segregation must stay. This was also the thrust of a major article he penned for the January 1943 issue of *Atlantic Monthly*, entitled "Nearer and Nearer the Precipice."

The momentum had shifted, and the more Logan thought matters over, the more he concluded that he, and not Couch, was right. Most of the contributors were on Logan's side, with Langston Hughes weighing in with the comment that "the southern intellectuals are in a pretty sorry boat. Certainly they are crowding Hitler for elbow room."[40] On January 14, 1944, Logan wrote Couch, threatening to sue him should the Press not publish *What the Negro Wants,* and five days later Couch relented. The book would be published, but only with a publisher's introduction disclaiming responsibility for the views expressed in the articles.[41]

39. Virginius Dabney to Couch, January 10, 1944, UNC Press Records.

40. Langston Hughes to Logan, December 21, 1943, RL(H)-I, box 15, "W. T. Couch."

41. Logan to Couch, January 14, 1944, Couch to Logan, January 19, 1944, UNC Press Records.

The "Publisher's Introduction" was a polished version of Couch's previously stated views on race relations. It opened, though, with a curious statement that "the authors of the present book are representing their people faithfully, that the Negro really wants what they say he wants, and that he reasons about democracy, equality, freedom, and human rights just as they do." Apparently Virginius Dabney had convinced Couch that despite "the psychopathic condition the manuscript reveals among Negro intellectuals,"[42] the book did indeed reflect the demands of Afro-America as a whole. Still, Couch continued to insist that this radicalization was not a result of the war, but rather was artificially induced by contemporary anthropological and sociological theory, especially that embodied in Herskovits's scholarship and in Myrdal's *An American Dilemma.*

In his view, the condition of African Americans was caused by their inferiority, but this condition—and race prejudice—could be overcome. What was required was that they recognize their inferiority and make a concerted effort to rise above their "natural" (i.e., less than civilized) ways. The "Negro's interest requires that he show qualities of greatness; that he not be so much concerned over the label 'equal,' but that he concentrate all his energies on being not merely equal to, but better than the white man."

The anthropologists and sociologists who were advocating racial equality were in effect encouraging the dismantling of a superior culture. *An American Dilemma* "was written under gross misapprehensions of what such ideas as equality, freedom, democracy, human rights, have meant, and of what they can be made to mean. I believe the small measure of these gained by western man is in serious danger of destruction" by the ideas in that book. Whites had the right to protect "their" values against encroachments of a people who lived in a "natural" state. Absent any indication that African Americans could achieve greatness, it was criminal to remove the barriers between the races. The alternative to segregation was biological integration and the dragging down of the white race. Myrdal and his fellow social sci-

---

42. Couch to Dabney, January 14, 1944, UNC Press Records.

entists were distracting African Americans from acquiring what they really needed—diligent work habits and self-control—in favor of something the majority would never allow them to have—the abolition of segregation.

Couch's statement became the Southern liberal's creed. Jackson Davis applauded it, and Virginius Dabney wrote, "It seems to me to be excellent, and to place the whole project in its proper perspective." Mark Ethridge told Couch that "your paper pretty well presents my viewpoint." Gerald Johnson, the North Carolina–born journalist and regular writer for the *New Republic* and columnist for the *Baltimore Evening Sun*, sent word to Couch that he was in favor of letting African Americans say what they wanted, but he did not favor giving it to them. "I like your introductory essay—" he wrote, "nimblest footwork I have seen in a cóon's age."[43]

Many reviewers received the book enthusiastically. Some Northern publications employed Southern whites to review *What the Negro Wants*. Paula Snelling, a close collaborator of Lillian Smith's, wrote a lengthy review for the *New York Herald-Tribune*'s book supplement, the *Weekly Book Review*. She found much to boost her spirits. The book would provoke a healthy soul-searching among white Americans, she hoped. But her optimism was tempered by the publisher's introduction, "which gives documentary evidence that the Anglo-Saxon mind here retains its old facility for throwing up verbal smoke screens when painful knowledge presses too close."[44]

The editors of the *New York Times Book Review* asked William Shands Meacham, the chairman of the Virginia State Board of Parole, and a trustee of the Hampton Institute, to review the anthology. Perhaps one-quarter of his article was devoted to a condemnation of miscegenation, even though intermarriage was only a minor theme in *What the Negro Wants*. Even the mere discussion of intermarriage "risks poisoning the atmosphere in

43. Jackson Davis to Couch, February 11, 1944, Virginius Dabney to Couch, February 25, 1944, Mark Ethridge to Couch, April 11, 1944, Gerald Johnson to Couch, October 9, 1944, UNC Press Records.

44. Paula Snelling, "To Be Counted as Human Beings," *Weekly Book Review*, November 12, 1944, p. 3.

which countless white Americans of good will would like to eliminate needless differentials." Once he had calmed himself, however, Meacham lent a sympathetic ear to the authors' demands for first-class citizenship. He was reluctant to grant full citizenship rights at once, but he welcomed the book as a refreshing change of pace. "Rationalization and sublimation have been the means by which we have tried to solve the American race problem, and this ably written book published by a Southern press is an outstanding example of the frontal approach."[45]

Not all educated Southern white opinion was so kind. H. C. Brearley, the reviewer for *Social Forces*, found little to like in the volume. Did the authors, he asked, speak for African Americans? No, for contrary to the book's claim, "realistically it is a collection of essays . . . by fourteen Negro intellectuals who were requested to say what they think the Negro wants." In his opinion, "Most of the writers make no effort to conceal the antagonism toward the whites that is characteristic of the upper class Negro." In fact, the most attractive essay was the publisher's introduction.[46]

African American reviewers hailed *What the Negro Wants* as a masterly statement. If anything, their reviews reinforced the unanimity of African Americans against segregation. J. Saunders Redding, writing for the *New Republic*, warned readers not to underestimate the authority of the contributors because their names were unfamiliar.

> They speak with authority. Ask any expert—and any expert would be any literate Negro. Indeed, the validity of this book is derived from the undisputable fact that the editor might have chosen fourteen other contributors and achieved the same general result.[47]

45. William Shands Meacham, "The Negro's Future in America," *New York Times Book Review*, November 5, 1944, p. 28.

46. H. C. Brearley, review of *What the Negro Wants*, ed. Rayford W. Logan, in *Social Forces* 23 (1945): 469–70.

47. J. Saunders Redding, "Fourteen Negro Voices," *New Republic*, November 20, 1944, pp. 665–66.

E. Franklin Frazier informed readers of *The Nation* that "The volume as a whole provides an excellent summary of the intellectual orientation of the majority of articulate and educated Negro leaders in the present crisis."[48] Reviewers at *Opportunity*, the *Journal of Negro History*, the *Crisis*, and the *Journal of Negro Education* all felt that *What the Negro Wants* was one of the most important books to date on race relations.[49] Not incidentally, with the exception of the reviewer for *Opportunity*, all the reviewers took Couch to task for his introduction. The *Chicago Defender* and the Schomburg Collection of the New York Public Library placed Logan on their respective honor rolls for 1944 in recognition of *What the Negro Wants*.[50]

The polemics over the publication of *What the Negro Wants* helped usher in a new configuration of forces in the struggle for civil rights in the post-war era. White Southern liberals had previously successfully argued that they knew best how to handle race relations and that the only alternative to their "mild" form of segregation was that of race haters like the Ku Klux Klan. They could parry the attacks by white social scientists who preached racial equality by claiming that they were the scholarly equivalents of outside agitators. In this fashion the Southern liberals like W. T. Couch clung to their national leadership on the race problem. The appearance, however, of a broad-based African American intellectual and political *movement* against segregation seriously undermined the Southern race liberals' moral authority. By acknowledging, however reluctantly, that the authors of *What the Negro Wants* did indeed represent the demands of African Americans, white Southern race liberals in effect gave up their claim to paternal omniscience on the race problem.

The Southern liberals' precarious grip on race relations leadership was further undermined by the growing legitimacy of

48. E. Franklin Frazier, "Wanted: Equality," *The Nation*, December 23, 1944, p. 776.

49. *Opportunity* 23 (1945): 158; *Journal of Negro History* 30 (1945): 90–92; *Crisis*, December 1944, 395; *Journal of Negro Education* 14 (1945): 67–68.

50. *Chicago Defender* to Logan, telegram, [1945], L. D. Reddick to Logan, February 19, 1945, RL(H)-II, box 19, "Citations."

civil rights among Northern white intellectuals.[51] If African Americans had previously felt compelled to align themselves with the less than satisfactory Southern race liberals because the only alternative was the Klan, this was no longer the case; they could, in the post-war era, stand up to the apologists of Jim Crow and still be fairly certain of substantial white support.

While the Southern liberals admitted they did not know "what the Negro wanted," they were unwilling to engage in good faith negotiations with African Americans. Even the most enlightened among them refused to come to terms with the system of Jim Crow. For example, Frank Porter Graham, the highly regarded president of the University of North Carolina, opposed President Truman's Civil Rights Commission report in 1948 because he feared it would defeat measures for voting rights and fair employment practices by raising the issue of social equality. In addition to weakening their own position, the actions of W. T. Couch and his fellow race liberals strengthened the African American leadership's convictions that segregation must be abolished. Some, like Rayford Logan, became more convinced of the duplicity of the Southern liberals.[52]

It would, of course, take some time for the conviction to percolate into direct action against segregation. In practice most African Americans who skirmished across the color line felt they were strong enough to tilt it, not abolish it. Until the end of 1950, the NAACP's carefully crafted legal challenges to inferior educational facilities for African Americans were designed to make the segregated schools truly equal. The Association's political calculus indicated that that was the outer limit to which American justice could be pushed. Then in November of that year, Thurgood Marshall went before the U.S. District Court in Charleston, South Carolina, to argue that black schools in

---

51. Walter A. Jackson, *Gunnar Myrdal and America's Conscience: Social Engineering and Racial Liberalism, 1938–1987* (Chapel Hill: University of North Carolina Press, 1990), 273–79.

52. For evidence of Couch's own personal capitulation, see Margaret Duckett to Couch, November 6, 1944, and Arthur G. Powell to Couch, December 31, 1944, UNC Press Records; on the capitulation of Southern racial liberalism, see Sosna, *In Search of the Silent South,* chap. 8.

Clarendon County were not equal. Judge Julius Waties Waring, a Charleston aristocrat who had been converted to the cause of civil rights, instructed Marshall to recast his case to challenge directly segregation.[53] Even in the early phases of the Montgomery Bus Boycott of 1955–56, African Americans demanded only truly separate-but-equal seating before insisting on an end to public segregation. What these instances show, however, is not an acceptance of segregation, but a calculation of what the movement could achieve.

The *What the Negro Wants* controversy helped clear the ground for this later phase of the civil rights movement. It synthesized African American opinion on segregation across the political spectrum. It also demonstrated with certainty to African American spokespersons the ineffectiveness of Southern racial liberals and their uselessness as political buffers against the Ku Klux Klan and other race haters. Shorn of illusions, African Americans were more ideologically prepared than ever to break through the color bar and wage a sustained assault on the system of segregation.

---

53. Richard Kluger, *Simple Justice* (New York: Vintage Books, 1977), 295–305.

For Further Reading

To learn more of the life, times, and scholarship of Rayford Logan, see Kenneth R. Janken, *Rayford W. Logan and the Dilemma of the African-American Intellectual* (Amherst: University of Massachusetts Press, 1993). August Meier and Elliott Rudwick, *Black History and the Historical Profession, 1915–1980* (Urbana: University of Illinois Press, 1986) discusses Logan's efforts, alongside those of Carter Woodson, Charles Wesley, W. E. B. Du Bois, and others, to build the discipline of Afro-American history. Logan's most important book, *The Betrayal of the Negro: From Rutherford B. Hays to Woodrow Wilson*, new enl. ed. (New York: Collier Books, 1965; reprinted New York: Da Capo, 1997), offers a framework for understanding the critical period of African American history from the end of Reconstruction until WWI that still stands the test of time. Logan's most productive years, both in terms of scholarship and politics, were in the 1930s, 1940s, and 1950s. Patricia Sullivan, *Days of Hope: Race and Democracy in the New Deal Era* (Chapel Hill: University of North Carolina Press, 1996), Brenda Gayle Plummer, *Rising Wind: Black Americans and U.S. Foreign Affairs, 1935–1960* (Chapel Hill: University of North Carolina Press, 1996), and Penny M. Von Eschen, *Race against Empire: Black Americans and Anticolonialism, 1937–1957* (Ithaca, N.Y.: Cornell University Press, 1997) provide domestic and international contexts for these endeavors. Logan often found himself jousting white liberals, as seen in the publishing history of *What the Negro Wants*. Walter A. Jackson, *Gunnar Myrdal and America's Conscience* (Chapel Hill: University of North Carolina Press, 1990), Morton Sosna, *In Search of the Silent South* (New York: Columbia University Press, 1977), and Jacqueline Dowd Hall, *Revolt against Chivalry* (New York: Columbia University Press, 1979), are three books that tackle the thorny problems of racial liberalism.

INTRODUCTION TO THE
1969 REPRINT

The intrinsic value of *What the Negro Wants* was enhanced in 1944 by the odd Introduction of W. T. Couch, Director of the University of North Carolina Press. He did not evoke as much added interest as the Watch and Ward Society would have done by banning the book (there is no sex, no obscenity, no sadism in *What the Negro Wants*). Mr. Couch, did, however, bestir the wonderment of scholars, perceptive reviewers and readers, and the volume became a minor literary *cause célèbre*.

Events proceeding publication have not been made public until now. In the early days of World War II, I was convinced of the need for a work on "The Negro and the Post-War World." Since the University of North Carolina Press well deserved its reputation for bringing out books which did not conform to the views of many Southerners, and since it had published in 1941 my *The Diplomatic Relations of the United States and Haiti, 1776–1891*, I submitted my proposal to Mr. Couch. The Press preferred the "here and now."

As Mr. Couch stated in his Introduction:

> "The book was written at the request of the Press. The idea in back of the request was that the country, and particularly the South, ought to know what the Negro wants, and that statements from leading Negroes might throw some light on this important question."

He and I agreed on equal representation of left-wing, moderate, and right-wing points of view and on the contributors holding those views.

But when I submitted the manuscript, he wrote me that I was "not publishable." I wrote him I had several options if the Press did not publish it. I could apprise Dr. Frank Graham, President of the University of North Carolina, of the decision; I could reveal the facts to the public and try to find another publisher; or I could consult my attorneys as to my legal rights. He replied that the Press would publish, provided the book contained an Introduction written by him. I accepted, but declined his offer to read it prior to publication. Acceptance would have been tantamount to endorsement of his statement.

Inasmuch as his Introduction was the principal cause of wonderment, readers of this reprint should examine it in its entirety. Three passages are particularly intriguing. He observed that Gunnar Myrdal's "*An American Dilemma: The Negro Problem and Modern Democracy* offers strong evidence that the authors of the present book are representing their people faithfully, that the Negro wants what they say he wants, and that he reasons about democracy, equality, freedom, and human rights just as they do." Mr. Couch then explained in several pages his views on three widely held theories "concerning the condition of the Negro in America." Teachers who use this book should require students to state as clearly as he does what those views were, especially why he believed *An American Dilemma* "was written under gross misapprehensions of what such ideas as equality, freedom, democracy, human rights have meant, and of what they can be made to mean."

In his closing paragraph, Mr. Couch stated: "While I disagree with the editor and most of the contributors on basic problems, there is much in the present book with which I have to agree." Nowhere in the Introduction was there any indication of what he agreed with.

It was my own belief that one specific in particular and two generalizations explain Mr. Couch's conclusion that the manuscript was not publishable. On few subjects was the South more intolerant than on its almost pathological objection to miscegenation and, even worse, intermarriage—especially when the white partner was a woman. One paragraph in the essay by Dr. W. E. Burghardt Du Bois violated this credo. During a trip to Germany in 1892, a blue-eyed German girl wanted to marry him. He "told her frankly and gravely that it would be unfair to himself and cruel to her for a colored man to take a white bride in America." This renunciation rankled nonetheless, especially since she had proposed to him.

What disturbed Mr. Couch more than anything else, I believed then and now, was the virtual unanimity of the fourteen contributors in wanting equal rights for Negroes. This general agreement surprised and pleased me as much as it probably shocked Mr. Couch. This virtual unanimity led some reviewers to criticize the book as being "repetitious." Therein lay, and lies, one of its greatest values.

I selected Dr. Du Bois, Langston Hughes, A. Philip Randolph, George Schuyler, and Doxey Wilkerson as representing *in 1944,* left-wing views. In 1944 is emphasized, because later their views shifted. Mr. Schuyler moved far to the right and was active in a number of right-wing organizations. On the other hand, Langston Hughes changed his bitterness as voiced, for example, in his poem "Good-bye Christ," to satires on the foibles of Americans; he was recognized as the "Poet Laureate of Harlem" and a near-great American author.

It is to the credit of Mr. Couch and the Press that the essay of Doxey Wilkerson, an avowed Communist in 1944, created no difficulties. To be sure, the Soviet Union's victories at Stalingrad, Leningrad, and Moscow helped enormously to turn the tide in favor of the Allies and to facilitate preparations for a 1944 landing in Normandy. On the other hand, domestic Communism caused almost as many shudders at home as did the victories of the Russians to the Nazis. Later Wilkerson severed his connection with the Communists but vigorously continued to urge necessary changes in the American society and economy.

Randolph, upon whom I only half facetiously conferred the "honorary degree" of "Doctor of Giant Killers" a few years ago, has moved to a more moderate position than in 1944. On the other hand, he has been the scourge of organized labor, repeatedly giving evidence of the wide gulf between pronouncements about equal opportunities and discriminatory practices. He richly deserves the kudos of "Elder Statesman of the Civil Rights Movement" in its nonviolent aspects.

Of all the essays, that of Dr. Du Bois must be read most closely within the perspective of the early 1940's. In my judgment (I first met him at the Paris sessions of the Second Pan African Congress, 1921, and "knew" him perhaps as well as did any one else), he was for most of his life what I have called "an authentic

American radical." In this connection, one passage in his essay has more than transitory value. He wrote: "I did not believe that the Communism of the Russians was the program for America; least of all for a minority group like the Negroes; I saw that the program of the American Communist Party was suicidal." Without reference to this essay, Dr. Herbert Aptheker, perhaps the most scholarly of American Communist theoreticians, included several preceding paragraphs in his editing of *The Autobiography of W. E. B. Du Bois,* 1968, and then gave this purported view of Dr. Du Bois: "I did not believe that the communism of the Russians was the program for America; least of all for a minority group like the Negroes; I saw the program of the American Communist Party was inadequate for our plight." I submit that there is more than a slight difference between "suicidal" and "inadequate."

The forces that led Dr. Du Bois to proclaim publicly in 1961 his application for membership in the American Communist Party are still a matter for conjecture, far beyond the scope of this Introduction. A long opus would be necessary for an analysis of the factors that led to the changes discussed above and to the careers summarized below.

The 1944 "moderates" or "liberals," as I call them, were Professor Sterling A. Brown, Willard S. Townsend, Charles H. Wesley, Roy Wilkins, and myself. With the exception of Townsend, who died in 1960, we have been honored by being called "Uncle Toms," especially by some Black Power militants.

The 1944 right-wing or "conservative" contributors were Mrs. Mary McLeod Bethune, Gordon B. Hancock, Leslie Pinckney Hill, and Frederick D. Patterson. Mrs. Bethune and Dr. Hill, who died before the beginning of "The Negro Revolution," maintained the "conservative" stance expressed in their contributions. Dr. Hancock has been less vocal but somewhat more militant in recent years. In 1956, Dr. Patterson, who had become President of the Phelps-Stokes Fund, was co-editor of *Robert Russa Moton of Hampton and Tuskagee,* published by the University of North Carolina Press, of which Mr. Couch was no longer director. The Preface, jointly signed by Dr. Patterson and the co-editor, W. H. Hughes, stated that Dr. Moton's views "touched the educational, social, economic and spiritual aspects of Negro life and, without exception, this has had a salutary and often decisive effect." I cannot agree with the statement, especially the words "without exception." On the whole, Dr. Patterson has remained a protagonist of the Booker T. Washington–Moton policy and practices of conciliation.

The second general reason for the difficulty about publication was, I believe then and more so now, the demand for equal opportunity in the fulfillment of obligations as American citizens. Even in 1944, when Negroes on many battlefields were giving "the last full measure of devotion," the myth of the Negro's avoidance of his responsibilities persisted. Despite similar evidence of this "last full measure" in the Korean War and the War in Vietnam, even some "friendly" writers continue to condemn Negroes for insisting upon equality of opportunity without allegedly accepting equality of responsibility.

I believe that in 1969 most Negroes want freedom of equality and freedom of opportunity. I believe also that the tide has begun to turn against the most militant Black Power advocates who want separate schools, a separate "black culture," a separate "black state," and guerilla warfare to achieve these goals and to overthrow the American government and society. With the support of men of good will, the goals and methods advocated in 1944 are still feasible and attainable. If these beliefs be true, this 1969 reprint of *What the Negro Wants* should accelerate the achievement of those goals within the framework of our imperfect American "democracy."

Rayford W. Logan
Professor Emeritus of History
Howard University

January, 1969

KENNETH ROBERT JANKEN is Associate Professor of Afro-American Studies at the University of North Carolina at Chapel Hill and author of *Rayford W. Logan and the Dilemma of the African-American Intellectual.*

WHAT THE NEGRO WANTS

WHAT THE NEGRO WANTS

Edited *by* RAYFORD W. LOGAN

Mary McLeod Bethune
Sterling A. Brown
W. E. Burghardt Du Bois
Gordon B. Hancock
Leslie Pinckney Hill
Langston Hughes
Rayford W. Logan
Frederick D. Patterson
A. Philip Randolph
George S. Schuyler
Willard S. Townsend
Charles H. Wesley
Doxey A. Wilkerson
Roy Wilkins

CHAPEL HILL

THE UNIVERSITY OF NORTH CAROLINA PRESS

Printed in the United States of America by
Van Rees Press, New York

PJ

CONTENTS

EDITOR'S PREFACE

Race relations in the United States are more strained than they have been in many years. Negroes are disturbed by the continued denial of what they consider to be their legitimate aspirations and by the slow, grudging granting of a few concessions. White Americans express alarm at what they call the excessive insistence by Negroes upon a too rapid change in the *status quo*. Serious riots have broken out in both Northern and Southern cities. Wild rumors inflame minds already aroused by actual facts. Dire predictions of what is going to happen as soon as the war is over surpass even these wild rumors.

This tension urgently requires a definition of terms and a clarification of issues by competent Negroes representing various shades of opinion. Fourteen Negroes who have devoted many years of study to America's most difficult and intricate minority problem have here presented their views within the framework of their own belief about the problem, of their conception of what the Negro wants and of the methods by which he can best achieve his aspirations.

The editor's role has been a minor one. He selected the contributors, four of whom might be called conservatives, five liberals, and five radicals. He in no way attempted to influence their opinions or conclusions. He has not tried to reconcile differences or to avoid repetitions. He has made no changes other than those required to assure uniformity of editorial style. The editor also arranged the contributions in the order in which they appear. He put first those that give in largest measure an overall picture, then those that represent particular organizations, and finally those that are more limited in scope.

The complete freedom enjoyed by all the contributors makes doubly significant the surprising unanimity with respect to what the Negro wants. Conservatives, liberals and radicals alike want Negroes eventually to enjoy the same rights, opportunities and privileges that are vouchsafed to all other Americans and to fulfill all the obligations that are required of all other Americans. Americans who profess to believe in democracy will have to face the dilemma of cooperating in the implementation of these aspirations or of limiting their ideals to white Americans only.

The editor wishes to thank the contributors for laying aside many other important duties in order to participate in this joint undertaking. Above all, he wishes to thank The University of North Carolina Press for creating the opportunity of presenting these essays to the American people. The publications by the Press already constitute a distinguished list of monographs designed to furnish an objective documentation of this grave problem and to further its solution. In this publication, as in others, it presents points of view that do not coincide with its own. This is, of course, constantly done among commercial publishers, is characteristic of most university presses, but is, I believe, noteworthy when done by a press in the South. This fact alone provides inspiration to those who believe that the democracy which we fourteen ask is not merely a fetish and a political and wartime slogan but a dream that may yet come true.

Rayford Whittingham Logan

Howard University
March, 1944

PUBLISHER'S INTRODUCTION

The wound of peace is surety,
Surety secure; but modest doubt is call'd
The beacon of the wise, the tent that searches
To the bottom of the worst.

THIS BOOK was written at the request of the Press. The idea back of the request was that the country, and particularly the South, ought to know what the Negro wants, and that statements from leading Negroes might throw some light on this important question.

Advice on the editorship and the authors was secured from the best sources available. It was stipulated that equal representation in the book be given to left-wing, moderate, and right-wing points of view. It was suggested that the editor form a committee to advise him on the problem of making the book as truly representative and as reasonable and faithful a statement as possible; and, further, that while he should leave his contributors free to say what they thought they ought to say, he should caution them against going to extremes they could not justify. The division of the subject and organization of the work, all editorial matters, large and small, were left entirely to the editor.

How far the book succeeds in carrying out the basic idea and achieving reasonableness, the reader may judge for himself.

A comprehensive investigation conducted in recent years under the auspices of one of the foundations, a two-volume summary of which has just been issued under the title *An American Dilemma: The Negro Problem and Modern Democracy*,[1] offers strong evidence that the authors of the present book are represent-

---

[1] Gunnar Myrdal, Richard Sterner, Arnold Rose, *An American Dilemma: The Negro Problem and Modern Democracy*, 2 vols., Harper and Brothers, 1944.

ing their people faithfully, that the Negro really wants what they say he wants, and that he reasons about democracy, equality, freedom, and human rights just as they do.

Three theories are widely held concerning the condition of the Negro in America. There is one which says his condition has been produced by his inferiority. In this view prejudice, and the additional burdens placed on the Negro on account of prejudice, are results, not causes. Those who hold this view ask why no Negro civilization of any importance has been developed in Africa, why there is so little intelligent interest among Negroes, even intellectuals, in what happens there. They insist that everything the Negro demands in America, he could get for himself in Africa, if he only had the ability to get it. Why, they ask, has Liberia been such a dismal failure? Why has it not been realized that a well-governed state in Africa, controlled by Negroes, could do more for the race than anything else that could be imagined? Why if race prejudice produces poverty— and if there is as little race prejudice in Brazil as is claimed—why aren't the people of that country accordingly prosperous and healthy? Why is the condition of that country far below that of the American South? Why has it not been understood, either by Negro leaders or by white advocates of equality, that no kind or amount of scientific investigation can settle questions like these in areas where Negroes live among white people? It can always be said, and cannot be disproved by any scientific procedure, they assert, that until the Negro shows he can govern himself and maintain a fair level of civilization it is reasonable to believe his condition is a consequence of his inferiority and his condition would drop to that of savagery if the white man were not present to hold him up.

Second, there is the theory that the Negro's condition is produced by inferiority,[2] but that this inferiority can be over-

[2] Several persons who have read this introduction for me have asked whether I mean by the word "inferiority" something innate or something produced by environment. I do not mean either one. I do not pretend to know how or why wide differences exist among peoples. Terms such as "innate" and "environmental" have to be used with extreme care; otherwise they may imply knowledge which at present no one has. The

come, and the prejudice resulting from it can be cured. The white man can help, but the main part of the task rests on the Negro. It is frequently argued, for instance, that it was only natural when the bonds of slavery were first broken for the Negro to wander around where he pleased, to work as he saw fit. Those who hold this view would answer, Yes, it was *only natural*. They would argue that the interest of the Negro demanded that he rise above what was "only natural"; that today the Negro's interest requires that he show qualities of greatness; that he not be so much concerned over the label "equal," but that he concentrate all his energies on being not merely equal to, but better than the white man.

Why, this group asks, is superiority so much feared and hated today? Were other men of their times equal in all respects to Lincoln and Jefferson? Was not Jesus a man, and as a man, equal to other men; but was he not also at the same time so far superior that no man has been his equal? Has the world suffered from the superiority of these men?

Further, they wish to know: Is there any sanity in the view now often stated that no one but a Fascist or Nazi can believe one people or race superior to another? Where does this put Abraham Lincoln, who once said (Peoria Speech, October 16, 1854) of the Negro and slavery:

> If all earthly power were given me, I should not know what to do as to the existing institution. My first impulse would be

---

myth, invented by the Greeks, of Athena springing full-panoplied from the brow of Zeus may be regarded as a representation of the arrival of intellectual superiority in the world. This representation is far better than current ones. It does not cover up with an appearance of knowledge something that remains a mystery. When the social scientist says that environment or heredity or anything else is the cause of the inferiority of any group, he is violating one of the first principles of modern science, which knows only an endless web of causation and recognizes no "causes" whatever of this or that. Such developments as the quantum theory and the principle of indeterminacy have made the gaps in this doctrine obvious, but strict causation still holds exclusive sway in modern science. Only the metaphysician is supposed to talk of "causes," and his talk, according to most exponents of science, is nonsense—an opinion with which I hope the reader will gather I do not agree. The social sciences are in complete confusion on this and related problems.

to free all the slaves, and send them to Liberia, to their own native land. But a moment's reflection would convince me that whatever of high hope (as I think there is) there may be in this in the long run, its sudden execution is impossible. If they were landed there in a day, they would all perish in the next ten days; and there are not surplus shipping and surplus money enough to carry them there in many times ten days. What then? Free them all, and keep them among us as underlings? Is it quite certain that this betters their condition? I think I would not hold one in slavery at any rate, yet the point is not clear enough for me to denounce people upon. What next? Free them, and make them politically and socially our equals? My own feelings will not admit of this, and if mine would, we well know that those of the great mass of whites will not. Whether this feeling accords with justice and sound judgment is not the sole question, if indeed it is any part of it. A universal feeling, whether well or ill founded, cannot be safely disregarded. We cannot then make them equals.

Can it be really true that the Great Emancipator was filled with race prejudice, that he was, after all, only a Fascist, a Nazi? Could any greater libel be imagined? Do these ideas, held by Lincoln, become signs of ignorance and viciousness when they are held by someone else?

The South, those who hold this second view may say, places numerous unnecessary burdens on the Negro—burdens which should be removed. But this cannot be done all at once. And it must not be done in such manner as to weaken the barrier between the races. This barrier cannot be made completely effective—but the fact that some people may cross it in secret does not mean that the barrier ought to be torn down. The barrier may be a tremendous handicap on the Negro; but removing it would result in something worse. The real problem of the Negro, they say, is in the Negro's mind, in his spirit, in his everyday actions in which he may either attempt to achieve genuine excellence and win victory over circumstance, or continue to be "only natural." If the Negro tries, every decent white man will help him—but if the white man thinks that he alone, that he, the white man, can raise the Negro, if he acts on this notion, imagining that he can relieve the Negro of what the Negro himself needs to do, he only fixes the inferiority of the Negro more certainly, more firmly. Of course, men ought to be well-fed, well-clothed, well-housed; of course, society has responsibilities to every individual, every group. If the South were wise, say those who hold this view, it would want in its borders all the superiority it could get, and it would want this most of all among Negroes. Genuine superiority is not a thing to be feared. The thing to fear is inability to recognize it; and equally dangerous is that pride which prevents the cultivating and following of superiority wherever it appears. The thing to fight—and once understood, it is clear it has to be fought—is the false kind of superiority, the kind that values the label more than the quality of the thing itself.

Third, there is the view that the Negro is not inferior to the white man, that he only appears to be so, that his condition is wholly and completely a product of race prejudice, and the consequent disabilities inflicted on the Negro by the white man. This is the dominant view of the day, is subscribed to by most sociologists and anthropologists, and is taught in many of the schools and colleges and universities of the country. It is the doctrine of *An American Dilemma*, the largest, best financed, and most elaborate investigation of the Negro problem ever conducted in America. As the authors of *An American Dilemma* say, "... the undermining[3] of the basis of certitude for popular beliefs has been

---

[3] The method of undermining illustrates the quality of the thinking characteristic of this field. It is assumed that one standard or set of standards cannot be shown to be superior to another—therefore no set of customs and habits, no culture can be regarded as superior to another. The existence of a valid basis for comparing and evaluating cultures is thus denied. According to this view, the white man who thinks the Negro came from an inferior culture is an ignoramus, and needs instruction in anthropology to illuminate his darkness. "Scientific thought," writes Melville J. Herskovits, "has for some time abjured attempts at the comparative evaluation of cultures...." In the book from which this is quoted, the author argues the Negro needs a past and he therefore sets out to provide him with one. He assumes that if the Negro is provided with accounts of his origins, if he is made conscious of his past, then whatever the specific content of that past, so far as history is concerned, the Negro is as well-equipped as anyone. In all such reasoning, the idea of comparison is present, and comparing is done, even though the words may not be used. Not infrequently an author who has scorned the idea that one culture may be

accomplished." (p. 149) "The popular beliefs rationalizing caste. in America are no longer intellectually respectable." (p. 1003) The central argument of their work is that the United States must either give up the "American Creed" and go fascistic, or accept an equality which would permit amalgamation. Amalgamation is not represented as being just around the corner or foreseeable in some predictable future. But the implication of the whole work is that if the white man were not obstinate, if he were only reasonable and would allow himself to be guided by "science," all race problems would evaporate overnight. (p. 117)

In the last ten years there have been numerous books, pamphlets, and articles presenting the same arguments found in *An American Dilemma*—that racial notions are responsible for Nazism, that race is a "modern superstition," a "fallacy," "man's most dangerous myth," that the concept of race has no scientific basis, that there is no scientific evidence of differences of ability among races, that mental tests have proved substantial equality, that custom, tradition, prejudice, rather than genuine differences in capacity are responsible for the status of the Negro in the South. *An American Dilemma* is exceptional only in that it was written under highly favorable and most reputable auspices, and is more com-

---

superior to others will slip into specific comparisons and attributions of superiority, apparently without realizing it. E.g., Ruth Benedict, *Race: Science and Politics*, p. 131 ff., Modern Age Books, 1940. Of course the fallacy in the assumption of equality is that equality cannot be discovered to exist, if it does exist, until after comparisons have been made. Obviously, if relationships of equality are possible, so are those of inequality —one cannot exist without the other. It would be interesting to speculate on which is more responsible for the second world war, the idea of racial inequality or the denial of universally valid standards. In considering this problem it should not be forgotten that the particular type of superiority delusion from which the Nazis suffer has grown out of the denial of universal values. In my opinion the same undermining which gave Nazism its opportunity has been going on, is still going on in this country, and the process, described above, seems to me to be it. See Melville J. Herskovits, *The Myth of the Negro Past*, pp. 2, 32, Harpers, 1941. For flagrant use of above methods see *An American Dilemma*, numerous passages, especially Chapter 4, p. 99; Chapter 35, p. 753. These two books are in the same series, part of the same elaborate study referred to above.

prehensive, more thorough, more readable and reasonable than the mass of material sharing its attitude.

In the last ten years how many books, pamphlets, articles written by authors of scholarly standing have questioned this view or attempted to support either one of the others? I do not know of any. There is no doubt the first two views above are "no longer intellectually respectable." Among educated, well-informed persons to express them in public today is strictly taboo. But is it possible there is nothing of any weight to be said for them? Is it possible that *An American Dilemma* is the final, authoritative word on this subject—that this third view is dominant because it is thoroughly buttressed with facts and sound reasoning?

Long ago I had to decide which of these views seemed to me most in accord with the facts and most reasonable. In my account I have made no attempt to hide the place where my faith lies, but I prefer to remove any possible ambiguity. I hold to the second view. The first seems to me possible. The third is obviously untrue. No one but a person who would look for mountains with a microscope could fail to see the large and important considerations that compel its rejection.

I believe the work referred to above, *An American Dilemma*, was written under gross misapprehensions of what such ideas as equality, freedom, democracy, human rights, have meant, and of what they can be made to mean. I believe the small measure of these gained by western man is in serious danger of destruction by widespread misunderstanding of the kind represented in *An American Dilemma*.

Rational considerations compel the rejection of current arguments on this subject. Among these considerations are the following:

1. It is frequently assumed that no culture[4] can be considered superior to another and that there are no universally valid standards. But if these assumptions are accepted, then there is no basis for criticism of any culture.

[4] It may be said that these remarks are perhaps applicable to cultures but not to peoples and races. Of course, civilization is not the creation of any one race or people—it is the work of many over a long period of time. But "a culture" and "civilization" are not the same things. A culture

2. Nor is criticism possible on the basis of any standards the people in a culture may say they have. If examination of what is

is the total expression of a people or race in a particular area over a period of time. Civilization, in its most essential character, is an accumulation of universal values from various cultures. A culture can be measured only by comparing its values with those of civilization. In this view, the culture of a people is a reflection of its essential qualities. How it is, why it is, that qualities appear and disappear, that a culture previously backward and stagnant may become vigorous and active, may receive old and develop new values, or may decay, I do not pretend to know; and I am inclined to be skeptical of claims of knowledge in this field. It is not possible to accept the view that any one race is perpetually superior, or that race determines culture. But it does not follow that races are equal. Ultimately perhaps they are. (What a panic among our social scientists if they should wake up and discover how many ultimates they have been harboring.) At any particular time one race may embody values higher than those embodied by any other race, and as long as it does this, a race may rightly be regarded as superior. Races, peoples, individuals, if they are to be judged at all, have to be judged by the values they embody and express. Denial of the possibility of such judgment is equivalent to a denial of knowledge of values and of civilization. It may be said the concept of race is vague, not susceptible of exact scientific delineation, therefore inadmissible in scientific discussion; that since races cannot be given scientific definition, their existence is "pure myth," "superstition." But are all those things "pure myth" or "superstition" which cannot be exactly defined? Who can exactly define "man"? Is man therefore a myth? ... Where dilemmas and contradictions are recognized, they can be reduced to a minimum and handled with some degree of rationality. To exclude them entirely is, of course, impossible. One of the chief characteristics of naïve thinking is facility and innocence in the expression of incompatible ideas. Social science developed by people unaware of the dilemmas at the basis of their discipline is likely to contain a maximum of such ideas. For example, it is not surprising to find Myrdal calling the question "Would you like to have your sister or daughter marry a Negro?" "stereotyped" and "hypothetical" (p. 55), and treating it as if it were silly (p. 1012), and then arguing for a "cumulative principle" (p. 75 f.) expressing exactly the meaning embodied in the question. The question says: *One concession will lead to another, and ultimately to intermarriage. You and I and our people might not be involved, probably wouldn't. Most likely for a long time, only a small number would be involved. But have we no duty to the remote future as well as to the present? And if you want to be fair, apply it to yourself. How would you like it...?* The only difference between the reasoning back of the question and Myrdal's "cumulative principle" is that Myrdal doesn't object to the possibility of intermarriage. In any rational consideration, if the theory that one concession will lead to another is silly when expressed by the typical Southerner, it is also silly when expressed by Myrdal.

said and done reveals a discrepancy, this becomes merely an additional item in the list of cultural characteristics. For instance, if people choose to talk (or write, as in the Declaration of Independence) as if they believe in equality and yet act in a manner that seems to show they do not believe what they say, the relativist (one who denies universal values) cannot do more than point out this fact—he cannot say this is bad, or dangerous, or hypocritical, and ought to be corrected. He has to accept it unless he abandons his rejection of universal standards.

3. An examination of anthropological works of recent years will reveal consistent and thoroughgoing application of relativistic principles to primitive cultures. The up-to-date anthropologist has no use for those earlier reporters on life in primitive societies who thought they saw cannibalism and other strangely perverted forms of living and dying. He deals tenderly with primitive customs and explains them as not really bad whatever they are. According to current anthropological doctrine, outside interference that does not respect long-established customs is likely to result only in degrading or destroying a primitive culture. But if all cultures are equal, the same applies to all.

4. It follows, of course, that relativistic anthropological and sociological arguments concerning race prejudice in western society cannot be effective in the way intended by those making the arguments. The treatment of certain classes of persons in Germany or in the South, in India or in Africa—all have to be looked at merely as phenomena of particular times and places, neither good nor bad. But nothing could be more abhorrent than this view. Those who promote it have to go along with other civilized people and refuse to accept it when they see its consequences. But in doing so they destroy their assumptions of equality and the non-existence of universal values.

5. The above are surface dilemmas, clear once they are pointed out. A more fundamental problem is that the assertion of equality is an assertion of values. To say that all men or all peoples or all races are equal is to assert: a) that certain qualities exist; b) that these qualities exist among men; c) that each and every man has exactly the same portion. Now to discover whether there is

any validity in the idea of the equality of all men, it has to be asked: What qualities, if any, are shared equally by all men? The author of the famous phrase "all men are created equal" also wrote: "I do not mean to deny that there are varieties in the race of man distinguished by their powers both of body and mind. I believe there are, as I see to be the case in the races of other animals." (Notes on Virginia.) What then did Jefferson mean when he used the word *equal*? According to his own statement (Letter to Henry Lee, May 8, 1825), among his sources were "the elementary books of public right, as Aristotle, Cicero, Locke, Sidney...." Now look at one of these authors, that one closest to Jefferson in time and fighting the divine right of kings exactly as Jefferson was. In his second *Treatise on Civil Government*, VI, 54, Locke says:

> Though I have said above 'That all men by nature are equal,' I cannot be supposed to understand all sorts of 'equality.' Age or virtue may give men a just precedency. Excellency of parts and merit may place others above the common level. Birth may subject some, and alliance or benefits others, to pay an observance to those to whom Nature, gratitude, or other respects, may have made it due; and yet all this consists with the equality which all men are in in respect of jurisdiction or dominion one over another, which was the equality I there spoke of as proper to the business in hand, being that equal right that every man hath to his natural freedom, without being subject to the will or authority of any other man.

It is impossible here to go further into the question of the exact content of the word "equal" as used in the Declaration of Independence. It should be clear that those who deny universal values cannot believe in equality, that they do not know what they are saying either when they deny the values or when they assert the equality. It is not improbable that they are ignorant of the nature of both.

Those of us who believe in universal values can also subscribe without reservation to Jefferson's idea of equality. This idea is more powerful than any high explosive. Handled with knowledge and skill it can civilize the world. Handled ignorantly or maliciously it can blow humane living out of existence and reduce man to a level lower than that of the savage.

Now it may be said: all this is mere rhetoric. What are these universal standards? Do they really exist? If so, where? Have they ever been demonstrated as valid and universal? Again, if so, where?

These questions may be pressed hard. The answers given them may be—often are—called empty and far removed from actual existence. But if there are no valid answers, how do the anthropologists and sociologists and social engineers (not to mention the rest of us) explain their zeal to reform the South? Are their efforts calculated merely to degrade or destroy? We can be certain this is not the case. On the contrary, there can be no question their motive is humane, is filled with conviction that there is a better and a worse, a good and a bad, that they know what these are, and that somehow the South, if not the world, must be brought up to their standards. When they pick the South, they assume—despite all their assertions of equality—either that the South needs their attentions because it is below par and they believe they can bring it up, or that it can stand their experimentation because it is strong and above the weaknesses of other cultures.

Along with the denial of universal values has gone another process of comparable importance. Since all people are equal, so the assumptions go, the explanation of apparent inequalities must lie in environment. All of us, in this view, are products of the conditions under which we have lived. No informed person would ever think of blaming the Ashanti, Dahomeans, or Yoruba for anything they do or do not do. If they had had the proper environment, so we are led to believe, they could have produced everything in which western man prides himself. And so it follows—how is not explained—it is your duty and mine to give them the proper environment. But, unfortunately, environment also embraces and determines western man. Prejudice is, of course, one of the things determined. Now when someone comes along and argues against prejudice, is he merely responding to the pressures of his environment and entitled only to a push that will finish him or send him in another direction; or is he to be understood as insisting that men ought to overcome their environment?

This should cause no difficulty. The latter is the obvious answer. Civilization would not exist if men had never overcome their environment. One group of men living in the presence of slavery gets an idea of freedom and gives that idea a form which lives for the future. Call it what you will, those men have done something that sets them apart, something that is worth remembering. Certainly the Dahomeans, or Ashanti, or Yoruba might have done the same; but neither they nor their descendants have yet done anything remotely comparable. Which proves exactly nothing as to what they may or may not do in the future. But whatever they do, we can be sure it will not be worth remembering if it can be explained wholly and completely by environment.

All of this has as much application to the South as to the Negro. The South, white and brown, must transcend the agitations, the hatreds, the foolish charges and counter charges, the pressures and threats of pressures with which it is encompassed. The white Southerner, reading this book, must remember that the task of the superior man is not to prate of being superior but to be really so. And that, in a world that seems determined to drag everything to one level, is no easy thing.

I have argued at length elsewhere ("The Negro" in *Culture in the South*) that many of the customs and practices and discriminations of the South are a terrible burden on the region and ought to be removed. But I have also argued, and see no reason to change my view, that "no worse punishment for Negro children in the South could be imagined than to send them to schools with white children." I believe that if complete elimination of segregation could be accomplished overnight—as many of the authors of this volume assume it ought to be—the consequences would be disastrous for everyone and more so for the Negro than the white man.

In spite of these beliefs, however, I am convinced the white Southerner would do well not to be too sure of his superiority. Two thousand years ago his ancestors were regarded by the civilized people of that time as savages incapable of enlightenment. Too many of us forget that even two hundred years ago the ancestors of the great majority of us were nobodies, considered inferior by nature. We forget too easily the ideas that enable us to stand up among men, any men anywhere. To be true to our heritage we must remember the admonition of Jefferson: "The mass of mankind has not been born with saddles on their backs, nor a favored few booted and spurred, ready to ride them legitimately, by the Grace of God." But, in Jefferson's view, if the masses are not to be ridden, they must not merely reject the leadership of the old aristocracy of birth and wealth, they must produce out of themselves and accept the leadership of an aristocracy of virtue and talent.

When the Press asked for this book it was hoped that serious attention would be given the possibilities for the Negro in America and elsewhere. The old complaints against the white man may be justified, but more than that, far more, is needed. More evidence that the white man is not considered responsible for everything, that the Negro himself has some responsibilities would help. Does the Negro have no opportunities in the South? Is the southern white man to blame for everything that happens? Do fate and the Negro have no part?

Do Negro leaders have any ideas on how educational processes can be improved? What is the Negro doing of importance in agriculture, in industry, in the professions? What is he inventing, discovering, writing? What is he contributing that is new and valuable, what does he want, what does he need in order to enable him to contribute more?

Is there need for a really great university for Negroes in the South? Can it be that Negroes in this region now have all the educational opportunities they can use? Which is the wiser course for the Negro: continuation of efforts to break down segregation in higher education—efforts which have no chance to succeed—or efforts to get the southern states to co-operate in supporting a first-rate institution for Negroes in some southern center?

Can Negroes and whites learn to work together, to develop and use all their talents, to live in peace and mutual respect—can they discover the meaning of human rights, can they learn to practice what they discover? Can they remain racially separate and distinct and at the same time avoid inflicting disabilities on each other? Does the white man have no right to attempt to separate cultural from biological integration, and help the Negro achieve the first and deny him the second? Can biological integration be regarded as a right? What happens to the case for the Negro if it is tied up with things to which he not only has no right, but which, if granted, would destroy all rights? If any two people have a right to lead their own lives, certainly any two others or ten or twenty million have a right to opinions on what ought to be allowed and what forbidden. To say that the twenty million have no right to make and enforce decisions that they think necessary to the well-being of all is to say that society has no right to govern itself. The assumption of a better, a more valid authority, one that can be understood and that ought to be accepted by all rational beings, one that speaks with the voice of reason and justice, is the only foundation for appeals against majority decisions. To say that two may be right and twenty million wrong is to say that there is a more valid authority, that it is the only trustworthy guide, and that all men ought to act in accord with it. But the spokesmen for minorities have followed the fashion of the times and denied the existence of any such authority. In doing so they have destroyed the only possible basis for their arguments, and have abandoned their only opportunity to help create understanding where confusion now exists.

What problem would be solved if the white South dropped all barriers and accepted amalgamation? Would anything be gained if overnight the whole population could be made one color? One of man's great problems in this world is to learn what is good, to learn to recognize the good in whatever form, under whatever circumstances, it may appear. Some day the social engineers may be able to make all men alike, indistinguishable from one another, and equally good. But until that has been done, men need most of all to learn to recognize and use good qualities whether they belong to tall or short, round or long skulled, colored or white. Booker Washington came nearer than anyone else to stating the problem of the Negro in its true terms. Envy, jealousy among his own people seriously hampered his efforts, curbed his program.

Nothing is more needed in the South today than rebirth of his ideas, restoration of the great leadership that he was giving.

I believe that regardless of the Negro's abilities the same justice that is good for the white man is good for the Negro. But this justice does not, cannot operate on the basis of a mechanical equality. To be just, distinctions and discriminations have to be made. If the distinctions and discriminations are made in directions that some people say are wrong—who can take such charges seriously in a world that denies the existence of any real right and wrong? I can and do, because I believe standards of right and wrong are necessary to civilization. Until the modern intellectual abandons his relativistic dogmas, he cannot criticize without expecting to be reminded that, according to his own doctrines, his opinion is merely his opinion and has no real validity. If he can quote "authorities," if something that calls itself "science" supports his views, if the assertion of opposed views is not intellectually respectable, what of it? What kind of "science" is it that has to support itself in this manner?

While I disagree with the editor and most of the contributors on basic problems, there is much in the present book with which I have to agree. It is unnecessary for me to go into this here in greater detail. I hope there is something beyond my opinions, and the opinions here expressed, to which all of us recognize allegiance. In our devotion to this, in our efforts to discover what it is, I would like to believe we are as one. In any case, I thank the participants in this volume for expressing their real opinions and making this book possible.

W. T. Couch

Chapel Hill, N. C.
April 13, 1944

WHAT THE NEGRO WANTS

THE NEGRO
WANTS FIRST-CLASS
CITIZENSHIP

By RAYFORD W. LOGAN

———

THE MATHEMATICS AND DYNAMICS OF THE PROBLEM

THE NEGRO PROBLEM in the United States is today a national problem spawned from two hundred forty years of slavery and the northward migration of Negroes incident to two world wars. It is our number one domestic failure and our number one international handicap. Common sense, devotion to our democratic ideals, and the imperatives of our national security and our moral leadership in world affairs demand its immediate improvement and ultimate solution.

We have been free for eighty years, one-third of the time that the Negro ancestors of most of us were slaves. This simple bit of arithmetic explains in large measure our third-class citizenship. It suggests also that we shall need another one hundred sixty years (approximately of course) to attain first-class citizenship, for human progress seems to require almost as long to destroy the vestiges of an institution as the institution had previously existed. This conclusion, I might observe, has been attacked by some critics as being unduly pessimistic; by others, as being incurably optimistic.

While this national time ratio of slavery to freedom is three to one, the regional ratios vary. It is highest in the South where slavery existed practically from the earliest days of settlement and where it was not abolished until eighty years ago. The ratio is lower in the North, for the original Northern states down to the Maryland-Delaware line had emancipated their slaves from forty to eighty years earlier than the American Civil War freed them in the South. The Ordinance of 1787, the Missouri Compromise of 1820, the Oregon Act of 1848 and the Compromise of 1850 made the Old Northwest, the Middle Northwest and the Far Northwest free territory. Until recently, there was much evidence for believing that the Negro problem in the United States could have been stated in the form of a proposition in which the acuteness of the problem was to X (the solution of the problem) as the duration of slavery was to the period of freedom.

Numbers have been the second important factor in determining the gravity of the problem. There is naturally a direct relationship between the time element and the numerical factor, for emancipation came generally last in those areas in which the number of slaves had been highest. When the four million slaves in the South were freed, elsewhere in the United States there were only some four hundred thousand Negroes.

Numbers today are becoming more important than the time ratio of slavery to freedom. Prior to the outbreak of World War II, race relations in the South had been gradually improving but race relations in the North had already begun to deteriorate. One fundamental reason for these changes was the considerable number of Negroes who had migrated from the South to the North. In the region from Delaware to Florida the Negro population had decreased from 33.7 per cent in 1910 to 26.4 per cent in 1940; in Kentucky, Tennessee, Alabama and Mississippi from 31.5 per cent to 25.8 per cent; in Arkansas, Louisiana, Oklahoma and Texas from 22.6 per cent to 18.6 per cent. The increase in New England had been only slight—from 1.0 per cent to 1.2 per cent. But the Middle Atlantic Region of New York, New Jersey and Pennsylvania had more than doubled from 2.2 per cent to 4.6 per cent. The East North Central (the Old Northwest) had similarly more than doubled from 1.6 per cent to 4.0 per cent. The West North Central and the Mountain Regions on the other hand had changed only slightly from 2.1 per cent to 2.6 per cent and from 0.8 per cent to 0.9 per cent respectively. But the Pacific Coast Region had doubled from 0.7 per cent to 1.4 per cent.

The importance of numbers is even more convincing when one breaks down the various regions. In the South race relations are generally most tense in those regions where the proportion of Negroes is highest. A young white Southern girl who is earnestly trying to formulate in her own mind an equitable attitude told me that she accepted all the criticisms that I had made, but then insisted: "But what are we going to do in a city where Negroes outnumber the whites? Accept the domination of the Negroes?" (Evidently she could not conceive that a numerically stronger race would permit equality to the weaker race.) Similarly race relations in the North are most tense in those states and cities where the Negro population has most considerably increased. The Negro population in Michigan, for example, had increased by more than five hundred fifty per cent. The exact increase in Detroit by 1943 can only be estimated, but several Detroiters of both races told me in January, 1943, that they expected a riot to result in part from this increase, and Detroiters of both races told me in January, 1944, that the riot had resulted in part from this increase.[1] As early as 1936 a movement was on foot to establish separate schools in Los Angeles and in some other cities of California. While segregation and other forms of discrimination have not been generally established farther north on the Pacific coast, cities like Seattle in which the Negro population has considerably increased reveal the usual connection between numbers and increased discrimination and segregation. Long-time residents of Washington, Philadelphia, New York, Brooklyn, Cleveland, and Chicago, for example, are convinced that a general deterioration in race relations has resulted when there has been a noticeable increase in the Negro population.

Numbers alone have not caused this deterioration in the North. Many of the Negro migrants have come from rural areas of the South and have naturally had difficulties in adjusting themselves to urban conditions. Many Negroes from the urban as well as from the rural South have had a lower cultural status than Northern Negroes who have had the benefit of better schools, frequently better homes, and daily contact with other superior

[1] See also Alfred McLung Lee and Norman Daymond Humphrey, *Race Riot*, New York, 1943.

culture-forming traits and manners. Most Southern Negroes have been understandingly eager to enjoy their new freedom. Moreover, many Southern whites who have migrated to the North have sought to establish Southern mores there.

The factor of numbers and of its concomitants has not merely assumed greater importance than the time factor of slavery and freedom. *The factor of numbers has made the Negro problem a national problem.* This nationalization of the problem may, as will be developed later, provide a substantial basis for its solution.

Meanwhile, however, this nationalization of the problem has aided the dynamic determination of the South that the Cause which it had lost on the battlefields of the American Civil War shall nevertheless triumph over the entire nation. That Cause has been its firm belief in a civilization based upon white supremacy. Contributory reasons for the South's crusade have been resentment arising from the loss of three billion dollars' worth of slave property, from its defeat in the Civil War, its subjection to the North and to Negroes during Reconstruction and the assignment to it of the rôle of the problem child. Desire for revenge and vindication has unquestionably given a proselyting fervor to the "Fighting South." Economic exploitation of cheap labor has undergirded the zeal. But both the greed and the zeal have been fortified by a firm conviction, originally perhaps only a rationalization, that God has ordained the Negro eternally to be a hewer of wood and drawer of water so that a superior people could develop the finest civilization that the world has known.

An illustration par excellence of this belief is the following story told by Mr. Ralph T. Jones in "The South's Standard Newspaper," the *Atlanta Constitution*. A crowd of Negroes remained standing in the rear of an Atlanta street car although there were many vacant seats in the front. Finally, a "decent, hardworking" colored woman asked the conductor if he would not, as the law requires, have a white man move to the front so that some of the Negroes could have seats. "The conductor replied: 'The white man can sit where he pleases.'" Mr. Jones commented that "that was one attitude." But the white man who had not been previously aware that he had been depriving Negroes of their lawful seats then moved to the front. "That was another attitude," Mr. Jones pointed out. He then drew the moral: "As to your opinion as to which of the two attitudes was right and which wrong, that will determine whether you are fit to bear the responsibilities which white supremacy places upon all white persons in the South."[2] Some readers need perhaps to be warned that Mr. Jones was in dead earnest. This attitude, which represents the thinking of many Southerners who sincerely think that they believe in "justice" to the Negro, is more discouraging than the rantings of politicians like ex-Governor Talmadge of Georgia, Senators Eastland and Bilbo of Mississippi and Representative Rankin of the same state.

But the idea of white supremacy has by no means been limited to the South. Some New Englanders who would not hold slaves bought them in Africa or the West Indies and sold them to the South; others made fortunes out of manufacturing slave-produced cotton and out of selling products for slave consumption. Riots in Philadelphia and Cincinnati prior to the Civil War attest the hostility of many workers in free territory to the presence of free Negroes. Northern advocates of the colonization or deportation of both slave and free Negroes used language that Hitler might have borrowed.[3] Many Northerners placed the Union above abolition. Mayor Wood of New York recommended on January 8, 1861, the secession of the city. "Copperheads" were by no means the only group that opposed the Civil War after it began—the "draft riots" in New York City in July, 1863, stemmed not only from opposition to the war but to Negroes in general. After the war, Northern Big Business as well as humanitarianism secured the ratification of the Fourteenth Amendment, and Big Business soon decided that it could make more money out of a stabilized racial situation in the South than it could out of agitation for Negro rights. The picture of an undivided North militantly fighting for the rights of the Negro is as great a myth as the spectre of a South in which every man, woman and child is adamant in his determination to deny to the Negro any opportunity for progress.

[2] December 12, 1942, p. 4.
[3] See my article, "Some New Interpretations of the Colonization Movement," *Phylon*, III (Fourth Quarter, 1943), 328-334.

The North, at all events, was in a receptive mood when Henry W. Grady of Atlanta began in the 1880's his intellectual conquest of the North with his eloquent speech, "The New South." He convinced his Phi Beta Kappa and business audiences that if the North, "which did not understand the Negro problem in the South," would only leave it alone, Southerners could be depended upon to treat the Negro with fairness and justice. (I can still remember the effect that this oration had on many of my classmates when we studied it in a Massachusetts college in 1916.) The South followed this encouraging initial victory by contracting intersectional marriages and by exporting its surplus population of not only poor workers but of intellectuals, professional and business men to the North. Southern revisionist historians have "proved" that slavery was all but idyllic, that the Civil War was an unconscionable and unnecessary blunder, that Reconstruction was an unmitigated orgy of black and Republican corruption. *Gone with the Wind* was the crowning achievement of a long list of books and movies that helped the Lost Cause to win popular support in the North.

Jacob Riis, Carl Schurz and other European intellectual liberals in the meantime fought for human rights, but great masses of laborers from European nations were not going to let a little thing like racial equality keep them from growing rich in the promised land. All too many members of racial and other groups fleeing persecution in their native land soon learned to outdo native born Americans in discriminating against Negroes. In the stern language of Oliver Cromwell: "Every sect saith 'Oh, give me Liberty,' but give him it and to his power he will not yield it to anybody else." Finally, when the migration incident to two world wars brought many Northerners into individual contact with many Negroes, most of these Northerners found that they had no substantial, practical, equalitarian philosophy, convictions or techniques. Many Northerners therefore gladly accepted Southern patterns since they were based upon a longer experience with a vexatious problem. The spread of these patterns to the North was made all the easier by reason of the fact that most Northern Negroes had deluded themselves into the fond and foolish belief that their static, relatively better situation could withstand a persistent, dynamic onslaught. Today, most white people, North as well as South, do not accept the Negro as an equal.

The Negro in general suffers more kinds of inequality than does any other minority in the United States, be it racial, religious, cultural, or economic. The association between the Negro's race and his inequality is therefore undeniable. Consequently, the achievement of equality will be extremely difficult, for racial differences have long been a most potent dynamic force in human relations. Even if "race" were nothing more than a "superstition," as Jacques Barzun terms it, it would be for that very reason a serious psychological hurdle. Even if racial attitudes and conduct are due in large measure to "prejudice," that fact similarly makes improvement a tremendous task. *Ideas are Weapons*, Mr. Max Lerner reminds us—false ideas as well as correct ones. Moreover, those who try to free themselves from superstition and prejudice find such conflicting conclusions among "scientists" that they may doubt, intellectually, the inherent equality of all mankind. Finally, most white persons, whether they be superstitious, prejudiced, or intellectual, believe that their fullest enjoyment of life—economic, political, cultural and social—demands the denial of full equality to the Negro.

The Negro problem in the United States is especially acute today. In normal times the great masses of Negroes, North and South, accept more or less silently the not too violent disregard of what they more or less vaguely consider their constitutional and legal rights and the equally nebulous ideals of the Declaration of Independence. But when our nation goes to war to assure the victory of the "democracies" over the "fascist" nations, we naturally become more insistent that democracy, like charity, should begin at home. We want an equal share not only in the performance of responsibilities and obligations but also in the enjoyment of rights and opportunities. We want the same racial equality at the ballot-box that we have at the income-tax window; the same equality before a court of law that we have before an enemy's bullet; the same equality for getting a job, education, decent housing, and social security that American kinsmen of our nation's enemies possess. We want the Four Freedoms to apply to black Americans as well as to brutalized peoples of Europe and to the other underprivileged peoples of the world. We insist that insofar as the equality asserted in the Declaration of Independence is applicable to all men, it should include us. We declare that our presence in this country for more than three hundred years, our toil, our honorable service in all our nation's wars, our demonstrated capacity for progress warrant our aspirations for eventual first-class citizenship and eventual full integration into the public life of the American people.

We do not stand alone. Even the conservative *Washington Post* admonished editorially that Negroes "can scarcely be expected to give full devotion to the democratic cause unless it affords some recognition of their legitimate aspirations." [4] But the more we assert these "legitimate aspirations," which the *Post* did not enumerate, the more the advocates of the *status quo* become determined to deny them. Mr. Duncan Aikman reported almost a year before Pearl Harbor, before these aspirations had become resoundingly vocal, that Southerners of various economic brackets were saying: " 'We're not going to let the Negro come out of this war on top of the heap as he did in the last one.' [!] That means," Mr. Aikman continued, "and plenty of Southerners stated it specifically, no Negro officers this time; no Negro skilled labor training and, if avoidable, not even any combat regiments." [5] Investigations by the National Association for the Advancement of Colored People, the National Urban League, and the Committee for Participation of Negroes in National Defense revealed at the same time a shockingly large number of Northern manufacturers and laborers, both organized and unorganized, just as determined not to use or permit to be used skilled Negro labor or to train it.

Negroes quite naturally became angry. Their anger increased when our entry into the war did not materially alter the situation. Fixed patterns of segregation in the armed forces that carried segregation into sections of the nation where it had not previously existed, limitations upon advancement, insults and violence inflicted upon men and women in uniform added to the resent-

[4] July 20, 1943, p. 8.
[5] *Washington Post*, February 26, 1941, p. 1.

ment. The insistence by the Red Cross that blood from Negroes for the blood bank should be labeled Negro—in spite of the facts that a Negro physician, Dr. Charles Drew, had made significant contributions to the development of the idea of the blood bank and that science denies that blood types are determined by race—provoked extreme bitterness. The failure to give adequate publicity to white America of the feats of Negro heroes also produced much caustic criticism. The conspicuous absence of the Chairman of the Senate Committee on Foreign Relations from official dinners given by the President of the United States to the Presidents of Liberia and of Haiti more than offset the fact that the Speaker of the House who is also from Texas rose above his racial provincialism sufficiently to perform his official duties. The discrimination imposed upon dark-skinned individuals from some Latin American nations, even when they were guests of our government, was not likely to decrease the resentment. American Negroes have been particularly distressed by the humiliations inflicted upon black French soldiers and sailors in this country. Reports of discrimination by Americans against Negroes in foreign theatres of war have cast an added pall of gloom. The little consideration given to Negroes in all parts of the world by many planners for world peace and the apparent acceptance of Prime Minister Jan Christiaan Smuts of South Africa as the spokesman for all of English Africa—all of these have caused many Negroes to ask bitterly, "What are we fighting for?"

The tension has at times become so great that periodically some "liberals," both North and South, have warned us to keep quiet. At least one rather well-known Southern colored educator publicly preaches the same doctrine. But most Negroes remember public lethargy on the Negro question in time of peace. They ask this question: If they can not assert their rights at the very time that they are risking their lives in the name of the very rights which they are asking, when will they receive consideration? We have no wish to obstruct the war effort. Rather we believe that the recognition and implementation of at least some of our legitimate aspirations will materially aid the winning of victory. Unfortunately, as this book goes to the press, the debates over the soldier vote bill, the publicly declared determination of some Southerners to filibuster the anti-poll tax bill to death reveal that the Old Guard dies but never surrenders. Many Negroes therefore remind themselves of the famous passage that William Lloyd Garrison wrote in the first issue of the *Liberator:* "I am in earnest. I will not equivocate—I will not excuse—I will not retreat a single inch. AND I WILL BE HEARD."

THE PROBLEM: DEMOCRACY THIRD-CLASS

Most Negroes in all parts of the United States have been relegated today to third-class citizenship. Our disabilities are greatest of course in the South. Poll-tax laws in eight states, the Democratic white primary which excludes practically all Negroes from voting for the candidates of the one party that rules the South, and outright intimidation violate the dictum of the Declaration of Independence that governments derive "their just powers from the consent of the governed." Segregation in schools, churches, theatres, restaurants, hotels, public transportation and in some cases in the places where they work and live constantly remind Negroes of their "inferiority." While happily the number of lynchings has greatly decreased, the threat of force prevents many legitimate aspirations. Instead of looking to the courts for protection, many self-respecting Negroes will forego their constitutional and legal rights because of the conviction that they will not be given a fair trial or will be humiliated by even the judges. Opprobrious epithets, unearned lofty titles such as "doctor" or "professor," or belittling names such as "boy," which any white man can use in addressing any Negro, hurt their pride and discourage their ambitions. The per capita expenditure for Negro education is much less than that for white children in all Southern states. Negro school teachers, with few exceptions, are paid less than white teachers with the same training and experience. Most Negroes are unskilled laborers in industry, domestic servants, or the most underprivileged farm workers. Most of the few semi-skilled and skilled workers receive lower wages than do most white workers performing the same tasks. There is hardly a single Negro above the custodial status in the administration building of any Southern state, county or

city. Intermarriage is of course forbidden in all the Southern
states.

In some respects Negroes in the Northern states fare much
better. They do have an effective vote and they send several
representatives to the state legislatures and to the city councils.
They hold many positions in the lower personnel brackets of
state, county and city administration and a few high positions.
They have greater protection in the courts and they enjoy more
civil liberties and relatively more civil rights. The threat of violence is less real. There is freer use of Mr., Mrs., and Miss, and less
public use of opprobrious and humiliating epithets. But segregation in the public schools, made easier by planned residential
segregation, is spreading. Segregation is also proceeding apace in
theatres, restaurants, hotels and on through trains to and from
the South. In cities in which there is any considerable Negro
population, segregation in the churches has long been almost as
general as in the South. The economic status of many Negroes
in the North is not appreciably higher than that of most Negroes
in the South. Gerrymandering and other techniques have thus
far limited to one the number of Negroes in Congress at any
one time. Intermarriage is forbidden by law in many Northern
states and contracted to only a limited extent in the others.

The national government has not greatly aided the Negro in
his struggle for equality. The Supreme Court has authorized
segregation if equal accommodations are provided, and it has permitted the Democratic party to exclude Negroes from its membership. Congress has not yet included most Negro workers
—domestics and agricultural laborers—in its social security provisions. The armed forces have followed a virtually iron-clad
policy of segregation in all parts of the country. While there are
more than three thousand colored officers in the army, they are
limited with few exceptions to the lower commissions. The Navy
had no known colored officers until recently and the Coast
Guard only a negligible number. Only recently has the Navy
permitted Negroes to serve again in capacities other than that
of messmen, and only recently has the Marine Corps abandoned
its traditional policy of excluding Negroes altogether. Most federal departments and agencies practise various forms of segre-

gation even in their Washington and some Northern offices, and none of them gives the Negro equal opportunity for promotion. There is probably not a single Negro occupying a policy-making position in the entire federal government. The President of the United States has not been able to secure full compliance even in the capital and in some parts of the North with his Executive Order 8802 which seeks to prevent racial discrimination in war industries.

Management also has generally discriminated against the Negro. Some firms, North and South, do not employ Negroes in any capacity. Many hire them only in menial and custodial capacities. Only a few give them skilled jobs and equal wages. Only a very small number permit them to hold executive positions. At the same time management employs in strategic positions in war industries men of German and Italian extraction although spies have been found among their number. Such recent gains as Negroes have made in industry have been due largely to the exigencies of the war.

Labor has been in many instances as hostile to Negro workers as has government or management, thus providing them with an additional pretext for not employing Negroes. "The solidarity of labor" is another myth as far as the history of American labor is concerned. More than thirty unions still bar Negroes from membership and many others grant them only limited rights. We can justly condemn these unions, most of which are A. F. of L., as "soulless corporations," the pet name that labor used to apply to Big Business. They resent any suggestion of government regulation for the purpose of changing their undemocratic practices. An A. F. of L. specialist on labor relations in the Office of Emergency Management told a committee of which I was a member in 1941 that "it is ridiculous to think that government can impose any restrictions on labor as far as its membership is concerned." The practice of establishing "auxiliary," that is separate Negro, unions the members of which are subject to the same obligations as are the members of the principal union but are denied the right to voting privileges and representation has of course raised the traditional American protest against "taxation without representation." As is well known, the C. I. O., on the other hand, has been the most aggressive organization in recent years in promoting not only economic equality for the Negro but also political and even social equality. Some Negroes express the belief that a long war may break down the undemocratic practices of the recalcitrant labor unions.

The United States has, in brief, developed a de luxe democracy. More than a century ago, some advocates of colonization or deportation of the American Negro outside the United States argued that the American democracy was for white men only since the Negro was not capable of assuming the full obligations of life in that democracy. Today the American government, management, and a large segment of labor and of the public, by denying the Negro equal opportunities, have "proved" to their satisfaction that we are not worthy of this de luxe democracy.

We have unquestionably provided some evidence for this argument. In times of prosperity we have bought too many fifteen-dollar green and red striped silk shirts, too many high-powered automobiles and fur coats, too much dog food and whiskey. We have been "stomping" at the Savoy when we should have been meeting to promote a better understanding of our problems and to concert plans for improving conditions. Many of us are boisterous in public. Too many are undependable on the job. Most of our leaders failed to prepare for the great opportunities and dangers that the European conflict portended— our first national conference on the participation of the Negro in national defense was held more than two years after Munich in connection with the induction into office of the President of Hampton Institute. There has been too much bickering between our own organizations. We do not yet have any coordinated effort to prepare for the peace conference.

But I believe that these shortcomings are largely attributable to our slave heritage, that they are characteristic of most recently liberated peoples, and that we shall eradicate them as this degradation fades into the past. I believe further that not only Frederick Douglass, W. E. B. Du Bois, Everett Just, Henry O. Tanner, Charles W. Chestnutt, Brigadier General B. O. Davis, Colonel Charles Young, the 99th Pursuit Squadron, Roland

Hayes, Paul Robeson, Marian Anderson, George Washington Carver and Booker T. Washington but also tens of thousands of decent, hardworking, thrifty Negroes have demonstrated beyond cavil our capacity to meet any test required of other Americans.

WHAT WE WANT

Negroes in the United States want first-class citizenship. There is, of course, still a considerable number who are willing to settle for less. This number is, however, growing smaller: a current expression among us asserts that "it is time for the leadership to catch up with the followship." There is also the growing conviction among us that the privileges and opportunities of the "talented tenth" are curtailed by the proscription of those privileges and opportunities to other Negroes, just as many white persons realize the danger for themselves in the proscription of these privileges and opportunities. In the name of democracy for all Americans we ask these irreducible fundamentals of first-class citizenship for all Negroes:

1. Equality of opportunity
2. Equal pay for equal work
3. Equal protection of the laws
4. Equality of suffrage
5. Equal recognition of the dignity of the human being
6. Abolition of public segregation

HOW TO GET WHAT WE WANT

I believe that a true application of the principles of democracy is the best way to gain this first-class citizenship. Thus, one of the fundamentals of democracy is acquiescence in the will of the majority. But, as Thomas Jefferson admonished in his First Inaugural Address: "All, too, will bear in mind this sacred principle, that though the will of the majority is in all cases to prevail, that will to be rightful must be reasonable; that the minority possess their equal rights, which equal law must protect, and to violate would be oppression."

I believe that we shall not gain these equal rights in the near future. The will of the majority is opposed to granting them now. We have, in truth, the same theoretical right to revolution that the Declaration of Independence asserts. In cold reality, thirteen millions, largely unarmed, have no chance to win equality by force from an adamant, powerfully armed one hundred twenty millions. The constant shifting of the Communist position has disillusioned most of the few who had put their hope in an American Communist Revolution. Most of us believe further that any real threat of such a revolution would provide American "fascists" with the very pretext that they seek in order to establish their own totalitarian government. The insistence by the Soviet Union upon the necessity for expanding her western boundary should disillusion those few who believed that Russia would have no ambitions which she would have to sacrifice at the peace conference in order to force American acceptance of Negro equality. And the infinitesimally small number who looked to Japan as their savior must now realize that Japan is not going to invade the United States.

Nor is the Negro problem going to be solved by the extinction of the Negro, by any Forty-Ninth State, by any Back-to-Africa movement. While Professor S. J. Holmes studiously avoided predictions, his carefully documented study must discourage those who believed with F. L. Hoffman, Edward Eggleston, and Dr. Raymond Pearl that, in the words of the last named: "Under conditions as they are, Nature by the slow but dreadfully sure process of evolution is apparently solving the Negro problem in the United States, in a manner which, when finished, will be, like all Nature's solutions, final, complete, and absolutely definite." [6] The proposal to establish a Forty-Ninth State in the United States for Negroes died a-borning about ten years ago. From Paul Cuffe to Marcus Garvey and Senator Bilbo, plans for the colonization or deportation of Negroes have failed to win the support of any considerable number of Negroes, or latterly of white Americans. Our roots are so deep in this country and our conviction of our obligation to help "solve the problem" so great

[6] S. J. Holmes, *The Negro's Struggle for Survival, A Study in Human Ecology* (Berkeley, 1937), especially pp. xi, 15-16, 214-224.

that, with few exceptions, we are determined to remain in the land of our birth and of our forefathers. My Negro grandfather was born in Fauquier County, Virginia, in 1829, the year in which Andrew Jackson first became President, three years after Thomas Jefferson and John Adams died, thirty years after George Washington died. I am an American. No Old Americans, no Europeans barely escaped from the Gestapo, no frustrated, pessimistic or ambitious Americans can make of me anything but an American. Besides, where would any considerable number of us go?

In recent years some Negroes have adapted an old American technique for the solution of the problem, namely, the March-on-Washington. Since I sat with Mr. A. Philip Randolph and Mr. Eugene Davidson in the all-day conference with Mayor LaGuardia and Mr. Aubrey Williams that culminated in the President's Executive Order 8802 of June 25, 1941, I can bespeak the power of a threatened march. There are, however, definite limitations on its power. Restrictions on travel have nullified it for the duration of the war and will probably curtail it in the crucial period when the European peace conference is held. Housing conditions in Washington and in many other "boom" cities during these same periods further restrict the number who would "march." Even under the best conditions, the March can be used only occasionally unless such a small number participated as to make the March appear to be a bluff. Constant vigilance would have to be exercised against *agents provocateurs* or outside hoodlums determined to create disorder or a riot. I definitely favor the March-on-Washington or on other cities only as a rare, dramatic, powerful weapon that should be used only when all other methods have failed.

Non-violent resistance, which the Fellowship of Reconciliation has developed in several cities, has achieved a limited success in breaking down public segregation. For example, a group of Negroes and of whites go to a restaurant that does not serve Negroes, thus demonstrating that at least some whites have no objection to eating with Negroes. Whatever happens, the group does not resort to violence. Sometimes this demonstration results in service. Evidently, however, repeated visits are necessary to have the service of Negro patrons accepted by management, waiters and customers as a fixed custom.

Consumers' and producers' cooperatives have been advocated almost as a panacea. But cooperatives in the United States, regardless of the constituency, have not achieved any signal success. Moreover, an extensive survey of cooperatives in ten European countries led to these conclusions: "From the things we learned and the figures we gathered could be woven an Aladdin tale of cooperative success. From a different selection of material could be built a story of cooperative blunders and class antagonism." [7]

My own methods for achieving first-class citizenship for the Negro take as their point of departure the fact that the Negro problem in the United States is today a national problem. This fact does not mean that all the problems are equally acute in all parts of the nation or even in the South. Likewise in a city one finds anomalies. In Washington, for example, Negroes are admitted to the ball park without segregation but are denied even segregation in the white movie houses. At one sports place they may buy seats for certain events but not for others. We eat at the Union Station, at the Supreme Court cafeteria and the National Art Gallery but not at most of the public restaurants elsewhere. The public schools are segregated but the street cars and buses are not. Two institutions of higher learning admit a limited number of Negro students; the others none. This crazy-quilt is found in practically all parts of the United States.

When I say that the problem is national, I do not mean that national action is the only approach to it. So long as we have a federal form of government, the states will possess many powers that must be utilized. Inhabitants of any locality naturally know the many nuances of inequality better than does an outsider. These inhabitants can meet more frequently for the discussion of their problems than can leaders, "experts," consultants and "men of good-will" from other parts of the nation.

What must be avoided, however, is the attempt of a group in any region or locality to solve its problems without the advice,

[7] Jacob Baker, Leland Olds, *et al.*, *Report of the Inquiry on Cooperative Enterprise in Europe* (Washington, 1937), pp. 1-2.

counsel, consultation, or even the "interference" of "furriners." Sectionalism has been the bane of American progress. Any attempt, therefore, to seek a sectional solution by only the inhabitants of that section runs counter to one of the most unmistakable lessons of our nation's history and of its inexorable trend. The world trend, moreover, is toward ever more distant horizons rather than toward provincialism.

The Durham, Atlanta, and Richmond conferences in which Southern Negroes and Southern whites drafted a program for the solution of the problem in the South must, therefore, be deplored so long as the participants come only from the South. So long as trains,. automobiles, planes, the telephone, telegraph, printing presses, and nation-wide business, church, educational, labor and other national organizations exist, the South will not be able to make the Negro problem in the South exclusively a Southern problem. So long as we have a national Constitution, a national Congress, a Supreme Court of the nation, and national armed forces, there can be no South apart from the rest of the nation. Northern Negroes and Northern whites have the right and the duty to accept or reject any program for the South just as long as the South is a part of the nation. The only way by which the South can make its problem exclusively a Southern problem is for it to secede from the Union and surround itself with a Chinese land, sea and air wall. Even then the radio and television would penetrate this medievalism.

Perhaps the soundest argument against this sectionalism is the fact that Northern Negroes accept most of the Durham statements as a sound document that could be useful throughout the nation. Since this is true, the obvious next step is to bring together Negroes and whites from all parts of the country to arrive at a statement for the nation. Regional or even local conferences might precede this national conference. But sooner or later Americans, not only Southerners or only Northerners, not only Bostonians or only Chicagoans, must pool their knowledge, their techniques, and their good-will for the solution of a national problem. If the Durham, Atlanta, and Richmond conferences result in such a national conference, as proposed in the second Atlanta conference, they will make a major contribution. If they remain exclusively Southern, they will be sowing the dragon seeds of sectionalism—and sectionalism was a fundamental cause of the only civil war in our nation's history. I happen to know that a statement drafted by a group of Negroes who were not participants in the Southern conferences was not published because of the opposition from some of the members of those conferences. Some Southern Negroes who had signed this "Northern" statement withdrew their signatures. This is an intolerable situation.

This gulf between Northern and Southern Negroes must be bridged at the earliest possible moment. Consequently, although "another conference" on the Negro is certain to provoke derision in some quarters, it seems mandatory. Not just another conference like a recent one, the net result of which was agreement on the necessity for cooperation among various organizations, but a conference with a carefully prepared agenda. Such a conference has a better chance for achieving a solid success than have some previous conferences for two reasons. First, the days of "the Negro leader" have passed. The idea was based fundamentally upon the Fuehrer or Il Duce concept. The death of "the leader" would have left us with the same kind of void that the United Nations encountered in their efforts to find some one with whom to negotiate after the overthrow of Mussolini. Happily also no one organization can speak for all Negroes. The passing of both the single leader and of the leadership of a single organization should facilitate the establishment of national coordinating committees similar to the Coordinating Committee for the Equitable Expenditure of Federal Funds for Public Education which helped to write many significant changes into the old Fletcher-Black-Harrison Bill, now Senate No. 637. This conference, I need not repeat, should consist of Northerners and Southerners, white and black.

Each organization should state exactly its program. Many of them are working for the same specific objectives. Some of them are employing the same techniques. Many are competing for funds from the same sources. Some local organizations have perfected techniques that might be employed on a national scale. The conference should also ascertain the progress being made in important fields of research. For example, several significant bibliographies and monographs are in preparation by various individuals and organizations. Is there unnecessary overlapping or duplication? What organization does not have its committee on post-war planning?

The ultimate outcome of the conference should be the establishment of coordinating committees on objectives, fund-raising, techniques, and research. Experience has demonstrated that coordinating committees are more effective than a topheavy, overall organization. The statement of objectives would make clear those areas with which no organizations are concerned and for which the same kind of coordinated effort must be established. From each of these coordinating committees should be chosen a representative to a national planning committee which would keep all the individual organizations and all the individual coordinating committees informed of the progress made and of the difficulties encountered. This national planning committee should also be responsible for the publication of a monthly magazine.

Since the problem is becoming increasingly national in scope, there is increasing need for coordination in the nation's capital. One organization already maintains a National Non-partisan Council on Public Affairs. It has done yeoman work. But one person with a secretary can not possibly follow all bills through the labyrinth of Congressional skullduggery, make weekly reports on all votes affecting us, contact enough friends of democracy to influence Congress, and at the same time see that necessary legislation is introduced. Moreover, since executive directives and administrative regulations have assumed at times even more importance than legislation, they too have to be watched closely. Only a lawyer can follow adequately judicial procedures and interpret properly judicial decisions. Only experts on labor problems are competent effectively to integrate the Negro into the increasingly powerful labor movement. Representatives of various individual organizations are attempting to do some of these tasks, practically all of these individuals while holding full-time positions. We must have in Washington the same kind of office that, for example, the C. I. O. has. It would be on a smaller scale, but I believe that a coordinated effort deriving support from all organizations would obtain sufficient financial resources to establish an office worthy of thirteen millions of people. As Sieyès said of the Third Estate, with some exaggeration, on the eve of the French Revolution: "We are nothing." We do not hope to become everything, but we should blame no one but ourselves if lack of coordinated effort prevents us from getting those rights that we so loudly demand. In every state and important city similar but smaller organizations should be effected.

At the same time that we organize this coordinated effort, we must subject ourselves to the most severe self-criticism. We must be sure that we are making the most of the restricted opportunities that we do have. We must recognize that although the argument "The time is not ripe" is frequently a subterfuge, timing is as important in our struggle as it is in the launching of other campaigns. We must determine the priority of our efforts in order to be certain that we do not expend our energy and resources upon relatively unimportant objectives.

In the following pages I submit an analysis of some of the major aspects of the problem. Although economic, political, cultural and social factors can not be isolated, they have been presented in this order as indicating their relative importance. The strategy is essentially that of this war—the capture of North Africa, Pantelleria, Sicily before beginning the attack upon the *Festung Europa.*

The growing force of organized labor provides the Negro with a golden opportunity if he can participate in it on a truly democratic basis. The participation is all the more imperative because of some evidence that reconversion of war industries is already resulting in the discharge of a disproportionately large number of Negro workers. If the recalcitrant unions will not of their own accord grant us equal rights, we shall have to resort to federal legislation just as labor had recourse to it against recalcitrant Big Business. The very fact that such federal control might serve as an opening wedge for other forms of control should constitute a potent reason for undemocratically organized unions to reform themselves. If existing legislation prevents the United States Supreme Court from exercising jurisdiction over conflicts between auxiliary and principal unions, the legislation should be changed to permit it. Truly equal participation in organized labor would deprive manufacturers of one excuse for not hiring Negro workers and would make unnecessary the establishment of separate plants or other units manned almost exclusively by Negroes.

The democratization of labor in industry would probably promote the democratization of government employees. Many Negro government workers assert that, with the exception of the states, the federal government is the most prejudiced large employer in the nation. Government like management has frequently invoked the opposition of white workers as justification for its discriminatory practices. Either the organization of government employees that would assume the pattern of democratically organized unions in industry or the influence of such unions should create a better atmosphere of employment first in the federal government and eventually in the state governments.

Since most Negroes are agricultural and domestic workers, they must be included in federal and state provisions for social security. The hoots of derision and the indifference that greeted the report of the National Resources Planning Board that envisaged this inclusion indicate the tremendous task before us. If, however, this inclusion should be made a separate item instead of a part of a "cradle to the grave American Beveridge Plan," there should be greater possibility of its enactment. At the same time we must endeavor to persuade the Southern states to make equal provision for Negroes under existing legislation. Negroes must also actively participate in all other measures that seek to solve the secular problem of achieving for all agricultural workers parity with urban workers.

As already indicated, the democratization of labor should make it increasingly difficult for management to deny Negroes equal opportunities. This fact is all the more important in view of the insistence by many employers that the Fair Employment Practices Committee appointed by President Roosevelt has no power to compel them to obey its directives. Even if a federal law were to give the Committee this power, its effectiveness would be largely nullified if at the same time unions refused to give Negro workers the same rights as any other workers. In the same way, the power of state fair employment practices committees could accomplish little unless organized labor is democratized.

This suggested program obviously looks to legislation as an important method for the redress of our grievances. Critics will immediately point out the weaknesses of this method. Did not President Grant say that the best way to repeal an unpopular law was to try to enforce it? The disastrous consequences of the attempt to achieve prohibition by legislation further support the argument. Unless, however, our government is going to degenerate into anarchy, then positive law and judicial interpretation and executive enforcement of laws must remain the fundamental basis for our institutions. Some critics seem to forget that many Americans are law-abiding citizens. While civil rights laws in Northern states, for example, are not always observed or enforced, the passage of such laws has generally assured Negroes greater enjoyment of those rights than prior to the passage. Moreover, legislation can give added strength to those who believe with Jefferson that "the minority possess their equal rights, which equal law must protect," can win over the lukewarm, and at the very least place the odium of lawbreaker upon those who violate the law.

Effective participation by Negroes in political affairs is necessary for the passage of legislation in their behalf. Experience has taught us that we can not rely upon our "friends." Our "friends" have permitted the second section of the Fourteenth Amendment to be disregarded ever since its ratification in 1868. That section provides that "when the right to vote at any election for the choice of electors for President and Vice President of the United States, Representatives in Congress, the Executive and Judicial officers of a State, or the members of the Legislature thereof, is denied to any male inhabitants of such State, being twenty-one years of age, and citizens of the United States, *or in any way abridged*,[8] except for participation in rebellion, or other crime, the basis of representation therein shall be reduced in the proportion which the number of such male citizens shall bear to the

[8] Italics not in the original.

whole number of male citizens twenty-one years of age in such State." It has been estimated that the Southern states have at least thirty electoral votes and as many representatives in Congress to which they are not entitled under the Constitution. If the Constitution were enforced, the power of obstruction exercised by the South would be considerably decreased. Consequently enforcement of this provision should be one of the first political goals of the Negro.

The abolition of the poll-tax requirement for federal elections in eight Southern States would remove this handicap from an estimated six million whites and four million Negroes. It can be argued that today any one who wishes to vote can find a dollar and a half or two dollars. In actual fact, the requirement is cumulative in four states. In Georgia, for example, the maximum legal payment may be $47.47. What is more essential is the fact that the poll tax is undemocratic. A man does not have to pay for the right to defend his country. Why should he have to pay for the right to vote for those who govern him? Moreover, many of the most reactionary representatives and senators would probably lose their seats if the suffrage were democratized by the abolition of the poll tax.

Abolition of the polltax in federal elections should be accompanied by the abolition of the poll-tax requirement for state elections. Probably more because of a desire to prevent Congressional action than of a desire to bring about state action, many Southerners have argued that if Congress and other "furriners" would leave them alone, they would abolish the poll-tax requirement. Proponents of state action pointed to the recent abolition by Tennessee. But the prompt decision of the Tennessee Supreme Court declaring the repeal unconstitutional has confounded these more or less sincere advocates of state rights. While it is difficult to discern any strong movement in the other seven states to accomplish repeal, the fight must be waged in them until the requirement is abolished.

Complete abolition of the poll-tax requirement will not, however, give Negroes in the Southern states effective voting power so long as the Democratic white primary prevents Negroes from voting to nominate the candidates of the one party that elects

practically all state officials, national representatives and senators. Probably before this book has been published, the Supreme
Court will have rendered its decision in Smith *v.* Allwright, the
fourth case in the relentless struggle to prevent the South from
being as totalitarian, politically, as Japan, Italy, Germany, Russia
—all nations in which a one-party government with a rigidly
restricted membership has ruled the people. If the decision up-
holds the Democratic primary, the struggle must be continued.
If the decision should declare the Democratic white primary
unconstitutional, the intelligent use of the ballot by Negroes
might reconcile the South to this democratization of the suffrage.

Improved facilities for Negro education in the South are imperative for reasons of an enlightened electorate, a better standard
of living and of cultural traits, and of national defense. The
passage of Senate Bill 637 which provides up to $300,000,000
of federal funds annually for education on the primary and
secondary levels has fairly adequate safeguards to prevent the
inequitable expenditure of these funds on the schools of the two
races. Without this aid the Southern states will not soon be able
to provide more nine-month terms, more transportation, more
accredited high schools and many other facilities for Negro
students. Insofar as the public schools can be used to promote
better race relations, as is being done with considerable success
notably in Springfield (Massachusetts), New York, and Chicago,
improved education for white children would result in some
democratization of the South. From the point of view of national
defense the need for the law is indisputable. Fifty per cent of
the Negro soldiers, most of whom are from the South, are in
the inferior group and an additional thirty-eight per cent in the
below average group on the basis of the "intelligence" tests.

Meanwhile, the fight must be continued to obtain equitable
expenditure of state funds. So long as a state, for example, provides three times as much for the per capita education of white
children as for Negroes, only a disproportionate allocation of
federal funds weighted in favor of colored students would redress the unfavorable balance. At the same time we must make
up our minds what we want with respect to graduate and professional education in the South. The Gaines Decision stated re-

peatedly that the "substantial equality" must be provided by the
states "within the states." Hence, out-of-state scholarships or
regional universities violate the decision. Many Negroes favor
them, however, because they argue that many of our Southern
colleges have not yet become first-class colleges and that the
establishment of separate graduate and professional schools will
make more difficult the eventual abolition of segregation. Since,
however, some of our Southern colleges have established graduate courses, the obviously sound procedure would be to make
them as strong as possible. After all, these colleges have come a
long way since as "universities" in the post-Civil War period they
were largely high schools.

General improvement in education would remove some of the
fear of the influence of an unenlightened electorate. As a matter
of fact, even the much derided Reconstruction legislatures and
conventions made some worthwhile contributions to American
life. In the words of Professor Arthur M. Schlesinger: "The
constitutions framed under these unpromising conditions embraced many excellent features, none more laudable perhaps
than the mandatory provisions for the inauguration of free
public-school systems." [9]

While this book is devoted almost exclusively to the Negro
problem in the United States, a brief reference to the international scene is required. Negroes in any part of the world suffer
from the inequality in other parts. Improvement in one area
would help in a limited measure to improvement elsewhere.
Moreover, while I am not optimistic about the establishment of
a supranational world machinery that will have the authority
to effect changes if they are opposed by powerful nations like
the United States, some tangible and intangible goals are not
impossible. Among them are the following:

A preamble to any new international covenant should assert
as categorically as did slaveholders in 1776 the essential equality
of mankind.

The new international covenant should proclaim the inter-

[9] *Political and Social History of the United States, 1829-1925* (New
York, 1925), p. 243.

national rights of man and give men as well as nations a status before international tribunals.

The statute or constitution of any new International Labor Organization should declare that no representative on it of management or labor should be a member of any firm or union that in practice discriminates against any worker on account of race, creed, color or national origin.[9a]

All positions on all international agencies should be open to all without discrimination on account of race, creed, color or national origin.

A definite plan should be adopted looking to the eventual self-government or autonomy of all colonial peoples, or the effective participation by Negroes in the government of those dependent areas in which commonwealth status may be preferable to detachment from the former governing power. This plan should also provide for the raising of the standard of living of the Negroes.[10]

Since the resolutions and conventions of all international agencies affecting the internal life of the United States would probably have to be approved by our Congress, it is all the more necessary that no undemocratic practices prevent the fullest participation by Negroes in the choice of members of Congress.

The crucial question remains: What should be the ultimate objective of this proposed action on both the national (including the state and the local) and the international scene? Should it be continuation of public segregation or should it be the eventual integration of Negroes into the public life of the American people? The answer to this question, indeed, vitally affects the achievement of the intermediate steps proposed. Many persons who say that they favor economic, political, and educational equality for the Negro oppose such equality in practice for fear

[9a] Professor Robert Brady of the University of California informs me that a "rank and file" movement among some of the younger men in the A.F.L. unions on the West Coast provides considerable hope for reform within the reactionary unions.

[10] Although I differ with Lord Hailey in the form of mandate system that he advocates, his little book, *The Future of the Colonial Peoples* (Princeton, 1944), is one of the strongest pleas made for eventual independence by any influential Englishman.

that it will lead to "social equality," by which most of them mean intermarriage. And the great majority of those who favor economic, political and educational equality in practice oppose intermarriage. On no aspect of the race problem are most white Americans, North as well as South, so adamant as they are on their opposition to intermarriage.

Now, Southerners especially fear that the abolition of public segregation would result in intermarriage.[11] The fact that mixed schools, mixed employment, even social mingling in the more liberal parts of the United States have resulted in very few mixed marriages does not prevent this real or fancied fear. Mrs. Eleanor Roosevelt may publicly state that mixed marriages are the personal affair of the couple if they are willing, in communities where they are not prohibited by law, to assume this additional burden upon a happy marriage. Some biologists and anthropologists have concluded that mixed marriages do not necessarily result in an inferior offspring and that, in fact, there is no pure race. Most white Americans remain nonetheless opposed to intermarriage and many of them to the abolition of public segregation as a possible first step toward it.

There seems to me to be an essentially sound answer to the fear of ultimate intermarriage whether it should result from the achievement of economic, political, and cultural equality under segregation (if that be possible) or from the abolition of public segregation. If, after either or both of these eventualities, laws or custom still rigidly oppose mixed marriages, there will be few more than there now are. If, on the other hand, laws and public opinion should change and there should be more mixed marriages —why, we shall all be dead in 2044 and the people will do what they wish. After all, most Southerners have accommodated themselves to the abolition of the "divine institution" of slavery.

I therefore definitely favor the eventual abolition of public segregation. It is not easy to define public segregation in such

[11] Other reasons for insistence upon segregation rest largely upon a real or alleged repugnance to close association with Negroes. Why, for example, should a fastidious white man or woman have to sit in a public carrier by a sweaty Negro? I also am fastidious and have an extremely sensitive sense of smell. But sitting by a sweaty white worker does not cause me to generalize about all white people.

a way as to assure the right of the individual to choose his private associates. Segregation in public carriers, hotels, restaurants, theatres and schools would obviously fall into this category. But what about private schools, theatres, country clubs, churches? As much as exclusion of individuals solely on racial grounds might be deplored as indicating the maintenance of racial animosities, it is difficult to see how government could prevent it. But it would seem indisputable also that if such a group were to receive government aid, then government could act. Naturally, many border line cases exist. The best thing to do, I believe, would be to gain wide acceptance of the principle of the abolition of public segregation and then determine each case as it arises. The Supreme Court, for example, has frequently stated that it will not assume jurisdiction over "political questions," but it has never attempted to enumerate all "political questions."

The education of public opinion would, of course, be preferable to government action. There is more ground for hope (or fear) in this area than some persons realize. I have been amazed to discover the reasons that led to a change of attitude on the part of many white Southerners. One recently told me that his change was due to his acceptance of the ethical ideals of a "religion." A young woman informed me in all seriousness that her whole attitude changed when she saw a colored girl in a class at Columbia University wearing better clothes than she did. The university of the arts has permitted Paul Robeson, Marian Anderson, and Roland Hayes to "convert" many hostile persons. Jesse Owens and Joe Louis in the sports and George Washington Carver in science have provided the first jolt to many minds steeped in stereotyped ideas. The formal educational work of The Commission on Inter-racial Cooperation, the Federal Council of the Churches of Christ in America, the Young Women's Christian Association, and of other agencies has demonstrated the effectiveness of organized efforts at good-will, tolerance, understanding, appreciation. I believe that a case history of "Why I Stopped Hating Negroes" would prove not only fascinating reading but also an encouraging revelation.

I can personally vouch for the fact that there is an essential element of truth in the conclusion of Dr. Clyde R. Miller,

Director of the Institute of Propaganda Analysis, that "Prejudice is a Disease: It *CAN* be cured."[12] Few Americans have hated or feared Negroes as much as I, in my youth, hated and feared "Poor White Trash." When I was graduated from college, I refused a position at Straight University in New Orleans because firearms could not be kept on the campus—I would not go South unless I could protect myself from the Southern "barbarians." Today, I firmly believe that I am without prejudice against any person because of his race or religion.

But the task of changing racial attitudes is a tremendous one. Such considerable progress had been made in the South on the eve of World War I that some enthusiasts were convinced that the race problem there was well on its way to solution, that even segregation would be voluntarily abandoned. But these enthusiasts must now realize that the number of converts to democracy was small and their convictions shaky. I believe, however, that the improvement was sufficient to justify the hope that a renewed, determined, improved campaign of popular education, supported by national, state and local legislation and by international influence as outlined above, will in the years after the war increase the number and strengthen their convictions. I believe that Professor Arthur M. Schlesinger was not too optimistic when in the closing sentence of his Presidential Address to the American Historical Association in 1942 he proclaimed his faith that

> The American character, whatever its shortcomings, abounds in courage, creative energy and resourcefulness and is bottomed upon the profound conviction that nothing in the world is beyond its power to accomplish.

Nothing, I would add, not even the race problem in the United States. I believe that it can be solved in the Liberal Democratic tradition. I believe that lumbering, blundering democracy will eventually overcome its enemies at home just as today it is crushing them abroad. I believe that the Dream of Democracy is worth fighting for if it takes another one hundred sixty years, or longer, for the Negro to win first-class citizenship. There is no defeat; there is only the postponement of Victory.

[12] Lecture at the Ford Hall Forum (Boston, February 27, 1944).

MY EVOLVING PROGRAM
FOR
NEGRO FREEDOM

By W. E. BURGHARDT DU BOIS

MY MIDNIGHT CLASSMATE

ONCE UPON A TIME, I found myself at midnight on one of the swaggering streetcars that used to roll out from Boston on its way to Cambridge. It must have been in the Spring of 1890, and quite accidentally I was sitting by a classmate who would graduate with me in June. As I dimly remember, he was a nice-looking young man, almost dapper; well-dressed, charming in manner. Probably he was rich or at least well-to-do, and doubtless belonged to an exclusive fraternity, although that I do not know. Indeed I have even forgotten his name. But one thing I shall never forget and that was his rather regretful admission (that slipped out as we gossiped) that he had no idea as to what his life work would be, because, as he added, "There's nothing which I am particularly interested in!"

I was more than astonished--I was almost outraged to meet any human being of the mature age of twenty-two who did not have his life all planned before him, at least in general outline; and who was not supremely, if not desperately, interested in what he planned to do.

Since then, my wonder has left my classmate, and been turned in and backward upon myself: how long had I been sure of my life-work and how had I come so confidently to survey and plan it? I now realize that most college seniors are by no means certain of what they want to do or can do with life; but stand rather upon a hesitating threshold, awaiting will, chance, or opportunity. Because I had not mingled intimately or understandingly with my Harvard classmates, I did not at the time realize this, but thought my rather unusual attitude was general. How had this attitude come to seem normal to me?

MY EARLY YOUTH

The small western New England town where I was born, and several generations of my fathers before me, was a middle-class community of Americans of English and Dutch descent, with an Irish laboring class and a few remnants of Negro working folk of past centuries. Farmers and small merchants predominated, with a fringe of decadent Americans; with mill-hands, railroad laborers and domestics. A few manufacturers formed a small aristocracy of wealth. In the public schools of this town, I was trained from the age of six to sixteen, and in its schools, churches, and general social life I gained my patterns of living. I had almost no experience of segregation or color discrimination. My schoolmates were invariably white; I joined quite naturally all games, excursions, church festivals; recreations like coasting, skating and ball-games. I was in and out of the homes of nearly all my mates, and ate and played with them. I was a boy unconscious of color discrimination in any obvious and specific way.

I knew nevertheless that I was exceptional in appearance and that this riveted attention upon me. Less clearly, I early realized that most of the colored persons I saw, including my own folk, were poorer than the well-to-do whites; lived in humbler houses, and did not own stores; this was not universally true: my cousins, the Crispels, in West Stockbridge, had one of the most beautiful homes in the village. Other cousins, in Lenox, were well-to-do. On the other hand, none of the colored folk I knew were so poor, drunken and sloven as some of the lower Americans and Irish. I did not then associate poverty or ignorance with color, but rather with lack of opportunity; or more often with lack of thrift, which was in strict accord with the philosophy of New England and of the Nineteenth Century.

On the other hand, much of my philosophy of the color line

must have come from my family group and their friends' experience. My father dying early, my immediate family consisted of my mother and her brother and my older half-brother most of the time. Near to us in space and intimacy were two married aunts with older children, and a number of cousins, in various degrees removed, living scattered through the county and state. Most of these had been small farmers, artisans, laborers and servants. With few exceptions all could read and write, but few had training beyond this. These talked of their work and experiences, of hindrances which colored people encountered, of better chances in other towns and cities. In this way I must have gotten indirectly a pretty clear outline of color bars which I myself did not experience. Moreover, it was easy enough for me to rationalize my own case, because I found it easy to excel most of my schoolmates in studies if not in games. The secret of life and the loosing of the color bar, then, lay in excellence, in accomplishment; if others of my family, of my colored kin, had stayed in school, instead of quitting early for small jobs, they could have risen to equal whites. On this my mother quietly insisted. There was no real discrimination on account of color—it was all a matter of ability and hard work.

This philosophy was saved from conceit and vainglory by rigorous self-testing, which doubtless cloaked some half-conscious misgivings on my part. If visitors to school saw and remarked my brown face, I waited in quiet confidence. When my turn came, I recited glibly and usually correctly because I studied hard. Some of my mates did not care, some were stupid; but at any rate I gave the best a hard run, and then sat back complacently. Of course I was too honest with myself not to see things which desert and even hard work did not explain or solve: I recognized ingrained difference in gift; Art Gresham could draw caricatures for the *High School Howler*, published occasionally in manuscript, better than I; but I could express meanings in words better than he; Mike McCarthy was a perfect marble player, but dumb in Latin. I came to see and admit all this, but I hugged my own gifts and put them to test.

When preparation for college came up, the problem of poverty began to appear. Without conscious decision on my part, and probably because of continuous quiet suggestion from my High School principal, Frank Hosmer, I found myself planning to go to college; how or where, seemed an unimportant detail. A wife of one of the cotton mill owners, whose only son was a pal of mine, offered to see that I got lexicons and texts to take up the study of Greek in High School, without which college doors in that day would not open. I accepted the offer as something normal and right; only after many years did I realize how critical this gift was for my career. I am not yet sure how she came to do it; perhaps my wise principal suggested it. Comparatively few of my white classmates planned or cared to plan for college—perhaps two or three in a class of twelve.

I collected catalogues of colleges and over the claims of Williams and Amherst, nearest my home, I blithely picked Harvard, because it was oldest and largest, and most widely known. My mother died a few months after my graduation, just as though, tired of the long worry and pull, she was leaving me alone at the post, with a certain characteristic faith that I would not give up.

I was, then, an orphan, without a cent of property, and with no relative who could for a moment think of undertaking the burden of my further education. But the family could and did help out and the town in its quiet and unemotional way was satisfied with my record and silently began to plan. First, I must go to work at least for a season and get ready for college in clothes and maturity, as I was only sixteen. Then there was the question of where I could go and how the expenses could be met.

The working out of these problems by friends and relatives brought me face to face, for the first time, with matters of income and wealth. A place was secured for me as time-keeper, during the building of a mansion by a local millionaire, in whose family an ancestor of mine had once worked. My job brought me for the first time in close contact with organized work and wage. I followed the building and its planning; I watched the mechanics at their work; I knew what they earned, I gave them their weekly wage and carried the news of their dismissal. I saw the modern world at work, mostly with the hands, and with few machines.

Meantime in other quarters a way was being made for me to go to college. The father of one of my schoolmates, the Reverend C. C. Painter, was once in the Indian Bureau. There and elsewhere he saw the problem of the reconstructed South, and conceived the idea that there was the place for me to be educated, and there lay my future field of work. My family and colored friends rather resented the idea. Their Northern Free Negro prejudice naturally revolted at the idea of sending me to the former land of slavery, either for education or for living. I am rather proud of myself that I did not agree with them. That I should always live and work in the South, I did not then stop to decide; that I would give up the idea of graduating from Harvard, did not occur to me. But I wanted to go to Fisk, not simply because it was at least a beginning of my dream of college, but also, I suspect, because I was beginning to feel lonesome in New England; because, unconsciously, I realized, that as I grew older, the close social intermingling with my white fellows would grow more restricted. There were meetings, parties, clubs, to which I was not invited. Especially in the case of strangers, visitors, newcomers to the town was my presence and friendship a matter of explanation or even embarrassment to my schoolmates. Similar discriminations and separations met the Irish youth, and the cleft between rich and poor widened.

On the other hand, the inner social group of my own relatives and colored friends always had furnished me as a boy most interesting and satisfying company; and now as I grew, it was augmented by visitors from other places. I remember a lovely little plump and brown girl who appeared out of nowhere, and smiled at me demurely; I went to the East to visit my father's father in New Bedford, and on that trip saw well-to-do, well-mannered colored people; and once, at Rocky Point, Rhode Island, I viewed with astonishment 10,000 Negroes of every hue and bearing. I was transported with amazement and dreams; I apparently noted nothing of poverty or degradation, but only extraordinary beauty of skin-color and utter equality of mien, with absence so far as I could see of even the shadow of the line of race. Gladly and armed with a scholarship, I set out for Fisk.

AT FISK UNIVERSITY

Thus in the Fall of 1885 and at the age of seventeen, I was tossed boldly into the "Negro Problem." From a section and circumstances where the status of me and my folk could be rationalized as the result of poverty and limited training, and settled essentially by schooling and hard effort, I suddenly came to a region where the world was split into white and black halves, and where the darker half was held back by race prejudice and legal bonds, as well as by deep ignorance and dire poverty.

But facing this was not a little lost group, but a world in size and a civilization in potentiality. Into this world I leapt with provincial enthusiasm. A new loyalty and allegiance replaced my Americanism: henceforward I was a Negro.

To support and balance this, was the teaching and culture background of Fisk of the latter Nineteenth Century. All of its teachers but one were white, from New England or from the New Englandized Middle West. My own culture background thus suffered no change nor hiatus. Its application only was new. This *point d'appui* was not simply Tennessee, which was never a typical slave state, but Georgia, Alabama, Mississippi, Louisiana and Texas, whence our students came; and who as mature men and women, for the most part from five to ten years older than I, could paint from their own experience a wide and vivid picture of the post-war South and of its black millions. There were men and women who had faced mobs and seen lynchings; who knew every phase of insult and repression; and too there were sons, daughters and clients of every class of white Southerner. A relative of a future president of the nation had his dark son driven to school each day.

The college curriculum of my day was limited but excellent. Adam Spence was a great Greek scholar by any comparison. Thomas Chase with his ridiculously small laboratory nevertheless taught us not only chemistry and physics but something of science and of life. In after years I used Bennett's German in Germany, and with the philosophy and ethics of Cravath, I later sat under William James and George Palmer at Harvard. The excellent and earnest teaching, the small college classes; the absence of distractions, either in athletics or society, enabled me to re-arrange and re-build my program for freedom and progress among Negroes. I replaced my hitherto egocentric world by a world centering and whirling about my race in America. To this group I transferred my plan of study and accomplishment. Through the leadership of men like me and my fellows, we were going to have these enslaved Israelites out of the still enduring bondage in short order. It was a battle which might conceivably call for force, but I could think it confidently through mainly as a battle of wits; of knowledge and deed, which by sheer reason and desert, must eventually overwhelm the forces of hate, ignorance and reaction.

Always in my dreaming, a certain redeeming modicum of common sense has usually come to my rescue and brought fantasy down to the light of common day: I was not content to take the South entirely by hearsay; and while I had no funds to travel widely, I did, somewhat to the consternation of both teachers and fellow-students, determine to go out into the country and teach summer school. I was only eighteen and knew nothing of the South at first hand, save what little I had seen in Nashville. There to be sure I had stared curiously at the bullet holes in the door of the City Hall where an editor had been murdered in daylight and cold blood. It was the first evidence of such physical violence I had ever seen. I had once made the tragic mistake of raising my hat to a white woman, whom I had accidentally jostled on the public street. But I had not seen anything of the small Southern town and the countryside, which are the real South. If I could not explore Darkest Mississippi, at least I could see West Tennessee, which was not more than fifty miles from the college.

Needless to say the experience was invaluable. I traveled not only in space but in time. I touched the very shadow of slavery. I lived and taught school in log cabins built before the Civil War. My school was the second held in the district since emancipation. I touched intimately the lives of the commonest of mankind—people who ranged from bare-footed dwellers on dirt floors, with patched rags for clothes, to rough, hard-working farmers, with plain, clean plenty. I saw and talked with white people, noted now their unease, now their truculence and again their friendliness. I nearly fell from my horse when the first school commissioner whom I interviewed invited me to stay to dinner. Afterward I realized that he meant me to eat at the second, but quite as well-served, table.

The net result of the Fisk interlude was to broaden the scope of my program of life, not essentially to change it; to center it in a group of educated Negroes, who from their knowledge and experience would lead the mass. I never for a moment dreamed that such leadership could ever be for the sake of the educated group itself, but always for the mass. Nor did I pause to enquire in just what ways and with what technique we would work—first, broad, exhaustive knowledge of the world; all other wisdom, all method and application would be added unto us.

In essence I combined a social program for a depressed group with the natural demand of youth for "Light, more Light." Fisk was a good college; I liked it; but it was small, it was limited in equipment, in laboratories, in books; it was not a university. I wanted the largest and best in organized learning. Nothing could be too big and thorough for training the leadership of the American Negro. There must remain no suspicion of part-knowledge, cheap equipment, for this mighty task. The necessity of earning a living scarcely occurred to me. I had no need for or desire for money.

I turned with increased determination to the idea of going to Harvard. There I was going to study the science of sciences—philosophy. Vainly did Chase point out, as James did later, that the world was not in the habit of paying philosophers. In vain did the president offer me a scholarship at Hartford Theological Seminary. I believed too little in Christian dogma to become a minister. I was not without Faith: I never stole material nor spiritual things; I not only never lied, but blurted out my conception of the truth on the most untoward occasions; I drank no alcohol and knew nothing of women, physically or psychically, to the incredulous amusement of most of my more experienced fellows: I above all believed in work—systematic and tireless.

I went to Harvard. Small difference it made if Harvard would only admit me to standing as a college junior; I earned $100 by summer work: I received Price Greenleaf Aid to the amount of $250, which seemed a very large sum. Of the miracle of my getting anything, of the sheer luck of being able to keep on studying with neither friends nor money, I gave no thought.

THE ENLARGEMENT AT HARVARD AND BERLIN

Fortunately I did not fall into the mistake of regarding Harvard as the beginning rather than the continuing of my college training. I did not find better teachers at Harvard, but teachers better known, with wider facilities and in broader atmosphere for approaching truth. Up to this time, I had been absorbing a general view of human knowledge: in ancient and modern literatures; in mathematics, physics and chemistry and history. It was all in vague and general terms—interpretations of what men who knew the facts at first hand, thought they might mean. With the addition of a course in chemistry in a Harvard laboratory under Hill, some geology under Shaler and history under Hart, I was in possession of the average educated man's concept of this world and its meaning. But now I wanted to go further: to know what man could know and how to collect and interpret facts face to face. And what "facts" were.

Here I revelled in the keen analysis of William James, Josiah Royce and young George Santayana. But it was James with his pragmatism and Albert Bushnell Hart with his research method, that turned me back from the lovely but sterile land of philosophic speculation, to the social sciences as the field for gathering and interpreting that body of fact which would apply to my program for the Negro.

I began with a bibliography of Nat Turner and ended with a history of the suppression of the African Slave Trade to America; neither needed to be done again at least in my day. Thus in my quest for basic knowledge with which to help guide the American Negro, I came to the study of sociology, by way of philosophy and history rather than by physics and biology, which was the current approach; moreover at that day, Harvard recognized no "science" of sociology and for my doctorate, after hesitating between history and economics, I chose history. On the other hand, psychology, hovering then at the threshold of experiment under Münsterberg, soon took a new orientation which I could understand from the beginning.

My human contacts at Harvard were narrow, and if I had not gone immediately to Europe, I was about to encase myself in a completely colored world, self-sufficient and provincial, and ignoring just as far as possible the white world which conditioned it. This was self-protective coloration, with perhaps an inferiority complex, but more of increasing belief in the ability and future of black folk. I sought at Harvard no acquaintanceship with white students and only such contacts with white teachers as lay directly in the line of my work. I joined certain clubs like the Philosophical Club; I was a member of the Foxcroft dining club because it was cheap. James and one or two other teachers had me at their homes at meal and reception.

Nevertheless my friends and companions were taken from the colored students of Harvard and neighboring institutions, and the colored folk of Boston and other cities. With them I led a happy and inspiring life. There were among them many educated and well-to-do folk; many young people studying or planning to study; many charming young women. We met and ate, danced and argued and planned a new world. I was exceptional among them, in my ideas on voluntary race segregation; they for the most part saw salvation only in integration at the earliest moment and on almost any terms in white culture; I was firm in my criticism of white folk and in my more or less complete dream of a Negro self-sufficient culture even in America.

In Germany, on the other hand, where after a stiff fight for recognition of my academic work, I went on fellowship in 1892, the situation was quite different. I found myself on the outside of the American world, looking in. With me were white folk—students, acquaintances, teachers—who viewed the scene with me. They did not pause to regard me as a curiosity, or something sub-human; I was just a man of the somewhat privileged student rank, with whom they were glad to meet and talk over the world; particularly, the part of the world whence I came. I found to my gratification that they with me did not regard America as the last word in civilization. Indeed I derived a certain satisfaction in learning that the University of Berlin did not recognize a degree even from Harvard University, no more than from Fisk. Even I was a little startled to realize how much that I had regarded as white American, was white European and not American at all: America's music is German, the Germans said; the Americans have no art, said the Italians; and their literature, remarked the English, is English; all agreed that Americans could make money but did not care how they made it. And the like. Sometimes their criticism got under even my anti-American skin, but it was refreshing on the whole to hear voiced my own attitude toward so much that America had meant to me.

In my study, I came in contact with several of the great leaders of the developing social sciences: with Schmoller in economic sociology; Adolf Wagner, in social history; with Max Weber and the Germanophile, von Treitschke. I gained ready admittance to two rather exclusive seminars, and my horizon in the social sciences was broadened not only by teachers, but by students from France, Belgium, Russia, Italy and Poland. I traveled, on foot and third-class railway, to all parts of Germany and most of Central Europe. I got a bird's eye glimpse of modern western culture at the turn of the century.

But of greater importance, was the opportunity which my *Wanderjahre* in Europe gave of looking at the world as a man and not simply from a narrow racial and provincial outlook. This was primarily the result not so much of my study, as of my human companionship, unveiled by the accident of color. From the days of my later youth to my boarding a Rhine passenger steamer at Rotterdam in August, 1892, I had not regarded white folk as human in quite the same way that I was. I had reached the habit of expecting color prejudice so universally, that I found it even when it was not there. So when I saw on this little steamer a Dutch lady with two grown daughters and one of twelve, I proceeded to put as much space between us as the small vessel allowed. But it did not allow much, and the lady's innate breeding allowed less. Before we reached the end of our trip, we were happy companions, laughing, eating and singing together, talking English, French and German, visiting in couples, as the steamer stopped, the lovely castled German towns, and acting like normal, well-bred human beings. I waved them all good-bye, in the solemn arched aisles of the Köln cathedral, with tears in my eyes.

So too in brave old Eisenach, beneath the shadow of Luther's Wartburg, I spent a happy holiday with French and English boys, and German girls, in a home where university training and German home-making left no room for American color prejudice, although one American woman did what she could to introduce it. She thought that I was far too popular with the German girls and secretly warned the house-mother. I was popular, but there was no danger in the American sense. I was quite wedded to my task in America. When blue-eyed Dora confessed her readiness to marry me "*gleich!*" I told her frankly and gravely that it would be unfair to himself and cruel to her for a colored man to take a white bride to America. She could not understand.

From this unhampered social intermingling with Europeans of education and manners, I emerged from the extremes of my racial provincialism. I became more human; learned the place in life of "Wine, Women, and Song"; I ceased to hate or suspect people simply because they belonged to one race or color; and above all I began to understand the real meaning of scientific research and the dim outline of methods of employing its technique and its results in the new social sciences for the settlement of the Negro problems in America.

PRELUDE TO PRACTICE

I returned to the United States, traveling steerage, in July, 1894. I was twenty-six years of age and had obtained an education such as few young Americans, white or black, had had opportunity to receive. Probably, looking back after the event, I have rationalized my life into a planned, coherent unity which was not as true to fact as it now seems; probably there were hesitancies, gropings, and half-essayed bypaths, now forgotten or unconsciously ignored. But my first quarter-century of life seems to me at this distance as singularly well-aimed at a certain goal, along a clearly planned path. I returned ready and eager to begin a life-work, leading to the emancipation of the American Negro. History and the other social sciences were to be my weapons, to be sharpened and applied by research and writing. Where and how, was the question in 1894.

I began a systematic mail campaign for a job. I wrote one public school in West Tennessee, not far from where I had taught school. The board hesitated, but finally indicated that I had rather too much education for their use. I applied to Howard University, Hampton Institute and my own Fisk. They had no openings. Tuskegee, late in the Fall, offered me a chance to teach mathematics, mentioning no salary; the offer came too late, for in August, I had accepted an offer from Wilberforce to teach Latin and Greek at $750 a year.

Probably Wilberforce was about the least likely of all Negro colleges to adopt me and my program. First of all I was cocky and self-satisfied; I wore invariably the cane and gloves of a German student. I doubtless strutted and I certainly knew what I wanted. My redeeming feature was infinite capacity for work and terrible earnestness, with appalling and tactless frankness. But not all was discouragement and frustration at Wilberforce. Of importance that exceeded everything, was the group of students whom I met and taught; most of the student body was in high school grades and poorly equipped for study. But filtering into the small college department were a few men and women of first-class intelligence, able and eager to work. As working companions, we made excursions into Greek literature; I gathered a class in German which talked German from the first day; I guided the writing of English themes and did a bit of modern history. Try as I might, however, the institution would have no sociology, even though I offered to teach it on my own time.

I became uneasy about my life program. I was doing nothing directly in the social sciences and saw no immediate prospect. Then the door of opportunity opened: just a crack, to be sure, but a distinct opening. In the Fall of 1896, I went to the University of Pennsylvania as "Assistant Instructor" in Sociology. It all happened this way: Philadelphia, then and still one of the worst governed of America's badly governed cities, was having one of its periodic spasms of reform. A thorough study of causes was called for. Not but what the underlying cause was evident to most white Philadelphians: the corrupt, semi-criminal vote of the Negro Seventh Ward. Every one agreed that here lay the cancer; but would it not be well to elucidate the known causes by a scientific investigation, with the imprimatur of the University? It certainly would, answered Samuel McCune Lindsay of the Department of Sociology. And he put his finger on me for the task.

There must have been some opposition, for the invitation was not particularly cordial. I was offered a salary of $800 for a period limited to one year. I was given no real academic standing, no office at the University, no official recognition of any kind; my name was even eventually omitted from the catalogue; I had no contact with students, and very little with members of the faculty, even in my department. With my bride of three months, I settled in one room over a cafeteria run by a College Settlement, in the worst part of the Seventh Ward. We lived there a year, in the midst of an atmosphere of dirt, drunkenness, poverty and crime. Murder sat on our doorsteps, police were our government, and philanthropy dropped in with periodic advice.

I counted my task here as simple and clear-cut: I proposed to find out what was the matter with this area and why. I started with no "research methods" and I asked little advice as to procedure. The problem lay before me. Study it. I studied it personally and not by proxy. I sent out no canvassers. I went myself. Personally I visited and talked with 5000 persons. What I could I set down in orderly sequence on schedules which I made out and submitted to the University for criticism. Other information I stored in my memory or wrote out as memoranda. I went through the Philadelphia libraries for data, gained access in many instances to private libraries of colored folk and got individual information. I mapped the district, classifying it by condition; I compiled two centuries. of the history of the Negro in Philadelphia and in the Seventh Ward.

It was a hard job, but I completed it by the Spring of 1898 and published it a year later, under the auspices of the University, as *The Philadelphia Negro*; a formidable tome of nearly a thousand pages. But the greatest import to me was the fact, that after years, I had at last learned just what I wanted to do, in this life program of mine, and how to do it. First of all I became painfully aware that merely being born in a group, does not necessarily make one possessed of complete knowledge concerning it. I had learned far more from Philadelphia Negroes than I had taught them concerning the Negro Problem. Before the American Academy, affiliated with the University, I laid down in public session in 1899, a broad program of scientific attack on this problem, by systematic and continuous study; and I appealed to Harvard, Columbia and Pennsylvania, to take up the work.

Needless to say, they paid not the slightest attention to this challenge and for twenty-five years thereafter not a single first-grade college in America undertook to give any considerable scientific attention to the American Negro. There was no thought or suggestion even of keeping me at the University of Pennsylvania. Before I had finished my work in Philadelphia, however, a Negro college, Atlanta University, had asked me to develop my program in Georgia. The days of the years of my apprenticeship were over. I entered on my life plan in the Fall of 1897.

THE PROGRAM OF 100 YEARS

The main significance of my work at Atlanta University, during the years 1897 to 1910 was the development at an American institution of learning, of a program of study on the problems affecting the American Negroes, covering a progressively widening and deepening effort designed to stretch over the span of a century. This program was grafted on an attempt by George Bradford of Boston, one of the trustees, to open for Atlanta University a field of usefulness, comparable to what Hampton and Tuskegee were doing for rural districts in agriculture and industry. At the Hampton and Tuskegee conferences, there came together annually and in increasing numbers, workers, experts and observers to encourage by speeches and interchange of experience the Negro farmers and laborers of adjoining areas. Visitors, white and colored, from North and South, joined to advise and learn. Mr. Bradford's idea was to establish at Atlanta a similar conference, devoted especially to problems of city Negroes. Such a conference, emphasizing particularly Negro health problems, was held in 1896. Immediately the University looked about for a man to teach history and political science, and take charge of future conferences. I was chosen.

When I took charge of the Atlanta Conference, I did not pause to consider how far my developed plans agreed or disagreed with the ideas of the already launched project. It made little essential difference, since only one conference had been held and a second planned. These followed the Hampton and Tuskegee model of being primarily meetings of inspiration, directed toward specific efforts at social reform and aimed at propaganda for social uplift in certain preconceived lines. This program at Atlanta, I sought to swing as on a pivot to one of scientific investigation into social conditions, primarily for scientific ends: I put no especial emphasis on specific reform effort, but increasing and widening emphasis on the collection of a basic body of fact concerning the social condition of American Negroes, endeavoring to reduce that condition to exact measurement whenever or wherever occasion permitted. As time passed, it happened that many uplift efforts were in fact based on our studies: the kindergarten system of the city of Atlanta, white as well as black; the Negro Business League, and various projects to better health and combat crime. We came to be however, as I had intended, increasingly, a source of general information and a basis for further study, rather than an organ of social reform.

The proverbial visitor from Mars would have assumed as elemental a study in America of American Negroes—as physical specimens; as biological growths; as a field of investigation in economic development from slave to free labor; as a psychological laboratory in human reaction toward caste and discrimination; as an unique case of physical and cultural intermingling. These and a dozen other subjects of scientific interest, would have struck the man from Mars as eager lines of investigation for American social scientists. He would have been astounded to learn that the only institution in America in 1900 with any such program of study was Atlanta University, where on a budget of $5000 a year, including salaries, cost of publication, investigation and annual meetings, we were essaying this pioneer work.

My program for the succession of conference studies was modified by many considerations: cost, availability of suitable data, tested methods of investigation; moreover I could not plunge too soon into such controversial subjects as politics or miscegenation. Within these limitations, I finished a ten-year cycle study as follows:

1896, *Mortality among Negroes in Cities*
1897, *Social and Physical Condition of Negroes in Cities*
1898, *Some Efforts of Negroes for Social Betterment*
1899, *The Negro in Business*
1900, *The College-bred Negro*
1901, *The Negro Common School*
1902, *The Negro Artisan*
1903, *The Negro Church*
1904, *Notes on Negro Crime*
1905, *A Select Bibliography of the American Negro*

I then essayed for the second decade a broader program, more logical, more inclusive, and designed to bring the whole subject matter into a better integrated whole. But continued lack of funds, and outside demands (like the request of the Carnegie Institution of 1907 for a study of co-operation) kept even the second decade from the complete logic of arrangement which I desired; finally, my leaving Atlanta in 1910 and at last the severing of my connection with the conference in 1914, left the full form of my program still unfinished. I did, however, publish the following studies:

1906, *Health and Physique of the Negro American*
1907, *Economic Co-operation among Negro Americans*
1908, *The Negro American Family*
1909, *Efforts for Social betterment among Negro Americans*
1910, *The College-bred Negro American*
1911, *The Common School and the Negro American*
1912, *The Negro American Artisan*
1914, *Morals and Manners among Negro Americans*

With the publication of 1914, my connection with Atlanta ceased for twenty years. Although studies and publications were prepared by others at the University in 1915 and 1918, the war finally stopped the enterprise.

What I was laboriously but steadily approaching in this effort was a recurring cycle of ten studies in succeeding decades; with repetition of each subject or some modification of it in each decade, upon a progressively broader and more exact basis and with better method; until gradually a foundation of carefully ascertained fact would build a basis of knowledge, broad and sound enough to be called scientific in the best sense of that term.

Just what form this dream would eventually have taken, I do not know. So far as actually forecast, it had assumed in 1914, some such form as this:

1. Population: Distribution and Growth
2. Biology: Health and Physique
3. Socialization: Family, Group and Class
4. Cultural Patterns: Morals and Manners
5. Education
6. Religion and the Church
7. Crime
8. Law and Government
9. Literature and Art
10. Summary and Bibliography

I proposed as I have said, to repeat each of these every ten years, basing the studies on ever broader and more carefully gathered data. Eventually I hoped to keep all the inquiries going simultaneously, only emphasizing and reporting on one particular subject each year. This would have allowed some necessary shifting or combination of subjects as time and developments might suggest; and adjustments to new scientific advance in fields like anthropology and psychology. The plan would have called in time for a large and well-paid staff of experts and a study of method and testing of results such as no group of Americans were engaged in at the time; beginning with a definite, circumscribed group, but ending with the human race. If it could have been carried out even imperfectly and with limitations, who can doubt its value today, not only to the Negro, but to America and to the still troubled science of sociology?

It was of course crazy for me to dream that America, in the dawn of the Twentieth Century, with Colonial Imperialism, based on the suppression of colored folk, at its zenith, would encourage, much less adequately finance, such a program at a Negro college under Negro scholars. My faith in its success was based on the firm belief that race prejudice was based on widespread ignorance. My long-term remedy was Truth: carefully gathered scientific proof that neither color nor race determined the limits of a man's capacity or desert. I was not at the time sufficiently Freudian to understand how little human action is based on reason; nor did I know Karl Marx well enough to appreciate the economic foundations of human history.

I was therefore astonished and infinitely disappointed, gradually to realize that our work in the Atlanta conferences was not getting support; that, far from being able to command increased revenue for better methods of investigation and wider fields, it was with increasing difficulty that the aging and overworked President, with his deep earnestness and untiring devotion to principle, could collect enough to maintain even our present activities. The conference had not been without a measure of success. Our reports were widely read and commented upon. We could truthfully say that between 1900 and 1925, no work on the Negro and no study of the South was published which was not indebted in some respect to the studies at Atlanta University. The United States Census Bureau and the Federal Labor Bureau asked our help and co-operation; institutions and philanthropies; authors, students and individuals in all walks of life, and in Europe, Asia and Africa, wrote us for information and advice. On the other hand, so far as the American world of science and letters was concerned, we never "belonged"; we remained unrecognized in learned societies and academic groups. We rated merely as Negroes studying Negroes, and after all, what had Negroes to do with America or Science?

Gradually and with deep disappointment I began to realize, as early as 1906, that my program for studying the Negro problems must soon end, unless it received unforeseen support.

THE CLOSING AND OPENING DECADES, 1900

For the American Negro, the last decade of the 19th, and the first decade of the 20th Centuries were more critical than the Reconstruction years of 1868 to 1876. Yet they have received but slight attention from historians and social students. They are usually interpreted in terms of personalities, and without regard to the great social forces that were developing. This was the age of triumph for Big Business, for Industry, consolidated and organized on a world-wide scale, and run by white capital with colored labor. The southern United States was one of the most promising fields for this development, with invaluable staple crops, with a mass of cheap and potentially efficient labor, with unlimited natural power and use of unequalled technique, and with a transportation system reaching all the markets of the world.

The profit promised by the exploitation of this quasi-colonial empire was facing labor difficulties, threatening to flare into race war. The relations of the poor-white and Negro working classes were becoming increasingly embittered. In the the year when I undertook the study of the Philadelphia Negro, lynching of Negroes by mobs reached a crimson climax in the United States, at the astounding figure of nearly five a week. Government throughout the former slave states was conducted by fraud and intimidation, with open violation of state and federal law. Reason seemed to have reached an impasse: white demagogues, like Tillman and Vardaman, attacked Negroes with every insulting epithet and accusation that the English language could afford, and got wide hearing. On the other hand Negro colleges and others were graduating colored men and women, few in the aggregate, but of increasing influence, who demanded the full rights of American citizens; and even if their threatening surroundings compelled silence or whispers, they were none the less convinced that this attitude was their only way of salvation. Supporting Negro education were the descendants of those Northerners who founded the first Negro institutions and had since contributed to their upkeep. But these same Northerners were also investors and workers in the new industrial organization of the world. Toward them now turned the leaders of the white South, who were at once apprehensive of race war and desirous of a new, orderly industrial South.

Conference began between whites of the North and the South, including industrialists as well as teachers, business men rather than preachers. At Capon Springs, on the Robert Ogden trips to Hampton and Tuskegee, in the organization of the Southern Education Board, and finally in the founding of the General Education Board, a new racial philosophy for the South was evolved. This philosophy seemed to say that the attempt to over-educate a "child race" by furnishing chiefly college training to its promising young people, must be discouraged; the Negro must be taught to accept what the whites were willing to offer him; in a world ruled by white people and destined so to be ruled, the place of Negroes must be that of an humble, patient, hard-working group of laborers, whose ultimate destiny would be determined by their white employers. Meantime, the South must have education on a broad and increasing basis, but primarily for whites; for Negroes, education, for the present, should be confined increasingly to elementary instruction, and more especially to training in farming and industry, calculated to make the mass of Negroes laborers contented with their lot and tractable.

White and Negro labor must, so far as possible, be taken out of active competition, by segregation in work: to the whites the bulk of well-paid skilled labor and management; to the Negro, farm labor, unskilled labor in industry and domestic service. Exceptions to this general pattern would occur especially in some sorts of skills like building and repairs; but in general the "white" and "Negro" job would be kept separate and super-imposed.

Finally, Northern philanthropy, especially in education, must be organized and incorporated, and its dole distributed according to this program; thus a number of inefficient and even dishonest attempts to conduct private Negro schools and low-grade colleges would be eliminated; smaller and competing institutions would be combined; above all, less and less total support would be given higher training for Negroes. This program was rigorously carried out until after the first World War.

To the support of this program, came Booker T. Washington in 1895. The white South was jubilant; public opinion was studiously organized to make Booker Washington the one nationally recognized leader of his race, and the South went quickly to work to translate this program into law. Disfranchisement laws were passed between 1890 and 1910, by all the former slave states, and quickly declared constitutional by the courts, before contests could be effectively organized; Jim-Crow legislation, for travel on railroads and street-cars, and race separation in many other walks of life, were rapidly put on the statute books.

By the second decade of the Twentieth Century, a legal caste system based on race and color, had been openly grafted on the democratic constitution of the United States. This explains why, in 1910, I gave up my position at Atlanta University and became Director of Publications and Research for the newly formed National Association for the Advancement of Colored People, of which I was one of the incorporators in 1911.

THE FIRST RE-ADAPTATION OF MY PROGRAM

Very early in my work in Atlanta, I began to feel, on the one hand, pressure being put upon me to modify my work; and on the other hand an inner emotional reaction at the things taking place about me. To note the latter first: as a scientist, I sought the traditional detachment and calm of the seeker for truth. I had deliberately chosen to work in the South, although I knew that there I must face discrimination and insult. But on the other hand I was a normal human being with strong feelings and pronounced likes and dislikes, and a flair for expression; these I could not wholly suppress, nor did I try. I was on the other hand willing to endure and as my dear friend, Henry Hunt, said to me in after years, I could keep still in seven different languages. But, if I did speak I did not intend to lie.

A characteristic happening that seared my soul took place in Georgia in 1899. A Negro farm laborer, Sam Hose, tried to collect his wages from his employer; an altercation ensued and Hose killed the white farmer. Several days passed and Hose was not found. Then it was alleged that he had been guilty of murder, and also of rape on the farmer's wife. A mob started after him.

The whole story was characteristic and to me the truth seemed clear: the habit of exploiting Negro workers by refusing for trivial reasons to pay them; the resultant quarrel ending usually in the beating or even killing of the over-bold black laborer; but sometimes it was the employer who got whipped or killed. If punishment did not immediately follow, then the mob was aroused by the convenient tale of rape. I sat down and wrote a letter to the *Atlanta Constitution,* setting down briefly the danger of this kind of needless race row, and the necessity of taking it firmly in hand in the very beginning. I had a letter of introduction to "Uncle Remus," Joel Chandler Harris, the editor, which I had never delivered. I took letter and article and started down town. On the way I learned that Hose had been caught and lynched; and I was also told that some of his fingers were on exhibit at a butcher shop which I would pass on my way to town. I turned about and went home. I never met Joel Chandler Harris. Something died in me that day.

The pressure which I began to feel came from white Northern friends, who I believed appreciated my work and on the whole wished me and my race well. But I think they were apprehensive; fearful because as perhaps the most conspicuously trained young Negro of my day, and, quite apart from any question of ability, my reaction toward the new understanding between North and South, and especially my attitude toward Mr. Washington, were bound to influence Negroes. As a matter of fact, at that time I was not over-critical of Booker Washington. I regarded his Atlanta speech as a statesmanlike effort to reach understanding with the white South; I hoped the South would respond with equal generosity and thus the nation could come to understanding for both races. When, however, the South responded with "Jim-Crow" legislation, I became uneasy. Still I believed that my program of investigation and study was just what was needed to bring understanding in the long run, based on truth. I tried to make this clear. I attended the conferences at Hampton for several years, to attest my interest in industrial training. There I was approached with tentative offers to come to Hampton and edit a magazine. But I could not be certain that I was to be allowed to express my own opinions or only the opinions of the school. Of those Hampton opinions, I became increasingly critical. In all the deliberations to which I listened, and resolutions, which were passed at Hampton, never once was the work at Atlanta University nor college work anywhere for Negroes, commended or approved. I ceased regular attendance at the conferences; but when later I was invited back I delivered a defense of higher training for Negroes and a scathing criticism of the "Hampton Idea." I was not asked to return to Hampton for twenty-five years.

About 1902, there came a series of attempts to induce me to leave my work at Atlanta and go to Tuskegee. I had several interviews with Mr. Washington and was offered more salary than I was getting. I was not averse to work with Mr. Washington, but I could get no clear idea what my duties would be. If I had been offered a chance at Tuskegee to pursue my program of investigation, with larger funds and opportunity, I would doubtless have accepted, because by that time, despite my liking for Atlanta, I saw that the university would not long be able to finance my work. But my wife and many friends warned me that all this eagerness for my services might conceal a plan to stop my work and prevent me from expressing in the future any criticism of the current Hampton-Tuskegee plan. I hesitated. Finally, in 1903, I published "The Souls of Black Folk" with its chapter, "Of Mr. Booker T. Washington and others."

This was no attack on Mr. Washington but it was a straight-forward criticism and a statement of my own aims. I received no further invitation to come to Tuskegee.

Events now moved fast. Opposition among Negroes to what now came to be called the Washington program grew. I took no active part in it, until Trotter was jailed in Boston for trying to heckle Washington. Then, in 1906, I called the Niagara Movement to meet at Niagara Falls and deliberate on our future course as leaders of the Negro intelligentsia. The manifesto which we sent out fixed my status as a radical, opposed to segregation and caste; and made retention of my position at Atlanta more difficult.

The presidents of Negro colleges, mostly white men, who began service with Reconstruction, were now beginning to retire or die of old age. Dr. Bumstead died in 1919. He was particularly disliked in the South because his white teachers and colored students ate together and because he gave up state aid rather than bar white students from his institution. He had been succeeded by a young man, son of Edmund Asa Ware, our first president. Young Edmund Ware was a good friend of mine and started his work with enthusiasm. But in raising funds he found himself against a stone wall; I do not know that he was actually advised to get rid of me, but I sensed his burden. I accepted the offer of the National Association for the Advancement of Colored People in 1910 to join their new organization in New York, as Director of Publications and Research.

My new title showed that I had modified my progam of research, but by no means abandoned it. First, I directed and edited my Atlanta study of 1912, *in absentia*, with the help of my colleague, Augustus Dill, my student and successor as teacher in Atlanta. Then in our study of 1913, I secured the promise of Dr. Dillard, of the Slater Board, to join Atlanta University in keeping up the work of the conferences. The work of research was to be carried on in New York, with a conference and annual publication at Atlanta. I was jubilant at the projected survival of my work. But on advice of President Ware, this arrangement was not accepted by the trustees. Ware was probably warned that this tie with a radical movement would continue to hamper the university. In August, 1910, I reported at my new office and new work at 20 Vesey Street, New York.

As I have said elsewhere, the National Association for the Advancement of Colored People "proved between 1910 and the World War, one of the most effective organizations of the liberal spirit and the fight for social progress which the Negro race in America has known." It fought frankly to make Negroes "politically free from disfranchisement; legally free from caste and socially free from insult." It established the validity of the Fifteenth Amendment, the unconstitutionality of the "Grandfather Clause," and the illegality of residential segregation. It reduced lynching from two hundred and thirty-five victims a year to a half dozen. But it did not and could not settle the "Negro Problem."

This new field of endeavor represented a distinct break from my previous purely scientific program. While "research" was still among my duties, there were in fact no funds for such work. My chief efforts were devoted to editing and publishing the *Crisis*, which I founded on my own responsibility, and over the protests of many of my associates. With the *Crisis*, I essayed a new role of interpreting to the world the hindrances and aspirations of American Negroes. My older program appeared only as I supported my contentions with facts from current reports and observation or historic reference; my writing was reinforced by lecturing, and my facts increased by travel.

On the other hand, gradually and with increasing clarity, my whole attitude toward the social sciences began to change: in the study of human beings and their actions, there could be no such rift between theory and practice, between pure and applied science; as was possible in the study of sticks and stones. The "studies" which I had been conducting at Atlanta I saw as fatally handicapped because they represented so small a part of the total sum of occurrences; were so far removed in time and space as to lose the hot reality of real life; and because the continuous, kaleidoscopic change of conditions made their story old already before it was analyzed and told.

If, of course, they had had time to grow in breadth and accuracy, this difficulty would have been met, or at least approached. Now in contrast I suddenly saw life, full and face to face; I began to know the problem of Negroes in the United States as a present startling reality; and moreover (and this was most upsetting) I faced situations that called—shrieked—for action, even before any detailed, scientific study could possibly be prepared. It was as though, as a bridge-builder, I was compelled to throw a bridge across a stream without waiting for the careful mathematical testing of materials. Such testing was indispensable, but it had to be done so often in the midst of building or even after construction, and not in the calm and leisure long before. I saw before me a problem that could not and would not await the last word of science, but demanded immediate action to prevent social death. I was continually the surgeon probing blindly, yet with what knowledge and skill I could muster, for unknown ill, bound to be fatal if I hesitated, but possibly effective, if I persisted.

I realized that evidently the social scientist could not sit apart and study *in vacuo;* neither on the other hand, could he work fast and furiously simply by intuition and emotion, without seeking in the midst of action, the ordered knowledge which research and tireless observation might give him. I tried therefore in my new work, not to pause when remedy was needed; on the other hand I sought to make each incident and item in my program of social uplift, part of a wider and vaster structure of real scientific knowledge of the race problem in America.

Facts, in social science, I realized, were elusive things: emotions, loves, hates, were facts; and they were facts in the souls and minds of the scientific student, as well as in the persons studied. Their measurement, then, was doubly difficult and intricate. If I could see and feel this in East St. Louis, where I investigated a bloody race riot, I knew all the more definitely, that in the cold, bare facts of history, so much was omitted from the complete picture that it could only be recovered as complete scientific knowledge if we could read back into the past enough to piece out the reality. I knew also that even in the ugly picture which I actually saw, there was so much of decisive truth missing that any story I told would be woefully incomplete.

Then, too, for what Law was I searching? In accord with

what unchangeable scientific law of action was the world of interracial discord about me working? I fell back upon my Royce and James and deserted Schmoller and Weber. I saw the action of physical law in the actions of men; but I saw more than that: I saw rhythms and tendencies; coincidences and probabilities; and I saw that, which for want of any other word, I must in accord with the strict tenets of Science, call Chance. I went forward to build a sociology, which I conceived of as the attempt to measure the element of Chance in human conduct. This was the Jamesian pragmatism, applied not simply to ethics, but to all human action, beyond what seemed to me, increasingly, the distinct limits of physical law.

My work assumed from now on a certain tingling challenge of risk; what the "Captain of Industry" of that day was experiencing in "kick," from money changing, railway consolidation and corporation floating, I was, in what appeared to me on a larger scale, essaying in the relations of men of daily life. My field of effort began to broaden in concept. In 1911, I attended a Races Congress in London. Had not the First World War so swept the mind of man clear of its pre-war thought, this meeting would have marked an epoch and might easily have made this Second World War unnecessary, and a Third, impossible. It was a great meeting of the diverse peoples of the earth; scarce any considerable group was omitted; and amid a bewildering diversity, a distinct pattern of human unity stood out.

I returned to America with a broad tolerance of race and a determination to work for the Internation, which I saw forming; it was, I conceived, not the ideal of the American Negroes to become simply American; but the ideal of America to build an interracial culture, broader and more catholic than ours. Before I had implemented this program in more than fugitive writing, World War fell on civilization and obliterated all dreams.

THE SECOND RE-ADAPTATION OF MY PROGRAM

I was forthwith engulfed in a mad fight to make Negroes Americans; a program I was already about to discard for something wider. The struggle was bitter: I was fighting to let the

Negroes fight; I, who for a generation had been a professional pacifist; I was fighting for a separate training camp for Negro officers; I, who was devoting a career to opposing race segregation; I was seeing the Germany which taught me the human brotherhood of white and black, pitted against America which was for me the essence of Jim Crow; and yet I was "rooting" for America; and I had to, even before my own conscience, so utterly crazy had the whole world become and I with it.

I came again to a sort of mental balance, when after the armistice, I landed in France, in December, 1918, charged with two duties: to investigate the stories of cruelty and mistreatment of Negro soldiers by the American army; and to sound some faint rallying cry to unite the colored world, and more especially the Negroes of three continents, against the future aggressions of the whites. For now there was no doubt in my mind: Western European civilization had nearly caused the death of modern culture in jealous effort to control the wealth and work of colored people.

The Pan-African congresses which I called in 1919, 1921 and 1923, were chiefly memorable for the excitement and opposition which they caused among the colonial imperialists. Scarcely a prominent newspaper in Europe but used them as a text of warning, and persisted in coupling them with the demagogic "Garvey Movement," then in its prime, as a warning for colonial governments to clamp down on colonial unrest. My only important action in this time, was a first trip to Africa, almost by accident, and a vaster conception of the role of black men in the future of civilization.

But here I was going too fast for the National Association for the Advancement of Colored People. The board was not interested in Africa. Following post-war reaction it shrank back to its narrowest program: to make Negroes American citizens, forgetting that if the white European world persisted in upholding and strengthening the color bar, America would follow dumbly in its wake.

From 1910 to 1920, I had followed the path of sociology as an inseparable part of social reform, and social uplift as a method of scientific social investigation; then, in practice, I had conceived an interracial culture as superseding as our goal, a purely American culture; before I had conceived a program for this path, and after throes of bitter racial strife, I had emerged with a program of Pan-Africanism, as organized protection of the Negro world led by American Negroes. But American Negroes were not interested.

Abruptly, I had a beam of new light. Karl Marx was scarcely mentioned at Harvard and entirely unknown at Fisk. At Berlin, he was a living influence, but chiefly in the modifications of his theories then dominant in the Social Democratic Party. I was attracted by the rise of this party and attended its meetings. I began to consider myself a socialist. After my work in Atlanta and my advent in New York, I followed some of my white colleagues—Charles Edward Russell, Mary Ovington, and William English Walling into the Socialist Party. Then came the Russian Revolution and the fight of England, France and the United States against the Bolsheviks. I began to read Karl Marx. I was astounded and wondered what other lands of learning had been roped off from my mind in the days of my "broad" education. I did not however jump to the conclusion that the new Russia had achieved the ideal of Marx. And when I was offered a chance to visit Russia in 1928, with expenses paid, I carefully stipulated in writing that the visit would not bind me in any way to set conclusions.

THE THIRD MODIFICATION OF MY PROGRAM

My visit to Germany and the Soviet Union in 1928, and then to Turkey and Italy on return, marked another change in my thought and action. The marks of war were all over Russia— of the war of France and England to turn back the clock of revolution. Wild children were in the sewers of Moscow; food was scarce, clothes in rags, and the fear of renewed Western aggression hung like a pall. Yet Russia was and still is to my mind, the most hopeful land in the modern world. Never before had I seen a suppressed mass of poor, working people— people as ignorant, poor, superstitious and cowed as my own American Negroes—so lifted in hope and starry-eyed with new determination, as the peasants and workers of Russia, from Leningrad and Moscow to Gorki and from Kiev to Odessa; the art galleries were jammed, the theatres crowded, the schools opening to new places and new programs each day; and work was joy. Their whole life was renewed and filled with vigor and ideal, as Youth Day in the Red Square proclaimed.

I saw of course but little of Russia in one short month. I came to no conclusions as to whether the particular form of the Russian state was permanent or a passing phase. I met but few of their greater leaders; only Radek did I know well, and he died in the subsequent purge. I do not judge Russia in the matter of war and murder, no more than I judge England. But of one thing I am certain: I believe in the dictum of Karl Marx, that the economic foundation of a nation is widely decisive for its politics, its art and its culture. I saw clearly, when I left Russia, that our American Negro belief that the right to vote would give us work and decent wage; would abolish our illiteracy and decrease our sickness and crime, was justified only in part; that on the contrary, until we were able to earn a decent, independent living, we would never be allowed to cast a free ballot; that poverty caused our ignorance, sickness and crime; and that poverty was not our fault but our misfortune, the result and aim of our segregation and color caste; that the solution of letting a few of our capitalists share with whites in the exploitation of our masses, would never be a solution of our problem, but the forging of eternal chains, as Modern India knows to its sorrow.

Immediately, I modified my program again: I did not believe that the Communism of the Russians was the program for America; least of all for a minority group like the Negroes; I saw that the program of the American Communist party was suicidal. But I did believe that a people where the differentiation in classes because of wealth had only begun, could be so guided by intelligent leaders that they would develop into a consumer-conscious people, producing for use and not primarily for profit, and working into the surrounding industrial organization so as to reinforce the economic revolution bound to develop in the United States and all over Europe and Asia sooner or later. I believed that revolution in the production and distribution of wealth could be a slow, reasoned development and not necessarily a blood bath. I believed that 13 millions of people, increasing, albeit slowly in intelligence, could so concentrate their thought and action on the abolition of their poverty, as to work in conjunction with the most intelligent body of American thought; and that in the future as in the past, out of the mass of American Negroes would arise a far-seeing leadership in lines of economic reform.

If it had not been for the depression, I think that through the *Crisis*, the little monthly which I had founded in 1910, and carried on with almost no financial assistance for twenty years, I could have started this program on the way to adoption by American Negroes. But the depression made the survival of the *Crisis* dependent on the charity of persons who feared this thought and forced it under the control of influences to whom such a program was Greek. In a program of mere agitation for "rights," without clear conception of constructive effort to achieve those rights, I was not interested, because I saw its fatal weakness.

MY PRESENT PROGRAM

About 1925, the General Education Board adopted a new program. It had become clear that the studied neglect of the Negro college was going too far; and that the Hampton-Tuskegee program was inadequate even for its own objects. A plan was adopted which envisaged, by consolidation and endowment, the establishment in the South of five centers of University education for Negroes. Atlanta had to be one of these centers, and in 1929, Atlanta University became the graduate school of an affiliated system of colleges which promised a new era in higher education for Negroes. My life-long friend, John Hope, became president, and immediately began to sound me out on returning to Atlanta to help him in this great enterprise. He promised me leisure for thought and writing, and freedom of expression, so far, of course, as Georgia could stand it.

It seemed to me that a return to Atlanta would not only have a certain poetic justification, but would relieve the National

Association for the Advancement of Colored People from financial burden during the depression, as well as from the greater effort of re-considering its essential program.

With the unexpected coming of a Second World War, this move of mine has proved a relief. However it only postpones the inevitable decision as to what American Negroes are striving for, and how eventually they are going to get it.

The untimely death of John Hope in 1936 marred the full fruition of our plans, following my return to Atlanta, in 1933. Those plans in my mind fell into three categories; first with leisure to write, I wanted to fill in the background of certain historical studies concerning the Negro race; secondly I wanted to establish at Atlanta University a scholarly journal of comment and research on race problems; finally, I wanted to restore in some form at Atlanta, the systematic study of the Negro problems.

Between 1935 and 1941, I wrote and published three volumes: a study of the Negro in Reconstruction; a study of the black race in history and an autobiographical sketch of my concept of the American race problem. To these I was anxious to add an Encyclopaedia of the Negro. I had been chosen in 1934 to act as editor-in-chief of the project of the Phelps-Stokes Fund to prepare and publish such a work. I spent nearly ten years of intermittent effort on this project and secured co-operation from many scholars, white and black, in America, Europe and Africa. But the necessary funds could not be secured. Perhaps again it was too soon to expect large aid for so ambitious a project, built mainly on Negro scholarship. Nevertheless, a preliminary volume summarizing this effort will be published in 1944.

In 1940, there was established at Atlanta, a quarterly magazine, *Phylon*, the "Atlanta University Review of Race and Culture." It is now finishing its fifth volume.

In the attempt to restore at Atlanta the study of the Negro problem in a broad and inclusive way, we faced the fact that in the twenty-three years which had passed since their discontinuance, the scientific study of the American Negro had spread widely and efficiently. Especially in the white institutions of the South had intelligent interest been aroused. There was, however, still need of systematic, comprehensive study and measurement, bringing to bear the indispensable point of view and inner knowledge of Negroes themselves. Something of this was being done at Fisk University, but for the widest efficiency, large funds were required for South-wide study.

The solution of this problem, without needless duplication of good work, or for mere pride of institution, came to me from W. R. Banks, principal of the Prairie View State College, Texas. He had been a student at Atlanta University during the days of the conferences. He took the idea with him to Texas, and conducted studies and conferences there for twenty years. He suggested that Atlanta University unite the seventeen Negro Land-Grant colleges in the South in a joint co-operative study, to be carried on continuously. I laid before the annual meeting of the presidents of these colleges in 1941, such a plan. I proposed the strengthening of their departments of the social sciences; that each institution take its own state as its field of study; that an annual conference be held where representatives of the colleges came into consultation with the best sociologists of the land, and decide on methods of work and subjects of study. A volume giving the more important results would be published annually.

This plan was inaugurated in the Spring of 1943, with all seventeen of the Land-Grant colleges represented, and eight leading American sociologists in attendance. The first annual report appeared in the Fall of 1943. Thus, after a quarter century, the Atlanta conferences live again.

To complete this idea, there is need to include a similar study of the vitally important Northern Negro group. The leading Negro universities like Howard, Fisk, Wilberforce, Lincoln of Pennsylvania and of Missouri, and others might with Northern universities jointly carry out this part of the scheme.

This program came to full fruition in 1944, when a report of the first conference was published as *Atlanta University Publication No. 22*. Then, without warning, the University retired me from work and gave up this renewed project.

SUMMARY

Finally and in summation, what is it that in sixty years of purposive endeavor, I have wanted for my people? Just what do I mean by "Freedom"?

Proceeding from the vague and general plans of youth, through the more particular program of active middle life, and on to the general and at the same time more specific plans of the days of reflexion, I can see, with overlappings and contradictions, these things:

By "Freedom" for Negroes, I meant and still mean, *full economic, political and social equality with American citizens, in thought, expression and action, with no discrimination based on race or color.*

A statement such as this challenges immediate criticism. Economic equality is today widely advocated as the basis for real political power: men are beginning to demand for all persons, the right to work at a wage which will maintain a decent standard of living. Beyond that the right to vote is the demand that all persons governed should have some voice in government. Beyond these two demands, so widely admitted, what does one mean by a demand for "social equality"?

The phrase is unhappy because of the vague meaning of both "social" and "equality." Yet it is in too common use to be discarded, and it stands especially for an attitude toward the Negro. "Social" is used to refer not only to the intimate contacts of the family group and of personal companions, but also and increasingly to the whole vast complex of human relationships through which we carry out our cultural patterns.

We may list the activities called "social," roughly as follows:

A. Private social intercourse (marriage, friendships, home entertainment).

B. Public services (residence areas, travel, recreation and information, hotels and restaurants).

C. Social uplift (education, religion, science and art).

Here are three categories of social activities calling for three interpretations of equality. In the matter of purely personal contacts like marriage, intimate friendships and sociable gatherings, "equality" means the right to select one's own mates and close companions. The basis of choice may be cultured taste or vagrant whim, but it is an unquestionable right so long as my free choice does not deny equal freedom on the part of others. No one can for a moment question the preference of a white man to marry a white woman or invite only white friends to dinner. But by the same token if a white Desdemona prefers a black Othello; or if Theodore Roosevelt includes among his dinner guests Booker T. Washington, their right also is undeniable and its restriction by law or custom an inadmissible infringement of civil rights.

Naturally, if an individual choice like intermarriage is proven to be a social injury, society must forbid it. It has been the contention of the white South that the social body always suffers from miscegenation, and that miscegenation is always possible where there is friendship and often where there is mere courtesy.

This belief, modern science has effectively answered. There is no scientific reason why there should not be intermarriage between two human beings who happen to be of different race or color. This does mean any forcible limitation of individual preference based on race, color, or any other reason; it does limit any compulsion of persons who do not accept the validity of such reasons not to follow their own choices.

The marriage of Frederick Douglass to a white woman did not injure society. The marriage of the Negro Greek scholar, William Scarborough, to Sarah Bierce, principal of the Wilberforce Normal School, was not a social castastrophe. The mulatto descendants of Louise Dumas and the Marquis de la Pailleterie were a great gift to mankind. The determination of any white person not to have children with Negro, Chinese, or Irish blood is a desire which demands every respect. In like manner, the tastes of others, no matter how few or many, who disagree, demand equal respect.

In the second category of public services and opportunities, one's right to exercise personal taste and discrimination is limited not only by the free choice of others, but by the fact that the whole social body is joint owner and purveyor of many of the facilities and rights offered. A person has a right to seek a home in healthy and beautiful surroundings and among friends and associates. But such rights cannot be exclusively enjoyed if they involve confining others to the slums. Social equality here denies the right of any discrimination and segregation which compels citizens to lose their rights of enjoyment and accommodation in the common wealth. If without injustice, separation in travel, eating and lodging can be carried out, any community or individual has a right to practise it in accord with his taste or desire. But this is rarely possible and in such case the demand of an individual or even an overwhelming majority, to discriminate at the cost of inconvenience, disease and suffering on the part of the minority is unfair, unjust and undemocratic.

In matters connected with these groups of social activity, the usage in the United States, and especially in the South, constitutes the sorest and bitterest points of controversy in the racial situation; especially in the life of those individuals and classes among Negroes whose social progress is at once the proof and measure of the capabilities of the race.

That the denial of the right to exclude Negroes from residential areas and public accommodations may involve counter costs on the part of the majority, by unpleasant contacts and even dangerous experiences, is often true. That fact has been the basis of wide opposition to the democratization of modern society and of deep-seated fear that democracy necessarily involves social leveling and degeneration.

On the whole, however, modern thought and experience have tended to convince mankind that the evils of caste discrimination against the depressed elements of the mass are greater and more dangerous to progress than the affront to natural tastes and the recoil from unpleasant contacts involved in the just sharing of public conveniences with all citizens. This conviction is the meaning of America, and it has had wide and increasing success in incorporating Irish, and German peasants, Slavic laborers and even Negro slaves into a new, virile and progressive American Culture.

At the incorporation of the Negro freedman into the social and political body, the white South has naturally balked and impeded it by law, custom, and race philosophy. This is historically explicable. No group of privileged slave-owners is easily and willingly going to recognize their former slaves as men. But just as truly this caste leveling downward must be definitely, openly, and determinedly opposed or civilization suffers. What was once a local and parochial problem, now looms as a world threat! If caste and segregation is the correct answer to the race problem in America, it is the answer to the race contacts of the world. This the Atlantic Charter and the Cairo conference denied, and to back this denial lies the threat of Japan and all Asia, and of Africa.

What shall we, what can we, do about it in the United States? We must first attack Jim-Crow legislation: the freezing in law of discrimination based solely on race and color—in voting, in work, in travel, in public service.

To the third category of social activity, concerned with social uplift, one would say at first that not only should everyone be admitted but all even urged to join. It happens, however, that many of these organizations are private efforts toward public ends. In so far as their membership is private and based on taste and compatibility, they fall under the immunities of private social intercourse, with its limitation of equal freedom to all.

But such organizations have no right to arrogate to themselves exclusive rights of public service. If a church is a social clique, it is not a public center of religion; if a school is private and for a selected clientele, it must not assume the functions and privileges of public schools. The underlying philosophy of our public school system is that the education of all children together at public expense is the best and surest path to democracy. Those who exclude the public or any part of it from the schools, have no right to use public funds for private purposes. Separate Negro public schools or separate girl's schools or separate Catholic schools are not inadmissible simply because of separation; but only when such separation hinders the development of democratic ideals and gives to the separated, poor schools or no schools at all.

Beyond all this, and when legal inequalities pass from the statute books, a rock wall of social discrimination between human beings will long persist in human intercourse. So far as such discrimination is a method of social selection, by means of which the worst is slowly weeded and the best protected and encouraged, such discrimination has justification. But the danger has always been and still persists, that what is weeded out is the Different and not the Dangerous; and what is preserved is the Powerful and not the Best. The only defense against this is the widest human contacts and acquaintanceships compatible with social safety.

So far as human friendship and intermingling are based on broad and catholic reasoning and ignore petty and inconsequential prejudices, the happier will be the individual and the richer the general social life. In this realm lies the real freedom, toward which the soul of man has always striven: the right to be different, to be individual and pursue personal aims and ideals. Here lies the real answer to the leveling compulsions and equalitarianisms of that democracy which first provides food, shelter and organized security for man.

Once the problem of subsistence is met and order is secured, there comes the great moment of civilization: the development of individual personality; the right of variation; the richness of a culture that lies in differentiation. In the activities of such a world, men are not compelled to be white in order to be free: they can be black, yellow or red; they can mingle or stay separate. The free mind, the untrammelled taste can revel. In only a section and a small section of total life is discrimination inadmissible and that is where my freedom stops yours or your taste hurts me. Gradually such a free world will learn that not in exclusiveness and isolation lies inspiration and joy, but that the very variety is the reservoir of invaluable experience and emotion. This crowning of equalitarian democracy in artistic freedom of difference is the real next step of culture.

The hope of civilization lies not in exclusion, but in inclusion of all human elements; we find the richness of humanity not in the Social Register, but in the City Directory; not in great aristocracies, chosen people and superior races, but in the throngs of disinherited and underfed men. Not the lifting of the lowly, but the unchaining of the unawakened mighty, will reveal the possibilities of genius, gift and miracle, in mountainous treasure-trove, which hitherto civilization has scarcely touched; and yet boasted blatantly and even glorified in its poverty. In world-wide equality of human development is the answer to every meticulous taste and each rare personality.

To achieve this freedom, I have essayed these main paths:

1. 1885-1910

"The Truth shall make ye free."

This plan was directed toward the majority of white Americans, and rested on the assumption that once they realized the scientifically attested truth concerning Negroes and race relations, they would take action to correct all wrong.

2. 1900-1930

United action on the part of thinking Americans, white and black, to force the truth concerning Negroes to the attention of the nation.

This plan assumed that the majority of Americans would rush to the defence of democracy, if they realized how race prejudice was threatening it, not only for Negroes but for whites; not only in America but in the world.

3. 1928-to the present

Scientific investigation and organized action among Negroes, in close co-operation, to secure the survival of the Negro race, until the cultural development of America and the world is willing to recognize Negro freedom.

This plan realizes that the majority of men do not usually act in accord with reason, but follow social pressures, inherited customs and long-established, often sub-conscious, patterns of action. Consequently, race prejudice in America will linger long and may even increase. It is the duty of the black race to maintain its cultural advance, not for itself alone, but for the emancipation of mankind, the realization of democracy and the progress of civilization.*

* After this book had gone to the press, Dr. Du Bois was appointed Director of Special Research of the NAACP. (Editor's note.)

WHAT THE NEGRO WANTS
AND HOW TO GET IT:
THE INWARD POWER
OF THE MASSES

By LESLIE PINCKNEY HILL

WHAT THE NEGRO WANTS

THERE IS LITTLE DOUBT now as to what the American Negro wants. Never, perhaps, has the Negro himself been more vocal or emphatic in his appeal, and never have so many helpfully approving, influential voices been raised in the surrounding white world. We have heard Mrs. Roosevelt, Sumner Welles, Pearl Buck and Wendell Willkie sounding forth the warning that all the legitimate aims of the war and of the peace may be lost if America fails to accord to its Negro minority freedom, justice and fundamental equality. Negroes want to be accepted by our American society as citizens who in reality belong, who have the respect of their fellow man and equality of opportunity for life, liberty and the pursuit of happiness. Negroes want what good men want in every democratic society. If they wanted less they would not deserve the status of citizens.

These desires, harmonized with those four great freedoms which the Allied Nations have proclaimed as universal war objectives, are widely published by press and radio. They are now carefully documented. Negro and white leaders in many parts of the nation, and inter-racial committees North and South have been at pains to set out, in language which Negroes themselves have formulated, most of the specifics of the social, political and economic aims of Negro striving. When Negroes meet in Durham, North Carolina, to develop a platform of agreements, it is significant that white leaders in Atlanta, Georgia, are sitting down very soon afterwards to make known to the world the attitude of the white South. Both groups, fortunately, are at last making the attempt to find acceptable bases for agreement.

The National Broadcasting System made history recently by presenting for the first time its own attitude on the highly controversial race question. Then it was that Wendell Willkie announced, and emphatically endorsed, at least six of the immediate aims of Negro effort:

1. Protection under the law and no discrimination in the administration of the law

2. Equality of education

3. Equality of expenditure for health and hospitalization

4. Elimination of all inhibiting restrictions in voting—through taxes or otherwise

5. Equal work opportunity and equal pay

6. The right to fight in any branch of the services

He might have included freedom from a generalizing press and from the usual moving picture presentation of the Negro as a scaramouch. These are minimum specifics. They are all, however, only items in the total urge of Negro life, under the impact of vast world forces, towards that status, precious now and consciously desired by all the peoples of the earth, in which equal recognition and full freedom will be accorded to the dignity and sanctity of all human personality in all human relations. The question is: How can the Negro achieve that status?

HOW CAN THE NEGRO GET WHAT HE WANTS—LEADERSHIP?

In attempting any answer to that question we have no lamp for our footing but the lamp of experience. Our light must shine from history, from the findings of all the sciences, and from the deathless words and example of those illumined spirits of every age and race in whom mankind has found inspiration and guidance. These all speak together of effort rooted in vision and long-enduring patience. No race or nation mushrooms up *en masse* into full-blown social acomplishment. No Rome was ever built in a day. There is no such thing as getting anywhere without going there. Time and the content we give it are always the final determinants.

And inasmuch as every people of whom we have record has been obliged to look to leaders through whose heart and mind they could express their hopes and define their directives—there is nowhere in history a single record to the contrary—it is clear that Negroes, whether in the disordered perspective-warping present time of tension and crisis, or in the outwardly calmer days of peace, will move forward only as the leaders whom they follow can effectively point the way. Of all the forces operating now towards the reaching of our aims and the molding of our future none is more potent for good or for evil than the force of this leadership.

Therefore I submit this fundamental thesis: The Negro will get the things he legitimately wants and strives for only if during the world crisis, and after it, he will follow leaders who have a known, articulate and unifying philosophy of life adequate to the exactions both of the crisis and to the still more difficult peace-time of reconstruction and rehabilitation. "The hungry sheep look up and are not fed." That was Milton's indictment of leaders whom he described as "blind mouths." But of another Leader it is written that the people heard Him gladly, that He spoke as one having authority because He brought the bread of life, the truth and a way. Who now will feed the discontented, disillusioned but waking masses of Negro people, and show them a path? What kind of leader must we magnify for a hindered but potentially great race?

We do not single out today any one all-dominating personality. There was a kind of social economy in the general uses made of the leadership of Frederick Douglass and Booker T. Washington. We have never had their equal in the responsibility these two men carried as referees in all the vexed issues confronting their people. They dispensed a vast patronage, made nominations to the government for all kinds of services available to Negroes, were called into conference in all parts of the nation where dangers threatened, spoke with authority to both races and by both were gladly heard. Neither was a university man, and the scholars often raised the old question of the source of their authority. But they possessed high elemental powers which they wielded unwearyingly and unselfishly for the common good. Negro aspiration in America for generations was to be typified by the vigor and achievement of these two spokesmen.

Today the scene has changed. Not even in George Washington Carver were Negroes generally aware of a consciously accepted influence. He was for long years rather a self-effacing prophet representative of new inter-racial values which only the future of our culture will explore. Today there are many leaders, and their development in Negro life is deeply significant and heartening. These are men and women who have strong influence and loyal following in all those areas of action and interest in which Negroes struggle. They are teachers and preachers, business men and women, journalists, authors and artists, social workers, labor organizers, politicians, parents, farmers and soldiers. They are spread over the land, North, South, East and West. Each, in his community, has some positive effect upon the social, moral, political and economic life of both races. Their compounded power is immeasurable. A thousand men and women with self-possession, informed outlook and active energy must, in the nature of things, promise more that is desirable in a democratic society than one compelling figure, however gifted or potent.

The most impressive single fact in this wide dispersion of leaders is the unanimity of their convictions. What can be said or attempted or done differs, of course, with the geographical locus. Atlanta and New Orleans cannot duplicate the precise procedures of Philadelphia or New York. Nevertheless, Negro leaders in all these places want the same thing. They want in Georgia and Pennsylvania, here at home, the same freedom for which the democracies say they are fighting on the other side of the Pacific in Burma or Munda. They want that sense of being acceptable and belonging which can be realized only when there is ungrudging respect for all human personality, whatever the accident of color. And the legitimacy and the necessity of these aspirations are now progressively acknowledged not only by our comparatively liberal North but even by brave and democratic spirits emerging in our South.

Now this manifold leadership can be wrought into effective power if it can be inspired and harmonized by a conscious philosophy that will constitute an unfailing frame of reference for leaders in every field. Not always can that philosophy be translated easily into the language of the masses, but to those masses it will invariably be consecrated. Gradually the people will feel its power. The leader's philosophy must look before and after. It must be the sanctuary of his spirit, the repository of his social and moral values, must keep him calm and resourceful under every challenge or provocation, and strengthen him to survive the strain of mental and physical exertion. It must be the power of that grace which in the old world, as Plutarch reports, kept the face of Phocion serene and unperturbed, and in our century, made Gandhi a figure of world concern.

Long ago I formulated for myself as a teacher, and thus perilously and inescapably a leader of youth, a brief but comprehensive personal philosophy of human relations, which time and experience have seemed to confirm. When I think or speak in detail of the racial scene here at home it is always against this universal background. I submit this philosophy to my responsible brethren in the United States or elsewhere who find themselves swept by the sudden but temporary alarms of tension and conflict, or challenged by the perduring blind pressures of prejudice.

A PERSONAL PHILOSOPHY OF HUMAN RELATIONS

The human family is one. The geographical or social factors that bind human beings together serve chiefly as conditioning settings from which proceed all those widely varying contributions, racial or national, that make up the culture of the world. Science continually proves the interdependency of all the races of man. Religion, education, politics and all the arts reënforce that proof. Race and nation are only terms by which we distinguish in this one human family vast aggregates of its members who have similar or identical characteristics.

* * *

No race or nation—as long as we think and behave under these concepts—can depend upon any other race or nation for its own advancement. Interdependency—now acknowledged everywhere —means fundamentally that each of the races must bear its own peculiar burden and, by working out its own salvation, help all the others.

* * *

Every race worthy of survival must make some definite and continuous contribution to the general welfare. Each, in good faith, must give as well as take. Rights must be balanced by obligations. Education must search out and develop every creative potentiality, large or small, and the whole group must magnify all the manifestations of genius.

* * *

No race can long survive or advance in full freedom if it fails to utilize its available resources and opportunities. These, left undeveloped, will be taken over and utilized, soon or late, by some other race.

* * *

Mandatory social objectives for the American Negro in his multi-racial environment must be adaptation and adjustment by cooperation. That indispensable cooperation will be powerfully assisted by strong personal self-control, good manners, intelligent tolerance, faith in the proved leaders and spokesmen of both races, and a reverent regard for the meaning and power of words. These are control factors directly related to the opening of opportunity for all kinds of participation and upgrading in the national service and elsewhere.

* * *

The greatest positive contribution the race can make to a deranged and demoralized civilization will be disciplined parents in upright, democratic homes wherein children are wanted and secure, and wherein they shall be taught respect for the laws of God and man, obedience to rightful authority, the universal need of self-sacrifice, responsibility for some worthy service to the family group, and the value of all work well done. Second only to the parent in all of this is the Negro teacher. Close to the school is the church. If these fail, the street will thwart home, school and church alike.

* * *

The race must keep all the friends it has in the dominant white world and work unceasingly to multiply them. Potent will be that discriminating intelligence by which Negroes will acknowledge the blessings they enjoy, as well as the wrongs they suffer. Praise must not be sacrificed to protest, nor protest to praise. No philosophy or procedure that produces racial hatred and antagonism can advance the common good.

* * *

World experience teaches that Negroes will make headway best by taking thought of one another and of their white friends in working out their common problems. Isolated individualism is impotent in an age whose genius is organization. By collective thinking every good mind, every skilled hand, every gift or grace of the spirit, every agency and every office is strengthened. In it there is room for all. It is the only guarantee of that effective group action required by the ordeal of war or the exigencies of peace.

* * *

The common foe of the whole human race is war, because war is a heinous and blasphemous negation of all right human relations. Nevertheless, a nation is often drawn into this disaster, and then every citizen becomes a guardian of his country's life. Then loyalty demands every sacrifice save that of honor.

* * *

In every emergency, the Negro race in America must give to the nation its unreserved allegiance. Wrongs will remain, but increasing opportunities and obligations will surpass them. Our democracy is not yet a satisfying reality, but Negroes are still free to live, strive and die to make it come in God's unhurried time. All else by comparison is trivial.

REALITIES BEYOND PHILOSOPHY

Beyond these sobering considerations there are two profound realities which no true leader can leave out of his reckoning—two visibly active manifestations that must broaden for him the base of an unshaken faith.

The first of these is the will of God which nothing can thwart. What is the will of God? The great religions teach that it is the will of God that men shall be brothers, that the truth shall be victor over lies, that men shall love mercy, do justly and walk humbly, that there shall be "beauty for ashes, the oil of joy for mourning and the garment of praise for the spirit of heaviness." It is the will of God, they declare, that brute force shall not prevail over the human soul, that every man shall know himself to be free and equal in his inalienable rights. They speak to the insufficiency of economic materialism, however impressive, by this brief teaching of all the humanities: "Man shall not live by bread alone but by every word that proceedeth out of the mouth of God." A thousand years was needed to document and verify the assurance of the most vigorous of all the saints that God has made of one blood all the nations of men. But the laboratories did in the end indubitably produce the proof.

So, in many tongues and symbols, come the eternal averments of prophet and poet. These are they who have brought the word of God from the mountain to the plain, registered that word in the great bibles, and manifested it in the lives which they themselves have set before us. "In the beginning was the word,...and the word was God."

The second reality, closely related and visible to our eyes, is the invincible power of the force of events. The complex of problems involved in race relations, here and everywhere, will not be solved by the syllogism. In these relations, logic seldom carries the issue, unless we think of the logic of the nature of things, the logic of stupendous events that come to pass without conscious human design. There is in the totality of things a power that passes out from all reasoned control into the fashioning of new worlds, new ideas, new values and vast new opportunities in new relations that were never deliberately planned or intended. This is the force of events—a force we can trust because it sums up in itself the whole aggregate of human conflict and striving, bringing the human family, in spite of itself, to higher levels of understanding, achievement, interdependency and well-being. We must get a place for logic and apply the rough tool wherever we can. We must continue to appeal to reason with all its implications. But let us not chafe nor lose vision when these fail us. Deeper down must go the pylons of our faith —down to the will of God, and to the revelations of that will in the force of events.

There is no logic nor reason, for instance, in the present polity or policy of nations that could expect Negroes to be sent to the defense of Australia. That is a white man's continent, unmistakably declared to be the white man's special preserve where no Negro is wanted. Years of logical argument and philanthropic appeal would not bear down the prejudice of white Australia against Negroes. But the mass pressure of a global war comes into play and takes the issue away from the local will. Down the gangplanks of the great ships long lines of clean, disciplined, eager black soldiers stream upon that land. They have not come to debate. They are silent about their rights. They do not by any uttered word ask white Australia to give up its race hating. They are there as soldiers of our American democracy to protect and strengthen that country for the freedom which coming centuries will widen and deepen for all mankind. And Australia, in spite of itself, must welcome those black men. And presently, out from the bush, crude, untaught black natives—the fuzzy wuzzies— come to the service of this same white community. They too come under world pressure as nurses, stretch-bearers, swift errand men. And they serve so well, overcoming so much evil with so much good, that recognition of a common humanity, even in these half-savages, breaks out in photograph, special communique and poetry. That was not planned, nor reasoned out nor intended. It is the all-compelling will of God. It is the force of events welding men into brotherhood. It is sublimity leaving our logic in shambles.

And those keen, young Negro air men flying now in advance of an assured Allied victory! How did they come to be? It was not by the cogent presentations of the earnest and honest citizens who opposed the flying field at Tuskegee. It was not by that Negro hating of prejudiced minds whose correct reasoning told them that if Negroes were taught to fly, they would be presently demanding a new recognition for technical service of the highest order, and then full equality everywhere. It was not by any upsurge of liberalism in government. It was again the tremendous demand of the emergency that took over the issue. The need that all the skills available in our total manpower should be gathered and sharpened towards the building of an incomparable air fleet, brought these Negro pilots into their flashing ships. While the debate went on, and logic struggled rightfully to defend and to oppose, the air field was laid out at Tuskegee. Keen young Negroes went into intensive training. They mastered mechanics and flying techniques. Presently they stood ready to serve not only their race and their country, but the future of civilization. They flew the wife of the President over Alabama, and they were flying in the spearhead of that brilliant sortie out of old Africa which was soon to humble Mussolini, make a mockery of Fascist race-hating propaganda, and break beyond repair the Axis powers. The logic of events wrought all this wonder.

And so with the commanding Negro general, magnificent in himself and in his service; so with the black captain commanding a ship bearing the name of a Negro educator; so with the colored citizen sharing increasing responsibility for government while men wearily debate the wicked poll tax; so with the Negro worker moving slowly but surely into every sphere of employment while the unions halt and haggle; so with the black scientist, artist and scholar transcending every embarrassment by the elevation of his spirit to see the beauty and the power of the manifest will of God.

It was the glory of our fathers that they responded to these ineffable intuitions and were persuaded of more things in the heavens and in the earth than are dreamt of in any philosophy. In desperate affliction they took the way of the spirit. Out of that spirit came preachers of the deathless word and a matchless body of imperishable song which has humbled and cleansed the souls of men in every part of the earth. When our greatest artist,

our supreme poet, our highest musician, our great unifying statesman or moral leader arrives, he will come, I think, clothed in
that same spirit.

EDUCATION OF THE MASSES

Now this philosophy and this reach beyond philosophy which
I commend to all our leaders makes no room for any kind of
laissez-faire. For we ourselves, all of us, must be part of that force
of events which is steadily advancing our cause by widening all
the boundaries of human freedom. Our leaders have a mighty
work to do in education. Always the average social and economic
level of the masses determines the status of any people anywhere
at any particular moment. Bringing up that average level is the
stupendous task of the hour.

Clearly must we understand in these dangerous days that the
goals which all our leaders have before them can be achieved, or
approximated, only in the degree to which the masses can acquire
inward power to react creatively to the demands of the prevailing cultural pattern. That power does not come by parades or
ultimatums. It cannot be given to any man or to any race or
nation. You cannot find it waiting at the end of any march.
Inward power is not the product of mass meetings. It does not
grow out of anger, vituperation or zealous self-assertion. It cannot be guaranteed even by legislation, since legislation is never
more effective than the enlightened public opinion which supports it. Pressure politics, as old as history, cannot create it. All
these things do come, and must come. But they are the variables—
stimulants in the long evolution of human society. They are part
of the whole social metabolism and coalesce with that totality of
social action whose grand result is the force of events.

But the mark of the authentic leader is his ability to look beyond all variables to that constant in the evaluation of social
status which is found always in a people's general condition. He
will think steadily in terms of the whole mass. His immediate
action will be determined always by his perception of permanent
ends. He will never forget that the things the people want and
must have can be achieved only by labor and sacrifice. Even

equality of opportunity can have little meaning unless those who have it are prepared to use it when it comes. To inflame the masses to immediate action is easy. To educate them is not easy. To demand rights is dramatic, but to bring into active conscience a sobering sense of responsibility by which rights may be balanced, retained and expanded is the patient, unheralded work of long-suffering consecration.

It is demonstrably then in education, I think, that our leaders will find their supreme task and challenge. They must bring to their labors much more than knowledge. To knowledge they must add reverence, to reverence a steady vision of the whole human struggle, and to that vision, sincerity and humility. For the whole body of the people must be enlightened. When leader and follower alike devote to that gigantic undertaking all the intelligence, all the energy and all the unselfish devotion they possess, progress will be long and painful.

Now, what are some of the fundamentals of the educative process which our leaders must everlastingly magnify and illustrate as they work to get what Negroes want? Returning to my philosophy, I draw forth from it definite and urgent mandates that must be reiterated until they are learned, believed and translated into conduct and achievement.

HOME, SCHOOL AND CHURCH

Of first importance always is the building of homes with all the sanctity, sacrifice and security of family life. Without this nothing else can prosper long. Here must be that basic grounding of the masses, from which all else must follow. Here our children must learn obedience to proper parental authority, respect for one another and for their elders, personal hygiene, good manners, thrift, understanding of the values of money and of property, the importance of unselfishness in sharing and doing well every kind of homely work, of being unfailingly dependable, and of reverence in the presence of holy things.

From such homes the whole group must get started towards those elements of learning which take form in reading, writing and numbers. Negroes must be taught the importance of identifying themselves with the whole family of man by acquainting themselves with the universal human record, supplemented and stimulated now marvelously by radio and moving picture. This is one way to broad sympathies and to spiritual freedom. And by the ability to reason even very moderately in numbers our people must see not only a schooling in the definition and measurement of values but also a defense against a caculating environment.

Out of these homes our masses must move faithfully to the church. It is tragically a common habit with our intellectuals to flout the house of God. They often think they have outgrown it. They examine it superciliously and dismiss it as of small emotional worth. They have left it. But they must come back to it. The real leader discerns that it is the man of the street whom he will find in this church, the working woman leading her child, and the unpretending poor. There with the common people he will find his proper fellowship. There he will be helped to keep quick within his own soul that word of the spirit without which all of his service will be vanity of vanities.

And with this three-fold grounding, under leaders who are not afraid of humility, our masses must take part actively and progressively in a great spread of miscellaneous interwoven necessities and opportunities as they move into wider areas of human relations. They must learn respect and gratitude for those of both races who unselfishly serve their interests. The citizen's right to vote they must hold as a sacred trust. Where they do not have that vote they must work unceasingly to win it, because without the ballot they are without the only protection a democracy can guarantee. They must be taught to compete in making homes clean and attractive. Multitudes of parent-teacher-preacher associations must teach hygiene and public manners, the importance of credit unions, cooperatives, and consumer buying. Every Negro worker must make good on the job to win the better wages that will support a higher standard of living. Masses of Negroes must learn to cultivate a little land, with joy in producing and conserving food. Boys and girls in much larger numbers must learn to play musical instruments, to dance beautifully, to sing and to cultivate flowers. Old and young must be taught to make useful things with their hands as well as with machines. They must support one another in initiating and developing all kinds of small business ventures. Literally tens of thousands of skilled and unskilled laborers, technicians, engineers, teachers, doctors, farmers, merchants, industrialists, managers, bankers, actors, writers, pilots, machinists, and social workers must be trained to innumerable services old and new. Thus time must be crowded with the purposeful self-discipline of hundreds of thousands of our people, if we are to lift the average level of our culture and get ahead to the things we seek.

And in all of this, if our leaders are wise, they will recognize and teach the need of an increasing interest and support from white America in spite of all the flurry and clashing of the races in many parts of the land. Without this genuine friendship and persistent cooperation Negroes will not get what they want and there can be neither peace nor attainment of democracy for either race.

EXAMPLE FROM THE ORIENT

Now these major propositions have countenance and support in many lands. Under limitations, I need to cite only one impressive illustration from the Orient.

China is a colossal example of a people, struggling, as Negroes struggle here, against ignorance, poverty, divisiveness, and exploitation. Yet they are getting forward painfully towards accomplishment. They listened finally to the voice of a leader with a unifying philosophy. In Chiang Kai-shek Negroes can recognize a great spiritual ally. How did he become the head of four hundred million human beings? It was by holding to the central conviction that the Chinese people could never reach the goal of national security, nor hope for victory against a powerfully organized aggression until the masses were awakened and prepared.

When it was clear, after the seizure of Manchuria, that Japan was moving to dominate the whole of Asia, the chancelleries of the world as well as the Chinese people themselves wondered why he did not immediately declare war and strike. He said the people were not ready. Young China, whatever the Hotspurs had to say, must learn good manners, self-service, obedience, industry, hygiene. Women must be emancipated, instructed, organized. There must be education for producing food and for making thousands of things required by the daily life of the people. There must be nursing, health teaching and cooperatives. The masses must be roused to a realization of their practical part in the vast bloody tragedy breaking upon them.

Chiang Kai-shek was called names. He was prodded. Friends left him. He resigned, was betrayed by close associates, was kidnapped, was even accused of playing the Japanese game for his own advantage. These are bitter experiences which, in varying degree, await the leaders of the masses everywhere. This man did not crack up under pressure and harrowing. He had a philosophy which kept firm his purpose and his faith. In early morning hours, he read the word of God, unashamed. From Confucius he turned for the dynamic of his spirit to that same Christ of the cross, in whose comforting words our fathers long ago found power unto salvation.

And what Negro has not been stirred by the story of the journeyings of China's young people to the far inland provinces with books and beds and tools, the meetings, the slow beginnings of teaching, the drills, the endless organization? Here was that hard, indispensable groundwork of preparation by which China was able to stagger up under merciless assault and the whole nation, though bleeding, to strain forward into increasing world esteem.

The Negro in this land, though differing from his oriental brother in unnumbered ways, can look with instruction and heartening upon this scene of unbelievable enterprise—this crowding of jealous time with multitudinous effort under deliberate self-discipline. It could never have come to pass if, at long last, there had not been working in all the Chinese provinces a purposeful body of individual leaders who finally caught and carried forward to the people an enlightened and practically implemented philosophy of unity and self-reliance. The scene and the circumstance of the Negro's striving are different; the principle is the same. In the course of human events, Chiang Kai-shek and the whole structure of his accomplishment may topple, but the record of his exalted adventure will remain for our chastening and profit.

MOBILITY

Our leaders must encourage our masses to move courageously from North to South, from South to North, whenever there is clear opportunity for that many-sided development which is demanded by the democratic society with which they must be integrated. Only by a free, intelligent mobility can labor itself, for instance, be properly distributed and evaluated. It is highly important, moreover, that the whole so-called Negro problem shall be seen not as a sectional but as a national and human concern. In the nature of things, and by the force of world events, mobility is both salutary and inevitable. Statesmen must plan for it. Education must enlighten and direct it.

There need be no fear of this healthful movement if our leaders, by a broad philosophy and wise procedure, guide it everywhere into channels of betterment and of inter-racial understanding. Everywhere they must make war upon the ghetto, whether in a city or in a section of the nation, whose natural products will always be vice, disease, delinquency, crime and social disaster.

Indignation and hasty judgment will stead us not at all when these shocks break upon us. Leaders must understand them and prevent them. "Examine," says Victor Hugo, "the road over which the fault has passed." And Thackeray graphically illustrates Victor Hugo's meaning. "Starve me," he writes, "keep me from books and honest people, educate me to love dice, gin and pleasure—and put me on Hounslow Heath, with a purse before me, and I will take it." The sources of delinquency, of tension and riot are as old as human unacquaintedness, indifference and neglect.

Before Negroes move in large numbers in any direction, therefore, leaders, cooperating with city officials and social agencies, must prepare the way in decent housing, in defining the job, and in facilities for recreation and education. Above all, they must bring together in the new locale the steady, cooperating good will of the strongest representatives of both races.

Never in America must Negroes, or any other people, be shut off and left unintegrated in any section of our land. The Indian reservations keep before us a perpetual warning.

SEGREGATION

Now, inasmuch as a progressive integration cannot for long years preclude the working together of masses of people of all races in separate groups and institutions, no discussion of what the Negro wants or of what he can do to get it can leave out the strangely complex meanings of segregation.

Recently in addressing the Pennsylvania State Negro Council I said:

It is high time that Negro leaders took a clear, objective view of themselves and of that phenomenon known as segregation, which the Jews have faced down through the centuries. We should have an understanding about segregation once and for all, and allow it no longer to baffle and defeat us as we move individually or by organization into the social action of our time.

Segregation is any convention or ritual or etiquette that preserves or extends the social distance between groups of human beings. It is not only spatial, institutional, physical. It is also a spiritual phenomenon. As the world grows smaller by the hour, segregation reveals itself as an evil thing when it is enforced by one individual or by one group upon another. But there is a self-imposed segregation operating all over the earth. That is the segregation by which people come together of their own accord for purposes bearing upon their general interests and their future prospects. Even this type of segregation carries often implications and results that are not in keeping with human solidarity and equality. Nevertheless, institutions and movements so initiated and developed rise everywhere. Negroes and Jews alike face both kinds of segregation—enforced and self-imposed—and from the effects of both kinds are everywhere endeavoring to find escapes. It is everywhere harassing business. For the surrounding white world has its own spread of segregated groupings as intense and sometimes as mischievous as any similar phenomenon in any part of the colored universe.

The challenge of the hour is that there shall come forth from both races leaders who shall be competent to develop engines of understanding and cooperative effort that may progressively break down the barriers that divide the human family. The bridges that must span the chasms between black man and white man, yellow man and brown man, Protestant, Catholic and Jew are difficult bridges to build. There is no ready blueprint adequate in detail for all times and places. The only prospect, therefore, of any sure progress toward that building, whether now or in the times that shall follow this war, is in the adoption by Negro and white leaders alike of a philosophy, or body of principles, that may be considered of universal application.

The essence of that philosophy I have already attempted to suggest.

TALENT AND GENIUS

And, finally, our leaders must help to make clear to the masses the glory that is shed upon the whole race and the bond which is established with all human progress when out of their midst arises high talent or genius. One Phocion, one Asoka, one John Pym may justify a nation. We have not been sufficiently alive to this fact. Even George Washington Carver was laughed at for years by intellectuals of both races as a strange, queer misfit. Now while all the trumpets are sounding for him on the other side, the nation builds a monument to his memory as a luminous first citizen and world benefactor. Our productive scholars are not yet properly acclaimed and encouraged, and our finest artists are just beginning to come into their own. Tanner had to leave America before his creative genius was revealed to the world. Roland Hayes was not in America but in London when, from the king's palace, he was launched upon his astonishing career. Illustrations abound. Let our leaders teach the masses that we must clear our eyes to recognize and support the high spirits moving already in our midst, to hear their words, to look upon their work with reverence and to follow the paths they are blazing. Genius and talent give dignity to the life of the people and bring them to recognition. Through genius the masses are impelled towards the highest goals.

SUMMARY

What does the American Negro want? Full citizen status in our American democracy. How shall he reach that goal? By the inward power of the masses. And how shall that power be acquired? Fundamentally, on the highest plane and on the humblest, by a leadership motivated by a world-encompassing philosophy which is rooted in the will of God—a leadership which, itself a vital part of the force of events, is consecrated in humility to the immediate and practical education of the people.

THE NEGRO
HAS ALWAYS WANTED
THE FOUR FREEDOMS

By CHARLES H. WESLEY

T HERE HAVE BEEN consistent approaches to social goals sought by American Negroes in order to secure what they want. Paths along which they have traveled have varied, but the objective of an improved status and an advancing standard of life have been always present in the striving. What the Negro wants is not foreign to what he has always wanted in the United States. Whether expressed or implied, the end has been envisioned despite the variation in method. The Negro has seen through the years that in spite of theoretical liberalism, discriminations have been practised against racial, religious and foreign-language groups, without the exaction of penalties upon the violators of our fundamental law and democratic tradition. The Negro has seen his countrymen condition his status through the operation of a rigid color line in economic, political, religious, educational and social practices. The Negro has seen the teachings of the physical and social sciences by many pseudo-scholars prostituted in order that the American people who are called "white" may secure some justification for their discriminations, separatist policies, exclusive programs and repressive activities against other American people who happen by the accident of birth to be darker in color. Among these minorities, none has experienced such treatment as the Negro-Americans.

They have wanted what other citizens of the United States have wanted. They have wanted freedom and opportunity. They have wanted the pursuit of the life vouchsafed to all citizens of the United States by our own liberty documents. They have wanted freedom of speech, where they were supposed to be silently acquiescent in all aspects of their life and not even to want to utter "a mumblin' word." For expressing what they thought, many Negroes were hounded, beaten and driven from their homes. They then developed the mask which grinned through shining teeth and the lips which hid behind the soul of protest. Many a shuffling, smiling, bowing and bending body of a servant and worker carried within a violence of opposition which the suppression of speech alone prevented. Many a public assembly has heard harmless platitudes, which freedom of speech would have changed into challenges of a social system holding the Negro as a chattel and a thing less than a man.

They have wanted freedom of religion, for they had been compelled to "steal away to Jesus" and to "go way down yonder" by themselves in order to worship God as they desired. They had to suffer the humiliation of the Negro pew and the Negro gallery if they would worship with other Americans. From the struggle over slave baptism to the last time a Negro sought to hold membership in a "white" church, there was a long story of the absence of the freedom to worship.

They have wanted freedom from want. They have been workers, for about one-ninth of the Nation's workers in 1930 were Negroes, but they were confined largely to the smaller wages and reduced incomes of household service, agriculture and the unskilled and menial labor of the mills, mines, lumber camps and transportation. This economic stratification has forced them into the least desirable jobs and paid them lower wages than white workers for the same work. War periods have witnessed booms of work, which have temporarily changed their wage scale. However, the Negro has remained a marginal worker and the competition with white workers has left him in want in many localities of an economically sufficient nation.

They have wanted freedom from fear. They have been cowed, brow-beaten or beaten as they have marched through the years of American life. In area after area, fear of bodily harm and fear for the future of self and family have dominated the life and thought of the Negro people. These have dominated their life experiences and created the exercise of escape mechanisms and psychological manifestations which have led to the false conclusion that the Negro is naturally submissive to superiors and apologetic to insults. They still want freedom to worship, freedom of speech, freedom from want, freedom from fear, and the freedom to be free.

Several methods have been employed to achieve these objectives in the past and in the present. What the Negro wants now should be seen from the basis of his strivings in the past. The historical view of the social scene shows endeavors along many fronts. The effort to present what the Negro wants must be made from this point of view or its validity will rest mainly upon a special interest basis, and the same facts may be subjected to an entirely different interpretation when viewed from another angle.

There have been several proposals and solutions to the so-called Negro Problem in the United States. These have varied with the passing years. They have been parallel in time and have differed with the social change of the problem. The first group of solutions were pre-Civil War ones which may be summarized under, first, insurrections and violent seizures of power; second, religious, philanthropic and ameliorative endeavors; third, colonization and expatriation; and fourth, organization and activities for freedom by Negroes and whites, individually and collectively.

Contrary to the accepted view, insurrection and violence were the earliest and most continuous of these programs to secure what the Negro wanted, although none of these efforts met with even temporary success. The more direct result was the adoption of laws and modes of control which would not only prevent the recurrence of these attempts but fixed more permanently the inferior status of the participants in these efforts. Beginning in 1639 near East Boston in Virginia, where the first recorded insurrection took place, to the outbreak of the Civil War, the Negro sought to use overt methods of freeing himself from the chains which bound him. These endeavors prove that the assertions of the docility, the humbleness and the satisfaction of the Negro with slavery are false. The mental picture of the Negro so willingly accepted is quite contrary to this fact of history.

Freedom and liberty are just as dear to the black or brown skin as to the white. Negro insurrections and rumors of them were the causes for the majority of severe slave codes and the legal control of free Negroes. During the early years of the colonial period, revolts occurred in the Northern states but as slavery declined in this section and grew more extensive in the South, the insurrections arose almost entirely in that section. While rumors connected free Negroes and white abolitionists with these revolts, the Negroes themselves from the depth of enslavement raised blows of protest more often than acquiescence. All of these insurrections ended in failures and instead of improving the Negro's status seemed in many places to have served to lower it.

Philanthropic and ameliorative efforts by individuals and groups were of greater influence. In the colonial period, the voices of John Eliot, Cotton Mather and Judge Sewell were raised against the slave trade and the endeavors of Anthony Benezet, founder of the present Benezet House in Philadelphia, John Woolman and others created sentiment for the amelioration of slavery in the North, and for the education of the Negro in this section. Individual Puritans and Quakers joined in this work. It is significant also in this connection that the first abolition society selected as its first title "The Society for the Relief of Free Negroes, unlawfully held in Bondage." This organization became known in 1787 as "The Pennsylvania Society for Promoting the Abolition of Slavery, the Relief of Free Negroes unlawfully held in Bondage and for improving the Condition of the African Race." Benjamin Franklin was elected its president and the society entered upon a vigorous campaign to carry out its purposes. Other state abolition societies with similar purposes were established. Particularly noteworthy were the abolition activities of a few individuals and groups in the South. The liberalism of the American Revolution, which gave rise to these societies, was soon forgotten, however, as economic factors became increasingly important in the national life. Negro leaders participated in these efforts to advance the status of their people, and among them were Richard Allen, James Varick, Lott Carey and a host of other religious interpreters. Slavery itself was ameliorated on many small plantations by the kindness of masters. Here, the institution became more social than economic. Intimate personal relations on the one hand were paralleled by distance on the other.

The organization movement of the thirties, known as abolition, in which Negroes and whites participated, gave some advancement to the status of thousands of Negroes, in spite of the abuse heaped upon it. Three members of the Executive Committee of nine of the American Anti-Slavery Society were Negroes. The Constitution of the American Anti-Slavery Society stated that its aim was "to elevate the character and condition of the people of color by encouraging their intellectual, moral and religious improvement, and by removing public prejudice, that thus they may, according to their intellectual worth, share an equality with the whites, of civil and religious privileges but this society will never, in any way, countenance the oppressed in vindicating their rights by resorting to physical force." Negro speakers and writers joined with whites to carry on the battle for freedom. Frederick Douglass, a slave and ship's caulker, became Douglass, the orator and editor; Sojourner Truth, the slave, became Sojourner Truth, the Abolitionist and Advocate of Woman Suffrage.

Negroes themselves organized societies for philanthropic purposes. The Free African Societies in Philadelphia, New York, Newport and Boston were organized for this purpose. The Moral Reform Society composed of free Negroes was interested in measures to improve the status of the free people of color. Negro women organized the Afric-American Female Intelligence Society for the advancement of the Welfare of Negroes and the Female Anti-Slavery Society of Salem, Massachusetts, composed of free Negro women, declared that their purpose was "to promote the welfare of our color." The Phoenix Society of New York had as its object the establishment of a fund for the "improvement of the coloured people in Morals, Literature and the Mechanic Arts."

A third program which was intended to improve the Negro's status was the Colonization Plan. The idea of removing the free Negroes to some territory outside of the United States had accompanied the anti-slavery movement from an early period. Negro insurrections had encouraged the development of the plan. The lot of the free Negro in this country was described by the proponents of this idea as so wretched and unworthy that colonization was suggested as the only remedy. In 1816 the American Society for Colonizing the Free People of Color of the United States was organized. The movement was advertised as one in which all parts of the country could unite for the improvement of the opportunities of free Negroes. Under this program the name Liberia or the Land of Freedom was adopted for a colony on the West Coast of Africa. In spite of continuous support from state societies as well as the national organization, the plan failed. With all of these efforts, between 1820 and 1830, the Society was able to send only 1,162 settlers to Liberia. Only a small number of American Negroes went to Liberia and the Americo-Liberians, although patterning the Liberian republic after the government of the United States, were outnumbered by the indigenous Liberian population by 100 to 1. Proposals were heard for colonization in Liberia, Haiti and other places again and again throughout the period prior to the end of the Civil War but no distinct practical success attended any of these endeavors.

The fourth program was the effort of the minority group to improve its status through the Convention Movement. Beginning in Philadelphia in 1830, the free Negroes of the United States held conventions for the consideration of their problems. The Convention of 1830 proposed the consideration by Negroes of emigration to Canada "as a measure of relief against the prosecution from which colored Americans suffered in the United States." At the Convention of 1832, there were eight states represented by delegates. In 1837, the last of a series of annual conventions which characterized the period between 1830 and 1837 were held. From this period up to the Civil War, conventions were held every year but many of them were local ones. However, they continued to be important milestones in Negro life. The call to a convention at Pittsburgh in 1842 declared:

> Two and a half million of our countrymen are in chains—
> our rights are cloven down so that we speak by sufferance.
> Mobocracy has disgraced almost every part of our country.
> Freedom of speech, the right of petition and of locomotion
> are denied us. Our trade is prostrate, our credit impaired,

and our prosperity paralyzed. Our religion is evil-spoken of, our institutions condemned, and our country is a hissing and a by-word before all the civilized nations of the globe. It becomes us to unite with one mind and heart to labor, with persevering zeal and efficiency, to bring slavery to a speedy termination.

These conventions did not accomplish much, beyond the issuance of calls and the adoption of resolutions. They did centralize the thinking of Negroes towards caste, proscription and oppression. These resolutions were not followed by definite actions, and yet, the organized life of the Negro would have been weak without these expressions of sentiment.

The Civil War brought fundamental changes in the status of Negroes in the United States. The victory of the Northern armies was the triumph of an industrial economy over an agricultural one. This triumph was followed by the legal destruction of slavery in the Thirteenth Amendment. This meant the destruction of the foundation upon which the Southern planter class had built its power and its system of life. The Northern industrial and political leadership led in the grant of an equal political status by the Fourteenth and Fifteenth Amendments to Negroes and Republican victories at the polls were thus assured for several years. The approval of these amendments by the state constitutional conventions did not carry with it an acknowledgment of a change in attitude and sentiment. The Military was necessary for the enforcement of this legislation. For in spite of legal provisions, Frederick Douglass in a speech in Boston in 1865 on the subject, "What the Negro Wants," declared that the Negro had been a citizen three times in the history of the government, in 1776, 1812, and 1865, and that in time of trouble the Negro was a citizen and in time of peace he was an alien.

The roles of master and slave or of superior white status and inferior black status were perpetuated by the so-called "Black Codes." The Freedmen's Bureau was an attempt to improve the Negro's status and to assist in his transition to freedom. It was engaged in the additional work of assisting the landless poor whites, also freed by the incidents of war. There was resentment in many localities and among the Confederate sympathizers against the work of this Bureau. The Civil Rights acts at first gave hope for a new day but the announcement of their unconstitutionality in 1883 showed how ineffectual legislation was without the support of public sentiment. The Ku Klux Klan and other hooded organizations began their reign of terror, and poor whites, seeing in the Negroes the symbols of their oppression, joined in acts of violence against them. Lynching developed as one of the vicious expressions of race hatred and racial exploitation. With anti-Negro sentiment growing in this way, the troops of the North were withdrawn in 1877 and the "Home Rule" was gradually regained by the White South.

Thereupon, the present system of subordination under which Negroes of the nation suffered was extended in this post-reconstruction period. Jim Crow legislation and separate race laws were enacted during the eighties to determine the status of the Negro. Standards were set for differences in jobs and the intercourse between the races was to be governed by social relations which were to maintain the Negro in an inferior status.

This status has been fixed by custom which has become as strong as statutory law. The fundamental reason for this situation is the belief in the inferiority of the Negro, a concept based upon the master-slave psychology and past poor white-Negro relationships. The presence of the Negro raises objection whenever he comes as an equal. As long as he is an inferior—a porter, a nurse, a sexton, a servant—he is tolerated. Whenever recognition is given to the status of inferiority, there is rarely any racial conflict. This belief is not peculiarly Southern, for although Northern sympathy could be aroused during slavery to a fairer consideration of the Negro by descriptions of Negro treatment in the South, there is no longer any rigidly marked sectional difference. Custom limits the Negro in the North just as legislation and custom circumscribe him in the South. An effective commentary in the *Independent* in 1920 upon this situation stated: "The omniscience of the South on the race question is only equalled by the mescience of the North." This condition is apparent in urban ghettos, disbarment from hotels and restaurants, the color line in the churches, lower wages for the same work, elimination from jobs, economic discrimination, and inequalities in education.

Separation with the consequent inferiority follows all along the line of Negro life.

Negroes have not meekly accepted this status. Some writers refer to a new spirit of resentment which has taken place among Negroes and they have described it as the spirit of the "New Negro." This is not entirely a correct description, as has been made clear by our description of the Negro's struggle for status prior to the Civil War. It is true that more Negroes appear to be less submissive in the face of oppression and inferiority but it is also evident that there have always been Negroes who were courageous and fearless leaders and actors in the organization and activity of opposition to oppression.

During the latter part of the nineteenth century, two main paths of this struggle were developed. The first was the path of conciliation which was pointed out by Booker T. Washington. In his Atlanta Exposition address in 1895, there appeared the clearest expression of this view. Dr. Washington expressed the belief that economic independence should precede social relations, and that the Negro should earn his rights before he demanded them. He would thus temporarily avoid the debatable issues. He urged:

> In all things that are purely social we can be as separate as the fingers, yet one as the hand in all things essential to mutual progress.... The wisest among my race understand that the agitation of questions of social equality is the extremest folly and that progress in the enjoyment of all the privileges that will come to us must be the result of severe and constant struggle, rather than artificial forcing. No race that has anything to contribute to the markets of the world is long in any degree ostracized. It is important and right that all privileges of law be ours, but it is vastly more important that we be prepared for the exercise of these privileges. The opportunity to earn a dollar in a factory just now is worth infinitely more than the opportunity to spend a dollar in an opera house.

He believed optimistically that the demonstration of merit by the Negro would lead to recognition. Said he: "The time will come when the Negro in the South will be accorded all the political rights which his ability, character and material possessions entitle him." He therefore urged the Negroes of the South not to migrate northward but, "cast down your bucket where you are—cast it down by making friends in every manly way with people of all races by whom we are surrounded. Cast it down in agriculture, mechanics, in commerce, in domestic service and in the professions." The program of industrial education then attracted the philanthropic interests and Tuskegee along with Hampton became expressions of the special development of this idea. Advances have been made by the Negro through these institutions and their programs of vocational education.

The fallacies in this argument that the Negro's status can be advanced by in-group progress along one path of material development and delay in other paths of life were clearly demonstrated by what has happened to wealthy, educated and talented minorities in Germany and Europe As long as the stereotypes of the Jew as the leech, the parasite, the non-conformist and the racial inferior in German society remained in the popular mind, his material progress and his educational and cultural advancement were achievements which could be used as a basis to intensify popular antagonism. The Jew could thus be made the scapegoat of national history. Without a doubt, this was one of the paths towards an improved status for the Negro but it was soon regarded by other leaders as not the only path nor the one which had priority over others.

The leaders of the second path regarded this approach as a surrender of real citizenship. They believed that manhood's rights were paramount in a democracy. Dr. W. E. B. Du Bois gave expression to this view when he said: "Manly self-respect is worth more than lands and houses" and, he added, "a people who voluntarily surrender such respect or cease striving for it are not worth civilizing." He believed that the Constitution was the guarantee of citizenship for Negroes as well as whites and that the ballot and the courts were necessities to the protection of the citizen. Said he: "I hold these truths to be self-evident, that a disfranchised working class in a modern industrial civilization is worse than helpless. It is a menace not simply to itself but to every other group in the community. It will be diseased, it will be criminal, it will be ignorant, it will be the plaything of mobs and it will be insulted by caste restrictions."

Organized expression was then given to this philosophy. In 1905 the Niagara Movement was launched at Niagara Falls. Its first convention was held in 1906 at Harpers Ferry where John Brown struck for freedom. This movement was planned as a direct break with the Washington program. An address issued at this time stated:

> We shall not be satisfied with less than our full manhood rights. We claim for ourselves every right that belongs to a freeborn American, political, civil and social and until we get these rights we shall never cease to protest and assail the ears of America with the stories of its shameful deeds towards us. We want full manhood suffrage and we want it now. Second, we want discrimination in public accommodations to cease. Third, we claim the right of free men to associate with such people as wish to associate with us. Fourth, we want the laws enforced against rich as well as poor, against capitalists as well as laborers, against white as well as black. We are not more lawless than the white race; we are more often arrested, convicted and mobbed. Fifth, we want our children educated. The school system of the country districts of the South is a disgrace to civilization and in few towns and cities are the Negro schools what they ought to be.

Four conferences were held by this movement and several legal contests were conducted through the courts by it.

About the time of the Springfield race riots in 1909 and the Berea decision of the United States Supreme Court which put an end to a mixed student body at Berea College, Kentucky, the idea of the National Association for the Advancement of Colored People was born. William English Walling, of Kentucky parentage, who had returned from a visit to Russia, said in September, 1908: "Either the spirit of the abolitionists, of Lincoln and of Lovejoy, must be revived and we must come to treat the Negro on a plane of absolute political and social equality or Vardaman and Tillman will soon have transferred the Race War to the North." With Oswald Garrison Villard, Mary White

Ovington, Charles Edward Russell, W. E. B. Du Bois and others as signers, a call was issued for a national conference.

This call concluded with the words: "Hence we call upon all the believers in democracy to join in a national conference for the discussion of the present evils, the voicing of protests and the renewal of the struggle for civil and political liberty." At the end of May, 1909, this conference was held and it was decided to form a permanent committee. Out of this plan there came the National Association for the Advancement of Colored People with Moorefield Storey of Boston as President and with W. E. B. Du Bois as director of publicity and research and later editor of the *Crisis* magazine which appeared in November, 1910. The platform adopted called upon black and white to stand together for the abolition of all forced segregation, equal educational advantages for colored and white, enfranchisement of the Negro and the enforcement of the Fourteenth and Fifteenth Amendments. This platform seems reasonable to us today but it was regarded as a radical one at that time. However, the association has had a steady growth through the years. It has disseminated facts about the Negro and courageously carried on the struggle for his improved status.

Negro Labor has sought to organize and to bargain collectively since 1869 to improve its status and secure what it wanted. Its experiences with the National Labor Union, the Knights of Labor and the American Federation of Labor have not been satisfactory and have not always resulted in an improved economic status. The appearance of the C.I.O., the Congress of Industrial Organizations, has brought new hope to Negro workers and has caused the American Federation of Labor to liberalize its policies. Negro workers in all walks of life are now thinking in terms of organization. They are organizing in separate bodies and they are organizing wherever the opportunities permit with white workers. The need for such organization is clearly apparent.

A strong movement for economic cooperation, particularly in sections where segregation had laid the basis for an in-group economy, was given activity in the National Negro Business League which was established in 1900 under the leadership of Booker T. Washington. Negro business was given considerable stimulus by this organization. Its annual meetings and its publications assisted in directing attention to this field of Negro life. As a result, there were Negro economic institutions which began to serve considerable numbers of Negroes. Closely associated with this same tendency was the cooperative movement. Small cooperatives were organized in Negro communities. This aspect of economic life was not developed as completely as was possible within the walls of a segregated economy.

Still other organizations with programs for advancing the Negro's status have also arisen. Among them were such smaller ones as the Constitution League, which made a gallant fight for the Negro troops at Brownsville, under the leadership of Gilchrist Stewart, and the National Equal Rights League, under the leadership of William Monroe Trotter, which was uncompromising in its fight against segregation.

The population trend towards the cities created interest among students of social conditions, and in 1905 several committees began to work for the improvement of conditions among Negroes. The first committees following these urban trends to handle this problem in New York City were The Committee for Improving Industrial Conditions of Negroes in New York, and The National League for the Protection of Colored Women.

In 1913 the National Urban League was incorporated under the laws of New York. The objects of the organization included the encouragement of the training of young men and women for social service, the improvement of workers in condition and efficiency through organization, the development of a vocational bureau, and an employment program and the endeavor to secure the cooperation of the employers of Negro labor. Health, housing, recreation, employment, crime and delinquency and the problems of school and home were its provinces. "Not alms but opportunity" was its slogan. White and colored leaders worked together in these efforts.

The depression struck the Negro squarely and left him frequently without a job. He found himself slipping down the economic ladder. Chain stores put his small independent stores out of business. Negro banks and financial organizations failed and their places were taken by white companies. Relief rolls were being filled with Negro employables. Studies of relief figures showed that Negroes were being added to relief rolls frequently in a proportion twice as great as whites. Here was the opportunity for the New Negro Alliance. With this background it began its program of "buy where you can work." In many neighborhoods Negro salespeople are seen where hitherto only white faces were seen. Its successful conduct of its picketing case against the Sanitary Grocery Company in the October term, 1937, of the United States Supreme Court is a significant milestone in Negro history. Other cities have followed this pattern and technique with similar successes. Among these groups have been the Vanguard League and the Future Outlook League. This program often directed attention to competition for jobs on the racial basis and widened the gulf between the white and black working classes. Every effort should be made to close ranks so that white and black may continue to work together and not against one another. However, some white labor organizations have joined with these organizations in their program of job-getting.

The National Negro Congress, composed of Negro organizations, was organized in 1936 and held its first Congress in Chicago. It declared that "the need for the establishment through united action of a strong movement against the social and economic repressions being experienced by the Negro made such a movement imperative." At its meeting in Chicago, 817 delegates from 585 organizations were present. The Congress grew out of the need for union among the several organizations and has been urging the creation of a United Front in action. Its work goes forward for the full participation of the Negro in the privileges of American democracy. Whites have participated with Negroes in the organization and deliberations of the Congress.

The outbreak of violence against Negroes following the First World War, represented by race riots in Washington, Chicago, Omaha, Elaine, Tulsa, and other places and the enforced stratification which took place in Negro life led to the adoption of several other techniques. One was a type of colonization plan originated by Marcus Garvey who came from Jamaica to the United States in 1916. He planned the creation of a Negro

Empire in Africa. He talked not only of a black state and a black emperor but also a black God, a black Christ and an African Virgin Mary. In 1921, before a crowd estimated at six thousand, he was proclaimed Provisional President of Africa. He became an international figure. His publication, the *Negro World*, carried his message to the peoples of color. The Black Star Line was incorporated but within a short time collapsed. Garvey was convicted of using the mails to defraud and was sentenced to the federal prison at Atlanta. After his term there, he was deported. Large numbers followed this dream of Garvey. He estimated his followers at from four to six millions, although this seems to be an exaggeration. Remnants of this organization may be found in various parts of the United States. It has, however, no large influence upon the Negro's status today.

Another movement of a radical nature appeared in 1917 when A. Philip Randolph and Chandler Owen began the publication of *The Messenger*, which declared that the Negro, being without political rights under the present government, was a victim of exploitation and the remedy was a radical social change. At one period *The Messenger* stated: "Under the Soviet System their right to vote would be based upon their service and not upon race and color." Affiliation was urged first with the Socialist Party and then with the Workers' Party of America. This cause was taken up by the Fourth Congress of the Third Internationale held in Moscow in 1922 which declared its determination to "fight for race equality of the Negro with the white people, as well as for equal wages and political and social rights." Communists began to make headway in Negro life and to suggest revolutionary ways of improving the Negro's status. The depression aided this trend to radicalism. A proposal was made by one group of Communists that there should be in the Black Belt, where Negroes formed the majority of the population, a plan for "self-determination." This would lead ultimately to the formation of a Negro Soviet Republic.

But Negro tenant workers in the South preferred their own organizations and solutions. The Sharecroppers Union in Alabama and the Southern Tenant Farmers Union, organized in Arkansas in 1935-1936, are evidences of the reactions. Locals were formed in other states. The purpose of all was to begin a process of economic self-emancipation through the cooperation of both races. Many have regarded these endeavors as the most hopeful sign of Southern cooperation in its most extensive economic sphere and among the largest number of Negro workers. The official leadership of these unions was in many cases interracial. The meeting places were, however, generally at Negro churches, for these were among the few places where such gatherings of both races could be held. These workers began to realize that the Southern leaders of agriculture were playing up race prejudice to keep the workers apart and to maintain their own dominance of Southern society. While it was reported that Communists were actively interested in these organizations, the evidence is also abundant that the tenants were beginning to stir themselves.

The March-on-Washington Movement has been the most recent organizational expression of an agency to secure what the Negro wants. This program involved mass pressure through nonviolent techniques upon government and people in order to achieve the democratic life for Negroes in the United States. The first gain under this program was the issuance by President Roosevelt of Executive Order No. 8802, which read in part: "There shall be no discrimination in the employment of workers in defense industries or in government because of race, creed, color or national origin." A second step was taken by the President in the appointment of the Fair Employment Practices Committee, which was empowered to investigate violations of this executive order and to "take appropriate steps to redress grievances." This movement continues to gather momentum and is at present the most important mass expression of what the Negro wants.

Two fantastic schemes to secure what is supposed to be best for the Negro deserve only passing consideration. One is the modern colonization plan sponsored by Senator Bilbo of Mississippi and others of "crack-pot" reputation on the Negro question. From the administration of Abraham Lincoln to the present day, similar proposals have been made, and even practical plans for this purpose have been complete failures. The time, effort and wealth necessary for such a proposal are major arguments against it as well as its injustice to American citizens. The proposal of a Forty-ninth State for Negroes is equally chimerical.

The friendship and cooperation of organizations of the dominant group interested in the Negro's status have been maintained for many years. Inter-racial committees have been at work. The Department of Race Relations of the Federal Council of Churches of Christ, the Commission on Race Questions and the Commission on Inter-racial Cooperation have also accomplished valuable work. The foundations, such as the Jeanes and Slater Funds, the General Education Board, the Rosenwald Fund and others have made significant contributions to Negro advancement. Negro welfare agencies such as the Y.M.C.A., the Y.W.C.A., hospitals, day nurseries, settlement houses and orphanages, schools and governmental agencies, state, municipal and national, especially in New Deal housing, are making notable gains in the improvement of the Negro's status in the United States.

All of these programs are temporary expedients, for in the final analysis the status of the Negro masses is bound up with the status of the other masses in the United States. It is fallacious to expect that permanent improvement can come by the raising of a separate racial economy within the walls of segregation. Bi-racialism has fitted the Negro into a secondary place in American life and has offered no valid solution to his economic and social problem. Improvements and change must come through co-operation between white and black workers of all types of the no-collar and white-collar variations, who know that they have nothing to lose except their chains. Protests, organization, political power, court decisions, job displacements, social and economic ameliorative measures, have their place but isolated victories gained may be more illusory than real for they can lead too often along blind alleys. Our minority, however, must keep up its fight along all lines, through a united front of all organizations of peoples who seek freedom, but we should recognize that some tactics are only opportunistic, and do not touch fundamental issues. For some programs to secure satisfactions for the wants of the Negro in the face of the larger and more dominant social and economic forces which control American life would tend to result in disillusionment.

There will be a vast gulf between what the Negro wants and what he can get in present social situations, even with the abnormal changes brought about by the war. This result has led and will continue to lead to frustration and outbreak. Suppressed wrath has finally found expression in inter-racial rioting and in-group violence. Nevertheless the Negro is now moving from "his place" in the social structure in all avenues of life. White liberalism, weakened by realistic examinations of its lack of democratic practices, may have enough life to meet this rising tide and continue to advance with it.

What then are the wants which must be faced in the future by our democracy? In answering this question it is difficult for one to endeavor to speak for the Negro. He must speak mainly from his own point of view, his faith, his hopes and his experiences.

1. *The Negro wants a revision of the concept of race and of racism.* Discriminations in industry, labor unions, education, the Jim Crow pattern for the Army and Navy are based upon fascist racism. The white people of the United States have strong and positive ideas about racial equality. They use these justifications for discriminations. Before the latter can be removed, there must be some change in the former. The Negro is pressing forward against these barriers but the assumption of racial equality is being resisted. The war, with its emphasis upon democracy and its apparent opposition to racial superiority, is continuing to raise the issue, and it will have to be met with sincerity. Speeches and well-meaning committees cannot solve it by themselves. There will have to be education on the subject of race. We shall have to learn that the doctrine of racism has no scientific foundation. It is, however, one of the most dangerous of dogmas. It was almost unknown prior to the period of the French Revolution. The first complete expression of racism was made by Count Arthur de Gobineau in his *Essay on the Inequality of Human Races* published between 1853 and 1857. The successors of Gobineau expanded these doctrines with pseudo-scientific investigations, which soon associated racist dogma with nationalism. Houston Chamberlain in 1899 with his *Foundations of the Nine-*

teenth Century developed the doctrine so that the Germans became a type of superior "chosen race." By 1914, race was closely associated with the national spirit in other countries, and here in the United States, we interpreted it to mean "white" people. This absurd scientific dogma became an instrument of justification for antagonism against a minority group. Actually the cause of racial antagonism goes deeper than the surface evidences of race. Competition for employment, poverty and the apparent need to guard a group's possessions from others who are unlike lead them to seek a scapegoat in the minority. The unequal rights of citizens based upon racial claims are so intermingled with racism that the exploitation and inequality from which the minority suffers are diverted into racial attitudes, which, passed from generation to generation, tend to become fixed. The schools can undertake to give their pupils instruction in the basic issues of race, rather than to continue the present hands-off program. Such instruction can be related directly to the welfare of democracy. The church, the movies, the library, the stage and radio can use their powerful influences in this endeavor. The newspapers of both white and black editorships can be employed as effective materials.

2. *The Negro wants a realistic interpretation of religion in terms of brotherhood.* The church is seen consistently to practise segregation and division, although its theory is universal. If it were not for the Negro Church, it is probable that there would be thousands of enemies of Christianity among Negroes. If the church does not desire to be known as a hypocrite in history and in fact, it must cleanse itself of segregation, discrimination and exclusion and begin to minister to all groups without the long-handled spoon. If the church would save itself, it must develop a crusading ardor for Christianity in relation to all men. The church can give the people the will to do, for facts will not suffice in this situation.

3. *The Negro wants ultimately the abolition of segregation in education and the equalization of educational opportunity as an immediate step.* The segregated Negro school is usually an inferior school and a disparity in the bi-racial system continues to develop. This is due largely to the fact that such a school is a re-

flection of the inferior economic and social status of the Negro. This inferiority is represented by inequalities in school terms, salaries, training of teachers, buildings and equipment. The inequalities extend from the elementary schools through the graduate school. Although the laws of some states prohibit educational segregation, it is not infrequently found, and these separate schools for Negroes are usually unequal evidences of the separation which reflects deeper maladjustments of the peoples, white and black.

It may be argued that the Negro in his present situation needs the separate school in order that his faith, pride and enthusiasm may be inspired and that the truth of history and social science may be made known to him. Nevertheless, if we abolish the racial causation for the school, namely, race prejudice and discrimination, this type of school is no longer an expedient but rather a fosterer of segregation. Ultimately, this segregated school should and will be abolished, and we shall have American youth educated in schools for Americans who will not be separated from one another by either class or race.

4. *The Negro wants to be considered a citizen of the nation under whose allegiance he was born.* His citizenship and presence in the states are as old as any other American's. He regards himself as an American among Americans. He was here in the United States when its fundamental documents of citizenship rights were adopted. He voted in at least five of the original thirteen states. There were nearly a half million free Negro citizens in 1860. Of 12,865,500 Negroes listed in the 1940 census, 99.4 per cent were native born and about 97 per cent were entirely of native born parents. The Negro is not an alien. This is his country and he knows it. He has developed with this nation and has been molded by its patterns of democratic life. He therefore feels himself entitled to all of its privileges—the ballot with the abolition of restrictions including the poll tax, the white primary and similar barriers; representation in political bodies and such community agencies as the jury, the school board, teaching staffs, hospital staffs and all civilian agencies; the best home that can be afforded without residential or other restriction; the privilege of association with or of forming a legal marriage with the person who is

willing to marry him, and to take the consequences as in all such cases, and not to be compelled to live a life of lies and deceits because of what is known as social policy, to which neither nature nor science give any measure of support; the right to work for equal wages wherever he is qualified and with whoever is equally qualified whether in government office, industry, agriculture or other activity; the right to be considered just as other applicants for any appointment in state, school, university or research organization either public or private; the right to serve as other citizens in the armed forces without discrimination in either camp or field, on the sea or in the air; and the right to enjoy all citizenship privileges and to accept all obligations and perform all duties expected by the nation of its citizens.

5. *The Negro wants democracy to begin at home.* As one was heard to say during the Detroit riots, "I would rather die for democracy here than in Germany." This attitude is typical of many Negroes. They want to secure freedom and democracy for the rest of the world but they also want these here at home. Some are already beginning to doubt that this war is for freedom or democracy. They are beginning to believe that it is a war to save an outworn civilization and to continue an old system of life represented in a nineteenth-century order. They are beginning to be disillusioned when they think of the result of the first world war to save the world for democracy. They want democracy to save itself for the world. The argument from silence in our democracy should give way to active participation in the extension of its practice. The future of our democratic life is insecure so long as the hatred, disdain and disparagement of Americans of African ancestry exist. The disappearance between the censuses of thousands of Americans of color through absorption into the "white" population group is an aspect of flight from this situation as well as the pursuit of other advantages which the change seems to provide. The unmolested ignorance of our democratic public mind about the Negro is one of the barriers to racial understanding. The Negro wants the education which is received by Americans to be one which includes not only information in the sciences, the arts and languages but also in democratic life as a whole, so that the citizen will adjust more rapidly to his

environment and to his fellowmen with an adequate and correct knowledge of them.

6. *The Negro wants not only to win the war but also to win the peace.* He desires that reality shall be given to the democratic faith for which he and others are fighting and giving their substance and their lives. He wants the peace to be free of race and color restrictions, of imperialism and exploitation, and inclusive of the participation of minorities all over the world in their own governments. When it is said that we are fighting for freedom, the Negro asks, "Whose freedom?" Is it the freedom of a peace to exploit, suppress, exclude, debase and restrict colored peoples in India, China, Africa, Malaya in the usual ways? Is it to be a freedom of racial arrogance, economic lordships, and social differentiation in the post-war era? Will Great Britain and the United States specifically omit from the Four Freedoms their minorities and subject peoples? The Negro does not want such a peace.

7. *The Negro wants freedom to work and to maintain, with others, the accepted American standard of living.* He is realizing that there are those who have themselves profited by race prejudice and have been motivating its increase among white workers. The owners of land and industry have often forged tighter the chains of poverty and caste upon white and black workers alike. They have used the old technique of "divide and rule" and have sought to encourage labor union strife as well as to inflate the pride of poor whites in regard to their former jobs and to debase wages and jobs by designating them for Negroes only. They have abandoned their Christian professions and bartered their souls in the long, bitter struggle to keep their profits and their White Supremacy. White and black workers need to realize that they must cooperate in order to achieve a higher living standard. Black workers seem to be willing to accept this challenge.

CONCLUSION

In all of these wants, there are ultimate, long-run proposals and more immediately approximate ones. Unless we begin the march now towards the long-run objectives, we shall never make the journey. These wants are not utopian and impractical in any other sense than that democracy is also. Unless we take these into consideration, we shall not be able to preserve freedom for other Americans, for it cannot be preserved by restricting its benefits to some and extending it to others.

The Negro's wants are not entirely selfish and do not affect his group economy alone. The settlement of his problem will lead to a realistic interpretation of democracy's faith. These wants are the tests of democracy. They are not necessarily new, although their expressions have taken different forms through the years. As a matter of fact, the Negro wants what he has always wanted, and yet he has had different ways of saying it.

And now, the colored peoples throughout the world wait for the answer to the question whether or not the struggle of World War II is one of freedom everywhere in the world or of freedom limited only to white people in the world and measured in broken doses to colored peoples. The answer to this question determines, on the one hand, the future status of the Negro, but on the other hand, it may sound the tocsin of another of civilization's advances or the death knell of democratic western civilization.

THE NEGRO
WANTS FULL
EQUALITY

By ROY WILKINS

———

In the time since Pearl Harbor there has been, perhaps, more heated and constant discussion of the so-called Negro problem in this country than in any similar period.

The war stimulated the discussion. The war stimulated the Negroes. The war alarmed many whites and threw practically the entire white South, including persons hitherto regarded as "liberals" on the race question, into hysterics.

For this war was *not* like other wars. As the second act to 1914-18, it was on a broader stage and the actors spoke plain lines from behind little make-up. The villains talked of "master races," of force, of the insignificance of the individual, of the might and power of the state, of the necessity of conquest and slavery.

These were things that 13,000,000 American Negroes, even though "educated" in Mississippi, could understand easily. If they had any difficulty with the words "fascism" and "totalitarianism" Hitler resolved their fogginess by speaking plainly of Negroes as half-apes. They knew where they stood.

Well, Hitler had made himself plain—what about those who opposed Der Fuehrer? What were they going to say? Britain's rule of her colonies is not exactly a secret to the dark people of the world. How would the perpetrators of the smelly Caribbean colonial policy (even then under fire and furious cover-up)

answer the man with the mustache? What would the rulers of
India, the overlords of Kenya, the collaborators with Smuts of
South Africa, the guardians of White Australia, say to Berchtes-
gaden? And America, bursting, as always, with indignation,
what would she, with her Dixie, say to the Wilhelmstrasse, the
Krupps, and the Wehrmacht?

From a ship off Newfoundland came the Atlantic Charter, but
before American Negroes, always cynical, could reason out its
weaknesses, Winston Churchill settled all speculation by reply-
ing to a question bluntly and unequivocally that the Charter
applied only to the nations of Europe conquered by Hitler. The
question had been cabled by natives in West Africa, who, like
their brothers behind the Jim Crow walls in America, just could
not believe the fine words of the Charter.

America, meanwhile, so accustomed to setting the Negro outside any moral and ethical considerations, had been going about
its business as though no conflict existed between its high pronouncements and its practices.

When, in 1939 and 1940, it began building up its army and
navy by voluntary enlistment, it took no Negro volunteers.
Negro lads stormed enlistment offices from coast to coast and
were turned down in batches of as high as 100. In Charlotte,
N. C., a Negro high school teacher who accompanied four of his
students to a recruiting office was set upon and beaten by a
sergeant.

The excuse was that there were only four regiments of Negroes in the regular army, that they were not too far under
strength since many men in them had re-enlisted as a career, and
that an act of Congress would be required to authorize the
formation of any more "Negro" units.

An official of the Army Air Forces wrote the NAACP a one-
sentence letter in the summer of 1940 saying it was "not contem-
plated" that Negroes would be admitted to the aristocratic air
forces.

All the while our leading statesmen, our radio stations, our
newspapers, were denouncing the dictators, racial and religious
bigotry, force and brutality. They were extolling democracy,
humanitarianism, equality of peoples. They were wringing their

hands and tearing their hair over the Austrians, the Czechs, the Danes, Norwegians and the rest.

Black America listened to the radio, read the newspapers. Here was language it could understand. If it was cause for international weeping that Jews were beaten in Berlin and scourged into a loathesome ghetto in Warsaw, what about a tear for black ghettos in America? If the aggressors in Central Europe and Asia should be quarantined, what about the aggressors on the racial front here?

So there was discussion among the Negroes. Many of the whites, caught up between their words and their deeds, saw the point but resolved stubbornly to give no ground. An old world was being shattered around them, their own words were promising the destruction of Hitlerism, but they insisted that "their own Negroes" should remain *in statu quo*.

Hitler jammed our white people into their logically untenable position. Forced to oppose him for the sake of the life of the nation, they were jockeyed into declaring against his racial theories—publicly. Europe was overrun. Britain had its back to the wall. It was a hop, skip and a jump from Ostend to the Thames estuary, and from there to the Hudson and the towers of Lower Manhattan. Latin America looked to Franco and Hitler. Australia was trembling. India and the whole Far East were watching and weighing.

America had to rally, to stave off disaster, to talk for time, to prepare to fight for its very life. It had to say: "Down with Hitlerism! Down with the Master Race theory! Away with racial bigotry!" If these words would rally men and gain precious support, perhaps our crumbling world could be saved.

But the irritation at having to say these things in their extremity, and the anger at the literal interpretation of them by the belabored Negro made our white people angrier and angrier in their insistence upon the status quo.

In the scholarly *Virginia Quarterly* for the Autumn of 1942, John Temple Graves, Southern editor and columnist, spoke his mind on "The Southern Negro and the War Crisis," bemoaning the stirring of the Southern Negroes in time of war by "Northern agitators," by the Roosevelt administration and Mrs. Roosevelt.

"Negro leaders outside the South...made the war an occasion for the most intensive campaign ever launched against any and every differential, minor or major, between white man and black," he wrote. "They have chosen to go crazy with their championings, scouring the land for trouble...making plain beyond question an intent to use the war for settling overnight the whole, long, complicated, infinitely delicate racial problem."

Hard on the heels of Editor Graves came Editor Virginius Dabney of the Richmond, Va., *Times Dispatch*, with an ominous article in the January, 1943, *Atlantic Monthly*, entitled "Nearer and Nearer the Precipice." Like Graves, Dabney decried agitators, shuddered at the thought of Negroes aspiring to political and social equality, reiterated the utter impossibility of abolishing segregation. He predicted that pressure of Negroes toward these goals would bring about "an interracial explosion which may make the race riots of the first World War and its aftermath seem mild by comparison...There may also be far-reaching and heavily adverse effects upon the colored peoples of China, India, and the Middle East—peoples whose attitude can be of crucial importance to the Allies in the war."

Latest expression, at this writing, has come again in the *Atlantic* for January, 1944, in an article, "How the South Feels," by David L. Cohn. No editor, but a business man of means, Mr. Cohn echoes Messrs. Graves and Dabney: segregation is here to stay, the agitators must beware, in fact, the whole problem is *insoluble*.

* * *

Now, it may be asked, what demands and what procedures aroused these furious pronouncements? What does the Negro want? Well, Negroes are demanding nothing new or startling. They are asking nothing they had not asked before Hitler came to power, before war had brought German armies within sight of the white cliffs of Dover. They are asking nothing inconsistent with the declared war aims of the United Nations. They are asking nothing inconsistent with the Constitution and the Bill of Rights.

They asked then, and they ask now simply complete equality in the body politic. They could not in self-respect ask less. If it has seemed in the past that certain segments of the Negro population and certain leaders have demanded less, closer study will show that the goal has always been complete equality. There is considerable evidence that that master politician on the race question, Booker T. Washington, carelessly nominated as the "half-loaf" leader, envisioned complete equality as the goal for his people. A shrewd man, thoroughly in tune with his time and its people, Washington *appeared* to be an appeaser and did his great work under that protective cloak.

It was inevitable that there should emerge, as the Negro made progress, a group which felt that the time had come for bolder words and more direct steps toward the goal. The Negro was here to stay. The terror of the Reconstruction had not wiped him out or submerged him completely. The years of lynching had not intimidated him. He was to be a citizen, with a citizen's rights, and the battle was pitched accordingly. The Niagara Movement, an all-Negro organization, came into being and later merged with the National Association for the Advancement of Colored People, formally organized in 1909.

From the very beginning the NAACP was for complete equality. It is not generally known that William English Walling, a white Kentuckian, wrote the words which stimulated the organization of the NAACP. In the *Independent*, of September 3, 1908, Walling had an article on the race riots in Springfield, Illinois, in the course of which he declared:

"Either the spirit of the abolitionists, of Lincoln and Lovejoy must be revived and we must come to treat the Negro on a plane of *absolute political and social equality*, [italics mine] or Vardaman and Tillman will soon have transferred the race war to the North.... Yet who realizes the seriousness of the situation, and what large and powerful body of citizens is ready to come to their aid?"

A little band of white and colored citizens responded to the Walling piece and issued a formal Lincoln's Birthday Call in 1909. Drafted by Oswald Garrison Villard, then owner and editor of the New York *Evening Post*, this call demanded equality of opportunity, equality before the law, an end to disfranchisement, abolition of segregation of the races, equality in education, and an end to mob violence. It voiced what was to be the recurring theme of the NAACP down the years: attacks upon citizenship rights of Negroes are attacks upon democracy and upon white Americans as well.

So, thirty-five years ago equality—political and social equality —was the stated goal of an organized body of white and Negro Americans. This, then, is no new World War II doctrine of the NAACP, trotted out to solve the race problem overnight. Yet Dabney could write in January, 1943: "The NAACP *now* [italics mine] is not only for 'absolute political and social equality,' but it has declared war to the death on all forms of racial segregation." The NAACP declared for this objective in 1909 and has been working assiduously toward its attainment ever since.

It is significant that this crusade has been conducted in the American tradition. There have been no cells of terrorists, no extra-legal activities. The pattern has been petition and protest, legal redress, lobbying, legislative activity, education, and persuasion. And, implicit and explicit in all activities, has been the theme of equality.

The earliest sustained work of the NAACP had to do with the crime of lynching. Security of the person from violence was a paramount problem, with lynchings in the early fifth of the century averaging more than 100 a year. In tackling lynching the Association had first to grapple with the cloak of sex which the defenders of lynching used to justify the crime. It determined by painstaking study that in less than 20 per cent of lynchings was *any sort* of sex crime charged, and that in only 16 per cent of the cases was rape charged. Thus, 80 out of every 100 victims of mobs were done to death for something other than crimes against white women.

Fifteen thousand persons took part in a silent protest parade against lynching down New York's Fifth Avenue in 1917. Charles Evans Hughes addressed a mass meeting in Carnegie Hall in 1919. The Dyer federal anti-lynching bill, forerunner of numerous others, passed the House in 1922 and was filibustered to death in the Senate shortly thereafter. Full and half-page display advertisements were inserted in daily newspapers in 1922, telling such a compelling story of the lynching evil that one Pacific Coast daily offered to carry the display without cost.

Pickets paraded before Albert Hall in London, decrying American lynchings. Feature articles appeared in dailies in far-away Sydney, Australia. Books, magazine articles, pamphlets, petitions, meetings and conferences spread the story. Filibusters merely helped scatter the education farther afield.

The story was getting across to America and the world that the Negro was a human being, was an American citizen presumably possessing inalienable rights which were being grievously and bestially violated, so that proud and free America could hardly hold its head high enough to escape the stench. Did we have courts? And to what end? Did we have a Constitution? For whom? What of our vaunted slogan, "Equal Justice Under Law"?

As the years went by, the skill and the pressure increased. Succeeding anti-lynching bills in the national capitol suffered the same fate as the Dyer bill: passage in the House, death by filibuster in the Senate, under both Democratic and Republican majorities. But the education went on, sped by the forces of opposition. Whereas in 1919 hardly any man of prominence, or any man of promising career would speak out against lynching, in 1938 when the last bill was killed in a 21-day filibuster, no man, or newspaper, or institution of any importance could be found to defend lynching. Public opinion had been completely reversed in twenty years, even to the extent that a number of Southern newspapers not only deplored lynching, but endorsed federal legislation against it.

The goal in this fight was equality: equality before the law, equality in security of the person, equality in human dignity. The campaign is not ended, but the point has been made, more than a toehold has been won. There will be, undoubtedly, more lynchings and more riotous outbreaks, but instead of being in the stream of public opinion, they will be counter to it; they will be against an established principle. As such they can be handled, just as any other crime is handled.

Hand in hand with the continuous struggle against lynching and mob violence went the legal battles in the courts of the land. In its thirty-five years of existence, the NAACP has carried twenty-one cases to the United States Supreme Court. It has won nineteen cases, lost one, and one is pending as this is written. In addition, it has handled thousands of cases in the lower courts.

The Supreme Court cases decided Constitutional rights of Negroes as citizens: equality in the body politic. Although the record is full of brilliant examples of legal procedure involving many questions, the outstanding example would seem to be the famous Elaine, Arkansas (Phillips County), riot cases which began in 1919 and ended in 1923. In this one action, covering 79 defendants, were the items of mob violence, mob domination of court procedure, service of Negroes on juries, and the enforcement of contracts.

Negro farmers of Phillips County had received no accounting from plantation owners on their cotton from June, 1918, to July, 1919. Feeling that they had been more than patient, they organized themselves into the Progressive and Household Union of America, engaged a law firm in Little Rock either to get a settlement or to sue the landlords. At a meeting in a small Negro church at Hoop Spur in October, 1919, a shot was fired into the church from the outside. The farmers stopped planning and returned the fire. A white man was killed and rioting ensued. Troops were ordered into the county. All available local and state police, as well as hundreds of deputized citizens joined the soldiers in a county-wide man-killing spree. Newspapers blazoned the affair as an "insurrection," thus justifying the wanton and indiscriminate killing of Negroes.

Eight hundred Negroes were arrested. A "Committee of Seven" held a kangaroo court and directed that 12 prisoners should die and 67 others be imprisoned. The courts faithfully followed directions. Five of the men were tried at one time and given death in a matter of six minutes. Counsel was provided by the court the day before trial, but did not consult with defendants, put no witnesses on the stand, made no address to the jury.

The Arkansas Supreme Court heard the appeals of the twelve men sentenced to death, granted new trials to six, affirmed the conviction of the others. On retrial the six were again convicted and again had their convictions reversed on the ground Negroes had been excluded from the jury panel.

From then on, the story is a complicated one of appeals, suits for various writs, changes of venue, transfers to federal courts, two unsuccessful attempts to get before the United States Supreme Court, one hairbreadth snatching of six doomed men from the death house, and finally, in 1922, a review by the highest court in the land.

In its opinion in this case, Moore *v.* Dempsey, 261 U.S. 86, handed down in February, 1923, the court reversed itself in Frank *v.* Mangum, 237 U.S. 309, and held that a trial in a court dominated by mob sentiment was not due process of law within the meaning of the Fourteenth Amendment. In the Frank case, arising in Georgia, the Jewish defendant, now known to be innocent, was convicted of attacking and killing a little girl, and then lynched. The court had held that since the forms of the law had been observed, it could not examine into the atmosphere of the trial. The Arkansas lawyers, out of the long, bitter legal tangle in the Elaine cases, bristling as they were with injustices crying aloud for attention, managed to get the story into their brief. A Negro and a white lawyer brought this battle to a victorious close by putting all 79 defendants "on the street."

But here again the objective was equality. Had it not been so, the Negro farmers would have accepted the status quo, would have agreed that *as Negroes* they had no right to demand, after the fashion of white men, an accounting for their crops. They would not have dared order suits to recover. They would not have dared shoot back. After the riot their lawyers and their friends and the NAACP would not have dared muster every skill in the tenacious fight, in a mob atmosphere, for their freedom.

Equality was the prize—equality of opportunity as farmers, equality in the courts of the land, the right to serve on juries, to avail themselves of writs, to have their motives, their provocations, their actions judged as free men among free men.

And this struggle for equality carried over into the quest for the purple badge of a democratic nation, the right to exercise the franchise. The very first case carried to the United States Supreme Court by the NAACP was a challenge of a then popular device for disfranchising Negroes, the Grandfather Clause. Inserted in many state constitutions in the South, this clause set forth, in varying language, that no person might vote whose grandfather was not eligible to vote in 1860. In 1915 the highest court held this clause to be unconstitutional, but, needless to say, the opinion did not enfranchise the Negroes.

Mindful that there can be no equality in a democracy where citizens are barred from the ballot box, the NAACP has kept up the campaign in the courts and in the public conscience to strike down the barriers. Two cases were taken up from Texas challenging the so-called White Democratic Primary, and the Supreme Court opinion went against the state. A third case was carried up by an independent group of Texas Negro citizens and the decision this time was in favor of Texas. A new case is pending, having been argued first in November, 1943, and re-argued in January, 1944.[1]

Along with these legal assaults on disfranchisement has gone a crusade against the poll tax requirement for voters which prevents an estimated 10,000,000 citizens (6,000,000 white and 4,000,000 Negro) from voting. If the poll tax can be eliminated and the Democratic primaries opened to Negro citizens, two stalwart props of inequality will have been struck down. Others will remain, not the least of which will be force and intimidation, but eventually these will have to go, also.

In the original Call to form the NAACP in 1909 there was this phrase: "recent history in the South shows that in forging chains for the Negroes, the white voters are forging chains for themselves." In no phase of this ever-continuing fight for equality for the Negro is this truism demonstrated more clearly than in the campaign for political equality. Here it becomes plain that the free ballot for the Negro means a greater and stronger democracy for *all* Americans. Tenaciously the NAACP has clung throughout the years to its thesis that inequality for the Negro opens the way to inequality for other Americans and thus weakens the nation.

[1] On April 3, 1944, the United States Supreme Court, in an eight-to-one decision, ruled that Negroes may not be barred from Democratic party primary elections in Texas.—Smith *v.* Allwright.

In the field of education the effort to achieve equality has gone steadily forward. Here, from the outset, America was receptive and responsive. Education is a fetish of our country; we have believed it somehow to be a magic cure-all. The chief inequality in education for Negroes lay (and still lies) in the system of separate, or segregated schools for the two races.

These inequalities in per capita expenditure, equipment, buildings, school term, teachers' salaries, and curricula, are too well known to be set forth in detail here. Most spectacular and easily-grasped illustration is the per capita expenditure for Mississippi, where the money expended for white children is roughly nine times as great as that expended for Negroes, although Negroes form 49 per cent of the population.

A vulnerable point in the system of segregation seemed to be the salary differential between white and colored teachers in the same local system, who have the same training and experience and perform essentially the same duties. These differentials have been attacked in courts by attorneys for the NAACP, acting at the request of individual teacher-plaintiffs, or organized groups of Negro teachers. The results have been reasonably successful, having forced equalization of salaries in localities in 13 states. The greatest single victory was that in Norfolk, Virginia, where an opinion was secured from the United States Circuit Court of Appeals which has tended to influence some local boards of education to equalize salaries on presentation of a petition, without actual court procedure.

Another vulnerable sector from the standpoint of the Constitution, was the denial of graduate and professional training to Negroes in tax-supported state institutions. In the famous Gaines case, where the University of Missouri was the defendant, the United States Supreme Court in December, 1935, held that a state either must supply equal separate facilities to Negroes for graduate and professional study or admit them to existing graduate institutions. Missouri chose to set up a separate law school for Negroes, and later a separate school of journalism, but the law school has been closed for lack of funds and students, and the journalism school is being staffed, beginning February 1, 1944, with faculty members from the University of Missouri.

The Gaines decision did not get a single Negro into a Southern graduate school, but it riveted the Negro's claim to equality under the Constitution; it set under way numerous plans for providing graduate instruction. One border state proceeded to admit a few Negro graduate students to its state university without publicity. Missouri seems to have demonstrated that a separate graduate institution is not the way out. A case is still pending in the courts against the University of Kentucky. The Negroes, members of state legislatures, heads of state universities, and white laymen are busy debating not whether the Negro is entitled to this training, but how it shall be made available. The right to it has been established as the law of the land: equality of opportunity.

The stubborn resistance to these latest moves in the field of education lies in the adherence to segregation as a pattern of life for the two races. The NAACP has maintained from the beginning that discrimination and inequality are inherent in the segregated pattern. There can be no equality *with* segregation. A hundred examples could be cited, but the Jim Crow public school system would seem to be all the proof needed. Complete equality, therefore, envisions the abolition of the segregated school.

On the economic front powerful obstacles to the attainment of equality have been encountered, but progress has been made. Equal pay for the same work has been the underlying theme. The sharecropping system of Southern agriculture has held millions of Negroes—and poor whites—in virtual economic slavery, impoverishing the entire region as it has impoverished its victims. Employers and trade unions, in and out of the South, have blocked industrial employment of the Negro. The "lock-out" of the Negro worker by many of the craft unions has been matched by the policy of many employers. Lately, by their pronouncements and practice of no discrimination, the industrial unions have eased the Negro's position and driven the crafts to the defensive.

But underneath, especially in the South, is the bugaboo of segregation. Workers at a war plant in Baltimore struck in the fall of 1943 to force the management to install separate toilets for Negroes. The Atlanta city council expressed opposition to the

establishment of a regional office of the Fair Employment Practices Committee in that fair city because it was proposed to have
Negro and white *clerks* working in the same office. A Negro
messenger, elevator operator, or cleaning man would have caused
no trouble. The bitter opposition to the CIO in the South stems
not alone from that region's aversion to organized labor, but from
the equality within the CIO and the non-segregation of its members. The fight on various organizations of tenant farmers and
sharecroppers had as one of its targets the non-segregation policy.

Like most other phases of the so-called Negro problem, this
denial of opportunity to Negro workers is not confined to the
South. Anti-Negro feeling has broken out in industrial plants in
many Northern centers, notably Detroit, where in June, 1943,
25,000 white workers quit the Packard plant because *three* Negroes had been upgraded, according to seniority rules, to work
on machines.

The NAACP has been hammering away for equality of opportunity in employment, attacking policies of discrimination
and exclusion, and instituting legal action in individual cases
deemed to advance the general cause. The first round in what
may be a notable achievement was won in January, 1944, when
a Providence, R. I., judge held that auxiliary unions, created especially for Negroes by the Boilermakers' union, were not legal
in the state, and that Negro boilermakers must be considered
members of regular locals. There is some indication that the
Boilermakers' international union may agree to alter its policy
and accept Negroes as full members. At any rate, there is an
important element within the union working toward this goal.

Most significant activity of the NAACP, in cooperation with
other groups, was the mobilization of pressure which resulted
in the issuance of an Executive Order by President Roosevelt in
June, 1941, forbidding discrimination in employment in any
war industry or government agency because of race, creed, color,
or national origin. The order also created the Fair Employment
Practices Committee, which has become a by-word as the FEPC,
during its short, stormy career.

Fierce opposition to FEPC has come from the segregationists.
Its work has been branded as an attempt to "tear down the social

fabric of the South," and in its one big case against sixteen Southern railroads, its findings that flagrant discrimination exists as a policy against Negroes as railroad firemen have been openly defied by both carriers and unions. Of course, FEPC activity is an attack upon the social fabric of the South, in the broadest sense of "social." It aims at equality of opportunity and reward, and any system or practice of any union or any employer, in the North or South, which operates to deny that opportunity may be considered under attack. The immediate cause for the creation of the FEPC was the shameless exclusion of Negroes from employment at a time when manpower was desperately needed to speed the war effort. The personnel managers who slammed doors in the faces of Negro applicants, and the union members who refused to work beside them were failing the nation in time of war. Something had to be done as a war measure. But the sure justification for the FEPC thesis lies not alone in the war of the present, but in the basic conception of the American democratic ideal.

It should be said that in normal peace times the Negro feels most strongly about economic proscription. He is insulted and humiliated in other phases of life and resentment will flare white hot at the moment. But on the limitation in employment his feeling is no spasmodic thing. He sees immigrants come to his America and get jobs he cannot get. He works as a "helper" all his life in a trade and teaches white apprentices who, in a few years, earn twice his wage and become his superiors. Each night he goes to his ghetto home. Each payday his working wife adds her bit to his bit to make a total barely sufficient to keep the household together, to keep the children in school, to pay the small insurance premiums. Or, he gets a high school or college education, but must content himself with jobs far below his talents.

He wants the bars down so that men may find their level, the dice players, business men, mechanics, professors, thieves, clerks, playboys, laborers, and the rest. He wants equality of opportunity to work at any job for which he is fitted, and to earn the pay and promotions that go with that job.

And then there is the whole area of relations encompassing

what may be called the movement of citizens, their enjoyment of public accommodations. The Jim Crow railroad car symbolizes to the Negro his proscription in public. Until this war arrived it was thought that resentment of the Jim Crow car was confined to Northern Negroes who had occasional business in the South. But it has been discovered that great masses of Negroes who have lived all their lives in the South and are familiar with its mores are bitter against the Jim Crow car, the separated seats in buses and trolleys, the filthy waiting rooms, the insolent ticket sellers and equally insolent sandwich counter attendants, both white and colored, and the arrogant, ignorant and brutal bus and trolley drivers. Contrary to some assertions, the flare-ups over these facilities have not been confined to Northern Negro soldiers in training in the South; if the truth be told, *all* Negroes except the minority of hat-in-hand variety deeply resent this separation. They took spontaneous advantage of the court decision in the case brought by former Congressman Arthur W. Mitchell of Illinois against the Chicago Rock Island and Pacific Railroad for denying him Pullman accommodations from Memphis to Hot Springs, Arkansas, a case which brought the opinion from the Supreme Court that Negroes may not be denied first class tickets or all accommodations which go with such tickets, including dining and lounge car facilities. Countless instances have been reported of Negroes in the Southern hinterland boarding trains and quoting this decision to conductors and others.

The Negro wants to be able to go to parks, playgrounds, beaches, pools, theatres, restaurants, hotels, taverns, tourist camps, and other places of public amusement and accommodation without proscription and insult. The question comes immediately: does this mean *with whites?* The answer must be in the affirmative. If the Negro's goal is complete equality, complete acceptance as a member of the American public, then he wants access to these accommodations on an equality with other Americans. The popular and instantaneous question of whether he wants to "thrust" himself "where he is not wanted" is supposed to flabbergast him. Who is "wanted" where, and by whom? During the Dewey racket-busting crusade in New York several years ago it was revealed that the king man in the huge organized prostitution ring lived in a tower apartment in one of the world's famous hotels on Manhattan's Park Avenue, the same tower apartments which housed a former President of the United States, which gave shelter to the First Lady of China, and to the former King of England! Yet a respectable Negro business man, tendering the correct tariff to the room clerk, would have been hustled out by house detectives like a criminal!

Is a hotel a membership club, or a theatre a drawing room? If a public bathing beach or pool or tennis court is restricted to "wanted" persons, why do we have the Racquet Club, Newport, Southampton, and their prototypes over the land?

In this general category comes the all-important matter of housing. The Negro wants to be free to rent or buy a house according to his standards and his means. If he can afford a $10,000 home, he does not want to be forced to build it in a $2,500 neighborhood. If he can pay $50 a month rent, he wants $50 in value, in a $50 locality; he does not want to be forced to pay $50 for a $40 home in a $30 neighborhood.

He wants all the municipal services—water, gas, light, sewerage, garbage collection, sidewalks and paving—on the same basis they are furnished to other citizens. Here again the pattern of enforced segregation is an obstacle and must be removed. Doubtless there will always be some voluntary segregation, as there is with other racial groups, but the ghetto must go. It does not seem to be known generally that in several communities in the South, Negro and white families live side by side in some streets without friction. Muskogee, Okla., among others, has such a section.

In this connection, as with other phases of the problem, the Negro is weary of the fallacious and oft-repeated argument that he is not a taxpayer, that white people bear the burden of such improvements as he receives. That this contention could be advanced seriously in this day of rudimentary economic intelligence among the masses of people only demonstrates the flimsy construction of the façade behind which the opposition parades.

These goals represent, then, what the Negro wants. The record of struggle toward the objectives is too long, too persistent, too studded with recurring efforts following failure to admit of doubt as to the ends sought. Here has been set forth only the latter phases of the fight—that covering the thirty-five years of the NAACP and the few prior years of the Niagara Movement. But these demands were voiced long before the Emancipation Proclamation. The great Frederick Douglass, chief spiritual father of the "no-compromise" school, was clamoring for full and complete equality even as a slave. Later he was to thunder his insistent message from platforms in the North and in England.

The leaders of the complete equality school have as their ancestors, besides Douglass, Sojourner Truth, Harriet Tubman, the insurrectionists Nat Turner, Denmark Vesey, and the rest. Behind these are the nameless hundreds whose indomitable spirits and will to freedom drove them from slave cabins through strange lands and unknown dangers to liberty in far Canada.

Not to be forgotten, too, are the mothers and fathers, newly-freed, who worked, sacrificed, and saved that their children might become what Mr. Lincoln's proclamation and the Thirteenth, Fourteenth and Fifteenth amendments said they should be. These people did not sacrifice for half-measures. They had had to take crumbs, but crumbs were not for their children and grandchildren. Their eyes were on complete equality.

All this explains the repeated challenges to the status quo, the long fight against lynching, the recourse to the courts again and again on the same issue. This explains the migrations to the North and West.

If these be the true yearnings of Negro Americans, how shall they be satisfied? That, now, is the problem of the American whites. In truth, the so-called Negro problem is really a white problem. In recent years the Southern whites have been trying to spread the responsibility for a solution to the nation as a whole; but any unbiased student must see that, regardless of the outbreaks here and there outside the South, the responsibility for initiating remedial action is upon the South. Indeed, nothing makes the Southerner froth more than attempts from without the South to do something about the situation. Governmental remedies for general situations which include the Negro have drawn heavy fire, even from so-called white "liberals."

What are the Southern whites going to do about it, aside from repeating over and over that they intend to do nothing, that the Negro must be satisfied with the status quo?

The Negro is here. He is thoroughly American. He thinks and lives in the American tradition. He learns from American text books about the Revolutionary war, about independence, the spirit of America—and equality. He reads the newspapers and magazines. He goes to the movies and he listens to the radio. Once every four years he has that wondrous educational experience, a Presidential election.

It ought to be apparent, therefore, that the Negro, even in peace times, cannot be insulated from the stream that is America. This is doubly true in a war where race, color, democracy, fascism, equality, freedom, and slavery are shouted from every microphone, screamed from every headline.

No "agitators" were needed to point out to him the discrepancies between what we said we were fighting for, and what we did to him. He did not need the NAACP to show him that it sounds pretty foolish to be *against* park benches marked "*Jude*" in Berlin, but to be *for* park benches marked "Colored" in Tallahassee, Florida.

It is pretty grim—not foolish—to have a black boy in uniform get an orientation lecture in the morning on wiping out Nazi bigotry, and that same evening be told he can buy a soft drink only in the "Colored" post exchange!

Yes, it's a problem for the white people. They have got to make up their minds. Pearl Buck puts it this way:

"But be that as it may, the real point is that our democracy does not allow for the present division between a white ruler race and a subject colored race, and we ought to make up our minds as to what we want and then move to accomplish it. If the United States is to include subject and ruler peoples, then let us be honest about it and change the Constitution and make it plain that Negroes cannot share the privileges of the white people. True, we would then be totalitarian rather than democratic; but if that is what we want, let us say so and let us tell the Negro so. Then the white Americans will be relieved of the necessity of hypocrisy and the colored people will know where they are. They may even settle down into a docile subject race, so long as we are able to keep the weapons of rebellion from them—and these include education."

Our country *could* eliminate the Negro as a citizen, but the dangers to other groups, and the precedent that would be set argue against it.

The Negro intends, from all present appearances, to "sit tight" on his demands. He cannot do otherwise, unless he means to retreat at a time when America and the world are moving forward. There is no indication that he intends this retreat. These goals, as has been shown, are no hastily manufactured items, incident to the beginning of World War II. They are the very warp and woof of Negro life. He stands ready to cooperate with anyone on their realization who recognizes them as the ends to be achieved.

It has been said that not all the armored divisions of both the Axis and Allied armies can force the South to revise its system of social segregation. It has been said again that if such a demand is made seriously, every white male below the Potomac will spring to arms and another civil war will rend the nation.

These are ominous pronouncements, calculated, through the threat of bloodshed, to give the Negro and his friends pause. But there is no sign of fright in the ranks of the darker Americans. They seem confident that the tides of social upheaval abroad in the world today cannot be channeled by the men and women north and south of the Ohio river who wish to keep them in "their place." The armored divisions will not have to be brought into play. The tremendous surges of the peoples of Russia and Asia and Africa may prove more powerful than tanks or guns. The urgent necessity for the building of a peace between the Western Powers and the rest of the world,. founded upon respect for the peoples outside the Anglo-American fold, will be a spur not to be lightly evaluated. Such a peace, in a shrunken world, could not avoid affecting the status of the Negro minority in our country.

And then there is the wholly unknown quantity of the attitude of our returning soldiers, white and black. There is no guaranty, as has been asserted by former Governor Sam Jones of Louisiana in a magazine article, that all the white soldiers of the South are fighting to maintain white supremacy. No doubt many of them are fighting for America as they have known it, and that would include white supremacy, but certainly many of them have had their eyes opened by their travels and by the blood and death which have respected no man because of his color.

Certain it is that the Negro soldiers are not fighting and dying to maintain the status quo for their race. The young Negro fighter pilots from Punta Gorda, Fla., and Emory, Miss., who were among those shooting down Nazi planes in the fierce fighting over the Anzio beachhead are not risking their lives to intrench further the way of life obtaining in their home towns. The Negro Marines in the South Pacific, the black engineers, the colored quartermaster units getting the supplies through the mud and heat and cold of the battle-fronts, are not working for the status quo. The lads who drove bulldozers in fifty below zero to build the Alaskan highway, who hacked their way through Burmese jungles to build the Ledo road, are not returning to run a bull-dozer on the Mississippi levees for 20 cents an hour. Nor will they take kindly, to put it in its mildest form, to surly suggestions as to their "place." Their place now is in front of the bullets of the enemy, and below the bombs in enemy planes. Bullets, or threats of bullets, are not likely to cause them to bow and scrape once they are home.

No, the threats of civil war will not turn the trick. The American demands of the Negro are there, made in the American manner, rooted in the American ideal. They are not to be brushed aside, and something more than fulmination and bluster is indicated from the opposition. The next move is up to white Americans, and particularly white Southern Americans.

MARCH ON WASHINGTON MOVEMENT PRESENTS PROGRAM FOR THE NEGRO

By A. PHILIP RANDOLPH

—————

THIS STATEMENT is being presented at an hour when the lamps of civilization are burning low. If the Axis powers win, the lamps may go out, and if they do, they may not be relighted in a thousand years. The lamps of enlightenment have gone out before. They may go out again. Thus, the Nazism of Hitler, the Militarism of Hirohito, and the Fascism of Mussolini and now Badoglio must be destroyed.

The cause of the United Nations must prevail.

But the colored peoples know from a tragic experience that it is not enough for the arms of the United Nations to win.

AIMS OF THE NEGRO

The oppressed darker races want something more.

They want much more.

They want the cause of true democracy to march forward.

They want the Brotherhood of man to triumph.

They want a durable and just peace.

They want security and plenty with freedom.

They want to put an end to the vile and sinister doctrine of the Master Race.

They want ethnic equality.

They want economic, political and social equality.

They want to abolish the racism and colonialism of the Anglo-American empire systems.

"Will this ever come?" ask the Negro bootblack, jitterbug, and Ph.D.

DARKER RACES MUST FIGHT FOR FREEDOM

It will not come if the Axis powers win.

It may not come if the United Nations win.

Albeit, it will not come automatically.

It will come only if the downtrodden peoples fight for it.

The darker races can get no solace from the proclamations of Prime Minister Churchill or President Roosevelt. With inept machiavellian diplomacy the Atlantic Charter states its concern only for the European countries under the Nazi yoke. And, Mr. Churchill observes in the unvarnished language of the "brass hat" imperialists, that he has not become the first minister of the King to preside over the liquidation of the British Empire. He also adds in a note of somber and sullen militant imperialism, that they will hold their own.

Thus the Negro, labor and liberals might well demand to know:

Are we fighting this global war to restore Singapore, Malaya, and Burma to Great Britain?

Will the peace reëstablish the ill-fated Italian Empire, and give back to notorious Belgium the African Congo? Are the "natives" of Africa to continue to live in slavery of the mandated colonialism of white powers?

FREE AFRICA

The March On Washington Movement proclaims the slogan of a free Africa. It joins the cry of a "Fight for a Free India and China." It hails the struggle for the freedom of the common man everywhere—the common man, whether black, white, brown, yellow, red, Protestant, Catholic, Jewish, native or foreign, worker, storekeeper, artist, teacher, minister.

NOT A WAR FOR FREEDOM

But be not deceived. This is not a war for freedom.

It is not a war for democracy.

It is not a war to usher in the Century of the Common Man.

It is not a Peoples' Revolution.

It is a war to maintain the old imperialistic systems. It is a war to continue "white supremacy," the theory of *Herrenvolk*, and the subjugation, domination, and exploitation of the peoples of color. It is a war between the imperialism of Fascism and Nazism and the imperialism of monopoly capitalistic democracy.

Under neither are the colored peoples free.

But this war need not be a world movement of reaction. The people can make it a Peoples' Revolution—a Revolution whose dynamism against Axis tyranny will be greater and more powerful because it will possess the fighting faith and crusading confidence of the masses of all colors and races. The people can cause this war to usher in the Century of the Common Man. This is the meaning of the call of Gandhi for an independent and free India. It is the reason for the stirrings of the "natives" of Africa, the war by the Chinese against the dominion of Nippon, the rebellion of the blacks in the Caribbean Islands against a bare subsistence wage, and the fight of the Negro people of the United States for equality.

CAUSE OF FREEDOM IN RETREAT

Let no Negro, in the pattern of the ostrich, bury his head in the sand and assert the denial of a raging storm of reaction that is now setting in against the Negro people. The Negro must face stark reality in all of its forbidding aspects. The fact is, the cause of freedom and democracy is already in full retreat everywhere. Fascism and reaction are on the offensive. It is obvious to the casual observer that the arms of the United Nations may win and democracy lose. Note that in England, the "Cradle to Grave Security Plan" of Sir William Beveridge has been practically turned down, and the National Resources Planning Board has met rebuffs with its post-war program of security and plenty for all in the United States of America.

The defeat of Senator Norris, the liberal of Nebraska; the expulsion of Leon Henderson, foe of inflation, from OPA; the lost fight to save Odell Waller; the vile and vicious attacks upon the First Lady, Mrs. Roosevelt, by die-hard Tories; the continuance of the infamous Dies Committee which has sought to smear, discredit and destroy Negro, labor and liberal leadership; and the enactment of the Smith-Connally Anti-Labor Fascist Bill over President Roosevelt's veto, are significant signs of the times. Yes, it is also important to add the torpedoing of the scheduled railroad hearings on racial discrimination by FEPC. Indeed the future looks dark. Developments point to the revival of the cry "back to normalcy," or the conservatism of Coolidge and the rugged individualism of Hoover, or maybe an era of furious Fascism with the Negro playing the chief role of the victim in America as did the Jews in Germany.

This is why the Negro must seek, discover and devise a program of liberation.

NEGRO MAY BEAR THE TORCH OF DEMOCRACY

A militant fight of the Negro for equality may save the day for the democratic way of life. But before a program of any oppressed minority or majority can be formulated, it ought to be determined what the group needs and wants. A discussion of needs and wants is timely because a group may need what it does not want and it may want what it does not need.

Since Negroes in the United States of America live under a democracy—of a sort—yes, a sharply limited democracy, especially, in terms of race, where public opinion, the most powerful single force in society, is created, or rather ought to be created by the free inter-play and free competition of ideas in the arena of public discussion, they, the Negroes, need and must have the status of free and equal citizenship. They must be free and equal to participate in and help shape and determine constructive and creative human action and human institutions for the advancement of the common good.

However, Negroes must be free in order to be equal and they must be equal in order to be free. These are complementary and supplementary rights and conditions. The existence of the one is a condition to the existence of the other. Under the terms of our liberal democratic traditions, the absence of freedom or equality means the absence of democracy. Men cannot win freedom unless they win equality. They cannot win equality unless they win freedom. By the same token men cannot remain free unless they remain equal. And they cannot remain equal unless they remain free. These are the axioms of a democratic progressive society. Their validity and verity are as unquestionable as the mathematical proposition, two plus two equals four.

This is why the historical experience of the modern world shows that political democracy can never be truly attained until it rests upon the underpinnings and is the correlative of industrial and economic democracy. There can be no true political democracy where equality is the ascendant note until there is a comparable dispersal of economic equality in our social order.

Now, the principle of the indivisibility of political, industrial, economic, and social democracy is a condition of total equality, political, industrial, economic, and social for all of the citizens of a given community. Just as a nation cannot survive half free and half slave, it cannot survive half equal and half unequal in terms of political, industrial, economic and social opportunity.

NEGROES NOT FREE

But the Negro is not free. He never has been free. He is not free because he is not equal to other citizens within the national framework of the laws, institutions, customs and practices of our so-called democratic government.

Why?

The answer is: The Civil War, the American liberal bourgeois democratic, socio-economic, political revolution failed to complete its basic historic mission.

While the liberal European bourgeois revolutions of the eighteenth and nineteenth centuries failed to attain their original and complete objectives, they, unlike the American Civil War, achieved the status of free and equal citizenship for the feudal serfs. But the American Revolution or Civil War was sadly aborted. It did not complete its course. It was much of the pattern of the Russian Revolution under the czar of 1905. What then is the historical path of a liberal bourgeois democratic, socio-economic, political revolution?

What are its basic aims?

They fall under the following main categories:

1. The overthrow of the old slave or feudal governmental regime and the establishment of a democratic republic.

2. The break-up of the slave or feudal economy and the creation in its stead of a free competitive capitalist order.

3. The translation of the power to rule from the agrarian slave or feudal class to the industrial and financial bourgeoisie.

4. The transformation of the slaves or serfs into free workers and independent proprietors.

5. The creation of an economic stake for the former slaves or serfs in the new social order.

6. The adoption of a universal and free suffrage.

7. The establishment of a free public school system.

8. The recognition not only of the right of the former slaves or serfs to vote, but to be voted for and to share in the operation and direction of the governmental apparatus, and to rule.

9. The economic unification of the national community.

10. The centralization of political power in a strong, federal or national system.

But what of the record?

Only a cursory examination of the historical, political and social economy of the United States of America will reveal that the American social revolution or Civil War was arrested and only those aims were realized that contributed to the consolidation of the power of the new ruling class, namely, the industrial and financial capitalists.

PRESENT TASK OF THE NEGRO

What then is the immediate task of the Negro?

It is to complete an uncompleted bourgeois democratic, socio-economic, political revolution.

What does it involve?

It involves giving life, reality, and force to those basic substantive, organic, social and political principles of freedom, equality, and justice, set forth in the Declaration of Independence, the Federal Constitution, and, especially, the Thirteenth, Fourteenth and Fifteenth Amendments, and the recent Rooseveltian Four Freedoms, in relation to the Negro people.

While the slave power was broken, the slave masters were not eliminated. They rose and seized the reins of state rule and served as industrial and plantation padrones of an absentee owning capitalist class of the North. Soon the newly emancipated slaves found themselves hedged in, limited and handicapped by the remnants, hang-overs and vestiges of a pre-capitalist era.

For a free suffrage, the Freedmen were given "Grandfather Clauses," poll taxes, white primaries and other restrictive registration devices that nullify the Negro's right to vote.

For a free public school system, the Negro received a segregated pattern in which the strongest lesson Negro students are taught is that they are inferior to white boys and girls.

For the status of free workers and independent peasant proprietors, Negroes by peonage, vagrancy laws, share-crop methods, and the notorious company store system, were reduced to the lot of serfs bound to the land, turpentine stills, and lumber mills, in a semi-capitalistic plantation economy. Moreover, the Freedmen were whipped and frightened into submission and docility by a lynch-rope, Ku Klux terrorism.

MEETING THE PROBLEM

How can this problem be met?

Naturally this question suggests methods.

Around methods invariably revolve multiple opinions.

Now the basic phase of the Negro problem is economic.
Why?

The origin of the Negro problem was economic, for it had its seat in the slave trade.

The reason for subjecting Negroes to slavery was economic. It had residence in cheap labor.

The reason for the abolition of slavery was economic.

It rests upon the rise of capitalist industrialism and the growing uneconomic character of slave labor in the production of cotton, rice, sugar and tobacco.

Verily, the biggest problem confronting Negroes today is economic, that is, getting work and wages to buy food, clothing and shelter.

Thus the March On Washington Movement sets forth as the cardinal and primary cornerstone of its program: economic action.

Economic

LABOR UNION

The major and paramount form of economic action by the Negro people must necessarily be the building of trade and industrial unions and the employment of the technique of collective bargaining. This is so because well-nigh 99 and 9/10 per cent of the Negro people are workers of hand and brain who earn their living in the sweat of their brow by selling their labor in the market for wages. Hence, the biggest business of the Negro consists in his selling at the highest price, that which he has the most of, namely his ability to work. But this business of the Negro worker selling his labor is not as simple as it sounds. For immediately he enters the market for jobs, he is met with a color bar in some of the trade unions, or prejudice on the part of some employers. Not only is he the last hired and first fired, but he meets this vicious cycle when applying for work or a union card. The employer rejects him because he does not have a union card and the union rejects him because he hasn't got a job.

Thus, the progress of the Negro in the modern industrial

system will depend in a large measure upon cleansing the labor unions and personnel manager systems of the sins of race prejudice. This is one fight Negro and white workers must wage which they cannot afford to lose since trade unions are the main bulwark of democracy. But this bulwark cannot stand if part of the workers possess economic citizenship and another part is economically disfranchised because of color and race.

The March On Washington Movement sets its face resolutely toward the complete integration of the Negro workers into the organized labor movement. If an industry in which Negroes work is controlled by the A. F. of L., they are urged to affiliate with this body. On the other hand, if an industry is under the control of the CIO, in which Negroes work, they are urged to affiliate with the CIO. If Negroes are employed in an industry which is not organized by either the A. F. of L. or CIO, they are urged to organize and become a part of one of these federated labor bodies.

COOPERATIVES

But, labor through trade unions may win decent wages at the point of production and lose them at the point of consumption, when, as consumers, the workers go back into the market to buy back, with their wages, the goods they produced with their labor. Consumers' cooperatives are agencies through which the workers can conserve and increase their purchasing power by eliminating the middle man, and buying from themselves on the Rochdale principle and they offer the Negro as well as white workers an important economic force for their liberation. The importance of the workers directing attention to the price of goods they buy is shown by the struggle now being waged to force OPA to roll back prices.

The cooperative movement is an important key to economic security and economic democracy for the worker and the little man.

EMPLOYMENT FOR NEGROES

No greater wrong has been committed against the Negro than the denial to him of the right to work. This question of the right to work is tied up with the right to live. But Negroes are not only denied the right to work on certain jobs but they are sentenced in some industries to a sort of blind alley position. For instance, the Negro may be employed as a Pullman porter but not as a Pullman conductor, although he demonstrates his ability to perform this service by running-in-charge, at a slight differential in pay.

A Negro may be employed as a waiter on the dining cars but not as a steward, although here, too, he demonstrates his ability to perform the services of a steward, in which event he receives a slight differential in pay. The Negro may operate as a brakeman or flagman but, because of custom, practice and tradition resulting from racial discrimination, he is not promotable to the job of train conductor, although all train conductors were former brakemen or flagmen. It is a matter of common knowledge that Negro train porters teach hundreds of white brakemen how to operate as train conductors. And Negro waiters break in white stewards, and Negro Pullman porters instruct white Pullman conductors how to make out their diagrams.

The March On Washington Movement rejects this economic discrimination and segregation of the Negro worker and calls for the abolition of the racial blind alley job.

The March On Washington Movement maintains that Negroes should be upgraded and assigned positions in industry, in the interest of industrial justice and efficiency, upon the bases of their merit and ability. It contends for the right of the Negro worker to break through the barrier of non-promotability so that a Negro Pullman porter may become a conductor; a Negro waiter, a steward, or a head waiter; a Negro brakeman or flagman, a conductor; and a Negro fireman, an engineer.

While the shortage of manpower, economic necessity, and the President's Committee on Fair Employment Practices have provided jobs in defense industries and the Government for Negro workers, practically over 75 per cent are still victims of discrimination when they seek upgrading in skill, and wages. Negro women, too, who are being put into war industries are suffering from all types of discrimination that are visited upon Negro men. For instance, Negro women are employed as porters in the terminal stations, but they are not allowed to perform responsible work in the railroad yards, such as white women are employed to perform. White women are being used as trainmen, but this privilege is denied to Negro women.

GOVERNMENT ALSO GUILTY

But private industry is not the only agency which sins against the Negro worker. The Federal Government is the chief offender. Hence, the March On Washington Movement fights for employment of Negroes in every part of the government, municipal, state and federal, from a porter or janitor to the highest form of technical, skilled, and professional service, upon a basis, naturally, of merit and ability.

Since Negroes, as workers and consumers, are tax-makers and tax-payers, they have a right to fight for placement in all types of employment in public utilities. Public utilities in every city should have their Negro motormen, conductors, bus drivers, mechanics, ticket agents, telephone girls, gas-meter readers, bookkeepers, stenographers, and foremen and also places in the higher supervisory and managerial brackets.

TECHNIQUE OF ACTION

But it is one thing to want a thing and another thing to get it. The whole world wants peace but how shall we get it? The workers want industrial democracy but how shall they get it?

Hence, there is nothing more important than method, technique, strategy in planning the solution of a problem.

MOWM employs the following pattern:
1. Negotiation
2. Inter-racial, inter-faith pressures
3. Mass marches
4. Picketing
5. Boycott
6. Seeking and developing trade union co-operation
7. Public relations
8. Membership in trade unions, the natural ally of the Negro

The March On Washington Movement, in seeking to secure employment for Negroes in industries hitherto excluding them, resorts first to the method of negotiation with the industrial management. Failing in this procedure, it seeks to coordinate inter-racial and inter-faith pressures to secure the consideration of personnel managers and the heads of industrial enterprises. When the aforementioned pressure proves ineffective, MOWM employs the non-violent direct action technique of mass marches. These marches are then reinforced by the relatively permanent picket line until some form of favorable action is secured.

Supplementing the technique of direct mass action is sometimes developed a boycott. The most basic and effective form of action consists in well directed and organized public relations to keep the public advised and informed that the reason for the campaign against a given enterprise and trade union is employment opportunities for Negroes.

Because of the progress of the closed and union shops and the maintenance of membership clauses for the benefit of trade unions, the fight for membership in all of the trade unions must and will be relentlessly waged by the Negro worker.

The March On Washington Movement assigns economic ignorance on the part of the white workers as a primary reason for the victimization of the Negro worker. Being in the main without knowledge of the far-reaching implications of monopoly capitalism and how all workers regardless of race, religion, color or national origin are the objects of exploitation, the white worker picks out the Negro as the scapegoat. But the white workers will change in their attitude towards the Negro as the forces of Fascism turn upon them and workers' education and economic pressure become more widespread.

EXECUTIVE ORDER 8802

Because the workers must eat, the March On Washington Movement made the fight for jobs in the early stages of the national defense program its cardinal plan of action. It was the coordination of the National Association for the Advancement of Colored People, National Urban League, civic, church, trade union, and educational movements into a formidable program to march on Washington that was largely responsible for the issuance of Executive Order 8802 and the establishment by the President of the Committee on Fair Employment Practices.

Here, the technique of non-violent direct action in the form of a March On Washington bore fruit. It was the continuous pressure of the March On Washington and the above mentioned group of organizations that rescued the Fair Employment Practices Committee from the War Manpower Commission and brought about the rescheduling of the railroad hearings that had been postponed indefinitely by the Chairman of the War Manpower Commission, Mr. Paul V. McNutt.

Political

But economics is only one arm with which the Negro people may fight for their liberation. The struggle of all oppressed peoples shows that economic action requires the supplementation of political action. To this end, the March On Washington Movement suggests as a major strategy for the effective employment of the political power of the Negro, the building of a national non-partisan Negro political bloc, with branches in the various local communities in the country. This does not require that Negroes come out of the Republican, Democratic, Socialist or Communist parties. But it does require that, when a crucial question of universal concern and importance to the Negro arises, Negroes will express their united political strength regardless of party politics. When this is done, it will strengthen the position of Negro leaders in the Republican and Democratic parties and make the white boss politicians more disposed to give serious consideration to all questions affecting the interest of the Negro. It will prove that Negroes are not so died-in-the-wool Republicans or Democrats that they will not ignore political labels when a crisis comes, for the benefit and advancement of the Negro. It goes without saying that any form of political action which favorably serves the interest of the Negro people also favorably serves the interest of our country. It is a matter of common knowledge that Negroes as Democrats do not amount to much.

They can get but little done for Negroes. Similarly, Negroes as Republicans are not very strong and their voice is seldom heeded. Negroes as Socialists or Communists are helpless, but when Negro Republicans and Democrats step forward in a united front expressed in a powerful non-partisan political bloc, they will be heard and heeded by political boss or mayor, governor, president, Senate or House Committees. The value of a non-partisan political Negro bloc consists in the fact that it represents power. It is well-nigh the law of the life of the politician that he respects nothing but votes. Politicians are seldom, if ever, moved by questions of principles, ideals, or human justice. Politicians are hungry for power and jobs. This is true of white and black politicians. They fear votes and the righteous wrath of the people. They will only do the right thing for the people when they are made to do so by pressure, public opinion and votes.

Therefore, upwards of 15 millions of Negroes need not forever play the role of political mendicants. They have power if they will mobilize by registering in mass for non-partisan political action. Such a political bloc should be financed by Negroes entirely. It is still true that the power over man's subsistence is the power of his will, and he who pays the fiddler calls the tune. Therefore, such a non-partisan political bloc should not accept any money from Republican, Democratic, Socialist or Communist party. It should be entirely free. It cannot be free if it is subsidized by any politicians.

HOW POLITICAL BLOC MAY FUNCTION

This piece of political machinery, during campaigns, could send speakers into districts to oppose the enemies of the Negro and support their friends on a basis of their record in office and public life. Literature on the issues and candidates could be prepared and distributed widely throughout the country, expressing the position of the Negro on them.

Whole page advertisements setting forth the position and demands of the Negro people should be carried in strategic papers, dailies and weeklies, during a campaign to let the world know that Negroes are not asleep or weak.

If such a powerful non-partisan political bloc is honestly, courageously and intelligently directed, it could transform the political status of the Negro people in our American community, put a Negro on the United States Supreme Court, Negroes on Federal courts, a Negro in the Cabinet, Negroes on policy making commissions, get Negroes their rightful share of jobs in government agencies, elect them to municipal and state legislatures as well as to the Senate and the House of Congress, abolish anti-Negro legislation, reverse anti-Negro court decisions, eliminate racial bias in administrative agencies, and secure for Negroes the respect enjoyed by other citizens. It could aid effectively in passing anti-poll tax legislation, put a federal anti-lynching law on the statute books and enable the Negroes to have their voice heard above the ranting and raving of the Bilbos and Rankins.

HOW BLOC CAN BE BUILT

A non-partisan Negro political bloc is not unprecedented. Already because of anti-labor legislation, the A. F. of L. and CIO, the Big Four Railroad Brotherhoods, and the National Farmers Union are seeking a common ground of political unity. They realize that as individual groups they are practically hopeless politically. But united they become a formidable power.

The technique of setting up such a bloc is simple, and consists in the federation of religious, fraternal, civic, labor, educational, women, business, and various political groups upon a minimum political program. This organization would be similarly constructed in local communities. It would mobilize its forces to operate the door-bell-ringing plan to reach every man, woman and child to get them to register and vote against a given political menace and to put literature into the hands of all citizens of the community. It would also conduct public forums to keep the interest and issues alive and focus attention upon the public evils.

This powerful non-partisan political bloc of Negroes would also serve the cause of labor, progressive, liberal and social legislation. It is pretty generally a matter of fact that the enemies of the Negro are the enemies of labor and progress and the enemies of labor are the enemies of the Negro. Note that the poll tax congressmen and senators who filibuster against legislation to free the Negro from mob violence and lynching and white primaries are the same leaders that pilot the fight to enact fascist legislation such as the Smith-Connally bill.

Such a bloc would necessarily use its force against reaction and on the side of progress. Why? The answer is Negroes are the victims of reaction and the beneficiaries of progress.

Nor is it difficult to see that the strategy of a non-partisan political bloc has its validity in the experience of the struggle of groups to achieve certain objectives. Big Business has the most powerful non-partisan political bloc in America. It has been built and is directed by the National Manufacturers Association. This bloc assails and opposes all liberal and social legislation. Farmers, too, have a non-partisan political bloc. It is represented by the American Farm Bureau Federation and the National Farmers Grange.

EXCLUDING THE COMMUNISTS

While Democrats, Republicans, and Socialists may be coordinated in such a non-partisan political bloc, Communists must be excluded. The reason is simple. It is silly and suicidal for Negroes to add to the handicap of being *Black*, another handicap of being *Red*. Moreover, the Communist Party seeks only to rule or ruin a movement. It has one objective. It seeks to use the Negro and labor or any group which may be at hand for the purpose of consolidating the foreign policies and fortunes of Soviet Russia. They have their feet in America but heads and hearts in Moscow. For this reason the Communists constitute a pestilence, menace and nuisance to the Negro people as well as to organized labor. It would be eminently unsound and destructive strategy for Negroes to tie up with Communists since the primary and fundamental interest of the Negro and labor are common and the same, but labor has long since recognized the danger of the Communist movement, and thus the A. F. of L. and CIO have condemned and repudiated the Communist party, its policies, program, tactics, and so forth, and have adopted the policy of throwing Communists out of the unions whenever they are discovered. Hence, Negroes cannot logically and with sound wisdom tie up with a movement such as the Communist which organized labor in America condemns and rejects. The history and record of this political cult shows that it conforms with rigid fidelity to the rapidly changing, unpredictable climate of Soviet Russia, without regard to the national interests of any other group. When the war broke, the Communists who had posed as the saviour of the Negro promptly dropped him like a hot potato. This was not the first time the Communists deserted the Negro. When Soviet Russia was seeking recognition from the United States government, Joe Stalin suddenly and unceremoniously halted the plans for the making of the well advertised, grandiose pro-Negro film, exposing the sins of America against the colored people, when he saw that such action would help Soviet Russia win the approbation of Southern politicians that might advance his interest in securing the said recognition.

Of course everyone is familiar with the fact that Communists were picketing the White House when Hitler invaded Russia, but with amazing celerity reversed their tactic and began preaching all-out war with a plague on the house of the advocates of peace.

NON-VIOLENT GOOD WILL ACTION

Discriminations against Negroes in restaurants, dance halls, theatres, and other public places of amusement and entertainment above the Mason-Dixon line are alarmingly quite general. There are few hotels in the big cities that freely admit Negro patrons. When approached for accommodations by Negroes, all sorts of ruses are resorted to. The well known excuse is that no rooms are available. It is difficult to meet this situation. But the March On Washington Movement has proclaimed its dedication to and advocacy of non-violent good will direct action as a method of meeting this discrimination.

It works in this way: White friends who believe in the right of the Negroes to exercise their civil liberties are organized, trained and disciplined with Negroes.

The technique works as follows:

The white friends who precede the Negro patrons to a table in a given restaurant or hotel or place of amusement, upon seeing the Negro citizens denied service, will thereupon join the Negroes in requesting conference with the management to discuss the reason for the anti-Negro policy. If the manager agrees to a conference, efforts are made by the Negro and white persons to convince the manager that he is violating the Constitutional rights of the Negro citizens, and if there is a civil rights law in the state, a copy of same is presented to the manager in proof of the claim that he is in conflict with the public law and policy of the state. If a conference is denied, civil rights action against the place in question may be filed, or another visit may be made to the place with a larger number of Negro and white friends and picketing may ensue, or the white and colored friends may decide to stage a sit down strike in the place to bring the issue to a head.

Before any form of direct action is engaged in, all the resources of negotiation are exhausted.

If in the process of attempting to exercise the right of Negroes to receive service in a given enterprise, the Negro and white friends are violently ejected from the place, the policy of the March On Washington Movement is not to fight back. Every individual who participates in such a project is pledged to non-violent action, to the extent of not even using violent language against the management or the employees. If a Negro or white friend seeking to break down the discriminatory barriers is physically injured, no effort will be made to secure financial damages for same, for it is considered as a part of the price which must be paid, in sacrifice and suffering, to eliminate an evil which has been acquiesced in and permitted to exist by the inaction and fear of the Negro people.

NON-VIOLENT ACTION IN THE SOUTH

The areas in which Non-Violent Good Will Direct Action will be initiated will be carefully studied and selected with a view to the avoidance of any unnecessary violent and destructive social explosions. MOWM recognizes that the barriers of racial discrimination in the Southern section of the country cannot be abolished overnight and that they must be approached in terms of the conditions of the racial climate of the community. But it also insists that a policy of do-nothing is also dangerous and provocative. Therefore, MOWM plans a series of Non-Violent Good Will Direct Action institutes throughout the country where techniques and strategy will be carefully evaluated and appraised with a view to their utilization in various fields of social interest. Thus, all persons who participate in these non-violent projects are required to go through a rigid training and discipline to develop self control and the requisite moral and spiritual resources and armament with which to meet the most trying ordeal in order that the principles of MOWM may not be compromised.

The March On Washington Movement takes the position that Negroes in the South can make an effective gesture against Jim Crow by setting aside a day when they refuse to send their children to a Jim Crow school. This will have a psychological value of focusing the attention of the South upon this social cancer.

The Jim Crow railroad coach in the South for Negroes can be scrupulously avoided as a leper on some given day set aside for that purpose. Street cars and buses in the South could also be boycotted on a given day. But these forms of social discipline and response can only follow well-planned educational programs.

Contrary to many hysterical and intemperate attacks upon Non-Violent Good Will Direct Action by some of the Negro intelligentsia and petty bourgeoisie that Negroes cannot comprehend and execute such a principle, this form of social protest and revolt was used by Harriet Tubman in her underground railroad for the escape of Negroes from slavery to the East and Eastern Canada before and after the Civil War. Migration movements of Negroes from the South are instances of Non-Violent Good Will Direct Action. Upon the introduction of the Jim Crow car in the South, following Reconstruction, thousands of Negroes refused to ride on them. They rode in hacks and wagons and sometimes walked in protest against this insult.

Instead of the strategy of Non-Violent Good Will Direct Action instigating and promoting violence and bloodshed, rioting and mob action, racial hatred and ill will, it is designed and will tend to eliminate these forms of racial irritation and conflict. Of course the MOWM does not contend that Non-Violent Good Will Direct Action is the final and complete answer to Jim Crow. It is only one method of attack.

WESTERN HEMISPHERIC POLICY CONFERENCE FOR FREE NEGROES

In addition to believing that winning democracy for the Negro is winning the war for democracy abroad, the MOWM is committed to the slogan of a free Africa, and links the interest of the Negro people in America to the interest of Negroes all over the world, including the Caribbean islands, Abyssinia, and other sections of Africa. While much is said from day to day in the public press about a free India and a free China, seldom is a word uttered or written in the interest of a free Africa. The old imperialistic principle of a mandate for the so-called weaker and backward peoples is likely to be dusted off and given the blessing of the peace conference unless public sentiment condemns it. Programs of health, education and the industrialization of Africa will receive but scant attention and interest unless an aroused public opinion demands it. Thus, the MOWM proposes to hold a Western Hemispheric Policy Conference for Free Negroes, when representatives of peoples of color, including the Hindus and Chinese, Arabs, Filipinos, and others may come together and discuss the problems of Africa and the darker races with the view to the formulation of well organized and scientific plans for the submission to the peace conference whenever and wherever it may be held. It is the purpose of MOWM to hold this aforementioned conference sometime before the armistice.

WORLD CONGRESS OF COLORED PEOPLES

In addition to the Western Hemispheric Policy Conference for Free Negroes, which will be held somewhere in America, it is the purpose of the MOWM to stimulate interest in the holding of a World Congress of Darker Peoples at the time the Peace Conference is held, and in the same city. The purpose of this Congress will be to discuss the findings of the Western Hemispheric Policy Conference for Free Negroes, and to formulate other programs concerning the status and future of the peoples of color in the world for submission to the Peace Conference, and to lobby and agitate for their consideration and acceptance.

It is the desire of the March On Washington Movement to co-operate with all existing organizations that may be concerned about the future of Africa and the Darker Peoples and in giving reality and force to the cause of their liberation, independence and progress.

MARCH ON WASHINGTON

Pivotal and central to the whole struggle in the Negro libera-tion movement at this time is the abolition of Jim Crow in the armed forces.

Many and varied opinions have been expressed about the merits and the danger of the March On Washington. The *Pitts-burgh Courier*, the journalistic spokesman of the petty black bourgeoisie, with bitter attacks, shrieks its condemnation of the March On Washington Movement because of the proposed march upon the nation's capital, viewing with alarm and a mor-tal, chronic fear the imagined consequence of such an adventure. It wants results without risks, achievement without action. Rest-ing upon the feather bed of de luxe, material comfort, it winces and cringes before the gathering forces of the Negro masses for direct action, though non-violent.

The MOWM is not unaware of the significance and value of every form of agitation and organization in the fight for Negro rights, including news articles and editorials in the press and magazines, sermons in the pulpit, orations on the public platform, programs on the radio, dramas and the movies, but it is com-mitted to the thesis that none of these agencies can and will pro-ject the cause of the Negro into the main stream of public opinion as effectively as direct action, mass action, and, of course, always, non-violent action.

The immediate, positive and direct value of mass action pres-sure consists of two things: One, it places human beings in phys-ical motion which can be felt, seen and heard. Nothing stirs and shapes public sentiment like physical action. Organized labor and organized capital have long since recognized this. This is why the major weapon of labor is the STRIKE. It is why the major weapon of business is the Lock-out and the Shut-down. All people feel, think and talk about a physical formation of people, whoever they may be. This is why wars grip the imagination of man. Mass demonstrations against Jim Crow are worth a million editorials and orations in anybody's paper and on any platform. Editorials and orations are only worthwhile and effective when they are built around some actual human struggles for specific social and racial rights and against definite wrongs.

Mass social pressure in the form of marches and picketing will not only touch and arrest the attention of the powerful public officials but also the "little man" in the street. And, before this problem of Jim Crow can be successfully attacked, all of America must be shocked and awakened. This has never been done, except by race riots that are dangerous socio-racial explosions. Moreover, mass efforts are a form of struggle for Negro rights in which all Negroes can participate, including the educated and the so-called uneducated, the rich and the poor. It is a technique and strategy which the "little Negro" in the tavern, pool-room, on the streets, jitterbug, store-front preacher, and sharecropper, can use to help free the race.

ALL NEGRO MOVEMENT

Now, the March On Washington Movement is an all Negro movement, but it is not anti-white, anti-American, anti-labor, anti-Catholic or anti-Semitic. It's simply pro-Negro. It does not rest so much upon race as upon the social problem of Jim Crow. It does not oppose inter-racial organizations. It cooperates with such mixed organizations as the National Association for the Advancement of Colored People and the National Urban League, and churches, trade unions. Its validity lies in the fact that no one will fight as hard to remove and relieve pain as he who suffers from it. Negroes are the only people who are the victims of Jim Crow, and it is they who must take the initiative and assume the responsibility to abolish it. Jews must and do lead the fight against anti-Semitism, Catholics must lead the fight against anti-Catholicism, labor must battle against anti-labor laws and practices.

This does not mean that Negroes should not invite Catholic, Jewish, Protestant, labor, and liberal business groups of white people to help them win this fight. Labor unions are only composed of workers, but they seek the help of clergymen, housewives and liberals who may be non-workers. During strikes, unions form citizens' committees to help them, but they do not take the citizens into the unions.

It is well-nigh axiomatic that while white and Negro citizens may sympathize with the cause of striking miners or auto-workers or lumber-jacks, the fact remains that the miners, auto-workers and lumber-jacks must take the initiative and assume the responsibility and take the risks themselves to win higher wages and shorter hours.

By the same token, white liberals and labor may sympathize with the Negro's fight against Jim Crow, but they are not going to lead the fight. They never have and they never will. The fight to annihilate Jim Crow in America must be led by Negroes with the cooperation and collaboration of white liberals and labor. And the fight against Jim Crow is the fight against fascism.

The petty black bourgeoisie are always hunting for some white angel at whose feet they may place the Negroes' problems. This provides a middle of the road or lofty, professional, neutral, so-called scientific objectivity or a severely critical but do-nothing attitude. At one time they unloaded their troubles on the G.O.P. on the grounds that it was the party of "Father" Abraham Lincoln. Then when the political pickings became slight they fled to the Democratic Jackass. Ere long they will learn that there is no fundamental difference between Democrats and Republicans, either with respect to Negroes or labor, that they are like two peas in a pod, two souls with a single thought—tweedledee and tweedledum.

RACE RIOTS

Now, what of the race riots that now bedevil the Negro and the country?

The March On Washington Movement urges Negroes to hold public meetings to discuss the epidemic of race riots now sweeping the country to bring the issue intelligently and boldly into the open.

People's committees should be picked in the meetings from the floor by the people and given the mandate to go to see the mayors of the cities, and to join with other committees of similar cities in a state to see the governor to urge and demand that commissions on race relations be appointed to study the labor, economic, housing, recreational and law enforcement agencies and policies and forces with a view to making recommendations to the mayor and governor to take measures to prevent riots, and to stop them promptly and effectively when they start.

These public meetings should also call upon President Roosevelt to appoint a National Commission on Race to perform the aforementioned task on a national scale. They should call upon Congressman Sam Rayburn, Democratic Speaker of the House of Representatives, and Congressman Martin, Republican Minority Leader to set up machinery for a Congressional investigation of the Detroit race riot and the riots in Beaumont, Texas; Mobile, Alabama; Los Angeles, California; New York City and other places.

The public meetings should also plan the formation of city-wide inter-racial inter-faith committees, composed of trade unionists, business, educational, political representatives which will serve as a public group of citizens to cooperate in the study and maintenance of law and order.

Such meetings should also call upon the President to send Negro and white troops into riot areas and to keep them there to insure the right and opportunity of the Negro workers to continue on the jobs with the white workers in the production of war materials, ships and planes to enable the United Nations to win the war and destroy Axis tyranny.

HITLER NOT CAUSE OF RIOTS

Now, Negroes must not be deceived into thinking that Hitler caused the Detroit race riot or any other riot. These riots are the result of our government's policy of segregation and discrimination against Negroes for decades. It had been going on long before Hitler was ever heard of, and race riots will continue long after Hitler is dead and forgotten, if our government does not stop the Jim Crow of Negro citizens and begin to integrate the Negro into the government, war- and peace-time industry on a basis of equality with their white brothers and sisters. Of course, everybody knows that these riots help the cause of Hitler and fascism. But let the Negro place the blame for these riots right where it belongs, namely, at the door of the past and the present administrations. This trick of getting Negroes chasing after Hitler as the cause of the race riots and tension diverts Negroes' attention from the true source of the riots which is America, and provides an opportunity for the government officials who are guilty to escape responsibility for not doing anything about it on the grounds that it is not possible to reach the cause.

NEGRO SOLDIER VOTE

What of the vote of the 400,000 or more Negro soldiers in the South? Because of recent legislation removing the obligation to pay a poll-tax by soldiers from the poll-tax states, Negroes have the opportunity to exercise considerable influence upon national political affairs in the coming presidential campaign. They can practically wipe out the menace of lily-white Republicans who are no better than Dixie Democrats. Because of superior numbers, the Negro soldier can be used to stage separate state Republican conventions and elect delegates to the forthcoming national convention and wield the balance of power in the selection of the next Republican candidate for President. This would enable the Negro to bargain for substantial concessions in the form of the Republican Party support of a national civil rights bill, anti-poll-tax bill, an anti-lynching bill and equal consideration of jobs in all categories in the government.

Negroes should also present themselves to register and vote in the Democratic primaries. But they should not appear as individuals. They should appear in groups of ten or more. Where there is more than one Negro appearing to exercise his constitutional right to vote, there is less likelihood for attempts at intimidation and fraud.

Negroes must also attack the rotten borough political system in the South. It can and must be destroyed. This fight will help save democracy in America.

Both major parties, Democratic and Republican, must answer for the fact that Negroes are deprived of the right to vote in direct violation of the Fourteenth Amendment. A flagrant evidence of the unwarranted power this disfranchisement gives the South is shown by the following figures from the 1940 census:

State	Total Population	Citizens over 21	Voters	Rep. in House
South Carolina	1,899,804	989,841	99,830	6
Washington	1,736,191	1,123,725	793,833	6
Arkansas	1,949,387	1,198,986	200,743	7
Connecticut	1,709,242	1,011,658	781,502	5
Georgia	3,123,723	1,768,869	312,539	10
Wisconsin	3,137,587	1,941,603	1,405,522	10

The national government does nothing in this situation to enforce that provision of the Fourteenth Amendment which directly states the representation of any state will be cut down in the proportion that it discriminates.

Negroes are denied an equal share of federal money appropriated under the Smith-Hughes and the George-Deen Acts for vocational education. The national government does nothing to see that this money is spent equitably.

Negroes are discriminated against in every aspect of life—in housing, transportation, health facilities, recreation, education and employment. This treatment has made the Negro bitter and determined that if Negroes have to serve in a Jim Crow army and risk their lives overseas for freedom, they are going to enjoy that freedom here. They wish to avoid race tension and conflict, but the major responsibility for avoiding conflict rests with those who refuse to change their thinking and practices in a period when great social changes are taking place.

The Republican and Democratic parties cannot escape responsibility for these conditions; therefore the March On Washington Movement, representing thousands of Negroes throughout the country, wants specific answers to the following questions:

1. What will the Republican party and its representatives in

Congress do to enforce that provision of the Constitution that reads: "No person shall be ... deprived of life, liberty, or property without due process of law?"

2. What will the Republican party and its representatives in Congress do to cut down the representation in Congress of those states which discriminate against Negroes in voting?

3. What will the Republican and Democratic parties and their representatives in Congress do to abolish Jim Crow in housing, transportation, education, recreation and other social services?

4. What will the Republican and Democratic parties and their representatives in Congress do to insure the permanency of the Fair Employment Practices Committee as an administrative agency to bring the techniques of intelligence, of fact and of justice, to the problems of breaking down discrimination in employment?

5. What will the Republican and Democratic parties and their representatives in Congress do to break down discrimination in the armed forces?

Finally, let me pose this challenging issue of the War.

Fellow Citizens!

ARE NEGRO AMERICANS CITIZENS?

Right here in our own country is one of the great issues of the WAR: SHALL WE HAVE DEMOCRACY FOR ALL OF THE PEOPLE OR FOR SOME OF THE PEOPLE?

This is a great moral issue since a war for democracy against Nazi racialism cannot consistently be prosecuted on a Jim Crow basis. This is also a great practical issue since racial antagonisms are grave handicaps in the national effort to win the war and plan the peace.

THE AMERICAN PEOPLE HAVE NOT MET THIS ISSUE.

THE ANSWER CAN NO LONGER BE POSTPONED TO THE QUESTION: ARE NEGROES AMERICAN CITIZENS WITH THE SAME RIGHTS AND OBLIGATIONS AS WHITE CITIZENS?

The Constitution states:

All persons born or naturalized in the United States and subject to the jurisdiction thereof, are citizens of the United States and of the State wherein they reside. No State shall make or enforce any law which shall abridge the privilege or immunities of citizens of the United States; nor shall any State deprive any person of life, liberty or property without due process of law; nor deny to any person within its jurisdiction the equal protection of the laws.

In these explicit words the Congress of the United States intended to help the newly freed people progress from slavery to free citizenship. But the promise of the Fourteeth Amendment, written into the Constitution itself, was never fulfilled. An undemocratic pattern of "white supremacy" and Jim Crow was evolved in the Southern states to take the place of chattel slavery. The shameful pattern has spread beyond the Mason-Dixon line and has infected racial relations throughout the country.

There are more than 13,000,000 Negroes in this country. Among them are laborers, labor leaders, tradesmen, poets, musicians, scientists, doctors, lawyers, social workers, teachers, ministers, writers and philosophers. The overwhelming majority are working people, whose toil and struggle have for more than 300 years helped build America.

Negroes are loyal to America and to the democratic principles for which our country stands. Though only 10 per cent of the population, Negroes, in 1940-41, furnished 16 per cent of all volunteers in the United States Army. They love their native land and have fought for it from Bunker Hill to North Africa.

BUT HOW HAVE THEY BEEN REQUITED?

They are discriminated against in the very armed forces which summon them to shed their blood for their country. They are drafted in Jim Crow quotas, trained in Jim Crow regiments, segregated in every possible way from their white comrades in arms. And all this despite the fact that Section 4A of the 1940 Draft Act states:

In the selection and training of men under this Act, and in the interpretation and execution of the provisions of this Act, there shall be no discrimination against any person on account of race or color.

We in the March On Washington Movement are disturbed by these things. We call on our fellow Americans to fight with us to wipe out these practices which violate both in spirit and in letter the Declaration of Independence and the Constitution.

We demand a democratic army and call upon the President as Commander-in-Chief to enforce the Draft Law which forbids discrimination.

We demand that Negroes be employed on the basis of their skill and intelligence in all branches of our federal service in every public and private industry. This means a functioning FEPC with power to end discrimination in training, in placement, in wages, in promotions and in membership in labor organizations. We demand equal education opportunities with equal access for the Negro student to all public tax-supported institutions. We demand the democratic right to vote without poll-taxes, white primaries and other devices which keep the majority of Southern Negroes a voteless group with no voice either in the selection of their representatives or a check on unjust public policies.

We demand an end to segregation in transportation, in housing, in health and recreational facilities and in all other social service.

We demand the enforcement of that provision of the Constitution which provides that "No person...shall be deprived of life, liberty, or property, without due process of law."

We demand the abrogation of every law which makes a distinction in treatment between citizens based on religion, creed, color or national origin.

We demand Negro and minority group representation on all administrative agencies so that these groups may help to determine policies for all people.

These demands are issues which concern all of us, both white and black, for every American has a stake in the fight against racial discrimination. For the rise of Hitler to power shows us racial prejudice is one of the most effective and dangerous tools of fascism. Just as the great mass of German people, their trade unions, their political parties and other organizations were crushed along with the Jews, so over here, reactionary forces will also strike down the trade unions, free religious and liberal institutions and the common people of America. The colored people of Asia, Africa, and Latin America will measure the genuineness of our declarations about a free world to the extent that we create a free world within our own borders.

In the name of America, past and future, in the name of the common interest of humanity, of the tenets of democracy, of those who now are dying and of those who live for freedom, we call upon all in the nation and the Christian Church to join in this struggle for human dignity and for the equality of all men and women.

In conclusion, let me add that the March On Washington Movement holds the following position:

1. It does not seek to overthrow the American Government. We shall uphold and defend it, but seek to purge it of its sins and make it better, and true to its ideals.

2. It does not seek to change the economic, political and social status of the Negro through bloodshed and violence.

3. It is determined to fight to abolish Jim Crow through non-violent, good will, direct action or constitutional obedience.

4. It does not seek to provoke race riots and increase race tensions and conflicts.

5. But on the contrary, it works to prevent race riots and decrease racial tensions by bringing the cause of race riots through the medium of public mass meetings, marches and public relations, into the open with frank and truthful discussion.

6. It is the general belief of the March On Washington Movement that the Negro would sooner or later be compelled to March On Washington to strike our heaviest blow against second-class citizenship, and the issuance of a national Proclamation to abolish Jim Crow in the armed forces by the President, just as Abraham Lincoln issued a Proclamation to abolish slavery during the Civil War.

7. The MOWM does not approach this problem with rancor, hatreds or fears. We approach it with the spirit of brotherhood, and good will. We believe in the essential decency of the great majority of the American people. We believe they will respond to a continuous challenge of the moral law of human unity and cooperation.

ONE AMERICAN PROBLEM
AND A
POSSIBLE SOLUTION

By WILLARD S. TOWNSEND

NOTES ON CHANGING ATTITUDES

THE INCREASING TEMPO of our present war is gradually introducing many profound changes in our common collective attitude towards the kind of world that must be constructed out of the shambles of the old order of fear, hate, and greed. Historically, changing attitudes under the stress and strain of war are not unusual. As a general rule, the horrible impact of war, both economic and military, has a tendency to force individuals, communities and even nations to re-examine their past ways of life and to search for new methods and ideas to solve and overcome old problems and prejudices. During these significant periods in the violent movement of social and economic forces, old methods, techniques and values are heaped upon the grave-yards of history and are replaced by what many choose to refer to as "revolutionary processes."

A study of the continuous movement of society and man's changing attitudes and relation to other men falls within the field of social science. Our more intelligent social scientists generally agree that man's attitudes and relation to other men are in a constant process of change. War, for the most part, acts to accentuate the need for change and to hasten the process.

Possibly, the most important emotional element responsible for changing attitudes on the part of individuals or a people in the throes of war can be traced to the many sacrifices made to prosecute the struggle. The very nature of the sacrifice and its intimate relationship to future well-being brings many to a real consideration of the kind of security to be accomplished as against the sacrifices being made. Total war demands equal sacrifices and more or less involves parallel dangers for the front line soldier as well as the civilian at home. A significant development within our present global conflict is that the common people of the world are making greater sacrifices and witnessing the destruction of human values at a pace unheard of in history.

This is, indeed, something for the little people of all races to consider since our past and present conflicts have placed the full burden of the sacrifices upon their shoulders. This war has not left them unaware of this point. Today, more little people are thinking seriously together of their common problems and the sacrifices they are making for an ideal that refuses to take any positive form in the minds and actions of a great majority of our politicians and statesmen. Their spirit of community responsibility has multiplied many times within the past fourteen years of the great depression and global war. Ideas are changing and unsolved problems are being re-examined with great sincerity. The little people are restless and are in motion as never before in the history of man.

"NEGRO PROBLEM" FUNDAMENTALLY SIMPLE

As with many other unsolved social, economic and political questions, the "Negro problem" today is receiving its fair share of critical re-examination. To the millions of toiling black and a growing number of white Americans, who constantly stand in the shadows of poverty, fear, disease and ignorance, the problem is, fundamentally, a simple one. It is as simple as truth itself. The problem only becomes complicated when conflicting self-interests become involved and shallow efforts are made to deny the truth through the creation of various and sundry defense mechanisms to forestall any attack upon this or that special interest. Therefore the extent of the complexity of the "Negro problem" is determined largely by its distance from simple fact and truth.

Each special interest group involved in the "problem" has manufactured its own peculiar defense mechanism and carved out its area of exploitation. For example, the "white supremists" insist that Negroes are a biologically inferior race and as such must be relegated to an inferior social, economic and political status. This untruth serves a double purpose. It lays the "moral" foundation for racial separatism and at the same time profitably exploits the fears and suspicions of both racial groups. The "black supremists" would have us believe that Negroes are "God's chosen people." The proponents of this untruth seek to develop an extreme degree of racial consciousness and community economic isolation which would give them a more fertile field for exploitation within the group. Beneath the surface these two extreme racial supremists have more in common with each other than they have with the racial group they ostensibly seek to make supreme. Both profit by ignorance and intolerance; both glorify the profit system and the myth of rugged individualism and both are extremely anti-labor.

To gain an adequate understanding of this problem it must be brought into focus with our general social and economic picture. Many Negro leaders with great influence have either mistakenly or consciously sought to view this problem as an isolated phenomenon and proceeded to wrap and tie this grave question with the tinsel and false glitter of racial isolationism and self-sufficiency. Within the Negro community, this has created much confusion and has made a great contribution to general social and economic illiteracy within the "white-collar" areas of the group.

Inequalities in our economic order are not initiated as the result of individual or stereotyped collective prejudices. It is exactly the other way around. Stereotyped prejudices result from inequalities and are merely by-products of the inequalities that are basic characteristics of our competitive "dog-eat-dog" economy. Within this economic structure there exist many areas of influence and power whose major task is to inflame race and class prejudices in order to perpetuate these inequalities. The many vicious attacks upon organized labor and the constant refusal to extend democratic opportunities to Negroes and other racial minorities are not a series of isolated and unrelated incidents, but are part and parcel of the whole organized pattern to keep America, economically, half free and half slave. This policy is subscribed to by many thousands through ignorance of the basic causes and disastrous results. These are the victims of propaganda.

THE ECONOMIC NATURE OF THE PROBLEM AND ITS INFLUENCE UPON THE DEMOCRATIC PATTERN

The complex modern problem of "race, creed and nationality" in our American civilization runs parallel with the opening of the flood gates of the Industrial Revolution following the Civil War. The stakes involved in this war, or the internal continuation of the American Revolution, were the determination of the base upon which our national economy would operate. This conflict resolved itself into a struggle between the plantation economy of the South, in which chattel slavery was the well established corner-stone in its methods of production, and the new industrial economy with its increased productivity and wage labor as its keystone. In the field of national politics, the agrarian South had used its dominant political role in determining domestic and foreign policies to offset any orderly evolutionary procession of the industrial revolution.

Prior to the Civil War the issue on the Negro was based in some degree upon Christian ethics and morality, especially by the abolitionists who saw in chattel slavery a challenge to their Christian consciousness and who had little or no concern with the broad implications found in the sweeping rush of historical events of the industrial revolution. The forces aligned with the new industrial economy only saw, as a necessity precedent to the enlargement of industrial profits, the need of uprooting chattel slavery as the main props upon which the agrarian economy rested and a forcing of the slaves into the competitive labor market as wage earners.

However, it was not until the 1870's that the full force of our modern problem of "race, creed and nationality" hit us squarely in the face. During these significant years of the 1870's we began to accumulate and develop many of our techniques for minority oppression and our undemocratic racial policies. These significant years brought to a close the period of Reconstruction (1865-76) through planter-industrialist agreement, and witnessed the ascendency to power of Northern industrial capitalism into every nook and crevice of American life. There the world-wide and domestic search for sources of cheap wage labor to feed the industrial machines began.

To keep labor cheap, divisions were fomented and old prejudices were institutionalized in order to maintain a "proper" political and economic balance within the new industrial order. Immigration of cheap labor from Europe to work on our railroads and in our mines and mills brought strange customs and cultures which we refused to integrate into our own. Americans began systematically setting these people apart. First came the Irish, who were the victims of native prejudice; then came the Italians, who met the same fate, and then the Poles, who faced the combined prejudice of native born, Irish and Italians. Americans eliminated the Indians by placing them on reservations, adopted the Oriental Exclusion Acts and disfranchised the Negro, organized the Ku Klux Klan, instituted racial segregation as a public policy and methodically went about establishing racial and nationality precedents which each succeeding generation would find more and more difficult to overcome as the problem increased in intensity.

THE MECHANICS OF INSTITUTIONAL POVERTY

It is not accidental nor is it wholly a matter of race prejudice that Negroes constitute a large percentage of that one-third of the nation that has been so aptly referred to as "ill housed, ill clothed and ill fed." The absence of accident and prejudice as a basis for this condition is due to the fact that our concentrated areas of great poverty and wealth operate under the controls of certain basic economic laws which create group inequities within our economy. In our economy, which places a premium upon unequal distribution of goods and services, great individual wealth cannot exist without widespread institutionalized poverty.

The phenomenon of poverty is the polar relation of wealth, just as night is the opposite of day or as top is the polar relation of bottom. We often wondered during the early days of the depression why the mechanics of our economy could ruthlessly destroy "surplus" farm crops while at the same time the fantastic spectacle of poverty and hunger haunted every community and hamlet in the country. The answer is simple. To distribute these goods among those facing hunger would violate the "sacred law" of inequity within our economy (as indicated by uncontrolled price fluctuations, high rates of profit and "reduced buying power").

To illustrate further this important point in reference to organized poverty and wealth, let us take the example of the South Sea Island untouched by the virus of our competitive economy. For the most part, the "natives" of Island "A" live in a community of peace, security, health and relative happiness according to their own moral and ethical code. There is no poverty, neither is there individual wealth because the simple crude economy of the island operates in a collective fashion for the well-being of all. There are no economic class lines nor is there any development of stereotyped group prejudices among the inhabitants of the island.

One blissful day, the "natives" awake to find themselves and the island discovered by the D.E.F. Fruit Company, which is in the business of selling bananas in the American fruit market. For the D.E.F. Fruit Company the potential wealth of that island cannot be realized until the inhabitants have been reduced to artificial poverty through a complete change from their former status of security and relative happiness. This is done through the simple process of expropriation and placing a fence around all the banana trees, which is their basic means of subsistence. From now on the new order of things demands that all those who desire to eat must first pick a certain quota of fruit for the D.E.F. Fruit Company, which is sent off the island and sold at a profit. So what was once a beautiful paradise becomes a cog in the machine of western industrial civilization.

The process of creating artificial poverty on the island does not stop there. The new economy demands creation of additional fences, since it is most difficult to force people to accept poverty in the face of abundance. Other fences are built to secure the first fence, until the islanders face a superstructure of fences and find it more and more difficult to safeguard themselves against poverty and insecurity. Formal laws are instituted and police power created to protect the "fenced in" bananas and the interest of the new "owners." Sacred property rights become the fetish of the expropriators in the administration of justice. Class divisions and prejudices among the "natives" are encouraged and developed by the old game of giving some more bananas than others. Such "natives" become overseers and stout defenders of the system. They begin to live in better huts, wear shoes and listen carefully to the missionaries, who have followed in the wake of the expropriators to give "moral" sanction to the "grab." (This is not an indictment of Christianity, but merely to indicate some selfish efforts made by our imperialists to use it for such purposes.) As the profits roll in and the outside demand for bananas grows, more areas are "fenced in" and the "natives" are forced into a smaller and circumscribed living space. With fewer and fewer bananas to eat for themselves, malnutrition and disease begin to show their ugly heads.

POVERTY PATTERN DETERMINES NATURE OF DEMOCRATIC INSTITUTIONS

This is a simple example of the nature of economic imperialism abroad, whose poverty pattern stems from the excesses of the profit motive. Remove the many outward and superficial trimmings and we easily discover that the same process is obtained in the creation of institutional poverty at home.

The practical operation of our democracy reflects in many forms the moral weaknesses of these applied economic principles. Our economic order is the base which determines the kind of companion institutions we will create. Therefore our political, social, cultural, welfare, religious, legal and educational institutions are greatly influenced by the prevailing economic structure. Economic equality is absent when 80 per cent of our national community receives the smaller share of the national income and the 20 per cent receives the larger share and in the same degree reflects these heavy strains upon the democratic process.

For a minimum health and decency budget for a family of five, the Heller Committee of the University of California and the United States Department of Labor have computed a $2,400 annual income minimum. This is a minimum figure based on actual immediate family needs and not a maximum figure which would insure greater democratic advantages. Compare this desired minimum average family annual income with actual income and you obtain the crux of the problem in round figures.

Studies made by the United States Federal Security Administration show that 40 million workers earned an average of $940 in 1940. This is exactly $1,460 short of a health and decency minimum. In relationship to minimum needs and real wages this actual average income is correspondingly reduced by higher unequal taxation and increased prices. It is this minimum income gap that takes the toll in disease, hunger, over-crowded housing, group fear and ignorance and presents itself as an immovable wall preventing the creation of an equitable democratic order and a practical realization of the Four Freedoms.

The relationship of the position of the Negro to this national income inequity can be found in the striking differences between the traditional low wage occupational areas of Negroes and whites, and the reduction of the income below the average annual maximum.

In March, 1940, farmers, farm laborers and other laborers constituted 62.2 per cent [1] of all employed Negro men as against 28.5 per cent of all employed white men. Other figures reveal that only 4.4 per cent of employed Negroes were working at the higher paid skilled and semi-skilled jobs and only 2.6 per cent of all workers employed in this category. Approximately 70 per cent of employed Negro women were found in service occupations as against 22.4 per cent of employed white women.

A study of agricultural income before the war reveals that the national income average was $528; for the South, where more than 95 per cent of the Negro farmers till the soil, this figure fell below $200 per year. This figure is much lower for the tenant

[1] See 16th Census of the United States, 1940.

farmer and share-cropper. In the field of domestic service, the average annual income fluctuates between $125 and $300. These two occupational areas, incidentally, are the ones that are excluded from the Social Security Act, the Wage and Hour Law and the National Labor Relations Act.

DEMOCRATIC ASSUMPTIONS SUBJECT TO EXPEDIENCY

With Negroes (and many whites) numerically "dominating" these impoverished occupational areas and the constant efforts made to perpetuate this condition of servitude, the major assumptions of democracy are continually subjected to certain social expediencies to safeguard the framework of inequity. The structure of economic inequality and its attendant evils of class division and institutional racial segregation and discrimination are pivotable social "stabilizers" within the body of profit economy. Otherwise a free democracy of equals could easily destroy these social cesspools of special interest.

Yet with each new violation of the assumption of democracy, we come closer in spirit to the methods and techniques of fascist totalitarianism.

The handling of Japanese-American citizens on the west coast is a recent example of government itself violating one of these democratic assumptions (civil liberties and the right of free movement) ostensibly as a military expedient. The removal of Japanese aliens to other points may have offered some logic, but the forced removal of Japanese-American citizens from their established homes and jobs clearly violated one of the accepted democratic ideals. To add insult to injury, Germans and Italians were left unmolested although they have figured in more known cases of sabotage and treason than Japanese.

If this was a case of misjudgment, which some suspect it was not, the recent proposal of Attorney-General Francis Biddle to President Roosevelt on possible methods of averting racial clashes similar to the Detroit riot is also cited. Attorney-General Biddle with unvarnished audacity suggested restricting the right of free movement of Negroes as a possible cure of racial friction. His proposal in this connection urged that:

Careful consideration be given to limiting, and in some instances putting an end to Negro migrations into communities which cannot absorb them, either on account of their physical limitations or cultural background. This needs immediate and careful consideration. When post-war readjustments begin, and jobs are scarcer, the situation will become far more acute. Witness the dislocation in cities caused by the migrations shortly after the last world war. It would seem pretty clear that no more Negroes should move into Detroit. Yet I know of no controls being considered or exercised. You might wish to have the recommendations of Mr. McNutt as to what could and should be done.[2]

There are other traditional violations of this assumption which flow from basic economic ills: restrictions on the right to vote, unequal educational opportunities, restrictive living areas, slums with their high rate of income going to real estate interests and the ever-present lynch mob and "lynch justice."

SOUTHERN "ECONOMY" AND ITS INFLUENCE ON THE PROBLEM

Again, to understand intelligently the economic, political and social status of the Negro in our American democracy, we must give a similar degree of consideration to the South and its peculiar pattern of "colony" economy operating as one of the many outposts and a feeder of raw materials within the structure of modern finance capitalism. This is highly necessary, because this hybrid economic pattern of the South greatly influences our national customs, social behavior and psychology in respect to the Negro and intensifies many of the problems which bar his enjoyment of the privileges of American citizenship.

While the problem maintains a surface sectionalism in many ways, its real solution lies within the framework of our total national economy. It is intellectually indecent for many of our "liberal spokesmen" in the North to spend the greater portion of their time berating the South for its obvious shortcomings while at the same time accepting the basic concept of inequities found hidden beneath the surface of such trivial innocent sound-

[2] Memorandum to President Roosevelt from Attorney-General Francis Biddle, July 15, 1943.

ing phrases as "individual initiative and incentive" and the recently revived hoax of "free enterprise" emanating from the well paid public relations experts of the National Association of Manufacturers.

The South is a land of many inequalities: inequalities that recognize no color line and have placed the brand of poverty, disease, fear and ignorance upon a great mass of whites as well as Negroes. These broad inequalities have caused the culture of the South to degenerate and left in their onward rush a bankrupt morality which makes it a fertile field for the continued existence today of wide areas of hate, stereotyped prejudices and mob violence.

Many of these inequalities have been forced by economic pressure from the outside and others have been adopted from within by political and social parasites as a self-defense mechanism. Whether they are forced from without or adopted from within is purely an academic question. The fact remains that these pressures upon the South are closely identified with the basic inequalities within our total economic framework: inequalities that permit the moral acceptance of dire poverty and its by-products in the face of great potential wealth in population, land and natural resources.

Approximately one-fourth of the population of the United States lives in the South, which receives only one-fifth of the national income. Of the 13 million Negroes in the country, 77 per cent are located in the South, and in Southern rural sections 90 per cent earn less than $1,000 per year, with an average of $480 per family as compared with the $1100 average for white Southern rural families. Two-thirds of the Southern Negro workers are engaged in agriculture and domestic service. In the urban centers of the South the average annual wage for Negro and white workers is $865 as compared with $1219 in other sections of the country. In farm ownership, one-fifth of the Negro farmers own their farms while one-half of the white farmers own theirs. More than half of the Negroes are directly affected by the farm tenancy system. In the field of educational expenditures $80.26 is the national average for each pupil. In the South, the average is $49.30 for each white child and $17.04 for each Negro youngster. Although representing 25 per cent of the population, the South has received only 6 per cent of the 80 billion dollars worth of war contracts awarded by the government.

THE SOUTH, AN ECONOMIC COLONY

The South is a land of many differentials: differentials that cut deep into the patterns of American life and which have caused it to be labelled "The Nation's Number One Economic Problem."

Here our primary interest is getting at the root of this problem. While the problem of the Negro and the poor white is acute, much valuable time and energy is being wasted and misdirected in a harmless rave and rant over the excesses of Southern racial discrimination. We have prima-facie evidence that they exist. We hear of these excesses every day; every Negro youth and adult can supply at least one first-hand experience; every well-meaning liberal has at least one good speech on the subject and every conference of Negroes has hashed and re-hashed their collective experiences. To this indignation, there is nothing new that can be added.

To drive at the heart of this number one economic problem, the innate character of Southern economy must be probed. The South appears, economically, to have been sinned against, as well as to have sinned. Its social patterns stem from the tradition and the historical background of slavery, with a caste consciousness left over from their feudal Anglo-Saxon ancestors.

Naked domestic imperialism is the controlling factor in this "number one economic problem." The South primarily operates as an economic colony and a feeder of raw materials for the industrial machines of the North. This, combined with its outdated agrarian individualism, glaringly reflects in its most vicious forms the basic inequities in our national economy. Extensive industrial development, with its changing social relationship, is rigorously controlled by the maintenance of discriminating freight differentials. These factors combine to create the age-old struggle of group competition, where whites seek to keep Negroes at the bottom, and find themselves held down by the inability of the Negro to rise.

THE PROGRESSIVE ROLE OF LABOR

Within the nature of our economy, labor, when constructively and aggressively organized, is the major productive force tending towards a complete eradication of all economic inequality, the pivot upon which our entire structure rests. Every effort should be made to understand the role of aggressive labor, for herein lies the key to the entire problem of common security and a democracy of equals in every sense of the word. Labor's aggressive historical role from the early days of unionization has been confined primarily to breaking down areas of inequality and a progressive extension of the democratic process. Universal suffrage, public schools, non-imprisonment for debt, minimum wages and social security are practical examples of the historical role of labor.

This is true despite the backwardness of certain sections of organized labor, whose inactive and defenseless position on industrial equality for Negroes is unsupportable and deserves the militant opposition of every worker in the country. However, it must be understood that discrimination against Negroes in the craft framework of certain sections of labor is used as a defense mechanism to support a weak organizational structure and flows from existing community over-all social patterns perpetuated by the economy itself. The solution to this problem is through a rapid extension of the aggressive industrial union forms of organization as characterized by the Congress of Industrial Organizations, whose policies and program negate much of the social and organizational backwardness within the American Federation of Labor.

The problems of aggressive labor and the Negro strike a close kinship. Not only is this true today, but it has been so since emancipation. Even leaders of the National Labor Union, the dominant trade union center following the Civil War, were conscious of this kinship. This is indicated by a speech made in 1868 by William Sylvis, president of the National Labor Union, at a workers meeting in Sudbury, Pennsylvania. He stated:

No man in America rejoiced more than I at the downfall of Negro slavery. But when the shackles fell from the limbs of those four million of blacks, it did not make them free men; it simply transferred them from one condition of slavery to another. . . . We are all now one family of slaves together, and the labor reform movement is a second emancipation proclamation.

To understand this kinship of common problems and the task of cementing the relationship of America's two great minorities in the struggle for a post-war future of hope, security and decency should engage the greater portion of our efforts today. To do so, we must understand the historical weaknesses and the present areas of strength in the joint struggle for security.

GROWING AGGRESSIVE STRENGTH OF LABOR

Today more than 12 million American wage earners and salaried employees are members of trade or industrial unions. Compare this with the 3 million organized workers 10 years ago and one can easily get a picture of labor's growth and increased influence in the United States. The tremendous growth of collective bargaining and the extension of influence upon the economy of our country leave no doubts that this growth and influence will continue to increase and that organized labor will assume a position of extreme importance in post-war America.

What this means to the Negro wage-earning community in its awakened efforts to advance its own security on a level with that of other sections of the working population is one of the major questions affecting the whole future course of American industrial democracy. The complete integration of black labor into the maximum productive capacities of American industry is a problem which must be courageously faced, and it presents new frontiers to be explored and settled by the vigorous movement of American industrial labor. This is not an easy task for the forward looking sections of the labor movement, who daily face the more difficult problem of maintaining living standards and warding off the attacks of those subversive forces who seek to destroy the growing effectiveness of the union movement.

Harmless outbursts, or giving way to emotional righteous indignation against the excrescences of racial discrimination in industry, will not scratch the surface of this problem. There are far too many powerful institutions with an economic stake in inequality and discrimination in industry to make this problem one which can be easily solved by methods other than those obtained through militant organization, with a real understanding of the nature and extent of the problem.

The greatest degree of discrimination against Negro labor flourishes in the industrial backwoods of craft and semi-craft unionism. More than 20 international unions organized on a craft basis exclude Negroes from their organizations through constitutional provisions. Ten of these are affiliated with the American Federation of Labor. The others are independent unions and the operating railroad brotherhoods. These unions which exclude Negroes entirely through constitutional provisions are roughly estimated to have a membership of 1,200,000. At least 9 other unions with an approximate membership of 1 million exclude Negroes through various other means, the ritual oath being one of them. Close to one-third of the craft and semi-craft union membership of the AFL and the entire membership of the standard operating railroad brotherhoods are officially committed either through constitutional provisions or ritualistic oaths to the task of maintaining "white supremacy" in labor by accepting into their ranks only those who are "white, sober and of good moral character."

Even this does not give the whole picture of the extent of craft union exclusion of Negroes within the socially and industrially backward sections of organized American labor. There are close to 30 additional unions which do not use the crude constitutional provision or ritualistic oath, but experience has proved that it is as difficult for Negroes to obtain membership in these organizations as in the ones mentioned above. There are also some organizations which do not practise outright exclusion but permit Negroes to create separate Jim Crow locals or auxiliaries under the control of the nearest white local. To these second-class members little or no voice is given in the operation of the organization and all negotiations and grievances with management in their behalf are conducted by white union officials.

A most vicious aspect of discrimination can be found in certain union-management "conspiracies" to eliminate Negroes from certain skilled well-paying jobs and certain industries. This is quite noticeable in the railroad industry, where Negroes have been methodically eliminated from the skilled and semi-skilled sections of the industry over the past several decades. This is done through agreements controlling seniority and the institution of employment policies of the companies designed specifically to (1) keep Negroes off skilled and higher paid jobs even when their seniority rights (the keystone of railroad employment and advancement), experience and skill entitle them to such advancement and promotion; (2) bar Negro youth as apprentices, even though they meet all qualifications. In the railroad industry, apprenticeship training for skilled jobs is a long established custom.

This technique is reinforced by railroad union-management agreements which serve to "democratize" in appearance this brutal undemocratic method of restricting this right of equality of opportunity. A classic example of the first steps usually taken in the whole process of eliminating Negroes from the skilled and higher paid jobs in the railroad industry can be seen in the recent case of the Negro locomotive firemen of the Florida East Coast Railroad. On this road, the entire force of locomotive firemen were composed of Negroes, as has been the past tradition of Southern railroads. Recently, the company entered into an agreement with one of the brotherhoods which states:

(a) Each engineer on the seniority roster of the Florida East Coast Railway Company, holding a seniority date prior to January 1, 1942, will be accredited with seniority date as fireman as of January 1, 1942, in the same sequence that his name appears on the seniority roster of engineers.

(b) Each engineer employed after January 1, 1942, will be given a seniority date of fireman as of the date he is employed as an engineer. An engineer promoted from the position outside hostler will be given a date as fireman as of the date of such promotion.

(c) Engineers accredited with seniority rights as firemen as of January 1, 1942, will not be permitted to exercise such rights in firing service until all of the colored firemen having seniority rights prior to January 1, 1942, have exercised such rights. Promotable firemen will be used in firing positions until fifty-five per cent (55%) are filled by promotable men.[8]

The substance of this agreement and its underlying subversive implications indicate that it will be used as the "legal" means to retard and possibly to defer permanently the further employment of Negro locomotive firemen. The actual meaning of the word "promotable" is white since Negroes are not eligible to "promotion" to engineers.

In 1940, the Class I railroads employed 1,421,222 persons of whom 127,642 or 9 per cent were Negro workers. Their average annual wage was $708 as against $1,359 for other employees. Approximately 97 per cent of these Negro workers were in the following job classifications: janitors and cleaners, extra gang, section and maintenance-of-way men, laborers and helpers, baggage room and station attendants, cooks, waiters and train attendants. In all the 111 other classifications of employees recognized by the Interstate Commerce Commission, there are only 4,015 Negro workers or 3/10 of 1 per cent out of a total of 1,297,563.[4]

Incidentally, these are the jobs where the greatest shortage of manpower exists and the ones declared essential by the War Manpower Commission. There were an estimated 2,000 Negro firemen in the South accounting for a good part of the 4,015 higher paid skilled and semi-skilled occupations held by Negro railroaders. This indicates that there is no more than one Negro worker for every one thousand white workers in the desirable job classifications.

The 1940 census shows that of the 46,185 railroad conductors, only 43 or less than one in one thousand were Negroes. Of 31,-554 telegraph operators only 35 were Negroes. In many other skilled and semi-skilled categories no Negroes are permitted. Not

[8] Special agreement between the Trustees of the Florida East Coast Railroad and the Brotherhood of Locomotive Engineers effective February 9, 1942.
[4] Railroad Retirement Board, *Compensation and Service Railroad Employees, 1940 Statistical Tables,* December 1941, pp. 1, 149.

only is this discrimination directed against Negroes, but Indians, Mexicans, Chinese, Filipinos and Japanese-Americans, as well.

The process of negotiated elimination and racial discrimination in the railroad industry does not stop here. In many instances federal agencies established under the Railway Labor Act have been molded to conform to this peculiar pattern of restricting the rights of minorities. A notable example can be found in the findings of the Attorney-General in an investigation of the administrative procedure of the National Railroad Adjustment Board. This board is composed of 18 management representatives and 18 railroad labor representatives charged with the responsibility of hearing disputes and grievances arising out of interpretation of agreements and making awards to railroad employees. The report states in part:

> Assertion of Claim: The agreements entered into by the majority unions with the carriers are regarded by the unions as peculiarly theirs, although they not only apply to the employees of the carriers who are members of the union, but the non-members as well. In some four hundred cases since the establishment of the Board, individuals have sought to assert claims before the Board. With the exception of a few isolated cases...no case asserted by an individual has ever been decided on the merits by the Board. The only way that an individual may prevail is by taking his case to the union and causing the union to carry it through to the Board. This means, of course, that...members of minority unions...as well as those who are ineligible to join a union, have no access to the adjudicatory processes of the Adjustment Board....
>
> The serious question with respect to rejection by the Board of claims of individuals arises when individuals who seek to assert their claims are for some reason ineligible to join the only union which could represent them. Such is the case, for example, with respect to some Negroes. In the organizations which do not admit Negroes to membership and which do not represent them effectively in asserting their claims, the system works in such a way as to deny equal privilege....Failure to maintain a semblance of equality between whites and blacks in respect of opportunity to

participate in selection of representatives to serve on the Board and opportunity to have their claims asserted effectively before the Board, opens to question the basic fairness of the system.

The maintenance of this brotherhood-management-government axis both to eliminate and restrict the rights of minority racial groups in the railroad industry converts racial discrimination into a profitable flourishing big business, where craft unionism declares dividends each year to their own compact membership at the expense of the lower paid unskilled Negro and other race minorities.

This briefly summarizes the extent of organized discrimination and exclusion within the craft structure of the American labor movement, and serves as an example of its actual operation in one industry. However, to understand the underlying causes for much of this discrimination and exclusion of Negro workers, we must understand the basic nature of craft unionism as it relates to the historical development of American industry and economy.

The sins and shortcomings of craft unionism extend far beyond the horizon of discrimination against Negroes and other racial minorities. Here again it exists as a by-product of inequity in our economic structure as reflected in the ranks of certain sections of labor, and again only through an effort to bring the Negro question into the general focus of this total problem, rather than isolating the issue, can black labor leadership assume competency and statesmanship in approaching a solution.

The very nature of craft unionism is one which seeks greater job control through limitation of employment opportunities, rather than an expansion of these opportunities which can be found in the practices and purposes of industrial unionism. Facing an uncontrolled expanding industrial economy plus the constant shift of workers from town to the frontier in search of new freedom and land, the early (and even present day) philosophy and goal of craft unionism was the artificial creation of a scarce, highly skilled labor market.

[5] Inquiry of the Attorney-General's Committee on Administrative Procedure Relating to the National Railroad Adjustment Board (1939), p. 90.

In the formulation of these aims and purposes, the philosophy of craft unionism meekly accepted the inherent weaknesses and inequalities found in the economy of scarcity, rather than direct an open, courageous challenge to the growing inequities found in the new industrial order. The emergence of the factory system which quickly revolutionized manufacturing processes made it impossible for the weak craft structure of unions to exert a parallel degree of pressure in behalf of living standards. As a result, these organizations operated mainly as defense weapons against the rising tide of industrial combination and cartelization. Lacking the organizational structure to take the necessary offensive in meeting the problem of working standards, the proponents of craft unionism fell back upon the defense mechanism of creating an "aristocracy of skilled labor." To create this so-called aristocracy, membership exclusion was exercised against the large majority of unskilled workers, whose lack of skill was more or less used to enhance the prestige and to gain higher standards for the tightly organized skilled workers. In addition to the general exclusion of the unskilled, other types of restrictions were employed to maintain the standards of the skilled, such as rigid apprenticeship, high initiation fees and dues, and the placing of Negroes and other non-white racial groups upon the sacrificial altar of craft unionism. In the legislative field efforts were made to restrict immigration, and the passage of the Oriental Exclusion Act was one of the early demands of the craft unionists. (Incidentally, this support of the Oriental Exclusion Act was reaffirmed at the August, 1943, meeting of the Executive Council of the AFL in Chicago.) In this safe role as trusted defenders of the *status quo*, the craft unions settled down to a comfortable life of "business unionism" and hardening of the arteries.

The movement for the elimination of these abuses and inherent weaknesses found in the structure of craft unionism began with the "radical" agitation for industrial unionism in the early 1890's. Frequent studies of the trend toward large scale industrial combinations and methods of mass production gave rise to the theory that labor's real effectiveness in the struggle for improved standards must be obtained by the development of workers' organizations that parallel the new structure of industry. This meant the inclusion of skilled and unskilled, native and foreign born, black and white. The broad implications of this theory meant the uprooting of all social and economic divisions within the ranks of wage-earners for a general offensive to improve and maintain the living standards of all workers. Group inter-dependence became the cornerstone of this theory. Individual prejudices may or may not exist, but they must necessarily be relegated to the background in order to accomplish the task of maintaining common security.

Perhaps the most ardent and uncompromising advocate of this new type of unionism during the early stages of its "theoretical" development was the scholarly Daniel DeLeon, organizer of the Socialist Trade and Labor Alliance and bitter foe of the social climbing "business unionism" of AFL President Samuel Gompers. The oldest and most outstanding examples of the organizational effectiveness of industrial unionism can be found in the United Mine Workers of America and the semi-industrial union, International Ladies' Garment Workers' Union. Both organizations, incidentally, were founders of the Congress of Industrial Organizations, which was organized after many unsuccessful attempts had been made to transform the ineffective craft structure of the American Federation of Labor.

Today the CIO stands as a national bulwark in the struggle to extend the democratic process into every phase of American life. Because of this, Negro labor today is perhaps the most articulate section of the Negro national community and is farther on the road to presenting a positive challenge to their problems as a race than any other section. Today more than 500,000 Negroes are estimated to be members of labor organizations. Ten years ago, Negro membership was less than 80,000. This great increase in organizational activity is due primarily to the extensive campaigns of the CIO in our mass production industries.

On the question of race discrimination, President Philip Murray of the CIO summarized the CIO's position in the following statement:

> Race discrimination is un-American. It is diametrically opposed to the guiding principles of the Congress of Industrial Organizations. It should be resisted immediately

and effectively by our responsible organizations wherever it raises its vile head. Negroes and whites are today fighting side by side, shedding their blood on distant battle fields for the protection of those of us who remain at home. Let us demonstrate our American Democracy and the fraternal spirit of the CIO by extending the Negro workers their full rights in American industry.

The CIO did not stop with fine speeches. It has waged a consistent fight against the poll-tax, and for housing, education and full integration of Negroes into industry. Under the militant leadership of James B. Carey, secretary-treasurer of the CIO, it has established the Committee to Abolish Racial Discrimination which operates as an integral part of CIO machinery. In addition, it has encouraged the development of a hard-hitting type of inter-racial local union leadership, which refuses to budge before the altars of race discrimination.

Today aggressive unionism becomes the major force for the extension of the rights and progress for the Negro race. It is the only segment of our society where Negroes and whites have been able to work together in common purpose. It has also become the political force through which civil rights acts may be enforced in states where they exist and efforts made to break down Jim Crow in states where it has a legal foundation.

THE ROAD TO A SOLUTION

If it is agreed that the basic problems of Negroes (and labor also) within our democracy flow from a general over-all system of economic inequity, it seems logical that attempting to apply cures to surface demonstrations of deep-rooted ills will only increase the irritation without removing the real causes. We must take the same attitude toward these diseases as the doctor toward a patient suffering from a malignant disorder. He does not apply salve to a cancer, but proceeds to diagnose the cause and works from that point to bring the patient back to full recovery.

Our patient is our economic order in this case. The deep rooted disease flows from structural inequity and institutionalized poverty. The "Negro problem" is a case of constant biliousness created by the disease. Aggressive labor contains the natural elements of vitamins A, B and C necessary for complete recovery.

To improve or remove the bilious "Negro problem" we must see it in its proper perspective and proceed to propose both a series of long range shifts in diet and exercise in our economic order and certain immediate hypodermics to remove much of the tension and strain around the Negro problem.

The long range over-all proposals are outlined as follows:

1. Development of an integrated and planned post-war economy in order to convert our vast industrial power for an all-out conquest of domestic poverty, in a practical realization of the Four Freedoms.

(a) An extension of the life of the National Resources Planning Board and the granting of full power to it so that it can make a complete study of our areas of economic wastage.

2. Fundamental shifts in the base of economic control of our national resources and services.

(a) Nationalization of transportation, production of raw materials and finished products, and public utilities with decentralized community controls.

(b) A well defined national agricultural policy designed to improve and maintain the standards of the working farmer and the city consumer, and to eliminate banker absentee control within our agricultural system.

(c) Encouragement of the growth of producers, consumers, credit and marketing co-operatives through a federally financed program of consumer and co-operative education, with bona-fide working farmer organizations and consumer organizations as joint sponsors.

(d) Closing of the economic industrial gap between the South and the rest of the country by removing all discriminatory differentials and moving industry closer to the source of raw materials.

(e) An equitable tax program through an elimination of all

sales taxes and unjust and special privileges. This includes requiring married couples to submit joint returns, taxing present tax-exempt state and local securities, increasing gift and estate taxes, corporate taxes and taxes on middle and high income groups.

3. Extension of government responsibility into the field of health, education and housing.

4. Broadening of our over-all social security program as outlined in some measure by the proposed Wagner-Murray-Dingell Bill, which includes broader coverage, unemployment compensation to members of armed forces, health and hospitalization insurance, disability insurance and maternity insurance for working mothers.

5. Development of permanent price and rent control legislation with strict enforcement.

6. A permanent public works program.

7. An over-all minimum wage and maximum hour law with the inclusion of the present exempt areas of employment. A 50 per cent increase over present minimum wages and 25 per cent decrease under present maximum hours.

8. A permanent National Youth Training Program patterned on the recent National Youth Administration.

9. Rapid extension of the industrial union form of trade union organization.

For immediate relief proposals to aid in improving the special problems of Negroes and maintaining the general welfare of the community include:

1. Passage of anti-poll tax legislation and the elimination of the "white primary" in the South.

2. Establishment of a Fair Employment Practices Board with powers similar to the National Labor Relations Board.

3. An extensive slum clearance and housing program, the lack of which is a major cause for mental attitudes, disease and high mortality rate among Negroes. Old restrictive covenants against racial groups must be eliminated.

4. Improvement and extension of educational and recreational facilities for Negroes.

5. Equalization of pay for teachers in the South and equalizing the per capita rate for Negro and white school children.

6. Creation of an experimental division within the army to test the validity of the idea that Negroes and whites will not work and fight together.

7. The appointment of a Negro as a Vice-Chairman of the War Manpower Commission with equal supervisory powers and one as Assistant Secretary of Labor. Full attention should be given to the full integration of Negroes into industry.

8. Dropping all discriminatory bars within federal employment.

9. An educational program within every Negro organization designed to improve community responsibility among Negroes. Equal rights demand equal responsibilities as citizens. Such a program should come through a co-ordination of efforts of all Negro organizations.

Another point that requires a great deal of sober consideration today and possibly during the post-war period is the question of racial strife and riots. Every metropolitan community and the nation as a whole should recognize the heavy strain each racial outbreak places upon the democratic ideal and a moral devaluation of our war aims.

The widespread development of these racial outbreaks indicates the widespread efforts that should be made to eliminate many of the immediate causes. It should be made clear that their causes are not found in any widespread agitation emanating from our enemies abroad and fifth column activity, but in too many instances from old ills mingled with the new tenseness of war and change. To pursue a course of organized action in order to head off further developments of these shameful outbreaks, each metropolitan industrial community should seriously consider the creation of responsible inter-racial commissions to function as a part of city government. This should be done in connection with the various Post-War Planning Commissions being established by many city governments. Such commissions should have their own budget and staff. The following outline should be a general guide for the work of the committee:

I. IMMEDIATE PROBLEM

The most immediate problem of the Committee on Racial (or Inter-racial) Relations, is to investigate existing conditions that might lead to race violence, and to study the situation and circumstances in which violence has already occurred. Some of these situations are well known, and material concerning them can be obtained from police officials, daily newspapers, social agencies and other similar sources.

Immediate steps should be taken in the following direction:

A. The Police Department

Interviews should be held with the commissioner of police, the chief of police, detectives and other police department personnel, to determine answers to the following questions:

1. What actual steps have been taken to insure better handling of inter-racial conflicts?

2. What are the tension areas in the city in which the police should concentrate their efforts in the event that racial friction developed?

3. Are there enough police to cover these areas and still have a pool of reserves at strategic points?

4. Have such vital points as the beaches and transportation transfer points in both predominantly Negro and white neighborhoods been taken into consideration?

B. Transportation Facilities

Similarly the heads of the transportation facilities companies should be interviewed to determine:

1. What types of friction have been reported on the surface lines, elevated lines and buses?

2. What steps, if any, have been taken to ease the friction?

3. What plans, if any, have been formulated to deal with outbreaks of racial friction on transportation facilities, if these occur?

C. The Mayor

The Mayor should be interviewed concerning the following questions:

1. What over-all plans have been drawn up to deal with outbreaks of racial friction in the city?

2. Under what conditions would the Mayor request assistance from the state police, the state militia and/or federal troops?

3. Are the mechanisms for requesting such assistance known to the proper city officials?

In addition it would seem advisable for the Committee to have its own personnel check certain troublesome areas to see how tense the situation is at present, and to observe the manner in which the police and transportation system personnel are handling the problem.

II. An Educational Program

A. Channels for a General Educational Program

1. The Office of Civilian Defense: There exists at present a mechanism which might well be utilized as a channel for education in the direction of securing better race relations. The Office of Civilian Defense was set up to deal with all problems on the home front that might negatively affect the war effort. Certainly racial friction is such a problem—and of the gravest import. Since the Mayor is the head of the OCD organization in many communities, he occupies an especially favorable position from which to direct the energies of the OCD toward improving race relations and averting race conflicts.

A first step in the utilization of the OCD for this purpose would be a meeting of block captains, to be addressed by the Mayor. The Mayor could explain to this group the importance of the problem in terms of war production, morale, and the achieving on the home front of the aims for which the armed forces fight abroad. Discussion from the floor could follow. It could be suggested to the block captains that they call block meetings to discuss the problem in each block. Where conditions warrant, local block committees could be set up to report trouble, and to discuss methods of alleviating friction wherever it was observed to occur.

A city-wide committee on inter-racial relations should be set up within the local office of Civilian Defense, to supervise this program.

2. Churches: The Mayor should request the Federal Council of Churches of Christ, Jewish Congregations and inter-denominational Protestants' organizations to appoint a committee from among their members to supervise the setting up of a religious education program on inter-racial relations, and request ministers of member churches to preach sermons on the problem. Sunday School discussion, particularly among the teen-age group, should be encouraged.

Similarly, the Archbishop of the Roman Catholic Church should be requested to send out a pastoral letter on this problem to be read from the pulpits of all churches.

3. Schools: Race relations could well be made a frequent item on the agenda of school assembly programs, in all of the public schools. (The same of course applies to parochial schools.) Probably a Committee on Curriculum of public schools should be asked to devote special attention to the problems of ways of integrating materials on race relations into the school program.

An especial effort should be made to make the consideration of the inter-racial problem an integral part of the curriculum at the high school level. In every racial disturbance (note particularly in this connection the recent Detroit riot) the teen-age group has played a highly conspicuous role in the disorders.

The Teachers Union should be asked to attempt to arouse consciousness among teachers of the significance of the problem.

4. Labor Unions: A Labor Committee composed of members of both AFL and CIO unions should be set up to formulate a program for incorporating material on race relations into the educational programs of the unions. AFL unions should be urged to participate especially, since in the past they have indulged in much discrimination toward Negroes.

B. Educating the Police

In all civic disorders, the behavior of the police is of paramount importance. Negroes feel—and there is much evidence to corroborate the correctness of this feeling—that they are mistreated by the police.

The Commissioner of Police should call together all members of the police force and read to them the Civil Rights Bill, if the state has one. There is reason to believe that many individual members of the police force are unaware of its existence. This could be followed by a general statement to the effect that it is the duty of the police to treat Negroes exactly as they treat all other citizens. In connection with the specific problems of averting riots, the pride of the force could be appealed to: "We will not let happen in our city what happened in Detroit. Our city is not that kind of a city. The police, as the custodians of law and order, can largely control the situation."

The Archbishop of the Catholic Church might be requested to attempt a special educational program for the Society of St. Jude—the Catholic fraternal police order. Educational materials on the problem of race relations and the duty of the police could be distributed in society meetings, and on the annual retreats.

C. Merchants and Sales People

Merchants associations, theatre owners and public institutions should be interviewed, having in mind the relieving of tensions developed by discourteous clerks and employees. Where clerks deliberately evade serving Negro patrons and deny them the common courtesies usually extended patrons, the belief is fostered that sooner or later flares will be precipitated.

D. The Press and Radio

Newspapers, books, magazines, and the radio are effective agencies to reach public opinion. They reflect human interests and community behavior. By clever manipulation of facts and interpretation they may emphasize some set of attitudes and inhibit or negate others. In recognizing this influence, frank discussions with publishers, editors, newspaper men and radio companies concerning the treatment of news are necessary. Uniform policy of fair and impartial purveyance of news affecting all groups must be requested.

III. LONG RANGE PROGRAM

Any long range program for removing the causes of racial friction must deal with the fundamental causes of unrest among Negroes—the disadvantages and disabilities to which they as a group are subjected. Most important among these are job opportunities, adequate housing, equal and adequate school facilities and equal and adequate health facilities. Any action which alleviates these now unfavorable conditions lessens racial tension—and the race problem will not be solved until these conditions are corrected.

To accomplish the proposals suggested here requires organization: organization both from a quantitative and a qualitative point of view. Since pressure appears to be the essence of our democracy, intelligent organization and understanding becomes the key for an adequate solution to all group and national problems.

It appears that the areas with mutual social and economic problems have a natural identity of interests and as such should draw closer together organizationally for mutual benefit. This suggests the dire necessity for a national clearing house for combining the political pressures of all liberal, labor, Negro, and religious elements in a united drive to insure the institution of a broad program of economic rehabilitation. International post-war conditions will necessarily influence any domestic economic problem. Therefore it becomes doubly important that the influence of this new combined pressure be felt in the making of the peace and international post-war organization.

This new alignment of forces must re-affirm its beliefs in the righteousness of justice, equality and human decency for all men against the degradation of organized poverty, hypocrisy and spiritual bankruptcy. It should lend all efforts to the eradication of these social and economic diseases, and exhort those who live after them to be satisfied with nothing less than the full dignity and honor of free men.

FREEDOM—
THROUGH VICTORY IN WAR
AND PEACE

By DOXEY A. WILKERSON

———————

THE NEGRO WANTS to be free. He wants freedom from every form of discrimination on account of race or color. He wants complete economic, political and social equality—in short, full democratic rights.

The Negro has always wanted—and fought for—his freedom. The past three centuries of Negro life in America record the unceasing struggles of the Negro people toward freedom. At times they have moved rapidly toward that goal, at times slowly or not at all, and at times they have been pushed backward toward greater subjection. But always the Negro people have struggled, and their goal has remained the same—complete freedom.

Now, in this period of unprecedented social and political change, the Negro people are struggling ever more vigorously for their freedom. They are fighting with the renewed confidence which this great liberating war has brought to the millions of "little people" the world over. They are fighting with the help of new and powerful allies which the national peril has brought to their side. They now move more rapidly toward freedom than at any time during the past seventy years. And they shall attain their goal of full democratic rights—far sooner than many people think.

There can be no doubt as to "What the Negro Wants." The crucial question now is: *How attain it?* How, during this period, can the progress of the Negro people toward freedom be most effectively advanced? This is the question to which the remainder of this discussion is addressed.

THE NEGRO AND THE NATION

The success of the Negro's struggles toward freedom has always been influenced decisively by the dominant economic and political trends in the nation as a whole. It is well to recall this historical relationship, for it holds the key to correct strategy and tactics in the continuing struggles of today.

During the 17th and 18th centuries, it was the increasing demand for more and more unpaid labor for the expanding cotton plantations of the South that led to the tearing of millions of African natives from their homelands and their enslavement on American soil. Similarly, it was the declining value of cotton production and the upsurge of democratic fervor during the American Revolution—in which Negro patriots fought gloriously —that led to the weakening of the slave system during the late 18th century. Oppressive restrictions on the slaves tended to be relaxed, the system itself seemed on the way out, and there ensued a period which Dr. Carter G. Woodson calls "the hey-day of victory for the ante-bellum Negro."

Following invention of the cotton gin and other technological developments, it was the tremendously rapid expansion of the now more profitable plantation system that led to the striking revival of the illegal slave trade during the first half of the 19th century. Earlier tendencies toward a paternalistic slavery gave way to an increasingly harsh and institutionalized system for the oppression of the then more enlightened, and hence more rebellious, slaves.

The 1860's witnessed a life-and-death struggle between the oppressive slave economy of the plantation South and the emerging and progressive capitalist economy of the industrial North. Both were forced by inner compulsions to expand. Inevitably they collided, giving rise to a struggle which was destined to decide the fate of American democracy—and hence, the status of the Negro people—for generations to come.

The North entered the Civil War with no intention to free

the slaves. "Save the Union" was the slogan behind which it sought to rally the people for struggle. But after a year and a half of vacillation and defeat, the democratic Union forces, led by Lincoln, were compelled to free and arm the slaves in order to save the nation. What had begun as a war with limited democratic goals was transformed through historic necessity into a truly revolutionary war of liberation.

Only then did the Union forces triumph, and they sought to consolidate their victory through the further extension of democracy in the South. The freedmen were made citizens and enfranchised. Democratic people's governments—representing coalitions of poor whites, Negroes, and abolitionists from the North—began to emerge in the Southern states. There was the prospect for the vigorous growth of democracy in the South.

Then came the fateful days of 1876-77, when the Republican party of the Northern bourgeoisie deserted the Negro people and betrayed the democratic revolution which the forces around Lincoln had won. The former Confederate slave-masters were restored to power. Ku Klux Klan terror and "white supremacy" propaganda were used to separate the Negroes and their allies. As a result, the forward march of democracy in the South was checked and reversed. An era of semi-feudalism took its place.

In the long, oppressive decades which followed the withdrawal of federal troops from the South in 1877, reaction again became thoroughly entrenched in power. The Negro people were disfranchised, intimidated, and forced back into a caste-like status which was but little different from that of slavery. The masses of poor whites, likewise, were deprived of their lands, disfranchised, and removed from effective participation in government. The new democratic people's governments were destroyed. The new state systems of free public schools promptly declined.

Moreover, democracy in our nation as a whole suffered directly from this triumph of reaction in the South. For example, our national Congress became saddled with a long succession of southern reactionaries whose political crimes against the American people are buttressed and made possible by the poll tax disfranchisement laws of the late 19th century period.

From even this brief, incomplete summary, the relevant historical lesson should be clear: In unity with powerful allies and aided by progressive economic and political trends, the Negro people have moved forward to greater freedom, and democracy for the nation as a whole has been advanced. However, when separated from their allies and confronted with reactionary economic and political trends, the Negro people have been defeated in their struggles toward freedom, and democracy for the nation as a whole has been severely retarded. *This is a fundamental lesson of history which Negro and all other progressive Americans must now come more fully to understand.*

The 1940's witness another sharpening conflict between powerful forces of reaction and progress, the outcome of which will decide the fate of democracy in our country and the world for generations to come. In this struggle, as during the 1860's, the freedom goal of the Negro people is again inseparably bound up with the survival goal of the nation as a whole. The attainment of both depends fundamentally upon victory over the fascist enemies of our nation and the organization of a just and durable peace.

It follows that effective struggles for Negro freedom today must be undertaken within the framework of the nation's struggle for survival. The crucial issue of this discussion, *how to attain* "*What the Negro Wants*," must be resolved, therefore, in terms of the Negro's relations to the larger struggles which now confront our nation and the world.

NEGRO FREEDOM REQUIRES VICTORY FOR THE NATION

During the early stages of our country's war with the Axis, there were widespread doubts among the Negro people as to what this conflict could possibly mean to them. These doubts were commonly expressed in such terms as: "Why fight fascism in Germany when we have fascism right here in America?"; or, "This is a white man's war in which the Negro has no stakes"; or, "It's good to see those little brown Japanese giving the whites the good beating they deserve." These were understandable emotional reactions of many Negroes who had grown bitter over continued denials of freedom in a nation they had given so much to build and defend. But the fallacies inherent in such expressions have now become apparent to most people.

It is now generally clear that the oppression suffered by Negro Americans, thoroughly unjust though it is, still represents something far removed from fascism. There is a fundamental qualitative difference between a government which deliberately proclaims the inherent inferiority of minority racial groups and uses the full power of the State to starve, murder and enslave them as a matter of "principle"; and a government whose theoretical foundations are democratic, which moves far too slowly—and at times not at all—to assure avowed democratic rights for its racial minorities, but which still provides the legal framework in which oppressed racial groups can struggle toward freedom—and win. It is the difference between hopeless slavery or extermination, on the one hand, and substantial opportunity progressively to enlarge the area of freedom, on the other.

It is now generally clear too that the welfare of the Negro in this war is inextricably bound up with that of the nation as a whole. The Negro is in this conflict, whether he willed it or not. Far from being a "white man's war" upon which the Negro people might look with detached neutrality, it is a mortal struggle in which the lives and destinies of both white and black are inseparably linked.

It is now generally clear also that color affords no bond of kinship between the Japanese war-lords and the Negro people. In China, the Philippines, and elsewhere, it has been well demonstrated that the fascist rulers of Japan are quite as brutal and thorough in their oppression of "colored peoples" as are their "master race" colleagues in Germany.

In short, the Negro people now know that an Axis victory would blast all hope for their freedom. It would subject our entire nation to the bestial policies of fascist oppression; and of all Americans, the Negro people would suffer most. Extermination would be their probable lot—or, at "best," a slavery more brutal and degrading than their forefathers ever knew.

Although the threat of an Axis victory to Negro freedom is now clear, there is far from adequate appreciation of the more imminent threat of a long, drawn-out war, ending in a "negotiated peace." There is now little likelihood of an Axis military victory. The more probable alternatives are an early and decisive victory for the United Nations, accompanied by unconditional surrender of the Axis and the complete destruction of fascist governments; or a prolonged war, leading to a military stalemate, and finally ending through the signing of peace treaties by the belligerent governments. Which of these alternatives is consistent with the freedom goal of the Negro people?

There is a curious notion, widely accepted in the Negro community, that the freedom of the Negro people would be furthered by prolonged extension of the war. It is frequently expressed in connection with some wartime improvement—or set-back—in the Negro's social-economic conditions, and is reflected by such statements as: "Lord, don't let this war end too soon." It rests upon the naïve assumption that since the war is now advancing the cause of Negro freedom, then more and more war should bring more and more freedom to the Negro people. There is a deceptive and dangerous fallacy in this argument which must be thoroughly exposed if wartime struggles for Negro democratic rights are to achieve maximum results.

It is Hitler and Tojo and their helpers in our country—and they alone—who would profit from a long, drawn-out war. Moreover, if their program were to prevail, the prospect for Negro freedom would be completely destroyed.

Just as there was a reactionary group of northern "Copperheads" who conspired to defeat the Union cause during the Civil War, so there is now a powerful clique of American defeatists and imperialists who are doing everything in their power to disrupt the war effort of our nation. They want to save Hitler and his fascist regime from defeat and destruction; and their basic strategy is to prolong the war.

Let none be misled into thinking that this "long-war" clique has any interest in advancing Negro freedom. Rather, they are the deadliest enemies of the Negro and all other freedom-loving peoples. Their goal is nothing less than a dominant and aggressive

American imperialism in the post-war world, supported by a domestic fascism here at home.

The tactics of this imperialist clique become more apparent every day. They employ every trick of demagogy to sabotage the win-the-war program of our Commander-in-Chief. They strive to create antagonisms within the Anglo-Soviet-American coalition, and to prolong the war by delaying the opening of the Second Front. They seek to substitute a "negotiated peace" for the Allied policy of "unconditional surrender." They hope to preserve fascist governments in Germany and the rest of Europe as a bulwark against the democratic upsurge of liberated peoples. They expect, thus, to establish the most favorable conditions for the rise of a fascist-imperialist regime in America.

This pro-fascist, imperialist clique consists of the most re-actionary sections of American monopoly capital. Its chief political spokesman is Herbert Hoover. Its *main* concentration is in the Republican Party, although it has powerful adherents in both major parties. Its main propaganda channel is the Hearst-McCormick-Patterson newspaper axis. Its immediate objective is to seize control of our government in 1944.

Should this defeatist cabal win in the 1944 elections, their ultimate plans for our nation would immediately become clear to all. They would try to lead our nation along the path which Hitler tried for Germany: conquest of foreign markets through military aggression abroad. But first, in order to keep the people from upsetting their plans, they would try to establish oppressive, fascist controls over our country.

This is why these Hoover-Republican appeasers and defeatists are doing everything in their power to disrupt the war effort and delay victory. This is why they attempt even to disfranchise our fighting men in the Army as a means toward winning the 1944 elections. They fear a quick and decisive Allied victory, for they know it would blast their dream of a fascist America moving toward the imperialist domination of the world. They want a long, drawn-out war, for they know this would give Hitler time to rally and make a successful bid for a "negotiated peace," thus leaving fascist regimes virtually intact in Europe and strengthening the forces of reaction in America and throughout the world.

These fascist-imperialist advocates of a long, drawn-out war are the common enemies of the Negro people and the nation. If they were to succeed in carrying through their program of reaction, the Negro's wartime gains would be engulfed and destroyed in the on-rush of American fascism, and the people as a whole would lose their liberty.

Quite apart from the dire political threat of this "long war" program to the freedom of the Negro and the nation, just think of the human suffering which prolongation of this war would bring. It would mean many more years of murder and slaughter of additional millions of men, women and children throughout the world. It would mean the further destruction of homes and factories and villages and cities. It would mean years longer before our sons and fathers and sweethearts in the armed forces could return home—and many more of them would never return.

This is the conspiracy into which any general acceptance of "long-war" propaganda would lead the Negro people. Nothing would more surely defeat the Negro's wartime struggles toward freedom.

The future of Negro freedom depends upon the triumph of the democratic win-the-war forces which are rallying in support of our Commander-in-Chief, and the defeat of the imperialist-appeaser bloc which now struggles for political supremacy. A long war would enhance the danger of a "negotiated peace" with fascism; it would enormously strengthen the reactionary enemies of the Negro people. An early victory would assure the unconditional surrender of the Axis and the destruction of fascist governments; it would tremendously strengthen the democratic labor and progressive forces who are the most effective allies of the Negro people.

It should be clear that the developing struggle for the unity of all progressive, win-the-war forces in America—in support of the Anglo-Soviet-American coalition for the quickest possible destruction of our Axis enemies—is fundamentally a struggle which the Negro and all other freedom-loving peoples must support. Along the path of victory for our nation and our allies, and along this path alone, can successful struggles for Negro freedom now proceed.

VICTORY FOR THE NATION REQUIRES
GREATER NEGRO FREEDOM

The implications of this war for the freedom of the Negro people do not arise solely from the negative threat of an Axis victory or a negotiated peace. Even more fundamental are the positive liberating tendencies which emerge from the progressive nature of the conflict. The democratic forces which this people's war has set into motion and continues to strengthen warrant full confidence in the further extension of Negro democratic rights.

This perspective of continued progress toward Negro freedom is rejected by many persons in our national life. Typical are the apparently divergent viewpoints of certain discouraged liberals and militant reactionaries. The thinking of both proceeds from a common defeatist error.

On the one hand, there are those Negroes and liberal white friends of the Negro who are so overwhelmed by the still existing crust of racial prejudice that they have lost all perspective, and with it all hope for a democratic America. They point with despair at the thousand and one anti-Negro discriminations in civil and military life. Despondently, they inquire: "If they treat Negroes this way in the very midst of the war, what hope is there for a progressive future?"

On the other hand, there are those die-hard reactionaries who loudly proclaim their everlasting allegiance to the principle of "white supremacy." They fight against every move to extend the boundaries of Negro freedom, and even jeopardize the wartime interests of the nation in their zeal to maintain the racial *status quo*. They are determined to "keep the Negro in his place."

The basic error of these two points of view, and the thing which unites them in a common defeatist outlook regarding Negro freedom, is their static approach to the social problems of this day. Both the despondent liberal and the militant reactionary fail to grasp what is really the most significant fact in the whole picture: our social pattern is not fixed and static, but is in process of flux. It is changing—*changing rapidly*. The nation's imperative requirements of victory in this war are subjecting the traditional fetters of the Negro people to terrific strain. One by one, the old bonds are breaking. A new and freer pattern of society is definitely in process of formation.

Negroes of little hope—and die-hard reactionaries too, for that matter—would do well to emulate the consistently dynamic approach of Frederick Douglass to the problem of Negro freedom in his day. He was quick to probe beneath the prevailing, but decaying, crust of reaction, and to seize upon the new and emerging forces of progress which he helped to nurture until they became dominant.

Douglass was under no illusions about the motives of the dominant forces in conflict at the start of the Civil War. He remarked that the war began "in the interests of slavery on both sides. The South was fighting to take slavery out of the Union, and the North fighting to keep it in the Union; the South fighting to get it beyond the limits of the United States Constitution, and the North fighting for the old guarantees;—both despising the Negro, both insulting the Negro."

Throughout the early stages of the war, when the Union forces suffered defeat after defeat from the Confederate armies, Douglass repeatedly urged Lincoln to free and arm the slaves. In his speeches he pointed out that the Union's cause would be victorious only when it took on an anti-slavery character, when it mobilized the Negro people on its side. Although his faith was often sorely tried, he continued to insist that the historic "mission of the war was the liberation of the slave."

When finally Lincoln did issue the Emancipation Proclamation, with its limited liberation of the slaves of the Confederate states, as a military necessity only, Douglass quickly realized that the imperatives of that developing situation would necessarily lead to the complete freeing of his people. He said: "I took the proclamation, first and last, for a little more than it purported, and saw in its spirit a life and power far beyond its letter. Its meaning to me was the entire abolition of slavery."

Even in the midst of the whirl of events of that period, Douglass correctly foresaw, *and struggled to achieve,* the transformation of the Civil War into an all-out abolition war for the freedom of his people. It was the new and developing forces of history, not those in process of decline, to which Douglass applied his energies. Herein lay a major source of his strength.

So, likewise, in his appeals to Negro men to take up arms in support of the Union cause, Frederick Douglass constantly emphasized the *changing* character of the War and the necessity for *struggle* to hasten this process of change. Thus, in his stirring appeal to the Negro people of New York, "Men of Color—to Arms!" just two months after the Emancipation Proclamation, Douglass' attention was focused, not alone on the existing state of affairs, but even more upon what it was in process of becoming. He declared:

> With every reverse to the national arms, with every exulting shout of victory raised by the slaveholding rebels, I have implored the imperiled nation to unchain against her foes her powerful black hand. Slowly and reluctantly that appeal is beginning to be heeded. Stop not now to complain that it was not heeded sooner... This is not the time to discuss that question.... Action! action! not criticism, is the plain duty of this hour. Words are now useful only as they stimulate to blows. The office of speech now is only to point out when, where, and how to strike to the best advantage.
> There is no time to delay. The tide is at its flood that leads on to fortune.... the sky is written all over, "NOW OR NEVER." .... "Who would be free themselves must strike the blow."

In a similar address to the Negro people of Philadelphia in July, 1863, Douglass hammered away, again and again, at the changed and still changing relations of the Negro people to the nation as a whole.

> Now, what is the attitude of the Washington government toward the colored race? What reasons have we to desire its triumph in the present contest? Mind, I do not ask what was its attitude before this bloody rebellion broke out.... I do not even ask what it was two years ago, when McClellan shamelessly gave out that in a war between loyal slaves and disloyal masters, he would take the side of the masters against the slaves.... These were all dark and terrible days for the republic. I do not ask you about the dead past. I bring you

the living present. *Events more mighty than men, eternal Providence, all-wise and all-controlling, have placed us in new relations to the government and the government to us.*

It is revealing to continue this quotation from Douglass' Philadelphia address, and to paraphrase in terms of the events of the present day.

"What that government is to us today, and what it will be tomorrow, is made evident by a very few facts. Look at them, colored men." Hundreds of thousands of Negro men and women are now perfecting skills and earning good wages in industrial employment from which they have traditionally been barred. Many thousands more find new expression for their talents in federal jobs where no black face has ever been seen before.

For the first time in the history of our country, a special agency of the federal government—the Committee on Fair Employment Practices—has been created for the purpose of blasting all remaining racial bars to the full employment of our people. Despite continued attacks from reaction, the President continues to fight for FEPC and to see it through each succeeding crisis. Also for the first time in history, another agency of our government—the War Labor Board—has handed down the unprecedented decision that the wages of white and Negro workers shall be equal.

One by one, the Jim Crow cafeterias in federal buildings in the nation's capital are being eliminated, and the few that remain are sure to go. The Presidents of the Republics of Liberia and of Haiti, black men, are greeted with all the ceremony and respect that the White House can command.

The Supreme Court of the United States completely reverses its position of a decade ago and hands down the historic decision that black men must be allowed to cast their ballots in the heretofore "white primaries" of the southern states. Despite the mediocrity which sits in the office of the Attorney General, the Department of Justice now moves, where it has heretofore refused, to wipe out the dual curse of peonage and lynching. Have no fear, the Attorney General will yet move to protect the rights of our people to vote in the states of the South.

In the armed forces of our nation, Negro men are fighting for their liberty in every branch of the service. A black man holds the post of Brigadier-General. Black men and white—in the good state of Georgia, mind you—pursue *together* their studies for officer's training on a basis of complete equality. Negro heroes are driving tanks and manning the great guns which spell disaster for our enemies. Negro pursuit flyers are giving a brilliant performance in the air, and other black men are now being trained as bombardiers. The Army's laggard Judge Advocate has relaxed, at long last, the traditional bars against Negro lawyers. In the United States Merchant Marine, white and Negro crews sail their Liberty Ships through submarine-infested seas under the command of Negro captains. Even though with reluctance and ill-grace, the Secretary of Navy has been forced not only to admit black men into the ranks of fighting seamen, but also to train them as officers.

Steps are taken toward the entrance of Negro players into organized baseball. A Negro journalist is appointed for the first time to the post of White House Correspondent. Twenty national Negro organizations unite in a manifesto declaring their support of the war and the independence of Negro voters as a political force in the nation. A Negro Communist is elected to the Council of the City of New York.

More than this, our people are finding new friends and allies in their wartime struggles for greater freedom. A Vice President of the United States insists, on one occasion: "There can be no privileged peoples"; and on another occasion calls for abolition of the poll-tax fetters upon our franchise, declaring: "Every citizen of the United States, without regard to color or creed...is entitled to cast his vote." An Under-Secretary of State proclaims: "Our victory must bring in its train the liberation of all peoples." An Eleanor Roosevelt, a Pearl Buck, a Wendell Willkie, and many others boldly throw their influence toward the further liberation of our people. The Atlanta Conference of Southern white liberals extends the hand of friendship and collaboration to the Durham Conference of Southern Negro leaders. The editor of an influential Richmond, Virginia, daily newspaper calls for the abolition of Jim Crow seating arrangements on street cars and buses—and gets an overwhelmingly favorable response from the public.

In the trade unions of our nations, especially in the great, democratic, industrial unions of the CIO, new bonds of comradeship are being forged between black workers and white. The power of organized labor is being thrown ever more frequently and effectively toward extending the democratic rights of the Negro people.

Negro Americans: These are but part of the changes now taking place in the relations of our people to our country. "The revolution is tremendous, and it becomes us as wise men to recognize the change and to shape our action accordingly."

Thus would Frederick Douglass address the Negro people of wartime America in 1944. He would see, not a static society of fixed racial discriminations and injustices, but a tremendously dynamic society in process of flux. He would see our nation, impelled by the necessities of a war it has simply got to win, moving more and more to extend the boundaries of freedom for the Negro people. He would look to the future with confidence.

It is important to emphasize that the Negro's wartime strides toward freedom are made possible by the inherently progressive nature of the conflict in which we are engaged. Henry Wallace says that it is continuation of the 150-year-old "People's Revolution," that it issues in the "Century of the Common Man."[1] Sumner Welles characterizes it as "A People's War."[2] Wendell Willkie calls it "A War of Liberation."[3] Earl Browder says it is "A People's War for National Liberation."[4]

These are not mere expressions of the ideals and hopes of "good men," but rather the realistic descriptions and interpretations of competent observers of world politics. The basic ideas they all seem to hold in common can be summarized in a few simple propositions: (1) Whatever may have been its origins,

[1] Address before the Free World Association, New York City, May 8, 1942.
[2] Memorial Day Address, May 30, 1942.
[3] *One World,* (New York, 1943).
[4] *Victory and After* (New York, 1942), Chapter 1.

this war has taken on the character of a life and death struggle for liberation on the part of nations now suffering the brutalities of Axis enslavement, and for survival on the part of other nations threatened with a similar fate. (2) It is not merely a war between opposing armies, but a war in which whole peoples are actively involved. (3) Because of the character of the forces in combat and the tremendous stakes at issue, this war has profoundly stirred the deep-seated, freedom-loving sentiments of the peoples of the earth, and has set them into motion. In the words of Vice President Wallace in his memorable "Free World Victory" address, "The people's revolution is on the march, and the devil and all his angels cannot prevail against it."

No undue significance is here ascribed to the wartime proclamations of statesmen as such. Their prophecies of a freer world to come are not important primarily because *they* make them. Rather, their importance arises from the fact that the liberating *policies* to which they give expression are *"dictated by the necessities of war, that they are necessary preconditions for Victory, for national survival."* [5] A few illustrations should suffice to make this premise clear.

China, the traditional prey of imperialist powers the world over, now sits as an equal on the Pacific War Council. There is every reason for confidence that her change of status among the nations of the world is permanent. It came about not through the benevolence of her allies, but because a strong, fighting, and united China is a basic requirement for their own survival in this death-struggle with the Axis foe. For precisely the same reason, the immediate post-war independence of the Philippines is now assured, and the liberation of Puerto Rico will yet be the order of the day.

The bitter lessons of the Malayan Peninsula and of Burma were not completely in vain. Even though slowly, the Allies are being forced to realize that, in this war, colonial peoples are more than pawns to be fought over; that the active support of the colonial masses is an indispensable requirement of victory. In Southeast Asia, in India, even in Africa, the liberating influence of this hard fact will yet find concrete expression.

[5] Browder, *op. cit.*

So it is with the Negro's wartime march toward freedom. In the course of this inherently progressive people's war, the further extension of democracy for the Negro has become an imperative necessity for national survival. Not only has our country been forced increasingly to integrate the Negro people into war production and the armed services in order to combat the military forces of fascism abroad; it has also been forced progressively to draw the Negro people into the democratic camp of national unity in order to combat the political forces of fascism here at home.

During the 1940's, as during the 1860's, the struggles of the Negro people for freedom and the struggles of the nation for survival have become inseparably merged. *Both must now move forward together.*

Let those Negroes of faint heart look about them, cast aside their unwarranted discouragement, and enter with full vigor and confidence into the common struggle for the survival of our nation and the liberation of the Negro people. The world is changing—changing progressively before their very eyes.

Let those modern Joshuas who now vainly command the sun of racial equality to cease rising likewise look about them. Their day in history is rapidly passing. Their out-moded edifice of "white supremacy" is crumbling before their very eyes. It will be swept away in the on-rush of mankind toward freedom.

This *is* a people's war of national liberation and survival—not purely, but *predominantly* and *decisively* so. Moreover, the liberating forces it has unleashed gather momentum every day. Despite the wishes and frantic struggles of reaction, a new society is being forged in the process of our nation's struggle for victory. As that struggle proceeds, the Negro people will continue to move forward toward their historic goal of freedom. This will happen, not merely because it *ought*, but primarily because it *must*. It is an essential requirement of victory for the nation.

THE NEGRO PEOPLE IN THE NATIONAL
FRONT FOR VICTORY

To assert that the progressive nature of this war "requires" the further extension of Negro freedom is not to minimize the importance of continued struggle. The changes now in process are not automatic, nor will they be in the future. The inherent liberating character of the war will not "solve" the problems of the Negro or of the nation as a whole; it but creates highly favorable conditions for the achievement of progressive solutions. Their realization will come only through deliberate and persistent struggle.

Quite the opposite point of view is advanced by important circles in our country. Curiously enough, it is embraced by both the Martin Dies type of reactionary and the John Temple Graves type of Southern liberal. Both find common ground in the proposition that, "for the sake of national unity," there must be a wartime moratorium on agitation for Negro democratic rights.

One of the clearest and most forthright answers to this specious argument is that given by the General Secretary of the Communist party:

There is another field of problems in which national unity demands a much more strict interpretation of equality. Typical...is the problem of our thirteen million Negro citizens. Here it would be disastrously destructive of national unity to try to make our peace with the status quo, which is a status of a shameful heritage from chattel slavery based on Hitler-like racial conceptions; and it would further undermine the United Nations, destroy confidence between the United States on the one side, and our allies and potential allies of the colored races on the other. We dare not, on pain of humiliating defeat in this war, rest complacently on the present status of the Negro citizens of the United States. *We must, as a war necessity, proceed to the systematic and relentless wiping out of every law, custom, and habit of thought, which in flagrant violation of our Constitution enforce an unequal status between Negro and white citizens of the United States.*[6]

[6] Browder, *op. cit.*, pp. 90-91. (Italics not in the original.)

Whoever now attempts to differentiate between the victory-goal of the nation and the freedom-goal of the Negro, setting one against the other, either fails to grasp or deliberately ignores the fundamental unity of the two. The nation's struggles toward victory now necessarily advance the cause of Negro freedom, and the Negro's struggles toward freedom likewise advance the cause of victory for the nation as a whole.

This wartime mutuality between the wartime interests of the Negro people and the rest of the nation serves to emphasize the necessity for ever more vigorous struggles for Negro democratic rights. It does more. It also suggests the direction and form which such struggles must assume if maximum results are to be achieved.

There are some Negro leaders who now propose to "bargain" with their embattled country, offering Negro support of the war "in return for" the correction of existing injustices. Their approach is fundamentally unsound in principle and stupid as a tactic of minority group struggle.

This is not a war which the Negro *may* support—if; rather, it is a war which the Negro *must* support—regardless. The lives and property of the Negro people, too, are at stake in this war. Moreover, all the social gains the Negro has made since slavery, and all he may hope to achieve in the future, are utterly dependent upon victory over the Axis forces of fascist enslavement. Nothing could more surely alienate the Negro people from the very progressive forces whom they must win as allies, nothing could more surely defeat their present and future goals of freedom, than for the Negro now to stand aloof from the developing national front for victory—petulant, impotent, and absurd. The Negro's support of this war is, and must be, unconditional. On no other basis can he now find solution for his problems.

There are also Negro leaders whose main stock in trade now is to denounce "the Government" and "white people" for still existing racial injustices, and to organize mass struggles of the Negro people, *as Negroes*, against both. They too are following a path which weakens the victory program of the nation and leads to the ultimate defeat of their adherents.

In the first place, the Roosevelt Administration has given convincing evidence of its sincere desire to advance the cause of

Negro freedom. Indeed, it has fought hard and achieved substantial results toward this end. For the Negro people now to join forces with the poll-tax Democrats and the reactionary Republicans in further undermining the strength of the progressive Roosevelt Administration would serve the interests neither of victory nor of Negro freedom. It would effectively retard the achievement of both. Again to quote Earl Browder:

> There is a loud-mouthed cult in our country which is willing to admit every weakness and error so long as they can blame it on the President. These are the demagogues of reaction. But there are too many honest democrats, progressives, and even labor men, who weaken the President's position by leaving all problems for him to settle, by failing to take energetic action themselves to help solve these problems. . . . No one has any right to criticize the President who is not himself in the midst of the hottest and most uncompromising fight to halt the mob of reaction now controlling the majority of Congress and threatening the whole country and its war effort.[7]

* * *

Second, although there is some justification for "all-Negro" liberation movements, the crying need of this period is for ever-broader unity between progressive white and Negro Americans to promote their common and mutual ends of victory and a democratic peace. Such Negro-white unity is not only more possible because of conditions created by the war; it is also more necessary.

Just as our nation would be in mortal peril if separated from her British, Soviet and Chinese allies, so would the Negro people face certain defeat if they allowed themselves to become separated from and placed in opposition to the other democratic forces of our country. Moreover, the strength of the whole progressive camp would thereby be weakened, and the goals for which this war is being fought would be placed in jeopardy.

The Negro freedom movement derives its main wartime strength from its integral relations with the victory program of the country as a whole. It necessarily follows, therefore, that

[7] *Policy for Victory* (New York, 1943), p. 66.

conscious struggles for Negro freedom during this period will achieve maximum results to the extent that they are carried on within the framework of the nation's struggle for victory. This premise is fundamental. From it there flow several practical implications for the wartime movement to extend the freedom of the Negro people.

First, organized struggles for Negro freedom must declare their unconditional support of the war effort of our nation. They must declare their full support of the win-the-war policies of our Commander-in-Chief. There must never be the slightest doubt about their genuinely patriotic character.

Second, demands for the correction of specific injustices must be raised as essential war measures to promote victory. Thus, racial bars to employment, abridgments of civil rights, denials of the franchise, discrimination in the armed forces, and the whole array of obstacles to Negro freedom should be challenged as obstacles to victory—which, in very truth, they are. Their removal should be demanded, not solely on the grounds of democratic justice, but especially also on the broader and even more urgent grounds of national security.

Third, organized movements for Negro freedom must direct their attention not only to specific issues of "Negro rights," but also to those larger wartime issues of the nation which profoundly affect the solution of the Negro's problems. They should fight implacably against the defeatist foes of our war effort. They should give aggressive support to such essential win-the-war measures as price and rent control, subsidies, a realistic tax program, an honest and democratic soldier vote bill, poll tax repeal, and the fullest use of war manpower. They should combat all defeatist efforts to disrupt the unity of our nation and of the United Nations. They should struggle to strengthen the program of the Anglo-Soviet-American coalition—for the quickest possible defeat and thorough destruction of fascism, for the organization of a just and enduring peace. Especially should they rally to the support of President Roosevelt and the election of a win-the-war Congress in the 1944 elections. In short, they must throw their full resources into the fight for all measures essential for winning the war in the shortest possible time. In the triumph of the cause of victory will the cause of Negro freedom achieve maximum realization of its goals.

Fourth, the Negro freedom movement must forge the closest possible unity among the Negro people themselves, and between the Negro people and their natural allies in the progressive white population and the organized labor movement. Petty organizational rivalries and factionalism should now be put aside. There should be uncompromising opposition to all reactionary attempts to use the "menace of communism" bogey as a tactic to divide, and thus defeat, the progressive organizations of the people. The growing virus of anti-Semitism must be fought. Above all, the Negro people must enter the labor movement in ever increasing hundreds of thousands, joining actively with their white fellow-workers in the solution of their common trade union problems, and turning the power of their unions increasingly to the related tasks of victory and Negro freedom.

Unequivocal support of this people's war of national liberation and survival. Demands for Negro liberation as a means of winning the war. Vigorous support of the win-the-war policies of our Commander-in-Chief. Solid unity of the Negro people with all other progressive, win-the-war forces of the nation. These are the basic essentials of a wartime program for the Negro people. Herein lie the correct strategy and tactics which will best advance the cause of Negro freedom. It is as an integral and struggling sector of the developing national front for victory that the Negro people can now make their most substantial progress toward attainment of "What the Negro Wants."

POST-WAR PROSPECTS FOR THE
NEGRO AND THE NATION

And once the war is won, what then of Negro freedom? Will not the Negro's wartime gains very shortly disappear? What, if any, basis is there for the prospect of continued progress toward freedom in the post-war world? The essential answers to these questions are largely implied in the preceding discussion. It is well to make them explicit.

There are those who see nothing durable in the wartime extensions of freedom for the Negro people. They believe these gains will vanish once the emergency from which they arose has passed. To them, these advances "must" be transitory because they were yielded under duress; they did not arise out of the chastened hearts of men. There are several considerations which suggest that this pessimism is quite unwarranted.

In the *first* place, the fact that wartime extensions of Negro freedom arise out of historic necessity, far from suggesting their weakness, is in reality their greatest strength. The history of human progress is a record of social gains which were impelled by the inherent logic of events and the struggles of mankind for freedom. "Humanitarianism" and "good will," noble sentiments that they are, have proved to be among the most unstable forces of history. They readily accommodate themselves to the necessities of time and place. It is well for Negro Americans to recall that the Emancipation Proclamation was not dedicated by noble sentiments, but rather by the stern requirements of military necessity.

Second, the events of this period are forging new relationships between the Negro people and the rest of the nation, relationships which, in themselves, are a substantial guarantee of permanence for the wartime extensions of Negro freedom. By way of illustration, consider the position of the new hundreds of thousands of Negro industrial workers, especially in comparison with the last war. After World War I, many—by no means all—Negro workers were ousted from their new-found jobs in the industries of the North. Not only were they members of a subordinate minority race, but they were also recent migrants to their communities, and many had been brought in as "scabs" and "strike-breakers." In the increased post-war competition for jobs, they found themselves in direct conflict with organized white workers into whose unions they had made but little headway. They were replaced.

After World War II, an entirely different situation will obtain. The pre-war influx of Negro workers into the trade union movement will have been enormously increased, especially in the great democratic unions of the CIO in basic industries. In the course of common wartime struggles on the industrial and political fronts, hundreds of thousands of Negro workers will have established firm relations of comradeship with their white fellow-workers. Their unions will have come more and more to take up the struggle for economic security and full democratic rights for the Negro people. Their jobs will be far more secure.

As in the industrial world, so in many other areas of our national life, the wartime experiences of the Negro people are fundamentally altering their relationship with their countrymen. New and different social structures are being built, and in their wake different attitudes emerge. In the development of these new wartime relationships, there lies a substantial basis for confidence that the wartime gains of the Negro people will abide.

Third, the future of the Negro's freedom in America will be decisively influenced by the quality of the peace which issues from this war, and here the prospect is far from discouraging. World War II cannot end in another Versailles, precisely because of the nature of the forces in combat, the inherent liberating character which the war has been forced to assume, and the power of the masses of freedom-loving peoples which it has set into motion the world over.

Contrast the anti-Soviet Pact of Munich, which unleashed the fascist military might upon the world, with the Anglo-Soviet-American Declaration of Teheran, which opens up an entirely new perspective for mankind. The capitalist and socialist worlds, once in serious conflict, are now firmly united in "complete agreement," on measures for the military destruction of fascism and the establishment of a just and enduring "peace which will command good will from the overwhelming masses of the peoples of the world." Precisely those three nations which represent the greatest concentrations of military, economic, and political power in the world have now agreed to "work together in the war and in the peace which will follow."

They reached this agreement because of historic necessity— the necessity to collaborate in order to survive. They have the determination and the strength to carry it out. And they *will* carry it out, for there is no other way to victory, and to peace "for many generations."

In a world bathed in blood by the reactionary policies of

Munich, this historic Declaration of Teheran represents an enormous achievement. It opens up the perspective of enduring peace and prosperity for all peoples. It inspires new hope and confidence in all progressive mankind. It lays the basis for the building of a truly progressive peace. It is, by far, the greatest possible guarantee of that kind of post-war world in which the Negro people can continue their march toward complete freedom.

Finally, a word should be said about the tremendous concern in certain quarters over "post-war plans" for the Negro's freedom. The position of the Negro people in the post-war world will not be determined by the blue-prints now formed in the heads of "planners." Rather, it will be determined by the relative strength of the pro-Teheran forces of progress and the anti-Teheran forces of reaction which now struggle for dominance in the world and in our nation. Especially will it be determined by the relations of the Negro people to these forces. Now to draft idealistic post-war plans for the Negro is not necessarily a harmful pastime—except that it tends to divert much needed energy from the really urgent task of today: to win the war at the earliest possible moment. It would be naïve to assume, however, that such "plans" will constitute an important factor in shaping the future of the Negro people.

The Negro's future is being decisively shaped by the struggles for victory and freedom today. Let the Negro people now exert their maximum strength toward winning the war. Let them fight for their own freedom within the framework of the nation's fight for survival. Let them do all in their power to hasten the unconditional surrender of the Axis and the complete destruction of fascism. Let them establish the firmest possible unity with the developing coalition of all other progressive win-the-war forces of our nation—fighting for the triumph of the Roosevelt Administration in the 1944 elections, for that speedy victory in war and that just and enduring peace which are the promise of Teheran.

Let the Negro people do these things *now*. This is their best possible guarantee of freedom in the post-war world. Along this path alone lies the ultimate attainment of "What the Negro Wants."

RACE RELATIONS
IN THE UNITED STATES:
A SUMMARY

By GORDON B. HANCOCK

———

THERE IS SOMETHING ominous and urgent in the race relational situation in the United States. This sense of urgency
is heightened both by the tempo of American life and by the
issues involved in the prosecution of the global war, the successful termination of which for the United Nations will have much
definite influence in the restatement of human policies and practices throughout the civilized world. Our commanding position
in the comity of the nations makes it imperative that we take an
inventory of our resources to the end that the post-war world
may not lack light on the one question that, above all others, will
largely determine whether World War II will be followed by a
just and lasting peace or whether it will be followed by World
War III and other wars that may bring world disaster. When
we consider how a righteously conceived League of Nations
most probably would have made impossible the present war, and
how the League as founded was doomed from the beginning by
reason of its race relational bias, it is difficult to restrain certain
apprehensions that are foisted upon us by the exigencies of the
current general situation. A brief survey, then, of the situation in
the United States may conceivably throw light on the general
situation throughout the world.

There is no way to avoid a head-on collision with the color
question. It has been raised everywhere by the white man who
dominates the Twentieth Century world, in which color con-

siderations have assumed a major importance. Although we are told by anthropologists that the white man did not appear upon the earth until the Bronze Age, within a comparatively brief time he has attained unto a position of dominance in the world that has thrown the darker peoples on the defensive in the struggle for survival. Today of the approximately two billion humans upon the earth, eight hundred twenty millions are classified as Caucasoid or white, six hundred fifty millions as Mongoloid and one hundred sixty-five millions as Negroid. It becomes obvious that Negroes are not only a minority in the United States, but that in the world picture they constitute a minority group, which fact has some serious implications in a world where life and survival are so largely conditioned by color considerations. Therefore when we survey the field of race relations in the United States, we are considering a world view in miniature and a satisfactory adjustment or lack of adjustment in race relations in the United States may bear heavily on the question throughout the world.

The color question is a social problem and, as such, is not essentially different from any other social problem; and by reason of this fact, it responds to the same processes of adjustment or maladjustment. Social problems by their very nature do not lend themselves to instantaneous and absolute solutions. To solve instantaneously and absolutely any social problem would conceivably make a hundred other problems quite as vexing as the one solved. Let us take the problem of poor health. Its complete and instantaneous solution would upset the entire balance of our social and economic life. What would become of all our fine physicians and surgeons and nurses and hospitals and their attendants and equipment? What would happen to all of our drug stores and drug manufacturers and their investments? Our famous health resorts and sanitoria and their workers would be distressed, to say nothing of the inevitable undertaker. The manufacture of alcoholic beverages would in all probability cease as would the production of tea and coffee and soft drinks, since all of these things are regarded as unnecessary to health, but serve rather the satisfaction of unhealthful appetites. This casual observation of the imaginary solution of the problem of poor health offers fertile suggestions as to what might conceivably result from a total and instantaneous solution of any one of our many social problems including the race problem. Our researchers and reformers have succeeded in creating in us an inordinate and unnecessary fear of problems in such a manner that much of the joy of life is dissipated in worries over various "problems." As a matter of fact problems are beneficent things; for every beneficent function of our bodies and every faculty of our minds have resulted from problems which have challenged the survival of mankind. The mind, the finest of all created mechanisms, not only arose in response to problems, but is at its best in grappling with them. The important thing about problems is not their number and variety and intensity, but the effect they have upon the character of men. Problems have been the levers that have lifted the Jews to the highest eminence in all recorded history and, in spite of the inhumanities perpetrated upon this people through many generations, the blessings they have brought to the world far outweigh the horrible sufferings they have endured. Every problem contains bristling possibilities for good, if the right mind or state of mind can be brought to bear. Strangely enough the world has moved gradually forward in spite of its problems. The tariff problem has never been satisfactorily solved by any nation, yet international commerce has flourished because of certain fortuitous circumstances which always inhere in the general situation. The real problems are in men and not circumstances.

SOME POINTS OF VIEW

The point of view we bring to the consideration of our question—any question—largely determines the fruitfulness of our efforts. There are three prevailing points of view on social problems, namely, the fatalistic, the alarmist and the scientific. The history of race relations in this country does not warrant or sustain the fatalistic point of view. Too much has already been accomplished to leave place for a species of fatalism with its accompanying cynicism. Man has wrestled too successfully with the problems of Nature to doubt that he will eventually master the problems of society. The race problem as a social problem contains nothing mysterious or magical. The same type of study and application that has made man master of so much of Nature's realm will make him victorious in the realms of human relations. No normally minded person can doubt that the mind that is fast overcoming the handicaps of time and space will overcome the problem of human adjustment. The very survival of mankind is indicative of a mastery that precludes the fatalistic point of view in the realms of race relations.

The alarmist point of view is no less specious and can only be explained by unfamiliarity with the dark and dangerous struggle that mankind has made down through the centuries of history and prehistory. It is true that men die but man lives on. The higher human values of love and life and justice and mercy and truth and right have survived every human crisis and this survival alone is one of the most significant facts of history. After the "Dark Ages" the genius of mankind flowered as never before and the fountains of life instead of drying up became deeper and sweeter; it will be even so after our present Dark Ages of World Wars. There is then no need of dire alarm for the darkness that enshrouds the color question throughout the world. The resurgence of a sweeping current of Negrophobia before even the fortunes of the current war are settled, and the dark shadows of Master Racism now projected into the world picture at one of history's most critical moments, are but transient phenomena in a world on which God and Time and Right have a mortgage. If the Jews could survive four hundred years of Egyptian slavery and live to give the world its God and its Bible and its Jesus Christ; if the Pilgrim Fathers could cross the deep and dangerous Atlantic Ocean in a sail-boat to lay the foundation of one of the mightiest nations of history; if the Negro could survive nearly three hundred years of wretched slavery and live to become a citizen in the land of his enslavement, greater things are still possible and little room is left for alarm.

The calm, deliberate and dispassionate consideration presupposed in the scientific approach to social problems is the antithesis of the emotionalism that too often characterizes our attempts to solve the riddle of race relations. Because from primitive times mankind made emotional adjustments to his environment and by these survived, it is increasingly difficult to divest our reaction of the emotional even though we know that the situation is thus made more confused and confusing. The temptation to give full rein to our "feelings" on matters of race relations is a serious and well-nigh compelling one to which most of us yield sooner or later in greater or less degree. Yet it is just as well for us to know that we thereby postpone the very adjustments we so earnestly seek and so seriously need. A calm and dispassionate appraisal of the race relational situation, presupposed in the scientific approach, contains the only hope that catastrophe in this realm may be averted. Furthermore, it is the scientific approach that affords the only reasonable basis for a "possibility complex" which is so essential to any constructive planning and programs of adjustment. Tradition plays a large part in this whole matter and thus runs athwart the finer impulses of the scientific approach and outlook. Tradition is the social germ plasm through which prejudices and false generalizations are transmitted almost without variation from generation to generation. And although we know that the most effective attack on the problem of race relations can be made through the younger generation, there is little hope when these have been born of prejudiced mothers, supported and protected by prejudiced fathers and taught by prejudiced teachers. The child has not an outside chance to be free! The difficulty of arriving at the dispassionate scientific view so essential to satisfactory adjustments in this area in no way obviates the necessity for such view. The very urgent fact that it is indispensable to effective achievement in this field is all that need concern us here.

To the three points of view mentioned we might profitably add another—the common sense point of view. In a scientific age it becomes academic heresy to posit common sense as a factor in the attempts at social amelioration. But it must not be forgotten that practicalization of life is the end of common sense, and long before the arrival of science as such, common sense held forth the light of progress and assured survival in the dim and dark millenia of prehistory. And even today science to be most effective must be supplemented with common sense. Only common sense can tell when an army must shift from the defensive to the offensive and vice versa. Although science may prescribe in medicine, the dosage is largely a matter of common sense. Common sense more than science must decide whether an attack is to be flank or frontal. In the long run Aesop's Fables, classics of common sense, will have greater bearing on current human problems than the cogitations of Aristotle, the Substance of Spinoza, the Reason of Hegel or the Relativity of Einstein. The greatness of Booker T. Washington hinges about his common-sense approach to the question of race relations; and although his doctrines have been gainsaid by many who are unworthy to unlatch his shoes, his basic approach was sound. In advocating industrial education for his people, he hoped thereby to achieve their full-fledged citizenship in this country. He knew, as we all have since learned, that the empty-handed knock in vain at the door of life. He reasoned that if the Negro could be made economically efficient he would stand a better chance of surviving even though his admittance to full citizenship be indefinitely postponed. This common sense alternative above all else marked the great wisdom and common sense that make Washington probably the greatest Negro in history. Common sense dictates that things which cannot be done one way may be done another; that practices and procedures must be conditioned to circumstances; that the cooperation of Kropotkin is just as essential to progress as the competition of Karl Marx; that minority groups must predicate their survival on strategy even as majorities predicate theirs on strength. Common sense would dictate to the dominant whites the impossibility of keeping the Negro quiet with a sub-citizen status when all history and all education are built around full citizenship and the ideologies thereof. Common sense precludes the possibility that Negroes in these war times make a frontal attack for full citizenship without a frontal counter-attack by the resisting white elements who in sheer desperation are threatening again to throw the color question into the politics of the South; and who are at present rumor-mongering in a manner that would provide excuses for a revival of their Reconstruction methods of dealing with the Negroes of the South.

The renaissance of common sense would be a blessing to the cause of race relations. Common sense tells us that we have had enough surveys on the Negro and that the time has come for some action—urgent action. The practical application and implementation of facts already found would be of far greater benefits than the interminable "researches" now carried on and projected in the name of getting more light on the Negro. The urgency of the situation demands action now and not further surveys.

THE QUESTION IN CROSS-SECTION: THE NATION

For a long time it was erroneously supposed that the color question was peculiar to the South, and that there was a peculiarly "Southern way" of viewing it. The North was long regarded as a haven for the Negro too hardpressed in the South. Because of a fortuitous combination of circumstances the Negro received his emancipation and enfranchisement from the North; he has been thus emboldened in his expectation of further deliverance from the same source. The Negro's almost religious devotion to the Republican party can be explained on the same ground. Only in recent years have Negroes in considerable number dared to break away from the Republican political standards and vote the Democratic ticket. But it is becoming more and more manifest that participation in the Democratic elections of the South is far more effective than supporting the Republican ticket the strength of which is too often far removed from the local situation to succour the Negro in his local urgencies. That is to say, Negroes are beginning to realize that it is more profitable, politically and otherwise, to vote for the mayors and councilmen of Southern cities who can help their local situation than for presidents and congressmen often too far removed from the scene of the trouble, thereby being powerless. The growing independence of the Negro voter is one of the healthiest signs of the moral growth of the Negro, and this fact promises excellent results in years to come. When the Negro shows that he cannot be politically herded, the white politician and office-seeker will make a higher bid for his political support; while the white South will have less fear of the Negro as a political factor. There is now no longer any characteristic "Southern way" of viewing things race relational. The northernization of the South is proceeding as is the southernization of the North. The process is facilitated by the accelerating improvement in communication and transportation. It has come about that meeting a prejudiced Northerner in the South and a liberal Southerner in the North are daily experiences for the casual traveler.

The national attitude on the race question is best epitomized in two instances, one falling in the realm of legislation and the other in the field of philanthropy. The Congress of the United States has stubbornly and persistently refused to enact anti-lynching legislation although such legislation is clearly indicated by the changing trends of public opinion within recent years. Such legislation has been thwarted more recently only by the employment of the filibuster and that these filibusters are invariably led by Southern congressmen is a fact no more significant than that these Southerners were not restrained by Northerners who might have—had they so desired—employed the cloture rules that would have made the filibusters impossible. The stark fact remains, the white North respects the sentiments of the white South far more than they respect the rights of the black South; and this means in the last analysis that the dispositions on the race issue are left in the lap of the South, which must bear full responsibility for any failure of race-relational policy and full credit for the success of such policy. The philanthropic foundations likewise refuse to make their contributions to Negro welfare in ways that might offend the white South. So careful are they in these matters that such funds as are distributed in the South are placed in the hands of white Southerners. Fortunately these men have been of larger mould; and the contributions of these foundations have been tremendously effective in the advancement of the Negro and the South. It is becoming more and more obvious that there will be no more "special dispensations" for the Negro in this country. His efforts and his ballot must henceforth be designed to advance the interests of the nation as a whole. When the nation prospers, he will prosper in less degree; when the nation comes upon adversity, the Negro will suffer in greater degree. The hopeful sign in the national picture is best seen in the almost generally defensive position of those who are committed to opposing the advance of the Negro.

THE NEGRO

The memories of the disillusionment that followed World War I make the Negro especially cautious in his appraisal of the present situation. In fact it is safe to say that there is a sense of justifiable frustration that characterizes the Negro's thinking on his own possibilities and limitations. Called upon to fight for freedoms that are denied him; baffled in his legitimate attempts to exploit current situations for opportunities of advancement; forced to stand aside with his scars and medals commemorative of his heroism and sacrifices while seditionists and saboteurs with their anti-Americanisms are feasted on the fat of this goodly land, it is no wonder that Negroes are becoming more and more restless and more and more resentful of their status as sub-citizens in a nation they have given so much to make great and mighty. To tell the Negro on the one hand that it is patriotic to live and die for principles and to deny him on the other hand the benefit of the principles for which he must die, is to leave him suspended between a fatalistic cynicism and a compensatory desperationism. The Negro however is becoming more and more determined to press his claims, reposing his faith in God and Time and Right.

The problem of leadership is one of the most acute intra-racial problems. The present frustration of Negroes can best be studied in its relation to a vigorous criticism that is ever and anon launched against Negro leaders. There are islands of leadership in an ocean of confusion. This means that in particular areas we find efficient leaders but in the general situation there is a marked leaderlessness that appals serious students of the question; for too invariably the leaders of the individual organizations are working at cross purposes so that the masses are left confused and baffled. The promiscuous attacks on Negro leadership ofttimes by the leaders themselves is a dangerous symptom in view of the fact that Negro leadership responsibilities are graver by reason of the white man's disinclination to be further responsible for Negro advance.

One of the saving graces of the white man is often his lack of unanimity in any program or policy of oppression. During the nearly three hundred years of slavery in America, there was never a time when the pro-slavery sentiment was unanimous. Not only at the North where slavery was not profitable did whites oppose slavery, but in the South where it formed the backbone of the agricultural economy there were whites who opposed it. Today there is in the United States a large segment of whites who are sternly opposed to the current practices and policies and preachments intended to perpetuate the sub-citizen status of the Negro. Although outnumbered—but not always hopelessly as is too often supposed—and at times painfuly cautious, these whites afford an invaluable liaison between the Negrophobes and the Negroes that saves the situation from threats of total loss. Interracialism has not been a total loss, as is so often erroneously supposed by the casual observers who emphasize the many things it has not accomplished rather than the fine things it has, without great fanfare. The modest methods of the interracialist have obscured many great and substantial achievements in the field of race relations.

The race integrity ideal of the white man the world over no less than in the United States is bound up with a Master Race complex that has reached its logical expression in Hitlerism. One of the indirect benefits that must surely come of Hitlerism is this bringing of the Master Race idea into boldest relief. This stark dramatization of the notion that more than any other is influencing the policies of the Twentieth Century world will prove to be one of the high lights of history from which it is quite conceivable that humanity may greatly profit. While nothing can be said against racial integrity, much can be said against the un-Christian, undemocratic and inhumane methods too often employed in the methods of its attainment. The integrity of both the white and Negro races stands better chances of preservation through a racial pride begotten of spiritual freedom than through force born of fear. There is an inverse ratio between race mixture and Negro advancement and this alone should relieve the morbid fears that too generally characterize interracial policies. There are many whites of the country who have grasped the significance of this fact and there is a growing feeling among whites favoring full citizenship for the Negro both as a fulfillment of race integrity idealism and as a fulfillment of the higher ideal of human brotherhood proclaimed in the Gospel of Jesus Christ. Strangely enough, too often these finer feelings are obscured beneath a lack of moral courage that is at times bewildering—a kind of "Pontius Pilatism"—that saps the moral life of the community. If the whites who know better and who care would implement their often carefully concealed notions of fairness and justice, the present of the Negro would not be so full of well-grounded apprehensions and his future would not be so full of uncertainty. Moral daring, then, is one of the great needs of the white man of this country and this precludes the "safety-firstism" that is too characteristic of too many situations. This becomes all the more deplorable in view of the large influence courageous men and women of the white South exert at sundry times in sundry ways. These whites fought the Ku Klux Klan to a standstill in its comeback attempt of recent years; these made a sustained and determined attack on lynching that drove this evil thing from the prominence it occupied in the sordid annals of man's inhumanity to man and they are irrevocably committed to its complete extermination. This group, conscious of the fact that the poll-tax qualification for citizenship was designed to limit the Negro's political participation, is now advocating its repeal. More recently these progressives are advocating the participation of Negroes in the primaries of the South. Strangely enough the Negro's campaign for the equalization of salaries in the South is having for the most part favorable consideration and determined opposition is conspicuous for its weakness. The Black Shirt movement in Georgia has never been able to get under way effectively in its avowed determination to guarantee to any white person any job—not Negro made—held by a Negro. This movement posits in its ultimate designs the social and economic damnation of the Negro. Whites have fought it to the bitter end. The white press of the South is becoming more and more favorable in its attitude towards the Negroes.

On the other hand there is an element of whites in this country determined to forestall any movements calculated to advance the Negro's cause. The threat to throw again the color question into the politics of the South is a straw that shows a threatening wind blowing in another direction. For better or worse this segment of whites have impressed upon the progressives the grave fears for the future of race relations in the South. The measure of the wrath of this group is best depicted in the hesitation of the white liberals that too often characterizes procedures in given situations. Assuming that the white progressives are conscientious, their great caution is a rough measure of the opposition they must face with any program for interracial amelioration. The recent riotous outbreaks and the pronounced antagonisms towards Negro soldiers and the rumor-mongering that too often serve as excuse for summary measures to suppress the Negroes are ominous incidents that weaken many of our former assurances. But it is here contended that the major problem of the progressive whites North and South is a problem of moral courage; lacking in this the outlook is not one of great promise. "Pontius Pilatism" is a grave liability in the premise!

ORGANIZED RELIGION

From every quarter comes evidence that the Christian Church is becoming ashamed of itself and of the too often passive roles it has played in the realm of race relations. It has come about that every major ecclesiastical organization is making some kind of pronouncement in opposition to the injustices, humiliations and deprivations which are too often the lot of Negroes. The Federal Council of Churches, the Methodist Episcopal Church, the Baptists, the Presbyterians, and especially the Catholics, all have some programs looking forward to facing the issues involved in the Christianization of Negroes. More and more indifference to the challenge of the race relational situation is becoming a badge of moral cowardice that the Christian Church is renouncing. It is a most significant and salutary fact that the races can come closer together in the name of religion than in any other capacity; why this great opportunity is not more thoroughly exploited is at times bewildering. Those Northern missionary societies that founded the Negro schools of the South wrought one of Christianity's most glorious achievements. They built better than they knew; for the fine leadership upon which the Negro race must lean so heavily is being supplied by these schools and their influences. That the support of these schools today is generally lacking or lagging is a disturbing fact. If the support declines faster than the responsibility of the Negroes can be developed, the religious leadership among Negroes will become a great problem in the near future. The lack of such leadership will be a tragedy.

The Negro church has borne the weight of responsibility for Negro advance in that it was the clearing house for the race's aspirations. Even now there are no indications that the Negro church is not without a large place in the future affairs of the Negro race. Nearly all of the race's fine beginnings in almost every field of noble and useful endeavor were launched in the church. For better or worse the Negro church is fast shifting its emphasis from things emotional to things more essentially related to strivings and contrivings of the race in its broader community relations. The coming of the current new cults ex- emplified in "Father Divinism," "Daddy Gracism" and "Elder Michauxism" is largely the result of an awakening in the Negro church that precludes the religious satisfactions that form the basis of these new cults. The growth of these cults is highly complimentary to the advance being made by the ordinary church with its advancing ministry. If somehow a ministry can be found for the Negro churches which represent the greatest moral and economic investment of the race, we shall have in these churches a lifting power the possibilities of which should inspire the at times faint of heart.

THE LABOR MOVEMENT

In the last analysis a people's welfare is correlated with its income. If we can determine the real income of Negroes it is easy to appraise their welfare and progress. Too often our exultation over our reputed progress is based upon the accomplishment and welfare of successful individuals rather than upon the total income of the race. Our progress cannot be measured merely in terms of the advantages of the favored few. Rather the composite income of the race in real wages becomes the more reliable index to Negro advance. The accumulations and achievements of Negroes warrant the belief that if given an opportunity, they, like any other group, will rise in the general level of life. But this opportunity means chiefly the ability to find sustained and adequate employment which affords the security without which life remains unfulfilled. Organized labor is fast occupying the most commanding position in the dispensation of employment opportunities in this country. Unfortunately the Negro's experience with organized labor has not been such as to give great assurance. Most of the Negro's labor is of the unskilled classification whereas labor organizations specialize in selling skilled labor on the market; this fact excludes Negroes largely from the benefits that come from bargaining power without which common labor becomes a species of slavery. It is safe to say that Negroes cannot posit a future brighter than their possibilities either of breaking more generally into the ranks of organized labor, or of organizing a movement of their own. For years I have advocated the latter course in view of the rigid exclusion practices organized labor has employed in its dealings with Negroes. In fact, the Negro laborer generally is disinclined to trust his fortunes with organized labor although ultimately the fortunes of all labor are the same; and the sooner both organized labor and the Negro realize this, the sooner will the labor movement in this country attain to its rightful place of power that its importance demands. Separate all-Negro organizations may be the answer to the questions raised by organized labor's too invariable inattention to the importunities of struggling Negro labor. More recently this course is being advised by serious students of the question who believe that only in this way can the Negro focus attention upon his precarious economic plight. It is being argued that Jews and Italians had to organize among themselves before they were accepted by organized labor. They had to become a threat to organized labor before they would be accepted into the organized ranks. This same procedure holds possibilities for Negroes. It is argued:

> The plight of the Negro laborer has never been presented to the American reading public in a manner which exploits all of the possibilities for building up good will towards him, or which tends to measure the racial antipathies which are directed against him.[1]

And then follows a subtle indictment against the Negro press which whether false or true should provoke serious circumspection. The very statement hurtles into the forefront of Negro thinking a charge that demands serious consideration:

> In reading most of the race papers one is impressed with the fact that they contain scarcely any labor news and have certainly little understanding of labor problems.[2]

Much is said from time to time about the Negro as strikebreaker. It is a highly debatable question whether the Negro by reason of his desperate economic condition is morally bound to support the unions that deny him membership. Those who feel that the Negro should refuse to break strikes and thus aid those who spurn his economic camaraderie are asking things of the Negro that presuppose a moral advancement to which humanity has hardly attained. To expect impecunious Negroes to turn suddenly in their hunger and wretchedness and play the role of philanthropists is expecting too much of a group living daily on the ragged edge of existence. A point worth considering in this connection is thoughtfully projected thus:

> Curiously enough many of the white workers who have since learned to berate Negroes for their willingness to act

[1] Horace R. Cayton and George S. Mitchell, *Black Workers and the New Unions* (Chapel Hill, 1939), p. 431.
[2] *Ibid.*, p. 432.

as strike breakers and to lower the standard of labor, themselves earned their place in industry a decade ago through similar strike breaking activities.[3]

In 1926 in an article in *Opportunity* entitled "When The Manna Faileth," it was pointed out that a well-defined movement was gathering momentum that demanded serious attention on the part of Negro leaders. This movement hinges about the displacement of Negroes by lowly whites who were using the color question as a means to their economic ends, which ends meant the elimination from all of the most lucrative jobs that afforded the backbone of the Negro's economic and social advancement. The movement reached the organizational stage in the appearance of the Black Shirt Movement in Georgia which was committed to the proposition that no Negro was entitled to a job that any white man wanted. The movement was thrown into bolder relief by the depression that followed World War I with its disproportionate unemployment among Negroes and with its higher incidence of relief among them. The tendency everywhere was to give available jobs to whites and more relief to Negroes. Such policy was a dire threat to the Negro, for the pride, progress and manhood of a race cannot be sustained on public relief, however lavish. Even today we need to give greater attention to this displacement movement, for it is still gathering strength which for the present is being concealed beneath the current war-time prosperity. If and when industrial proscription against Negroes is tied up with the veiled philosophy of racial integrity, it becomes doubly dangerous. The following statement is tremendously provocative:

Some of those who are opposed on racial grounds to giving the Negro industrial opportunities commensurate with his abilities, when pressed to admit the unreasonableness of such attitude on other grounds, may fall back on the argument that this would increase the likelihood of intermarriage. The reasoning which in certain of its elements is logical enough is that the more that industrial opportunities are

[3] Herman Feldman, *Racial Factors in American Industry* (New York, 1931), p. 33.

opened to the Negro, the more frequently will individuals
rise to places of importance, wealth and authority; they will
lead to the heightening of the prestige for many Negroes,
to their cultural development and to closer contacts or relationships between superior Negro men and women and
white persons of the opposite sex; inevitably their intermarriage will become more frequent leading to a reduction
of the whites to the more common level of the Negro, or
mulatto.

It is fair to assume that intermarriage would become less
rare if Negroes of the country were freely admitted to a
higher industrial status. But it is true that the prospects are
overdrawn by those who fear miscegenation, and there is a
tendency to overlook the extreme social antagonism against
intermarriage in this country which imposes a deterring
penalty upon the white person who takes this step and as
well to some extent upon the black. The social ostracism
visited upon such mating normally stands in the way of
intermarriage. Moreover, industrial relations do not of necessity impose social relationships outside.[4]

The foregoing statement senses and suggests a subtle design in
the economic and industrial restrictions thrown about Negroes
that has some disquieting implications. If these practices and
policies of economic exclusion become too prevalent, great tribu-
lations lie ahead for the Negro worker and the Negro race.
Quite as convincing as the argument just referred to is the more
practical observation that the social and economic advancement
of the Negro has not resulted in greater intermarriage but definitely less. In fact there are reasons to believe that every opportunity given the Negro to rise to high levels and standards of life
are so many measures which insure the mutual integrity of both
races.

It was consideration of these threatening developments in their
relations to Negro welfare that has led to the promulgation of
the doctrine of the "Double-Duty Dollar" which has gained considerable currency in recent years. Summed up it advocates
spending, wherever possible, Negro dollars with Negro business,
on the assumption that the dollars thus spent not only secure the

[4] *Ibid.*, p. 73.

goods and services indicated but they make jobs and employment for Negroes, thus doing double duty. The doctrine in its amended form contends that the same results are obtained when Negro dollars are spent with those whites who employ Negroes. It is not boycott in the same sense suggested by such slogans as "Don't-Trade-Where-You-Cannot-Work" which have achieved considerable notice and not a little advantage here and there about the country. There is no boycott implied in the doctrine of the "Double-Duty-Dollar" for generally Negro retailers buy from white wholesalers and this fact unmistakably eliminates the element of boycott. The impossibility of these self-help attempts has been thoroughly projected by many of the finest scholars of the race. It is contended that there can be no separate economy for Negroes. This contention would scarcely be disputed by even the most casual economists; yet the fact remains that the Negro is forced by circumstances to sink, begging for jobs; or swim, trying to make them; his heroic efforts deserve commendation rather than disparagement. Although we know a separate economy is impossible we also know that hard-pressed groups must find practical solutions of their problems rather than scholarly analyses. But even while many of our master minds were disparaging these self-help movements, our practical business men have been exploiting them with such astounding success that their achievements are becoming heralded as outstanding examples of Negro enterprise and possibilities. These self-help movements are essentially defensive and while they may not be thoretically sound, they are tremendously effective in the premise.

The problem then of getting Negro labor ready for labor organizations and getting these organizations ready for the Negro easily becomes one of the most pressing of the major problems confronting the Negro and the nation. Whether this can be accomplished by merely pressing upon the labor organizations themselves or by organizing Negroes to cooperate with white labor if possible, or to compete with it if necessary, is a question pressing for an immediate answer. Without some sustaining economic opportunity the Negro's future in this country leads uphill and into the dark. We read:

The future of the Negro worker is problematical. There has been definite improvement in his economic status, and there is reason to believe that even greater improvement is likely in the future. The rapidity of his progress will depend upon many factors. Much depends upon the Negroes themselves and those of the race who have the capacity and determination to assist themselves and other Negroes. The Negro can do most himself to demonstrate the invalidity of the charge of incompetence and inefficiency which is so commonly made against him. The expansion of educational and training facilities will do considerable to equip him for the performance of skilled tasks and the assumption of heavier responsibilities in industry and business. Cultivation of the Negro's interest in the labor movement will contribute greatly to his protection through collective bargaining. He will be helped greatly if he is taught the risks he runs and the injury he does his race by acting as strike breaker. Increased political solidarity of the colored people will help them secure a reasonable opportunity in public service. Whatever can be done to lessen public prejudice against colored people will pave the way for the general improvement. In the future as in the past the Negro will be an important factor in the production of wealth in this country.[5]

This sympathetic statement predicates the future of the Negro on two things, namely the Negro's own resourcefulness and efficiency and on the removal of prejudice. It is the slowness of the latter process that beclouds an otherwise reasonably hopeful picture.

EDUCATION

No nation in the world can compare with the United States in superbly equipped and heavily endowed colleges and universities. But strangely enough there was even before the outbreak of war a confusing uncertainty in the whole education field. In almost every well-endowed college and university there is under way some "experiment" in education and "plans" are appearing

[5] Gordon S. Watkins and Paul A. Dodd, *Labor Problems* (New York, 1940), p. 521.

over night. There is a serious questioning of the present policies and programs and objectives in education. Much of our education today is wholly detached from the question of moral discipline; and religious training for the most part is entirely absent from the curricula of most of the schools; where it still holds place it is of the sketchy variety. In spite of the fact that most of our great institutions of learning were conceived by the church and by the church long sustained for the training of ministers and missionaries, religious education is by no means common among them. The general tendency is for these institutions upon the attainment of anything bordering on financial security to declare themselves non-sectarian and this usually means the subtle renunciation of emphasis on moral and religious training. This of course alludes to institutions founded in the Protestant faith. Catholics invariably adhere to their system of religious education. The confusion in the field of education in general is more confounded in the field of Negro education. The education for Negroes is generally geared to the liberal arts traditions the same as sixty years ago. Industrial education advocated by Booker T. Washington forty years ago has never attained any appreciable favor with Negroes; for it suggested too vividly the occupational ideology of Negroes in their slave status when manual and menial tasks consumed their energies.

When we consider the "preparational" nature of American education and the practical nature of Negro life in its vocational aspects, we can the more clearly perceive the lack of coordination and correlation with life that education in its philosophy subsumes. At present every stage of our education is a preparation for a succeeding higher stage with the result that the only preparation for life in its practical aspects is found for the most part in the professional schools. Some efforts have been made to correct this to be sure; but the fact remains that the serious criticisms leveled at education and the persistent efforts being made to change the current situation indicate clearly the unsatisfactory educational adjustment in this country. It is however among Negroes that the faultiness of the system produces the more unsatisfactory results; for a group disadvantageously circumstanced cannot afford the waste motion resulting from an education not geared to life. It is true that our present education has produced our ablest leaders; but the time has come when we need a system that produces followers. A thorough-going system of industrial and technical education projected and propounded by Negro teachers who believed in it would be one of the finest departures in education imaginable. So long as Negroes resent any attempt on the part of whites to suggest and commend the more practical types of education, it is imperative that Negroes themselves take the first steps in the revision of the educational programs affecting so intimately the fortunes and future of their people. This appears logically to be a departure to be emphasized by our Land-Grant Colleges. It would be most tragic if whites awakened to the larger opportunities of a more practical education before Negroes, who must live by it or perish without it. It is one of the pressing problems confronting the leaders in the field of education. It cannot be evaded much longer. Unless education guarantees the economic foundations without which a race's future cannot be built, then a revision in the concepts and programs of education is indicated. In the last analysis it is the education that is geared to the demands of the situation rather than that which satisfies the pride that promises survival.

THE DURHAM CONFERENCE

What is probably the most constructive departure in race relations since the emancipation of the Negro was made in the historic conference held at Durham, North Carolina, October 20, 1942. Sixty of the most influential Negroes of the South representing all shades of thought and occupational affiliation met of their own free will and accord—and at their own expense—and drew up a statement now known as the Durham Manifesto, which has had a far reaching effect on the thought and thinking of this country. Six thousand copies of the printed statement have been sent upon request to every state of the Union where interested persons are seeking more intimate knowledge of a document that has had such dramatic reception throughout the country. The conferees not only brought forth the statement, but assumed the financial responsibility for its publication. This forthright statement by a group of Southern Negroes caught the imagination of the country and the first edition of seven thousand copies is nearing exhaustion. A prominent churchwoman recently requested sufficient copies to supply the missionary circles of her entire state where it is to be used for study groups. In the *Statement of Purpose* we read:

The inception of this conference hinges about the tragedy that took place at the close of World War I, when returning Negro soldiers were met not with expressions and evidences of the democracy for which they had fought and for which thousands of their fellow race men had died. Instead, there was a sweeping surge of bitterness and rebuff that in retrospect constitutes one of the ugliest scars on the fair face of our nation. Interracial matters were left adrift and tragic was our experience and distressing was our disillusionment. Today the nations are again locked in mortal combat and the situation is desperate and dangerous, with the scales of fortune so delicately poised that we dare not predict what a day may bring forth; but this we know, that the Negro is again taking the field in defense of his country. Quite significant also is the fact that whereas the pronounced anti-Negro movement followed the last war, it is getting under way before the issues of the current war have been decided. In an hour of national peril, efforts are being made to defeat the Negro first and the Axis powers later. Already dire threats to throw again the Negro question into the politics of the South is becoming more and more dangerous. This is a direct challenge to the Negroes of the South who have most to gain if this threat is throttled and most to lose if it is fulfilled.

The purpose then of this conference is to try to do something about this developing situation. We are proposing to set forth in certain "Articles of Cooperation" just what the Negro wants and is expecting of the post-war South and nation. Instead of letting the demagogues guess what we want, we are proposing to make our wants and aspirations a matter of record, so clear that he who runs away may read. We are hoping in this way to challenge the constructive cooperation of that element of the white South who express themselves as desirous of a New Deal for the Negroes of the South.

In our "Articles of Cooperation" we are seeking for a common denominator of constructive action for the Negroes and this element of whites who are doing many of the things that we want done, and cannot do ourselves. In other words, we are proposing to draft a "New Charter of Race Relations" in the South. The old charter is paternalistic and traditional; we want a new charter that is fraternal and scientific, for the old charter is not compatible with the manhood and security of the Negro, neither is it compatible with the dignity and self-respect of the South. It ever leaves the South morally on the defensive! The Negro has paid the full price of citizenship in the South and nation, and the Negro wants to enjoy the full exercise of this citizenship, no more and no less.[6]

The Durham Manifesto broke down the whole area of race relations into seven categories relating to political and civil rights, industry and labor, service occupations, education, agriculture, military service, social welfare and health. The statement was widely and favorably received throughout the nation, with white and Negro press not only lavish in their praise of the document but generous in the space allotted to its publicity. By its very nature it presupposed a like conference of the Southern whites which met in Atlanta, April 8, 1942, attended by over a hundred representatives from all the Southern states. The righteousness of the Negro's cause and contentions were readily conceded and full assurances of cooperation given in any reasonable plan for the achievement of the objectives outlined in the Durham Manifesto. Members of a Collaborating Committee were named to meet with a like committee representing the Durham Conference. The Collaboration Conference was held in Richmond, June 16, 1942, attended by sixty-six committeemen representing the Durham and Atlanta conferences. The Durham statement was heartily indorsed and was accepted as the "blue print" for the improvement of race relations in the South. The profound and sympathetic understanding evinced by the participating con-

[6] Southern Conference on Race Relations, *Statement of Purpose* (Durham, 1942), p. 3.

ferees can best be appreciated by an excerpt from the final report which reads in part:

> This is the problem of two great peoples caught up in the midst of transition between the powerful heritage of the past and the mighty pull of the future. For here is the white South, a great people often doing little things and good people often doing bad things. And here is the Negro South, caught as always between the upper and nether millstones of conflicting forces and as also paying the price of extraordinary transition from level to level of cultural achievement, and needing plenty of understanding and cooperation. And here is the white South inexorably conditioned by cultural complexes, suffering terribly, too, and needing sympathy and help as few peoples have ever needed in the annals of man. And, even more important, the two, white South and black South, are part and parcel of the nation whose people need, scarcely less than the two regional peoples, the sense of time and wisdom....
>
> This is a rare challenge to the leadership of the South; to the white leadership to find new ways of cooperation and to justify increased confidence of Negro leadership in the white South; to sense the difficulties involved and to meet increasing demands without slowing down their essential efforts.[7]

A Continuing Committee was appointed to take "affirmative action" in carrying out the spirit of the conference. The "affirmative action" recommended by the Richmond Conference removes all doubt as to the determination of both groups to prosecute vigorously the courses indicated, thus implementing the sentiments of the South for amicable race adjustment.

Curiously enough the Durham Manifesto stirred the imagination of the country as to the possibilities of its course so that statements came from many quarters. One of the most conspicuous of these studied reactions to the Durham Manifesto came from the white clergy of Virginia who outlined, with the Durham statement as a basis, their own program for the implementation of the statement. It reads in part as follows:

[7] Collaboration Committee, *Report* (Richmond, Virginia), June 16, 1943.

We recommend the report of the Committee speaking for the Southern Conference on Race Relations, held at Durham, North Carolina, October 20, 1942. While we cannot endorse every item in that statement, as published, we unreservedly respect the report for its seriousness, its frankness, its understanding, its openmindedness and its specific practical nature. We urge the objective attitude it manifested be adopted by groups of both whites and Negroes as they, separately and collectively, seek a solution to the problem of race relations.

All things considered, it is safe to say that the ground work for some constructive developments in race relations has been laid by the Durham, Atlanta and Richmond Conferences and that great things are possible if ways and means and moral courage can be found to implement the spirit of these pronouncements. If the South can be organized by states and counties into councils on race relations committed to the implementation of this spirit of the new South, there are evidences that we are heading somewhere in particular in the area of race relations. Somebody has said that the study of philosophy is like unto a blind man, in a dark room, looking for a black cat that is not in there. No such futility surrounds honest efforts at interracial adjustment in the South; for what we are trying to do must be done in defense of the Negro, the South and the nation.

RE-PROPOSING THE NEGRO SANHEDRIN

The late Kelly Miller, long associated with the faculty of Howard University and one of the most picturesque figures on the horizon of Negro history, was long an advocate of a clearing house for Negro thought and opinion which by its very nature would resemble the ancient Sanhedrin of the Jews. Although he made little or no headway with the enterprise, the notion has much to commend it. A minority group circumscribed as is the Negro needs some instrument or tribunal whose combined opinion would be authoritative in a way that would give balance and direction to Negro thought and ambition. Separately in their various organizations, Negro thought has ample expression but its very diversity becomes a handicap in the general realization of the Negro's aims; for the authority is so decentralized that it lacks compelling powers such as the situation so often demands. Some super-council or Sanhedrin could conceivably facilitate the advancement of the race by bringing definiteness of direction for our moral and material energies which are too often dissipated into "waste motion" resulting from confused counsels. From the days of Booker T. Washington, there has been a prevailing faith in the efficacy of individual leadership. The very suggestion is intriguing to the ambitious. The vain attempt to be a leader has not only spoiled many a useful citizen but many situations and circumstances holding possibilities of better things. A Sanhedrin would obviate the necessity of these individual leaders with their concomitant ambitions and too often their concomitant jealousies and intra-racial politics.

Some of the questions that a Sanhedrin might consider follow: Shall we call ourselves Negroes or colored people? In our struggle for full-fledged citizenship, shall we assume a defensive or offensive position? In the first case we fight back when fought; in the second we carry the fight to the other fellow and "fight fire with fire." Which formula of social and economic deliverance shall we adopt, that of Karl Marx or that of Jesus Christ? The former is materialistic while the latter is spiritual, exemplified so dramatically today in the life and labors of Mahatma Gandhi. In our fight for our rights shall we make a frontal or a flank attack? That is to say shall we serve notice that we are going to have everything or nothing or shall we move step by step towards our desired goal? Light football teams resort to deception and strategy while heavier teams with great power use "power plays." What proportion of our moral and material energies shall we use fighting segregation and what proportion shall we employ making the most of it, to gain strength with which further to fight it? Shall we exhaust our energies on efforts at integration or shall we make the very most of a separate economy that is forced upon us, thus gaining strength for the long tomorrow? Shall we adopt the same type of education current among the whites or shall we seek a type of education that meets the needs of the millions of Negroes who must live by the labors of their hands rather than a type that meets the needs of the few Negroes in the higher brackets of life? In the first case we too often satisfy merely our pride; in the second we satisfy the demands of an inexorable situation. Should Negroes in their public utterances and through their press tell everything they know about things and situations, or should they have a reserve such as whites invariably have? It is argued that while it is a good thing for a mind to be open, it is not a good thing for it to be "wide open." Too often the too free speech of Negroes puts the enemies of their advancement on guard against measures designed to ameliorate conditions affecting Negro life. Shall Negroes concentrate their fighting energies on segregation, or should they concentrate on prejudice, the cause of segregation? Segregation is incidental; prejudice is fundamental! If prejudice is eradicated, segregation as a system will collapse; if segregation is abolished without the eradication of prejudice, the race relational situation would scarcely be improved, for prejudice will find other manifestations quite as vexing as segregation. Should Negroes allow themselves to be used as strike-breakers? Strike-breaking often makes the unorganized Negro laborer a menace to organized labor. It is better to be a menace than to be disregarded. The Jews and Italians became menaces before they became members. To scab or not to scab? is one of the bristling questions that a Negro Sanhedrin could ponder. What part of our energies should we devote to protest and what part to a program? Is the doctrine of the Double-Duty Dollar worth promulgating or should we renounce it and advise Negroes to trade most conveniently and most economically regardless of racial considerations? Strangely enough the most lucrative positions held by Negroes are based either upon the principle of the Double-Duty Dollar or upon the practice of segregation. There are hundreds of such questions that could be laid before a Negro Sanhedrin for final decisions. This would eliminate much "waste motion" such as results when every man is his own interpreter of events and situations.

SOME DANGER SPOTS

There has been successfully built up in the Negro a "fight" psychology. Henceforth the Negro need not be expected to take it lying down! In many situations he is called upon to be a man; naturally in the situations involving his legitimate rights and aspirations he may also be expected to be a man. Limited in his fight against the dominant white group, there is danger that his fight energies be released against his own people. In sheer frustration Negroes may unconsciously strive against one another in a manner that may seriously hamper their advancement. Already there is a well-defined tendency utterly to "destroy" those of different opinions as may be seen from a casual study of some sectors of the Negro press where the very term "conservative" is often bitterly derided. Smearism is a species of annihilationism which might have disastrous consequences among Negroes when given too free play.

There is danger that race prejudice may be commercialized. Today both whites and Negroes are using the race appeal as a means of better business. From the beginning it was not supposed that segregation as a social device would be employed to handicap the Negro in his legitimate economic pursuits. Today it has come about that the principle and practice of segregation are being employed to limit the Negro economically in a manner foreign to its original design. This unmistakably reveals the commercialization of prejudice. In addition to its uses as a social device, segregation is fast becoming a trade mark. There is danger that Negroes as a minority group may accept the materialistic interpretation of life and human affairs which in its final implications leads to the ruthlessness and brutality so characteristic of natural selection. This is doubly dangerous for minority groups. As with a materialistic concept of life so with the quantitative interpretation of progress. A qualitative concept of progress better becomes minority groups. There is danger in current political reversions so vividly exemplified in the return of dictatorship, and in the patent breakdown in international morality so clearly discernible in Hitler's attempted conquest of Europe and in Mussolini's rape of Ethiopia which had the silent assent of the powerful nations which alone could have prevented it. The coming of propaganda is a threat in many ways against minority groups. Propaganda explains more than anything else why the Negro has been damned in the eyes of the world. Propaganda deals in half-truths which are too often detrimental to minority groups by reason of their inability to finance their whole truths. The man who can finance propaganda is in the last analysis the only one guaranteed its advantages. Like science, whether it is good or bad depends upon whether or not it falls into the hands of a good or bad person. There is also danger that Negroes may trust too implicitly in courts and constitutions. These have their fundamental place in the struggle; but some terrible things have happened to Negroes in spite of them. They are not substitutes for cooperation and understanding. There is the major danger that Negroes may gravitate too largely towards the larger urban centers. The most casual demographic generalization reveals that there are relatively few old people, children and mental defectives in the city, the reason being, where the struggle for existence is fiercest the weaker groups are eliminated first. Economic and political weakness, like physical weakness, predisposes the weaker groups to extermination. We read:

> The fate of the Negro will be decided on the farms and in the small villages of the Southern states. The future development of agriculture in the South will have much to do with deciding the issue....
> The way that urban migration will influence the two races will doubtless depend mainly upon economic forces. Naturally these will be determined partly by the industrial development of the cities and partly by the conduct of agriculture. In both these fields the advance of science may bring about much greater changes than we are likely to anticipate. If for any reason land ownership in the South should come to be concentrated in the relatively few large holdings employing chiefly Negro labor, while the white workers are led to seek the opportunities afforded by the cities, the Southern whites will be largely replaced by Negroes. If on the other hand agricultural employment should be carried on mainly by white labor thereby causing the Negroes to trek to the cities, the future of the Negroes will be dark in-

deed. In the latter case the only way in which Negroes would avoid extinction, would be to acquire such adjustment to urban life as to make possible an adequate productive rate. With their present low replacement indices this achievement is not likely to occur. [8]

From the foregoing it is imperative that the Negro himself should decide whether he will seek the more immediate economic and social advantages of the city or the ultimate biological advantages of the country. Upon this decision may conceivably depend the survival of the Negroes in this country. And finally there is the danger that the white man may decide to pay the fearful price of attempting to subjugate permanently the Negro with its consequent deterioration of the moral stamina of the nation. Such a course would have fearful consequences for the white man and the Negro.

SOME HOPEFUL SIGNS

The interracial situation to which we are addressing ourselves is by no means hopeless, for there are reasons not only for great encouragement but for genuine and abundant hope. It was a long way from Jamestown where Negroes were sold and bought as slaves to Richmond, Virginia, where on June 16, 1943, representatives of the white and Negro South sat in solemn conclave as equals about a common discussion table, seeking ways and means to meet the common challenge. The press of the South is becoming more and more liberal in its attitude towards Negroes; the Negrophobe politician is on his way out; the educational advance of the South precludes the profitless endeavors to shut forever the doors of full citizenship in the face of deserving Negro citizens; the sails in the soul of white youth are catching a new breeze that is driving in a new direction; the church is awaking to the challenge of color, which is also a challenge to its own integrity and survival. In the world of the future as in the world of the past, the ultimate determinant of survival is

[8] S. J Holmes, "The Trend of the Racial Balance of Births and Deaths" in Edgar T Thompson, ed., *Race Relations and the Race Problem* (Durham, 1939), p. 95.

character and there is no known correlation between character and race. The most hopeful sign resides in the great power of a favorably changing public opinion. This is the mightiest weapon for the Negro's deliverance. Whatever the Negro does to influence this opinion in his behalf will weigh most heavily in the scales of final adjustment. Whether the Negro seeks the more immediate advantages of urban life where he must live by the Double-Duty Dollar plus a super-efficiency, or whether he seeks rural life with its greater assurances of his survival, it is public opinion that will stay the floodgates of merciless competition and ruthless race prejudice. This larger public opinion must come through the school-room, the church, radio and especially the press. In the last analysis the foundations of a favorable public opinion must be laid in individual character, for which there is no substitute. The survival value of character can be be seen in the history of the Jews. It promises no less for minority groups of other peoples. H. G. Wells recently said that there was a race between education and catastrophe and in the current war there are evidences that catastrophe has taken the lead. Viewed from the angle of race relations it might in equal truth be said that there is a race between public opinion and Negro extermination; for it must never be forgotten that spreading segregation in its ultimate implications means the extermination of the Negro. Only a public opinion sensitive to the Christian ideal can save the interracial situation in the South and Nation. That this public opinion is in the making is the source of an abundant hope!

"CERTAIN
UNALIENABLE RIGHTS"

By MARY McLEOD BETHUNE

———

IT IS A QUIET NIGHT in December, 1773. A British merchant ship rides easily at anchor in Boston Harbor. Suddenly, some row boats move out from the shore. Dark stealthy figures in the boats appear to be Indians in buckskin jackets and with feathers in their hair; but as they reach the ship, clamber abroad, climb down into the hold and carry out boxes of the cargo, the muffled voices speak English words. Their voices grow more excited and determined as they open the boxes and dump the King's tea into the ocean. The Boston Tea Party is in full swing. Resentment has reached flood tide. "Taxation without representation is tyranny!" The spark of the American Revolution has caught flame and the principle of the "consent of the governed" has been established by a gang disguised as Indians who take the law into their own hands. In this action a small and independent people struck out against restrictions and tyranny and oppression and gave initial expression to the ideal of a nation "that all men are created equal, that they are endowed by their Creator with certain unalienable Rights."

It is a Sunday night in Harlem in the year of our Lord 1943. Along the quiet streets dimmed out against the possibility of Axis air attack, colored Americans move to and fro or sit and talk and laugh. Suddenly electric rumor travels from mouth to ear: "A black soldier has been shot by a white policeman and has died in the arms of his mother." No one stops to ask how or why or if it be true. Crowds begin to gather. There is a rumbling of anger and resentment impelled by all the anger and all the resentment of all colored Americans in all the black ghettos in all the cities in America—the resentment against the mistreatment of Negroes in uniform, against restriction and oppression and discrimination breaks loose. Crowds of young people in blind fury strike out against the only symbols of this oppression which are near at hand. Rocks hurtle, windows crash, stores are broken open. Merchants' goods are tumbled into the streets, destroyed or stolen. Police are openly challenged and attacked. There are killings and bodily injury. For hours a veritable reign of terror runs through the streets. All efforts at restraint are of no avail. Finally the blind rage blows itself out.

Some are saying that a band of hoodlums have challenged law and order to burn and pillage and rob. Others look about them to remember riots in Detroit and Los Angeles and Beaumont. They will look further and recall cities laid in ruins by a global war in which the forces of tyranny and oppression and race supremacy attempt to subdue and restrain all the freedom of the world. They are thinking deeply to realize that there is a ferment aloose among the oppressed little people everywhere, a "groping of the long inert masses." They will see depressed and repressed masses all over the world swelling to the breaking point against the walls of ghettos, against economic, social and political restrictions; they will find them breaking open the King's boxes and throwing the tea into the ocean and storming the Bastilles stirred by the clarion call of the Four Freedoms. They are striking back against all that the Axis stands for. They are rising to achieve the ideals "that all men are created equal, that they are endowed by their Creator with certain unalienable Rights, that among these are Life, Liberty and the pursuit of Happiness." With the crash of the guns and the whir of the planes in their ears, led by the fighting voices of a Churchill and a Franklin Roosevelt, a Chiang Kai-shek and a Stalin, they are realizing that "Governments are instituted among Men" to achieve these aims and that these governments derive "their just power from the consent of the governed." They are a part of a peoples' war. The little people want "out." Just as the Colonists at the Boston Tea Party wanted "out" from under tyranny and oppression and taxation without representation, the Chinese want "out," the Indians want "out," and colored Americans want "out."

Throughout America today many people are alarmed and bewildered by the manifestation of this world ferment among the Negro masses. We say we are living in a period of "racial tension." They seem surprised that the Negro should be a part to this world movement. Really, all true Americans should not be surprised by this logical climax of American education. For several generations colored Americans have been brought up on the Boston Tea Party and the Declaration of Independence; on the principle of equality of opportunity, the possession of in-alienable rights, the integrity and sanctity of the human per-sonality. Along with other good Americans the Negro has been prepared to take his part in the fight against an enemy that threatens all these basic American principles. He is fighting now on land and sea and in the air to beat back these forces of op-pression and tyranny and discrimination. Why, then, should we be surprised when at home as well as abroad he fights back against these same forces?

One who would really understand this racial tension which has broken out into actual conflict in riots as in Harlem, Detroit, and Los Angeles, must look to the roots and not be confused by the branches and the leaves. The tension rises out of the growing internal pressure of Negro masses to break through the wall of restriction which restrains them from full American citi-zenship. This mounting power is met by the unwillingness of white America to allow any appreciable breach in this wall.

The hard core of internal pressure among the Negro masses in the United States today is undoubtedly their resentment over the mistreatment of colored men in the armed forces. The Negro faces restrictions in entering certain branches of the service, resistance to being assigned posts according to his ability; and above all there is the failure of the Army and his government to protect him in the uniform of his country from actual assault by civilians.

Letters from the men in Army camps have streamed into the homes of their parents and friends everywhere, telling of this mistreatment by officers, military police and civilians, of their difficulties in getting accommodations on trains and buses, of numerous incidents of long, tiresome journeys without meals and other concrete evidences of the failure of their government to protect and provide for its men, even when they are preparing to fight in defense of the principles of that government.

They need no agitation by newspaper accounts or the stimulation of so-called leaders. These things are the intimate experiences of the masses themselves. They know them and feel them intensely and resent them bitterly.

You must add to these deep-seated feelings a whole series of repercussions of the frustrated efforts of Negroes to find a place in war production: the absolute denial of employment in many cases, or employment far below the level of their skills, numerous restrictions in their efforts to get training, resistance of labor unions to the improving and utilization of their skills on the job. Pile on to these their inability to get adequate housing even for those employed in war work, and often, where houses are available, restrictions to segregated units in temporary war housing. At the same time they see around them unlimited opportunities offered to other groups to serve their country in the armed forces, to be employed at well-paying jobs, to get good housing financed by private concerns and FHA funds.

Even those observers who have some understanding of the Negro's desire to break through all these restrictions will charge it to superficial causes, such as the agitation of the Negro press and leaders; or they counsel the Negro to "go slow." It is as though they admit that the patient is sick with fever and diagnosis reveals that he needs twelve grains of quinine, but they decide that because he is a Negro they had better give him only six. They admit that he is hungry and needs to be fed, but because he is a Negro they suggest that a half meal will suffice. This approach, of course, is a historical hang-over. It is a product of the half-hearted and timorous manner in which we have traditionally faced the Negro problem in America.

In order to maintain slavery, it was necessary to isolate black men from every possible manifestation of our culture. It was necessary to teach that they were inferior beings who could not profit from that culture. After the slave was freed, every effort has persisted to maintain "white supremacy" and wall the Negro in from every opportunity to challenge this concocted "supremacy." Many Americans said the Negro could not learn and they "proved" it by restricting his educational opportunities. When he surmounted these obstacles and achieved a measure of training, they said he did not know how to use it and proved it by restricting his employment opportunities. When it was necessary to employ him, they saw to it that he was confined to laborious and poorly-paid jobs. After they had made every effort to guarantee that his economic, social and cultural levels were low, they attributed his status to his race. Therefore, as he moved North and West after Reconstruction and during the Industrial Revolution, they saw to it that he was confined to living in veritable ghettos with convenants that were as hard and resistant as the walls of the ghettos of Warsaw.

They met every effort on his part to break through these barriers with stern resistance that would brook no challenge to our concept of white supremacy. Although they guaranteed him full citizenship under the Constitution and its Amendments, they saw to it that he was largely disfranchised and had little part in our hard won ideal of "the consent of the governed." In the midst of this anachronism, they increasingly educated his children in the American way of life—in its ideals of equality of all men before the law, and opportunities for the fullest possible development of the individual.

As this concept took hold among the Negro masses, it has evidenced itself through the years in a slow, growing, relentless pressure against every restriction which denied them their full citizenship. This pressure, intensified by those of other races who really believed in democracy, began to make a break through the walls here and there. It was given wide-spread impetus by the objectives of the New Deal with its emphasis on the rise of the forgotten man. With the coming of the Second World War, all the Negro's desires were given voice and support by the world leaders who fought back against Hitler and all he symbolizes. His efforts to break through have responded to Gandhi and Chiang Kai-shek, to Churchill and Franklin Roosevelt.

The radios and the press of the world have drummed into his

ears the Four Freedoms, which would lead him to think that the world accepts as legitimate his claims as well as those of oppressed peoples all over the world. His drive for status has now swept past even most of his leaders, and has become imbedded in mass-consciousness which is pushing out of the way all the false prophets, be they white or black—or, be they at home or abroad.

The Negro wants to break out into the free realm of democratic citizenship. We can have only one of two responses. Either we must let him out wholly and completely in keeping with our ideals, or we must mimic Hitler and shove him back.

What, then, does the Negro want? His answer is very simple. He wants only what all other Americans want. He wants opportunity to make real what the Declaration of Independence and the Constitution and Bill of Rights say; what the Four Freedoms establish. While he knows these ideals are open to no man completely he wants only his equal chance to attain them. The Negro today wants specifically:

1. *Government leadership in building favorable public opinion.* Led by the President himself, the federal government should initiate a sound program carried out through appropriate federal agencies designed to indicate the importance of race in the war and post-war period. The cost of discrimination and segregation to a nation at war and the implications of American racial attitudes for our relationships with the other United Nations and their people should be delineated. Racial myths and superstitions should be exploded. The cooperation of the newspapers, the radio and the screen should be sought to replace caricature and slander with realistic interpretations of sound racial relationships.

2. *The victory of democracy over dictatorship.* Under democracy the Negro has the opportunity to work for an improvement in his status through the intelligent use of his vote, the creation of a more favorable public opinion, and the development of his native abilities. The ideals of democracy and Christianity work for equality. These ideals the dictatorships disavow. Experience has taught only too well the implications for him and all Americans of a Nazi victory.

3. *Democracy in the armed forces.* He wants a chance to serve his country in all branches of the armed forces to his full capacity. He sees clearly the fallacy of fostering discrimination and segregation in the very forces that are fighting against discrimination and segregation all over the world. He believes that the government should fully protect the persons and the rights of all who wear the uniform of its armed forces.

4. *The protection of his civil rights and an end to lynching.* He wants full protection of the rights guaranteed all Americans by the Constitution; equality before the law, the right to jury trial and service, the eradication of lynching. Demanding these rights for himself, he will not be misled into any anti-foreign, Red-baiting, or anti-Semitic crusade to deny these rights to others. Appalled by the conditions prevailing in Washington, he joins in demanding the ballot for the District of Columbia and the protection of his rights now denied him within the shadow of the Capitol.

5. *The free ballot.* He wants the abolition of the poll tax and of the "white primary"; he wants universal adult suffrage. He means to use it to vote out all the advocates of racism and vote in those whose records show that they actually practise democracy.

6. *Equal access to employment opportunities.* He wants the chance to work and advance in any job for which he has the training and capacity. To this end he wants equal access to training opportunities. In all public programs, federal, state and local, he wants policy-making and administrative posts as well as rank and file jobs without racial discrimination. He wants a fair share of jobs under Civil Service.

7. *Extension of federal programs in public housing, health, social security, education and relief under federal control.* Low income and local prejudice often deprive him of these basic social services. Private enterprise or local government units cannot or will not provide them. For efficiency and equity in administration of these programs, the Negro looks to the

federal government until such time as he has gained the full
and free use of the ballot in all states.

8. *Elimination of racial barriers in labor unions.* He demands
   the right of admission on equal terms to the unions having
   jurisdiction over the crafts or industries in which he is employed. He urges that job control on public works be denied
   to any union practising discrimination.

9. *Realistic interracial co-operation.* He realizes the complete
   interdependence of underprivileged white people and Negroes, North and South—laborers and sharecroppers alike.
   He knows that they stay in the gutter together or rise to
   security together; that the hope of democracy lies in their
   cooperative effort to make their government responsive to
   their needs; that national unity demands their sharing together
   more fully in the benefits of freedom—not "one as the hand
   and separate as the fingers," but one as the clasped hands of
   friendly cooperation.

Here, then, is a program for racial advancement and national
unity. It adds up to the sum of the rights, privileges and responsibilities of full American citizenship. This is all that the Negro
asks. He will not willingly accept less. As long as America offers
less, she will be that much less a democracy. The whole way is
the American way.

What can the Negro do himself to help get what he wants?

1. In the first place, he should accept his responsibility for a
   full part of the job of seeing to it that whites and Negroes
   alike understand the current intensity of the Negro's fight for
   status as a part of a world people's movement. As individuals
   and as members of organizations, we must continue to use
   every channel open to affect public opinion, to get over to all
   Americans the real nature of this struggle. Those of us who
   accept some measure of responsibility for leadership, must
   realize that in such people's movements, the real leadership
   comes up out of the people themselves. All others who would
   give direction to such a movement must identify themselves
   with it, become a part of it, and interpret it to others. We

must make plain to America that we have reached a critical stage in the assimilation of colored people.

We have large and growing numbers of young and older Negroes who have achieved by discipline and training a measure of culture which qualifies them for advanced status in our American life. To deny this opportunity creates on the one hand frustration with its attendant disintegration, and, on the other, deprives American civilization of the potential fruits of some thirteen millions of its sons and daughters.

Through our personal and group contacts with other racial groups, we must increasingly win their understanding and support. Only in this way can the swelling force among minority racial groups be channeled into creative progress rather than exploded into riots and conflicts, or dissipated in hoodlumism. While we seek on the one side to "educate" white America, we must continue relentlessly to make plain to ourselves and our associates the increased responsibility that goes with increased rights and privileges. Our fight for Fair Employment Practices legislation must go hand and hand with "Hold Your Job" campaigns; our fight for anti-poll tax legislation must be supported equally by efforts of Negroes themselves to exercise fully and intelligently the right of franchise where they have it.

2. We must challenge, skillfully but resolutely, every sign of restriction or limitation on our full American citizenship. When I say challenge, I mean we must seek every opportunity to place the burden of responsibility upon him who denies it. If we simply accept and acquiesce in the face of discrimination, we accept the responsibility ourselves and allow those responsible to salve their conscience by believing that they have our acceptance and concurrence. We should, therefore, protest openly everything in the newspapers, on the radio, in the movies that smacks of discrimination or slander. We must take the seat that our ticket calls for and place upon the proprietor the responsibility of denying it to us.

We must challenge everywhere the principle and practice of enforced racial segregation. We must make it clear that where groups and individuals are striving for social and economic status, group isolation one from the other allows the rise of misunderstanding and suspicion, providing rich soil for the seeds of antagonism and conflict. Recently in the city of Detroit, there was no rioting in the neighborhoods where whites and Negroes lived as neighbors, and there was no conflict in the plants where they worked side by side on the assembly-lines. Whenever one has the price or can fill the requirements for any privilege which is open to the entire public, that privilege must not be restricted on account of race.

Our appeal must be made to the attributes of which the Anglo-Saxon is so proud—his respect for law and justice, his love of fair-play and true sportsmanship.

3. We must understand that the great masses of our people are farmers and workers, and that their hopes for improvement in a large measure lie in association with organizations whose purpose is to improve their condition. This means membership in and support of labor and farmer unions. Within these organizations it means continuous efforts with our allies of all racial groups to remove all barriers which operate in the end to divide workers and defeat all of their purposes. The voice of organized labor has become one of the most powerful in the land and unless we have a part in that voice our people will not be heard.

4. We must take a full part in the political life of our community, state and nation. We must learn increasingly about political organization and techniques. We must prepare for and fight for places on the local, state, and national committees of our political parties. This is a representative government and the only way that our representatives can reflect our desires is for us to register and vote. In a large measure the whole of our national life is directed by the legislation and other activities of our governmental units. The only way to affect their action and to guarantee their democratic nature is to have a full hand in electing individuals who represent us. The national election of 1944 represents one of the most crucial in the life of this nation and of the world. The Con-

gressional representatives that are elected to office will have a large hand in the type of peace treaty to be adopted and the entire nature of our post-war domestic economy. All of our organizations and individuals who supply leadership must fully acquaint our people with the requirements of registering and voting, see to it that they are cognizant of the issues involved and get out to register and vote.

Negro women and their organizations have a tremendous responsibility and opportunity to offer leadership and support to this struggle of the racial group to attain improved cultural status in America. We have always done a full part of this job. Now, with large numbers of our men in the armed forces and with considerable numbers of new people who have migrated into our communities to take their part in war production, we have a bigger job and a greater opportunity than ever. Our women know too well the disintegrating effect upon our family life of our low economic status. Discrimination and restriction have too often meant to us broken homes and the delinquency of our children. We have seen our dreams frustrated and our hopes broken. We have risen, however, out of our despair to help our men climb up the next rung of the ladder. We see now more than a glimmer of light on the horizon of a new hope. We feel behind us the surge of all women of China and India and of Africa who see the same light and look to us to march with them. We will reach out our hands to all women who struggle forward—white, black, brown, yellow—all. If we have the courage and tenacity of our forebears, who stood firmly like a rock against the lashings of slavery and the disruption of Reconstruction, we shall find a way to do for our day what they did for theirs. Above all we Negro women of all levels and classes must realize that this forward movement is a march of the masses and that all of us must go forward with it or be pushed aside by it. We will do our part. In order for us to have peace and justice and democracy for all, may I urge that we follow the example of the great humanitarian—Jesus Christ—in exemplifying in our lives both by word and action the fatherhood of God and the brotherhood of man?

THE NEGRO WANTS
FULL PARTICIPATION IN
THE AMERICAN DEMOCRACY

By FREDERICK D. PATTERSON

———

MOST AMERICAN NEGROES are not allowed to forget the fact of their racial identity during any but the briefest periods of their lives. This enforced consciousness of race with its connotation of inferiority is a deterrent in varying degrees upon practically all Negroes. Only a few are consequently able to achieve in a fully normal way their life's ambitions. Indeed, the limitations and proscriptions imposed upon Negroes make them the most discriminated against minority in the United States.

These limitations and proscriptions, easily imposed because of "high visibility," have no necessary relationship to previous status or to scientific justification. The ignominy of the slave background is applied even to those who are the descendants of a long ancestry of free Negroes. Many competent genetecists and anthropologists deny that there is any conclusive evidence to prove that one race is inherently inferior to another. But the Negro more than any other minority in America has been misrepresented, misjudged, and maligned. Denied his rightful opportunities to develop as a normal being, his every shortcoming has been cited as evidence of his "inferiority" and "depravity." Even his ancestral African culture has been ridiculed and undervalued in attempts to prove his innate inferiority.

Students of the race problem in the United States associate degrees of ignorance, poverty and disease with a people's environment. Crime and disease will thrive among any people who live in crowded slum areas. Ignorance, the pernicious results of extreme malnutrition, and general backwardness are the almost inevitable products of sharecropping and tenant-farming. The fact that Negroes have been able not only to survive but in many instances to rise above, the squalor of their humble beginnings and attain worthwhile goals has won faith in the vitality and intrinsic worth of the race.

The majority of Negroes, nevertheless, are lagging behind the standards attained by white Americans. As limitations and proscriptions are removed, the Negro people as a whole will measure up to their fullest opportunities in a manner that will equal the achievements of others. This fact is already being abundantly shown. Crime and juvenile delinquency rapidly diminish when housing projects provide a wholesome environment. Home ownership among Negro families on modest but stable incomes is rapidly increasing. Where the franchise is enjoyed, Negroes are usually found on the side of good government. Like other good citizens, they want economical and honest administration; good schools; paved streets; adequate fire and police protection; as wide an enjoyment of the Four Freedoms as is practicable; and whatever other progress the community can afford.

In spite of these evidences of increasing ability to meet American standards of citizenship, the underselling of the Negro continues. Today, just as during slavery, this occurs for the purpose of keeping him in economic bondage and with him the laboring class of whites in both rural and urban areas. The race hatred which is fanned periodically in both the North and the South derives indeed rather from this economic fact than from social implications. Whenever circumstances or convenience dictates, the social factor in race relations is simply ignored.

The social factor, moreover, has been in many instances exaggerated. The argument that the common use of restaurants and public facilities by Negroes and whites will lead inevitably to race intermixture has much evidence to the contrary. Many States are comparatively free from the meaner forms of segregation and yet the number of mixed marriages is negligible. Further, aside from the desire to escape the debasing environment of slum or blighted areas, Negroes generally prefer to live among their own race. They are, of course, compelled to do so in many cities in which covenants or other restrictions prevent them from living in the more desirable sections. In the small towns of the South the Negro is yet living to a large extent on the far side of the railroad tracks, where the pavement, sewer system and supply of running water are frequently non-existent.

Negroes are neither satisfied with nor unduly irritated by the constant reminder of their racial identity. They are definitely annoyed by the uncertainties likely to arise in any given situation, as for example in the great social question of shaking hands with a white person. Even after this crisis has passed, the Negro is still uncertain of the degree to which normal courtesies will be extended. He must be on his guard in order not to appear either boorish or too eager.

Two other factors are important since they determine in great part the reaction of this large minority group to the section in which most of the thirteen millions of us still reside. The first is that in addition to the constant humiliation of segregation there is the lack of equity of accommodations. The term "separate but equal" is rarely lived up to. Most Negroes abhor segregation, therefore, not only because of the implied inferiority or unworthiness involved, but also because they are reasonably sure that whatever provisions are made for them on public carriers or otherwise will suffer by comparison with those provided for members of the white race at the same price. Nowhere is this violation more flagrant than in the case of school facilities. In those counties where the Negro population is the heaviest, there will be found the greatest neglect of Negro children, while the white children of this same community enjoy a corresponding opulence in facilities. These flagrant abuses are often shamelessly administered by county boards of education who make no pretense of fair distribution of educational funds on a population ratio basis.

The other point which looms large in the Negro's attitude toward the South is the fact that he is living dangerously in terms of his physical safety and that of his family. Most Negroes in the South, intelligent or otherwise, dread an altercation with a white person. Even if the threat of lynching is not serious, they feel reasonably sure that their side of the issue stands little chance of getting a fair hearing. In many instances, falling into the hands of the law results in more violent mistreatment for them than if they had attempted to handle the matter themselves. If the case comes to trial, the odds are greatly against them that the decision will be just if either the plaintiff or the defendant is a white person. For ordinary infractions of the law, the penalty is apt in many cases to be unnecessarily severe. Or, what is more likely, the arresting officer will be abusive. Owing to a complete understanding of these facts by most Negroes and their desire to avoid the extreme unpleasantness and humiliation involved, the number of such instances is kept to a minimum. It is these dangers rather than the actual mistreatment or violence that makes life for the Negro in the South a daily depressing experience. Yet, the degree of accommodation which the Negro has attained permits him to make sport of many of these potentially difficult and humiliating experiences.

Many Southern white people, it is true, feel a definite friendship for the Negro. But this runs largely to individuals. At the same time, Negroes are of the opinion that Northern white people feel some sense of justice toward the Negro as a race but often little friendship of a personal nature. Southern whites, in noting the preferences which many Negroes exhibit for the North, fail to understand why this should be true. They do not appreciate the fact that when one Negro is lynched, the entire race is not only humiliated but threatened. At the time that friendship is most needed, these occurrences erect a strong and cold wall which separates the two races and sets at naught the many instances of kind deeds and mutual helpfulness which are nowhere more evident or more feelingly rendered than in the South.

Many Negroes see much of the better side of the South. Acts have varied from the giving of funds in the promotion of education to extra-official and confidential happenings that have spared them humiliation and hardship. All the more remarkable has been the fact that some of these gestures have involved the most sensitive spots in race relations. Naturally these favorable experiences temper understanding of the problem and have forced many to see it more in terms of its individual than its racial aspects. These experiences reveal at once the futility of race hate and the necessity to approach all aspects of the problem on the basis of facts.

The rapid migration of the Negro to all sections of the nation, and with him many white people of the South, is producing a standard attitude toward the race question over the nation which inclines in the direction of the Southern pattern. In many instances the attitude of sections outside of the South toward the Negro, as they now receive their initial first hand contact, is more severe than that to be found in the South generally. It may very well be that the South, having had years of experience in inter-racial contact, will move forward in constructive measures with greater assurance and rapidity than most non-Southern sections of the nation. The South at least has evidence built up over many years of the purposefulness and normality of the strivings of the Negro race. It also has ample evidence that given the opportunity the Negro people are capable of normal development along all lines. It remains, then, for the South to realize that the full extension of opportunities to all is the only way to promote the full economic and social development of the region. Once this concept is fully matured, the South can move forward in friendship and understanding. Already it is evident that Southern political demagogues are finding this section less of a fertile soil than formerly for sowing the seeds of distrust through dire predictions of Negro domination. The recent race riots that have come in the South as a part of the wave of national hysteria could easily have been more severe but for the growing sanity and basic wisdom of the Southern people, black as well as white.

It is therefore out of this hodgepodge of good and evil, or as Dr. Howard Odum of the University of North Carolina says, of many good people doing bad things, that we shall attempt to see what next steps may wisely lead us in the direction of the democracy this nation eventually hopes to become.

WHAT THE AMERICAN NEGRO WANTS

The American Negro wants to become a fully participating citizen in every sense of the word. He wants this participation not only or merely for the sake of himself but also because he believes in democracy as a way of life for this nation and because his concept of democracy leads him to feel that this citizenship status is essential to the complete realization of our national destiny. "A government of the people, by the people and for the people" implies ALL in each of these connections. No government by or for the people is possible until all people understand their government and have the freedom and privilege of expressing themselves in regard to it. This hinges upon the inalienable right to share with the nation's people those minima which they have determined to be essential to the general welfare. When these minima are guaranteed to all of the nation's people without regard to race, creed or color, such people are uniformly better able to serve the nation both as individuals and in terms of their collective strength. We, as Negro people, must, therefore, look forward to the extension of every guaranty of full citizenship. We believe that whether these things come now or later, there can be no compromise in stating them as objectives. The Supreme Court has ruled that the full enjoyment of the blessings of democracy is an individual rather than a race or group right. If this concept is adhered to, there can be no question that whatever is available as a privilege of citizenship for any of the people must be available to all of the people. This means equal opportunity for education, freedom of speech, the right to worship according to the dictates of one's conscience, the right to vote—when the standard qualifications of voting are met—and freedom from all forms of discrimination which only serve to embarrass and single out for ridicule an individual because of his color. To those who ask, "Is not discrimination involved in all forms of segregation?" the answer seems unquestionably "yes." One cannot dodge the issue by making a distinction between the two, although there is difference in the degree of discrimination to be found in the segregated pattern. Any form of segregation based on race, creed or color is discriminatory and imposes a penalty inconsistent with the guaranties of American democracy. The more conservative element of Negroes differ from those who hold the most radical views in opposition to segregation only in terms of time and technique of its elimination. In any statement which attempts to speak unequivocally in terms of ultimates, all Negroes must condemn any form of segregation based on race, creed or color anywhere in our nation.

The extension of the full privileges and responsibilities of democracy to the Negro people should not be seen as a threat in any way to the sanctity of the homes of American white people or as an abridgment of any kind of their rights. When Negroes are extended their full rights as American citizens, there will be much in the way of needed growth that will not come except through time and experience. That is as it should be, and the fact that it is required is not a reflection on anyone.

Democracy is a form of government and a way of life whose tenets require full participation by its adherents. Each citizen experiences and enjoys democracy in proportion as he fulfills the responsibilities related thereto. The proper discharge of these duties is possible only through the experience which participation will give. As long as participation is denied, the citizen is unable to share in the democratic process. It seems unquestionable, therefore, that there is no privilege of American democracy that Negroes do not want as the inherent individual right of every citizen in the United States.

HOW ARE THESE RIGHTS, PRIVILEGES AND RESPONSIBILITIES TO BE SECURED?

It is much easier to state what the Negro wants than it is to state the methods or procedures by which these wants are to be satisfied. The fact that the Negro people do not have the enjoyment of the full guaranties of democracy today is based upon the existence of a number of factors, some of which are only secondarily related to considerations of race.

The Negroes' liberation from the bonds of slavery as unlearned and poverty-stricken people placed them in the great class of laborers and made them part and parcel of the economic problems of this group. We find them, therefore, in addition to limitations and proscriptions which they suffer as members of the Negro race, carrying the enormous handicaps of unskilled workers in industry or agriculture, and suffering all of the privations which came to this group through an era of rugged individualism and the ruthless exploitation of an outmoded economic system which in many instances has been oblivious of the rights of the masses of working people. The above consideration has forced the Negro to be a permanent ally of labor and has made him a proponent of whatever measures have been intended to secure a wider distribution of income with the establishment of certain essential minima in terms of health, housing, education and related factors of living.

It would appear that the Negro may expect to receive more justice and a greater measure of the blessings of democracy in proportion as he finds himself working in statesman-like fashion for those measures which have to do with the general upbuilding of our nation and the extension of rights to the underprivileged regardless of race, creed or color. It has been made clear in the economic and social studies of recent years that our nation, though young, has had an interesting history with a vigorous past. The early pioneers found a country filled with abundant wealth, but one which was undeveloped and thus burdened with many obstacles to be overcome. These early American settlers showed that they possessed the rugged pioneering spirit necessary to harness the resources which they found and gave to us one of the greatest of industrial nations. The rapid growth which was enjoyed with abundance on every hand served to develop a rugged individualistic and often wasteful approach which only now is beginning to reveal its seriousness as we take stock of the fact that millions of acres of virgin timber have been destroyed and millions of acres of soil have been eroded beyond the point of reclamation. Our minerals have been mined to the vanishing point, and we find ourselves—with all of our modern knowledge— unable to stop the vicious waste which is going on apace.

More important even than the recognition of the waste of natural resources has been our revelation of what has happened to our human resources which, after all, are the fundamental wealth of any nation. Our economy was based on the unreal notion that any individual who was healthy, normally ambitious and willing to work could someday acquire a sizable fortune. We have moved ahead allowing the process of rugged individualism to grind under the heels of industry and a not less ruthless and exploitative agriculture, hundreds of thousands, if not millions of souls who we now believe never had a decent chance to make the most of their abilities. Industrial exploitation has created our slum areas in urban centers and given rise to all of the concomitant ills imaginable. Too frequently rural areas with their agrarian economy have made exploitation of sharecroppers and tenants as well as of the soil a technique of survival with a steady impoverishment of both the land and the people. This has been aided by sectional differences, with the South serving as the orphan of a national situation in which it has the most people to support and the least wealth upon which to feed, clothe, educate and employ them. It is an area developed largely by means of Eastern and Northern capital. Most of the surplus earnings of the region have come from cheap labor and vigorous exploitative practices and have been drained off to other sections to enhance their already stable and superior financial position.

Negroes, who constitute practically one-third of the Southern population of some 25,000,000 people and who belong largely to the class that has been most vigorously exploited often as a technique of survival, have a vital interest in all measures which look to changing the unbalance of things both economic and social in the Southern picture. The guaranties to all of the people of this nation of minimum housing, health benefits, education, jobs, old age pensions, security for unemployment and the elimination of poll tax, are measures which Negroes regard as essential in correcting the ills described above. One of the fundamental approaches to the solution of the Negro's problem as an underprivileged American is that he should become aware of these economic conditions which hold him, along with thousands of whites, in virtual bondage. Another fundamental is that he ally himself with those who wish to make the American democracy more socially sensitive so that it will extend to those who are disfranchised in more ways than in terms of the ballot the chance for a decent existence. This can be done without destroying the economic structure of the nation in terms of those splendid aspects which have made this nation a great one. The extent to which these measures are designed, and success attends the attempt, to benefit all of the people in keeping with the guaranties of democracy, to this extent will the Negro people find themselves greatly improved in their economic and social relationships. Fortunately this can be done without any particular reference to race.

Already we are beginning to see the change take place. New and better schools for Negroes, as well as for whites, are being constructed. In many instances, it is true, an unfortunate disparity in the quality of buildings and in the salaries of teachers and other personnel still exists. Increasingly, however, education is being recognized by the several states of the South, and of the nation, as an obligation which they must discharge in terms of their total population. Nowhere are signs more evident in this regard than on the campuses of the state-supported institutions for Negroes in the South. Some of them in the past ten or twelve years have come into completely new physical plants the quality and accommodations of which in terms of the programs being administered seem entirely adequate. Not a few of these institutions are also being enabled to pay salaries in keeping with the standard of the state and comparing favorably with the national scale. Some of these things, no doubt, are coming to pass because of decisions of the courts requiring equal pay for teachers doing equal work, but an important share of them is coming as a general recognition of the relationship of education for all the people to the establishment of sound democracy.

What is true of education can also be said of other areas of living, such as employment in industry and such social benefits as old age pensions and greater development of health facilities which assure the indigent of all races an opportunity to receive some of the abundant medical and surgical care which they need. This human rather than racial approach should be applied to all aspects of the problem. The emotional quality which is always attached to the consideration of purely race issues leaves much to be desired in the working out of prompt and effective solutions. The sooner white people can be brought to regard the Negro's plight in terms of the economic and social oppression which he experiences rather than in terms of any innate inferiority, the sooner all can unite in working for a solution in a calm and unemotional way which will simply recognize that rights and opportunities of human beings are involved.

We have a striking example confronting the American people at present as to what the churning up of race antipathies will do to a nation trying to gird itself for war. If during the period of peak employment and high wages our nation is plagued by considerations of race, it becomes a matter of great urgency as we prepare for the post-war period, when adjustments are going to be doubly hard to make, that we accustom ourselves instead to thinking in terms of the over-all rights, opportunities and responsibilities of the American people rather than in terms of race. This will make possible the reconversion to peace with a minimum of interracial friction. The American people may face at best a difficult and prolonged period of adjustment that will bring economic dislocation with unemployment and hardship to many. It is hoped that the brunt of the burden of this readjustment will not fall upon the Negro. It therefore becomes almost a matter of national mental hygiene to help encourage this approach to the solution of the nation's problem.

It is perfectly clear, however, that the foregoing does not constitute the sole or total approach to the matter of the proper adjustment of Negroes in American society. Entirely aside from discriminations which Negroes suffer because of their relationship with a great mass of workers in this country, there are also specific injustices which they experience because of race, and only a direct, specific approach to the correction of these things in terms of the elimination of the effects of race prejudice will do any real or lasting good. As already indicated, Negroes have suffered greatly from a general underrating including their contributions to this nation both in war and in peace. At the same time they have been confronted with an overrating of everything which has had a white origin.

Those who sincerely wish to correct this situation, which is in reality bad for both races and distinctly inimical to any harmonious working together of all of the peoples of this nation as a unit, will seek to change conditions which play up all of the unfavorable aspects of the Negro particularly in the public press while ignoring or playing down his racial identity in connection with those laudable achievements of which any American could rightfully be proud. Those who are working for the compilation of Negro history in America should be encouraged and particularly should those who write textbooks be urged to bring the Negro in for his fair share of credit for the contribution which he has made to this nation since its very inception. Anything which serves to reveal to the minds of children and adults the Negro's worth as a contributing citizen and not simply as a charge or ward of the nation will inevitably be reflected in improved race relations and in the desire to see the Negro people receive their just due. As this nation becomes increasingly literate, it is all the more important that the people receive an unbiased and fairly developed literature which will tend to make for greater American unity by showing the total contribution which all of the nation's people have made to the growth and development of our country. The portrayal of invidious and unwholesome distinctions between groups based on circumstances over which those groups have no control only serves to divide them. All writers, therefore, should be brought to realize the significant responsibility which they carry for the development of American unity. It is fitting to commend those newspapers—Southern as well as non-Southern—that have already taken cognizance of this fact and that are doing much to give credit where credit is due in terms of Negro achievement. The effect of this will be not only to change the attitude of white America toward black America but to change the attitude of black America both toward white America and toward itself. One of the great depressing factors in Negro life is that the Negro people have so thoroughly accepted the ideas that they were non-contributors and that they were not expected to meet the American standard and participate in the American ideal that many of them have developed complexes which deny them the opportunity to make the full contribution of which they are capable. Obviously, to the extent to which this is true the entire nation suffers.

There are a number of other ways in which Negroes come to public notice. Most of these reveal black people in none too favorable light. Those who wish to help should endorse and encourage efforts which are underway at the present time to change this state of affairs. They consist of: (1) requesting and working for a change in the reporting of crime in which race should not be played up; (2) obtaining recognition for achievement in the daily press; (3) securing the inclusion of historical contributions in historical texts; (4) assuring favorable recognition of Negroes as citizens in children's school books; and (5) attaining the assignment of something other than the usual roles of servants and buffoons to Negro actors in the movies.

In those cases of discriminatory practices involving Negroes which have legal sanction there appears to be no other point of attack except through a direct challenging of the law which denies to one-tenth of the population the protection and equality which it guarantees to the other ninety per cent. This forthright attack has brought and will bring a number of sweeping victories in behalf of democracy. These will place Negro citizens on a plane with all other citizens of our nation in terms of their individual rights.

Those laws and practices which deny to the Negro equal pay to that received by whites for the same type and equality of work are a scourge to democracy, and nothing less than a forthright uncompromising effort should be made to secure their change. This does not mean that immediate changes can always be effected. There can obviously be circumstances under which attempts at salary equalization may result in a schedule of adjustment which will require a period of two or three years to bring complete parity. Where a lack of funds dictates this course and where another approach would cause a corresponding and unnecessary hardship to white teachers, wisdom would appear on the side of the gradual process. If, however, such a proposal is not made in complete sincerity or no effort to right a patent injustice develops, there is no course open other than that of an unrelenting use of every available legal means to secure correction.

The extension of the franchise is another and transcendingly important right, denied only to Negroes on the basis of race, which Negroes themselves should seek with whatever legal and other honorable means at their disposal. As long as this fundamental guaranty of citizenship is withheld, many of the other inequities based upon race will be continued. The refusal to extend the right and responsibility of voting to Negroes in most of the Southern states is a deliberate injustice to an important segment of the population and an absolute deterrent to good government. The ballot is withheld partly through groundless fear and partly as a tool of unscrupulous politicians who secure their privileges through the numerical population strength of their states while denying to an important share of that strength a voice in their choice.

Several Southern states are correcting this evil without resorting to the subterfuge of the "private" primary. There is a growing realization that Negroes are equally interested with their white neighbors in good government. The fundamental soundness of extending the franchise to all who meet the qualifications, regardless of race, along with the inconsistency of its denial with the avowed tenets of democracy, gives great hope that efforts to correct this situation will meet with decreasing resistance. The Negro people owe it to themselves and to the nation which receives their allegiance to leave no stone unturned until this fundamental democratic right is secured.

When this is done, Negroes will use it just as will their white fellow citizens. They will, however, in the full possession of the ballot constitute a far more potent asset to themselves and to good government than is now the case. As long as the Negro is a nonentity in the determination of the kind of government under which he must live, there may be expected a continuation of many of the injustices from which he now suffers. Law enforcement officers and public servants generally feel no necessity for a just administration of the law for the Negro people. Too frequently the behavior of these public officials is determined by the avowed interests, good or ill, of those who elect them. If justice and fair play are to have sway, they will result only from the balanced judgment which will be possible when all citizens exercise the responsibility and right of voting. There is no single advance that may be made that will prove of greater benefit in establishing the Negro people as full-fledged participating citizens than the granting of the franchise.

The present status of race relations in America is intricate and involved. Its improvement is not subject to any one point of attack. It is made up from the failings and inadequacies of both groups, white and black. If the solution is ever to be realized, it must come from a frontal attack on all areas requiring adjustment. If there is any failing within the Negro group today, it is probably that of trying to find a panacea or cure-all. Negroes are yet at the stage where they are vying with each other for ascendency in terms of technique or method. Experience indicates that until a combined effort is made there is little hope for anything more than a piecemeal solution of the problem.

First of all then, if the Negro is properly to secure for himself the measure of justice and security which he desires as an American citizen, there is needed sound planning on the part of Negroes themselves—planning that will encompass the over-all relationships involved and which will seek to put at work those who can best work at some particular aspect or relationship. If this is done, one of the values which will accrue will be the development on the part of the Negro himself of a plan of action. It is not sufficient simply to declare the failings of America toward the Negro; it is also necessary for the Negro to plan a dynamic program which he can initiate that will help bring his way the things which he has failed up to now to receive at least in full measure. If this is done, it will be in opposition to that stream of thought which has placed great stock in revolutionary ideas in America, and which believes that the Negro by taking a passive or waiting role will come into his own out of the economic and social confusion now engulfing the nation and the world. Strong issue must be taken with this point of view. In spite of the fact that much in the old order will need to pass as we come into a new economic and social relationship which encompasses not only our nation, but the world, we shall have to make our prog-

ress slowly if permanent improvement in our way of life is to
result.

The Negro himself must assume an important responsibility
for stimulating and sharing in this process of progress by evolution in his own thinking and action. It is possible to place such
great stress on the ultimate that we forget the step by step methods which are necessary in order to bring the ultimate to pass.
At this stage of the American Negro's development and in the
presence of the attitude which the majority of people seem to
have toward him, he may well afford to place great emphasis on
the securing of opportunity. This must be opportunity for a
varied participation for significant numbers of Negroes rather
than that of simply getting one or two in hitherto unexplored
and uninvited fields. Negroes prefer that this opportunity should
come to them untrammeled by conditions of segregation or discrimination. If, however, choice is limited to a segregated opportunity, or no opportunity, experience indicates the former as
more desirable. If the most is made of segregated opportunities
now, those who are developed thereby will do much, by showing the insignificance of race in terms of accomplishment, to
break down segregation and other barriers to normal participation.

Acknowledging the present situation in which participation
is not possible on any large scale for the Negro without some
consideration as to race, Negroes should work in an organized
way for the staffing of all institutions maintained at public expense for Negroes by Negroes. In a few instances there are yet
high schools in the South which have white principals. These
principalships are simply being used as a training ground for
people who are moved on to white schools as a promotion or they
become a dumping ground for superannuated people. They deny
to the Negro an opportunity for leadership under the bi-racial
concept of the South. In this the race is denied both the opportunity for growth through a desirable outlet for its talent and
for the earning power involved. This is likewise true of institutions for the insane, alms houses, public health programs, hospitals, and other institutions maintained by tax support. The element of injustice is so evident in this situation that it is difficult

to see how any really organized approach to the securing of this additional opportunity and provision for worthwhile participation on the part of Negroes can be denied. Moreover, if we add up the total income involved in this situation in the entire South, we shall find that it runs into millions of dollars—millions of dollars that would encourage our youth to new heights of development in order to secure these opportunities and millions of dollars which our race as a poverty-stricken group needs as it attempts to live in better homes and enjoy in fuller measure those things which the American people regard as essential to normal living.

If the Negro is to come fully into his own, we must take into account the conditions which surround seventy-five per cent of the Negro people in the South where the bi-racial pattern is most rigid. In view of decision rendered by the U. S. Supreme Court in the Gaines case in which it is stated that "education is an individual right," we find the whole question of higher and professional education for Negroes brought to a focus, and very much in need of a sensible and practical solution. In most instances it seems reasonable to state that Negroes will not be allowed to enter the state universities available to white students in the South either now or in the near future. This may occur with limited numbers in the border states in which courses, such as law involving small numbers, are in question. The Supreme Court has expressed the opinion that education is an individual right and that individual Negroes, who seek college and professional education including graduate work, are entitled to any and every offering which is available to youth of any other race within the confines of the state. The question is whether or not the sound approach is going to be to ask that this requirement of the Supreme Court be lived up to in letter or in spirit.

The South is greatly lagging behind the nation in terms of per capita wealth and no aspect of its public benefits shows this more than its educational facilities. Institutions for white students suffer by comparison with those in other sections. And those which have hitherto been available to Negroes suffer greatly by comparison with Southern white state colleges to say the least. The question which confronts Negroes, then, is, will they insist that the South go through some sort of gesture in each individual state and set up courses in name only, which will comply with the Supreme Court decision, or will they take the initiative or at least cooperate in working out some plan which will bring to individual Negro students the highest quality of education obtainable within the finances available? This latter approach seems to be the only sound one.

The working out of this problem will not be fundamentally different from that which the South is finding necessary in terms of its white students. The practical working of this method would be to see to it that all work done on an undergraduate basis in the state-supported institutions should measure up to the standards of the rating agencies and be class "A" work. In the case of graduate and professional education where the demand is limited, the sound approach would seem to be that now taking place on a small scale in which certain centers are selected for development in specific areas of work. Then through sensible cooperation and contribution from neighboring states this work is promoted in such a way that the offerings will be of the best and students will be educated in terms of regions rather than in terms of state lines. The soundness of this approach is such as to make it amenable to adoption, and its adoption will guarantee in the end the best possible education for Negro youth which should be our goal.

The present duplication which takes place within the confines of every state and results in a most unsatisfactory level of attainment would be eliminated. Since the two medical schools that are available to Negroes are not full and have just reached their stage of maturity after long years of travail, it would be little less than tragic for unsatisfactory medical schools to be developed within the confines of the several Southern states for Negroes where there are medical schools for whites. In fact, there is no need for new medical schools for whites and they could well strengthen by a regional approach some of those which they have. The University of West Virginia has adopted this method in its recently stated plan to contract with the University of Virginia for the two final years of medical studies. This plan has the sanction of the West Virginia legislature which makes of it a completely legal transaction.[1] The great need for graduate work in teacher education makes this an offering that should probably be provided on a state basis. The strong facilities which are necessary for undergraduate professional instruction makes this a not too difficult transition.

Of the more than five and one-half millions of employable Negroes, the vast majority, according to census reports, are in the unskilled occupations. Approximately thirty per cent are domestic and personal service workers. In spite of all that may be done in the up-grading of these workers into the semi-skilled and skilled brackets, for a long time to come most of these people will remain in the unskilled labor class. Any program, therefore, which looks to the sound economic development of the Negro race would have to give important attention to the welfare of this group. In all probability Negroes face a large unemployment problem after the war with keen competition for all jobs including those in the unskilled brackets, and they also face a situation in which machine production will develop shorter hours of labor for all with increased need for recreation and directed leisure time activities. This is coupled with the increasing tendency for women to find employment outside of the home. There will be both keen competition for service occupations and a greater need for the kind of service which will replace many of the activities which the home has been accustomed to perform. As this competition grows keen and an educated public demands service of a superior type for its need in every area, no worker, even those who occupy the so-called unskilled brackets, can afford to be without some specific training. Schools are being established for hotel workers, laundry workers, dry cleaning and pressing businesses and workers in retail and wholesale food establishments of almost every conceivable variety.

It is of fundamental importance in terms of the economic income of this great mass of workers that educational programs of whatever type needed be organized in order that Negro work-

[1] The extent of useless of duplication with an obvious sacrifice in quality is revealed in *American Council on Educational Studies*, Series I, Vol. II, No. V, p. 27. Sixteen colleges of pharmacy were found in a radius of 388 miles.

men may present as satisfactory qualifications for these jobs as any other group. Most of these opportunities for schooling will have to be of the in-service type located in the cities and areas where the jobs are, so that workers of low income may study and improve themselves in their spare time. If the masses are to be properly served, there is a splendid opportunity for a limited Negro leadership to be trained specifically and extensively in terms of so-called service occupations. A new outlet is envisioned for Home Economics people who have been trained through their first degree in college or those who understand public health and personal hygiene. There is an opportunity for those who are trained in building maintenance, power plant work and the like in order that the custodial services in the increasing number of office buildings may be of a greatly improved and satisfactory variety. The time has come when the extension of a practical democratic concept must lead many people to understand the importance of the jobs which they are doing and not to regard their occupations as either lowly or unworthy of their best efforts.

One of the possible weaknesses in the educational programs for American youth in general, and Negroes in particular, has been the fact that the areas of mass employment and opportunity have been completely overlooked. A trained leadership giving serious attention to these areas would have meant much in increasing the earning capacity of these jobs and standardizing the conditions under which the workers are employed. It would appear extremely probable that this indifferent and *laissez-faire* attitude will not be able to succeed in the post-war world and those who are interested will do well to regard this as one of the pioneer areas in which important progress may be made. Houston, Texas, and Little Rock, Arkansas, through pioneering efforts of well-trained Negro women, have pointed the way to a splendid resource in this regard. It is important that whatever antiquated notions have retarded our full development in the past be completely discarded as we move forward into the future in an effort to secure the economic adjustment which is so important to the development of the group as a whole.

In all probability the high wages which are now prevailing

in these areas and the growing appreciation of the fact that every human being must have a decent wage in order to live satisfactorily will prove an encouraging asset to those who wish to make improvement along this line. Those schools and colleges which find it possible to add such courses to their curriculums or to organize extension programs whereby members of their staffs may go into the community and render this important service will greatly enhance their service to the community and will receive a corresponding recognition which will help them in the development of their total programs.

The fields of nutrition and child development have made important advances in the past few years and these are destined to achieve even better results in the future. Any program of education or of progress which can encompass the entire group of Negro people, or any other people for that matter, cannot overlook this great area of promise in post-war development. This should be coupled with the development of small businesses rendering these types of service where a great deal of capital is not needed and where the community stands increasingly in need of the type of service which is organized on a small basis. There is needed, therefore, the kind of vision and imagination on the part of *our* leadership which will take these comparatively simple jobs, see in them the opportunity for careful study and along with some program of organized finance, such as is possible under a cooperative arrangement, and start many new businesses for the Negro group. These businesses will not depend solely on Negro patronage and will be businesses which will form a desirable outlet for the trained youth of the Negro race. There are splendid examples to be found, although these are too few in number, showing what the possibilities are, in almost every field of endeavor. The vigorous program which attempts to ferret out these opportunities is destined for a large measure of success.

SUMMARY

An attempt has been made to set forth the peculiar position in which American Negroes find themselves as citizens who are without their full privileges. They are at times confused, embarrassed and mistreated. They recognize that they have been permitted to make substantial progress and many of their relationships are normal. They find the special restrictions which are imposed upon them out of keeping with professed national ideals. Negro youth particularly and the present generation of adults, having experienced no status except that of free men, fail to understand much of the treatment they receive which can be explained only in terms of the inferiority associated with a status of slavery.

Negroes, having no ideology other than that of democracy, cannot consistently behave in any pattern except that which seeks complete freedom of expression and assures them the same rights, privileges and responsibilities as are possessed by other Americans. They ask not for special privilege, but for the opportunity to achieve in accordance with their individual abilities as human beings.

To bring about the full participating status desired, the writer believes there must be organized, simultaneously, efforts, as thoroughly coordinated as possible, in several directions. This will consist in part of a vigorous and sustained combat against injustices. This effort should be constituted in the main by sound, practical and realistic programs which recognize clearly the limitations which exist and attempt to overcome them by the most feasible methods. A few such methods have been suggested, many more are necessary and possible. As these are applied with increasing effectiveness the problem of race with its manifold aspects will move steadily toward a solution that will be consistent with our national ideals in their economic, social, and Christian principles.

THE CAUCASIAN PROBLEM

By GEORGE S. SCHUYLER

———

BY A PECULIAR logical inversion the Anglo-Saxon ruling class, its imitators, accomplices and victims have come to believe in a Negro problem. With great zeal and industry those controlling the media of information and instruction have succeeded in indoctrinating the whole world with this fiction. It is written into the laws, accepted by organized religion; it permeates our literature, distorts our thinking and is deeply imbedded in our customs and institutions. So successful has been this propaganda that even its unfortunate victims often speak of it with the same conviction with which many people talk of guardian angels, ghosts and malignant spirits. It is the "stop thief" technique at its best—a great testimonial to the ingenuity of exploiters with a bad conscience; for while there is actually no Negro problem, there is definitely a Caucasian problem.

Continual reference to a Negro problem assumes that some profound difficulty has been or is being created for the human race by the so-called Negroes. This is typical ruling class arrogance, and, like most of the faiths circulating in our civilization, has no basis in fact. It has been centuries since any Negro nation has menaced the rest of humanity. The last of the Moors withdrew from Europe in 1492. Since that time not one of the numerous industrially retarded but socially complex African states has molested the rest of the world with the possible exception of pirates of the Barbary Coast. They have neither possessed the means nor the inclination to do so, and they lived more or less happily in isolation until the coming of the European with his Bibles and bullets.

The so-called Negroes did not inaugurate the trans-Atlantic slave traffic, although some profited from it. They have not invaded anybody's territory for almost a millennium. They have passed few if any Jim Crow laws, established no Jim Crow customs, set up few white ghettos, carried on no discriminatory practices against whites and have not devoted centuries to propaganda attempting to prove the superiority of blacks over whites. The last Negro writing with that slant was in the Tenth Century. We seek in vain during modern times for any record of Negroes having destroyed any white cultures, having ravished and debauched white women wholesale, or having stolen white manhood. On the other hand the history of the world since 1815 is crowded with references to wars, campaigns and expeditions by Caucasian Powers against almost every African and Asiatic nation.

Of the international capitalists who control the lives of over a billion colored people practically all are white, and so, also, are the technicians, brokers, lawyers, generals, admirals, artists and writers who serve them. Colored people are largely excluded from this select group and relegated to the economic fringes of society where labor is long and hard and pay is short and seldom. The occasional exception here and there only emphasizes the point. The only sense in which there is or has been a Negro problem is in the colored folk's natural human aversion and opposition to conquest, enslavement, exploitation and debasement during the long and bloody period of Caucasian military ascendency.

With the exception of such camouflaged colonies as Haiti, Ethiopia, Liberia and Egypt, all the Negro countries have been overrun long since, their rulers killed or exiled and their peoples chained and exploited like those of the European lands currently under Nazi rule. The colored countries in Latin America and Asia are either directly the victims of aggression and occupation by Caucasian powers—chiefly Anglo-Saxon and their imperialist satellites—or they are controlled indirectly by native dictatorships backed by white international bankers and their tax-supported armed services. Where and when the opportunity presented itself, the other Caucasian countries did likewise or to the extent of their abilities. Thus, Russia subjugated the people of Siberia, Spain slaughtered her way to empire in the Americas and the Philippines, Germany and Italy grabbed remnants in Africa and Asia, and Denmark gathered a few islands in the Caribbean. Portugal, Holland and Belgium have assembled valuable real estate and subject peoples in Asia and Africa, although the Japanese have rudely relieved these British satellites of some of their ill-gotten gains.

The only nation that has become a problem to the Caucasians is Japan which was the hired gunman of Anglo-Saxondom until the beginning of this decade, checkmating Russia and helping to weaken, undermine and debauch China. Only when the Nipponese bandit went into business for himself and practised what he had been taught, equipped and financed to do by erstwhile employers, did he become a problem.

While we may dismiss the concept of a Negro problem as a valuable dividend-paying fiction, it is clear that the Caucasian problem is painfully real and practically universal. Stated briefly, the problem confronting the colored peoples of the world is how to live in freedom, peace and security without being invaded, subjugated, expropriated, exploited, persecuted and humiliated by Caucasians justifying their actions by the myth of white racial superiority. Put bluntly, that is the concern uppermost in the minds of all intelligent and sensitive colored people whether they live in Birmingham, Boma or Benares. They are nauseated by the fictions and hyprocrisy cloaking military aggression and crass materialism, and everywhere today their dream is to rid themselves of the whole Caucasian problem which is basically the same throughout the colored world.

Whether he be as wise as Einstein or as saintly as Jesus, the colored man must everywhere accept a subordinate position. There are restrictions on where he may live, on what work he may do, with whom he may associate, how and where he may travel, on his right to choose his rulers, on his education, on whom he may marry, and, in many places, on where his last remains may be interred. The problem is worse in Kenya or Australia than in Mississippi or Sierra Leone, but the general pattern is similar. It is no easier for him to get bed and board in

London than it is in Washington, D. C. Whether in the Transvaal or in Texas, he is at the bottom of the industrial hierarchy—except in war time when the system is imperilled and every man is expected to do his bit for democracy. He observes that the press, radio and cinema are primarily for the entertainment and benefit of white people and almost never for colored people. He has become painfully aware that generally throughout the world he is treated by white people as a pariah. Whether in Fiji or Florida, the black man's burden is this vicious color caste system which makes his world a cultured hell. On the other hand, the white man's burden is his guilty conscience which he sublimates with racial fictions to which he laboriously accommodates his morals and ethics.

The term Negro itself is as fictitious as the theory of white racial superiority on which Anglo-Saxon civilization is based, but it is nevertheless one of the most effective smear devices developed since the Crusades. It totally disregards national, linguistic, cultural and physical differences between those unable to boast a porcine skin, and ignores the findings of advanced sociologists and ethnologists. Avoiding the consideration of such obvious differences between colored people, it facilitates acceptance of the fiction of similarity and identity which is easily translated into a policy of treating all colored people everywhere the same way.

The once-popular American ditty, "All Coons Look Alike," was a musical statement of the Anglo-American color philosophy already embodied in the law and hallowed by custom and tradition. So likewise was the thought expressed in that other popular American song of the turn of the century, "I'd Rather Be a White Man Than a Coon, Coon, Coon." In the word "nigger" (the overall-and-jumper version of "Negro") we have a term conveying this thought throughout the Caucasian—and especially the Anglo-Saxon—world. To a lesser extent it circulates also among the satellite Belgian, Dutch and French ruling classes, and among the other white aristocracies. Almost everywhere the colored people are "niggers" or they are called by the less biting synonyms: "native," "kaffir," "fellah," "boy" or "coolie," which serve the same purpose. In the United States the childish device of attempting to make "Negro" respectable by using a capital "N" seems to have deceived everyone except a realistic, and therefore insignificant, minority of thinkers.

Of course "white" and "Caucasian" are equally barren of scientific meaning but are similarly useful for propaganda purposes. There are actually no white people except albinos who are a very pale pink in color. A white skin would be a diseased or dead skin. If the name "Caucasian" is meant to imply racial purity or unusual paleness, it is certainly fallacious because the original home of the Caucasians, from which some romantic scientist assumed the present Europeans migrated, contains some 150 to 300 different "races" or types, and, as Ruth Benedict points out: "Caucasians have no characteristic cephalic index or body height, no specific hair color or eye color; their noses may be Roman or concave; even the color of their skin is extremely variable." Aryan, of course, is a language designation, and anybody using an Indo-Iranian tongue is an Aryan regardless of appearance; while Nordic, as a description of the Northern European blondes presumed to be a pure race is somewhat invalidated by the belief of some anthropologists that they are bleached Bantu who originally came north out of Africa and followed the receding glaciers.

However, the point is that these general terms "Negro" and "Caucasian," "black" and "white" are convenient propaganda devices to emphasize the great gulf which we are taught to believe exists between these groups of people. It is significant that these divisions very conveniently follow the line of colonial subjugation and exploitation, with the Asiatics and Africans lumped together smugly as "backward peoples," "savages," "barbarians" or "primitives": i.e., fair prey for fleecing and enslavement under the camouflage of "civilization."

Prior to the rise of the present imperialist Powers on the wings of piracy and conquest, and during the period when the African states were still intact and powerful, colored people were generally known as Saracens, Moors, Ethiopians, Africans or by other nationalistic names which conjured visions of pomp, tradition, glory and might, or they referred to some specific locality. Before the inauguration of the slave traffic, Europe knew these people as warriors, merchants, physicians, sailors and artists; but afterward they ceased being Mandingoes, Yorubas, Fulanis or Vais and, merged in common servitude, they became "niggers," or the more dignified "Negroes." These terms became in time synonymous with servitude and debasement, and still are.

The slave was a piece of property, a thing. Learned clerks argued long and heatedly over whether or not he was a human being and possessed a soul. The term Negro or "nigger" implies that he is still a thing, a member of a robot-like mass of inherently inferior beings essentially the same regardless of intelligence, education, skill, profession or locality, and in any case of lower status than any white person though the latter be a criminal or imbecile. Thus the so-called Negro race is a melange representing every known variety of human being with nothing whatever in common except a common bondage and a common resentment against enforced poverty and pariahdom, and an increasing determination to rid the world of the Caucasian problem which hampers its progress and development.

The racial fiction has been industriously spread over the world with the extension of white hegemony. The Anglo-American immigration policies excluding Orientals from the United States, Canada and Australia, have been part of the white supremacy doctrine introduced to Asiatics. It is noteworthy that while these colored peoples are excluded from white lands, the Caucasian missionaries, soldiers, sailors, racketeers, merchants, salesmen and investors have swarmed over the South Seas and Asia carrying the torch of civilization which, as René Maran has well said, "consumes everything it touches."

Wherever they landed, they insisted upon and got special privileges, thanks to superior arms. Soon there were special Caucasian concessions, courts, and "spheres of influence" throughout Japan and China backed by ubiquitous detachments of troops and occasional cruisers. India fell to the British adventurers. The former Chinese imperial provinces of Thibet, Manchuria, Burma, Malaya, Cochin-China, Annam, Cambodia, Tonkin and Laos got white overlords. The erstwhile independent kingdoms of the East Indies languished under the heels of Dutch freebooters whose regime became so cruel and corrupt that it shocked Sir Stamford

Raffles, founder of Singapore, when he took over as governor during a temporary transfer to the Union Jack in 1811. The numerous paradises of the Pacific, those lovely, languorous emeralds set in the azure seas, became sugar and pineapple plantations or mining concessions of absentee owners and worked by peons.

The white man became the sahib, tuan or master, living aloof in luxury with the prettiest "native" women (whom he abandoned when he returned home). The "native" saw his land taken, his crops appropriated, his labor stolen, his leaders debauched or imprisoned, his culture undermined and destroyed, his family and friends debased by alcohol and opium, and their lives shortened by malnutrition and disease. Along with this imperialism went various forms of Jim Crowism and humiliation. It is not singular that these Asiatic colored folk are in revolt against white rule. To them the Caucasian problem means the same thing that it does to the serfs of Georgia, of Trinidad and of South Africa.

Turning to Latin America we see basically the same problem. There is to be found the same white economic and financial ownership and control of natural resources and public utilities administered by white or mestizo politicians financed and maintained by foreign loans and subsidies. As an inevitable corollary we find the Indio-African masses impoverished and degraded, with the little islands of whites living in affluence and looking down upon them as "spigs." Significantly enough the more highly colored Latin American countries are regarded as having failed to live up to the democratic ideal whereas the "white" lands like Argentina, Chile and Costa Rica—equally torn at intervals by internal revolts and bossed by alien-supported dictators—are hailed as successes. A more sinister aspect of this economic domination is the spread among the white and near-white Quislings of the Nordic-superiority nonsense prevalent elsewhere. Both Waldo Frank and Donald Pierson have recently noticed this development in Brazil, although so far it is happily restricted to only a few.

It is noteworthy that most Latin American nations are careful to send only white or near-white diplomatic and consular representatives to England and the United States. The experience of Haiti on this point is very illuminating. From 1804 to June 5, 1862, the United States refused to recognize Haiti although there were American legations in twenty-one countries of less commercial importance to America, and although many other nations, including Great Britain, had done so. The reason was clear. Senator Thomas Hart Benton of Missouri very succinctly stated the case for the opponents of recognition:

> Our policy towards...Hayti has been fixed...for three and thirty years. We trade with her, but no diplomatic relations have been established between us....We receive no mulatto consuls, or black ambassadors from her. And why? Because the peace of eleven states will not permit the fruits of a successful negro insurrection to be exhibited among them. It will not permit black ambassadors and consuls to...give their fellow blacks in the United States proof in hand of the honors that await them for a like successful effort on their part. It will not permit the fact to be seen, and told, that for the murder of their masters and mistresses, they are to find friends among the white people of these United States.[1]

President John Quincy Adams quickly concurred in this view.

Later in 1852 when a system of "partial recognition" was prepared, the Emperor Soulouque upset the apple cart by appointing an American to be a Haitian consul at Boston. Secretary of State Daniel Webster refused to accept an appointee bearing that title, implying recognition, but stated that any person "not of African extraction"[2] would be welcomed as a commercial agent. Even when the Haitians promised to send a diplomatic representative to Washington so light that he would be indistinguishable from the other members of the diplomatic corps, the United States was adamant—until the slaveholding South seceded and thus lost its grip on American foreign policy. The lesson has not been lost on other countries.

In the Caribbean area where American "penetration" is most marked the color line has kept pace with Yankee imperialism.

[1] *Congressional Debates*, 19th Cong., 1st sess., cols. 330-332.
[2] Ludwell Lee Montague, *Haiti and the United States* (Durham, 1940), p. 59.

Cuba, Panama and Puerto Rico have become well acquainted with this phase of the Caucasian problem. Since the taking over of naval and air bases in the British West Indies, American missionaries of Negrophobia have alarmed the "natives" by insistence upon Jim Crow set-ups and practices formerly unknown even in those English colonies.

Only when we understand the universal character and international ramifications of this Caucasian problem are we able to see how faithfully it follows the pattern in the United States, with important differences and variations. Here the so-called Negroes are a small minority living in the midst of a great majority. They use the same language and have the identical culture. They arrived with the whites—and before most of them. Both peoples have made important contributions to the development of this civilization which both regard as their own. The colored Americans are perhaps more American than most of the whites since they have practically no foreign connections. The ruling class here encourages the white generality to believe they control the government, but it does not permit the colored minority to share this illusion. The thousand and one devices and artifices used to prevent the colored people's full enjoyment of citizenship rights and privileges fully attest to that.

The position of the colored subject in England, although born to the soil, is equally unenviable, and in some ways is worse. Neither ruling class, unlike the rest of the Europeans, is willing to accept the colored person for what he may be as an individual, perhaps because such exceptions are regarded as undermining the color caste system. There are exceptions but their paucity only emphasizes the rule. Maintaining this international bi-racialism in the face of the growing demand of colored people everywhere for justice, equality and opportunity is what white spokesmen mean by "the Negro problem." It is the same problem which confronted the French in Indo-China and Africa, the Dutch in the East and West Indies, and the British in Burma, Malaya, India, Africa and the Caribbean.

Students of the Caucasian problem will admit that Negrophobia has spread far beyond the upper and middle classes and has penetrated the lowest stratum of white society. But they are aware that the ruling class and its intellectual gendarmerie set the fashion in prejudices as they do in clothing, habitations and hairdo. The uncannily accurate polls of public opinion have proved that these few shape the thought of the masses, rather than the other way around. There is much evidence that the color prejudice of the masses is not too deeply rooted. For one thing there has always been a natural trend toward fraternization between the common folk, regardless of skin color, as shown by the strenuous efforts throughout American history to prevent it and by the progressive lightening of the color of American Negroes.

It is clear that the numerous laws and regulations enacted to halt association between the colored and white people on a plane of equality have been written and passed by the few and not by the many. It was the "pillars of society" who insisted upon racial segregation. Jim Crow schools, railroad coaches, bus compartments and waiting rooms would not exist if those who are influential in American society had opposed them. They have not frowned upon the self-appointed missionaries of racial purity. Wherever permitted, the common people have established the democratic relations that should exist in a free country.

Even after three centuries of Negrophobic indoctrination, no deep-seated revulsion or antagonism has prevented 15,000 interracial marriages and countless clandestine relations in all parts of the country. It would be extremely difficult to find a community in the United States where members of the two groups reside and where no intimate interracial relationship between both sexes of both "races" exists. It is well known that white people from the most Negrophobic areas will move to other and more liberal communities and speedily adjust themselves to eating with, riding alongside, working and living with colored people with extremely little friction and scarcely a murmur of protest. The growth of Negro ghettos in large cities can be traced chiefly to avaricious realtors eager to roll up bigger profits through artificial scarcity of habitations. The fact that almost every one of these ghettos has been permitted to expand with increased Negro migration indicates that profits rather than principles were behind the original restrictions.

The United States government has bowed without exception

to the will of the ruling class in these matters. No one seriously contends that it is a government of the people. Although colored and white soldiers served side by side in the early wars of the Colonies and the Republic, the federal government segregated them in separate units during and after the Civil War. Following the First World War it restricted colored sailors to service only in the mess departments of its warships. It is not hard to guess why Negroes have had such difficulty in gaining admission to the military and naval academies, or to the citizens' training camps. It is no accident that at least nine-tenths of the colored soldiers and even a large percentage of colored sailors serve as stevedores, laborers and in other "service" branches. It has remained for the French General Henri Giraud to state bluntly the reason for this policy in the case of the Jews. The same reasoning is doubtless behind the American and British restrictions, but inherent hypocrisy militates against such frank statement. Ordered General Giraud: "Jewish commissioned and non-commissioned officers and men in the reserve will generally be assigned to special non-combatant and work units. This measure appears necessary in order to avoid having the entire Jewish population gain the title of war veteran, which might prejudice the status given these people after the war."

The Panama Canal Zone, built largely with Negro labor and run autocratically by the War Department, is a strictly Jim-Crow set-up operating under "silver" and "gold" euphemisms, with the whites naturally coming under the name of the more valuable metal. In practice this means the operation of two sets of public places, separate housing and a double standard of pay and promotion. The American people did not insist that this be done. Nor did they demand that the War Department divide the Puerto Rican National Guard regiment so that light islanders served in one branch and dark folk in the other, with the result that brother was often separated from brother.

Segregation and discrimination have been systematically practised in the United States Civil Service, and although identifying photographs on applications (as Negro traps) are no longer required, it just happens that colored workers seldom seem to occupy certain positions, especially those of the white collar variety where they might have to meet the general public. The student of these tortuous artifices must ever wonder how much time and effort is spent by tax-paid officials on working out these schemes devised to prevent just treatment of fellow citizens. The same meticulous care in protecting white supremacy is to be observed in all other departments of the government, and this is not done at the insistence of the white masses. It is also significant that such public positions as Negroes held fifty years ago are in many instances unobtainable today.

The United States Supreme Court is certainly far removed from the pressure of the masses of white Americans, and yet it has distorted and twisted out of all semblance to the originals those Constitutional amendments guaranteeing full rights of citizenship to all citizens regardless of creed or color. By its interpretations of the Constitution, colored citizens have been systematically reduced to the status of half-men. It has consistently supported segregation as a genuflection to State's Rights while denouncing discrimination—knowing full well that the two are inseparable when applied to a weak minority. No mob has as yet stood at the doors of the Justices' chambers compelling them to concoct unjust decisions blessing the anti-intermarriage laws of two-thirds of the states which Hitler so slavishly copied. They did these things in obedience to the Negrophobic philosophy of our dominant class.

Congress, which has always faithfully represented the American propertied interests, administers the District of Columbia. In this, the capital of the world's allegedly greatest democracy, a colored citizen is and always has been a pariah. No mass upheaval has prevented the District Committee from ending this shameful situation, and thus making it possible for Negroes to be free in at least one place in the Republic. The District could certainly have as liberal civil rights laws as New York, Illinois, Connecticut and New Jersey where the masses of white people actually vote and, in the main, are no more liberal and tolerant than the inhabitants of the nation's capital, who do not vote and thus exercise no control over their civic administration.

The students of the Caucasian problem do not find it surprising that those who control the government are no more liberal than those who operate it. This small minority of financiers, industrialists and merchants has made perhaps the greatest contribution to the problem by barring Negroes from the mechanical trades and technical professions, from commerce and finance. This "cold pogrom" has caused more bitterness among colored people than any other American racial policy. It is not a policy which can be blamed on organized white labor, as American business is wont to do, because only a few industries and businesses, up until a decade ago, were organized by the unions. The rest were open shop, free to hire and fire whom they chose without interference. Invariably they chose the racially chauvinistic course, and then declared it was done because their unorganized hands objected to working alongside Negroes. The successful interracial employment policy of Henry Ford, the greatest industrialist, gave the lie to these excuses.

Unquestionably a score or more of unions of skilled workers have made the Caucasian problem more difficult by adopting constitutional or ritualistic provisions barring colored workers from membership, and thus from earning a living. But here they have been upheld and encouraged by the courts of justice (?) and by the overwhelming majority of the employers. If there had been any solid front of business and financial interests against color discrimination in industry, it would have never found a foothold. The fact that under war time stress thousands of employers have lowered the color bar with little protest and no decrease in production shows that it could have been done years ago.

While numerous labor unions have been and are guilty of color discrimination, and have contributed much to keeping the colored people hanging on the economic fringes of society, it is seldom recognized that organized labor as a whole has been more liberal than organized business, organized religion or organized education. If there are a score of labor unions from which Negroes are barred there are thousands of churches and schools which do not accept them, and an equal number of business and professional organizations where, to say the least, colored members are not welcome.

However, there can be no question about the increasing public aversion of the white masses to Negro equality. Fundamentally, racial relations have worsened as the propaganda of white supremacy has sunk deeper and deeper; and the Aryan policies of government, the courts and business have become more widespread while national leaders denounced Hitler, Goebbels and Rosenberg. Bi-racialism has become the accepted practice in America as in South Africa at the time when the shouts are loudest in praise of freedom and democracy. In most instances this has meant the exclusion of Negroes, legally and in practice, because even the United States is not rich enough to maintain two sets of facilities of equal quality and quantity, even if the desire were there.

Thus, on a little higher scale, America is following the African and Asiatic practice. The basic philosophy of the white rulers here is the same as that elsewhere. It is not a national problem but a world problem. But curiously enough, as the Caucasian problem has grown worse, there has been an increasing denial of the white supremacy philosophy and of the whole racial mysticism by more and more authorities on the subject. Not only is the superiority of one race being vigorously denied but the whole concept of race is being effectively challenged. This phenomenon dates chiefly from the First World War. Numerous books and articles disproving the racial basis of supremacy have been written and circulated. Anti-discrimination clauses in state and federal laws and regulations have increased yearly. Even some of the sternest Negrophobes deny that they are prejudiced against colored people and state their opposition to color discrimination. A few school and college textbooks have been written and adopted which attempt a rational approach. It is becoming infrequent for newspapers to wave the red shirt of racial antagonism as was the wont of so many in the not-so-distant past. All of the leading magazines are "right" on the race question—or at least they do not now flaunt their phobia. All unions of the Congress of Industrial Organizations have anti-discrimination clauses in their constitutions. Several A.F. of L. unions have become more liberal on the question. Official pronouncements of the various Christian church groups begin to breathe the spirit of Jesus on the matter of color—although practice falls far, far short of the ideal. Three times in the past twenty years the House of Representatives has passed anti-lynching bills and it recently voted against the poll tax. Interracial committees have grown and flourished all over the country. It has become not uncommon to see news items in Southern papers about Negroes who have *not* committed rape, robbery or arson.

But unhappily this dramatically sudden change has come too late. The die has been cast. The snowball has reached such proportions and velocity that only some determined and revolutionary program can stop it. A small but growing number of white people in the United States and elsewhere realize that this is a Caucasian rather than a Negro problem and have been trying to do something about it. But the process of indoctrination has gone much too far for all the ordinary remedies. A few books, articles and pamphlets, a few polite committees, occasional radio speeches and sonorous pronouncements from politicians—these will not suffice to re-condition the public mind. We cannot teach racial fictions from 1619 to 1919, and then expect people to change overnight to brotherly love and neighborly justice.

In the early days there was fraternization, intermixture and intermarriage between the masses of Negroes, whites and Indians in all the colonies. Had this process been permitted to continue publicly and unhampered, there would now be no Caucasian problem. But those in authority insisted on all sorts of legal and extra-legal devices to enforce bi-racialism. Through the years it became a social distinction and an economic advantage to be non-colored. Despite this advantage of being white, the masses gradually lost their freedom and their hopes in a progressively regimented machine of feudalism draped in the habiliments of democracy. As they sank lower and lower into a proletarian status, they clung the more desperately to the one possession that could not be taken from them—their superior status as whites. This lifted them a notch higher than somebody else; and to a drowning man, an inch is as good as a mile. By virtue of their absence of color, they can go wherever they please—if they have the money; marry whom they wish—if·they have the money;

live where they choose—if they have the money. The problem, of course, is to get the money. Nevertheless it is comforting to know that nature has put Utopia within reach.

Having become used to this situation by long conditioning, the people are more reluctant to change their habits, even if it can be demonstrated beyond doubt that those habits are wrong. People are not motivated by what is right but by what they *believe* to be right—and the general white public believes that discrimination and bi-racialism are right because they have always been told so. So the white supremacy propaganda has become a Frankenstein's monster which, having largely served its purpose, the more intelligent members of the ruling class would fain destroy but now are terrorized by their creation. Of course it must be admitted that they are not as eager for change as they were when the Afrika Korps was pounding toward Alexandria, when the panzers were on the outskirts of Moscow and half our Pacific fleet lay on the bottom of Pearl Harbor.

On the other hand, while a few whites have realized that the so-called Negro problem is actually a Caucasian problem, millions of colored people have arrived at the same conclusion. For some years after emancipation there was a general belief among American colored people that they were responsible for their lowly status, and that all they had to do was to measure up to the requirements of Anglo-Saxon society and they would be accepted as individuals on their merits. Similar views were held by bright and ambitious colored folk in other parts of the world before they discovered the difference between Caucasian professions and practices. To be sure there was a skeptical minority which had so little faith in the big white brother that it urged emigration. But these fellows were shouted down by the chorus of optimists.

However, as Negro literacy increased, and the true nature of the problem was brought home by reading, travel and experience, disillusionment and pessimism took possession. This great awakening came shortly after the realization that the war for democracy had been a war for white democracy—and little of that. When the deluge of propaganda died down, they discovered that they had been carried "back to normalcy." This increasing disillusionment has driven the Negroes within themselves, bringing about a group solidarity as basically unhealthy as that of the whites, but just as real. It has developed a racial chauvinism countering that of the whites which has dangerously deepened the gulf between the two peoples who are actually one people. The study of African history and civilization, the fostering of Negro business, the support and growth of the Negro press, the power of the Negro church, and the general development of anti-white thinking is a reaction to social ostracism and economic discrimination. Race, which began as an anthropological fiction, has become a sociological fact. Socio-economic bi-racialism advanced as a "solution" for the color question has brought about a psychological bi-racialism which may bring about an entirely different "solution."

An antagonism has developed on *both* sides which is increasingly similar to that between two Balkan nations. From being regarded as something present in and yet apart from American life and institutions, the Negro is coming to regard himself in the same way. He is thinking about solving the Caucasian Problem by his own actions rather than by healthy cooperation. He can scarcely be blamed for feeling this way, being a product of his environment. This reaction is not confined to the colored people in the United States, but exists wherever they have been the victims of white subjugation, exploitation and humiliation. It is a development which can only end tragically unless some way can now be found to re-condition colored and white people everywhere so that they will think of themselves as the same.

What chance is there of doing this? It would require a revolutionary program of re-education calling not only for wholesale destruction of the accumulated mass of racialistic propaganda in books, magazines, newspapers, motion pictures and all the present laws and regulations which recognize the racial fiction and are based upon it, but for a complete reorganization of our social system. It would have to include the complete abolition of Jim Crow laws and institutions; the rescinding of all racial pollution laws barring marriage because of so-called race; a complete enforcement of the letter and the spirit of the federal constitution, and the ending of every vestige of the color bar in industry, commerce and the professions. The words "Negro," "white," "Caucasian," "Nordic" and "Aryan" would have to be permanently taken out of circulation except among scholars and scientists. There would have to be an end of gathering population statistics by so-called race. Government service in all its branches, state and federal, would have to be thrown open to all on the basis solely of merit, and promotions made accordingly. It would probably be necessary to have drastic laws against manifestations of color prejudice and discrimination, just as we have legislated against kidnaping, arson and murder which are certainly no more serious from the viewpoint of national welfare.

It is extremely doubtful if the colored people here or anywhere else will accept anything less than this, and if they do it is very likely to prove unsatisfactory. The alternative is to drift toward an international color war. Already there is a dangerous feeling abroad among colored people that they have been treated so badly that they want nothing more to do with white people. This mood is circulating rapidly as science shatters distance in the modern world.

This is a time of mass action and mass thinking. While privately white and colored persons still get on fairly well, it is the public attitudes which will more and more prevail until the leavening influence of the former is eventually destroyed; and those who once were and still could be friends stand against each other as enemies. If there is sincerity and determination in the hearts of the mighty, there is still time to make a new world where tolerance, understanding, mutual respect and justice will prevail to a greater degree than men have ever dared dream. True, this means a complete about face on the part of the white world, but this is only right since the race problem is of its own making. The alternative here and abroad is conflict and chaos. We shall have to make a choice very soon.

MY AMERICA

By LANGSTON HUGHES

―――――――

THIS IS MY LAND, America. Naturally, I love it—it is home— and I am vitally concerned about its *mores*, its democracy, and its well-being. I try now to look at it with clear, unprejudiced eyes. My ancestry goes back at least four generations on American soil and, through Indian blood, many centuries more. My background and training is purely American—the schools of Kansas, Ohio, and the East. I am old stock as opposed to recent immigrant blood.

Yet many Americans who cannot speak English—so recent is their arrival on our shores—may travel about our country at will securing food, hotel, and rail accommodations wherever they wish to purchase them. *I may not.* These Americans, once naturalized, may vote in Mississippi or Texas, if they live there. *I may not.* They may work at whatever job their skills command. *But I may not.* They may purchase tickets for concerts, theatres, lectures wherever they are sold throughout the United States. *Often I may not.* They may repeat the Oath of Allegiance with its ringing phrase of "Liberty and justice for all," with a deep faith in its truth—as compared with the limitations and oppressions they have experienced in the Old World. I repeat the oath, too, but I know that the phrase about "liberty and justice" does not fully apply to me. I am an American—*but I am a colored American.*

I know that all these things I mention are not *all* true for *all* localities *all* over America. Jim Crowism varies in degree from North to South, from the mixed schools and free franchise of Michigan to the tumbledown colored schools and open terror at the polls of Georgia and Mississippi. All over America, however, against the Negro there has been an economic color line of such severity that since the Civil War we have been kept most effectively, as a racial group, in the lowest economic brackets. Statistics are not needed to prove this. Simply look around you on the Main Street of any American town or city. There are no colored clerks in any of the stores—although colored people spend their money there. There are practically never any colored street-car conductors or bus drivers—although these public carriers run over streets for which we pay taxes. There are no colored girls at the switchboards of the telephone company— but millions of Negroes have phones and pay their bills. Even in Harlem, nine times out of ten, the man who comes to collect your rent is white. Not even that job is given to a colored man by the great corporations owning New York real estate. From Boston to San Diego, the Negro suffers from job discrimination.

Yet America is a land where, in spite of its defects, I can write this article. Here the voice of democracy is still heard— Wallace, Willkie, Agar, Pearl Buck, Paul Robeson, Lillian Smith. America is a land where the poll tax still holds in the South—but opposition to the poll tax grows daily. America is a land where lynchers are not yet caught—but Bundists are put in jail, and majority opinion condemns the Klan. America is a land where the best of all democracies has been achieved for some people— but in Georgia, Roland Hayes, world-famous singer, is beaten for being colored and nobody is jailed—nor can Mr. Hayes vote in the State where he was born. Yet America is a country where Roland Hayes *can* come from a log cabin to wealth and fame— in spite of the segment that still wishes to maltreat him physically and spiritually, famous though he is.

This segment, the South, is not all of America. Unfortunately, however, the war with its increased flow of white Southern workers to Northern cities, has caused the Jim Crow patterns of the South to spread *all* over America, aided and abetted by the United States Army. The Army, with its policy of segregated troops, has brought Jim Crow into communities where it was but little, if at all, in existence before Pearl Harbor. From Camp Custer in Michigan to Guadalcanal in the South Seas, the Army has put its stamp upon official Jim Crow, in imitation of the Southern states where laws separating Negroes and whites are as much a part of government as are Hitler's laws segregating Jews in Germany. Therefore, any consideration of the current problems of the Negro people in America must concern itself seriously with the question of what to do about the South.

The South opposes the Negro's right to vote, and this right is denied us in most Southern states. Without the vote a citizen has no means of protecting his constitutional rights. For Democracy to approach its full meaning, the Negro *all over* America must have the vote. The South opposes the Negro's right to work in industry. Witness the Mobile shipyard riots, the Detroit strikes fomented by Southern whites against the employment of colored people, the Baltimore strikes of white workers who objected to Negroes attending a welding school which would give them the skill to rate upgrading. For Democracy to achieve its meaning, the Negro like other citizens must have the right to work, to learn skilled trades, and to be upgraded.

The South opposes the civil rights of Negroes and their protection by law. Witness lynchings where no one is punished, witness the Jim Crow laws that deny the letter and spirit of the Constitution. For Democracy to have real meaning, the Negro must have the same civil rights as any other American citizen. These three simple principles of Democracy—the vote, the right to work, and the right to protection by law—the South opposes when it comes to me. Such procedure is dangerous for *all* America. That is why, in order to strengthen Democracy, further the war effort, and achieve the confidence of our colored allies, we must institute a greater measure of Democracy for the eight million colored people of the South. And we must educate the white Southerners to an understanding of such democracy, so they may comprehend that decency toward colored peoples will lose them nothing, but rather will increase their own respect and safety in the modern world.

I live on Manhattan Island. For a New Yorker of color, truthfully speaking, the South begins at Newark. A half hour by tube from the Hudson Terminal, one comes across street-corner hamburger stands that will not serve a hamburger to a Negro customer wishing to sit on a stool. For the same dime a white pays, a Negro must take his hamburger elsewhere in a paper bag and eat it, minus a plate, a napkin, and a glass of water. Sponsors of the theory of segregation claim that it can be made to mean equality. Practically, it never works out that way. Jim Crow always means less for the one Jim Crowed and an unequal value for his money—no stool, no shelter, merely the hamburger, in Newark.

As the colored traveller goes further South by train, Jim Crow increases. Philadelphia is ninety minutes from Manhattan. There the all-colored grammar school begins its separate education of the races that Talmadge of Georgia so highly approves. An hour or so further down the line is Baltimore where segregation laws are written in the state and city codes. Another hour by train, Washington. There the conductor tells the Negro traveller, be he soldier or civilian, to go into the Jim Crow coach behind the engine, usually half a baggage car, next to trunks and dogs.

That this change to complete Jim Crow happens at Washington is highly significant of the state of American democracy in relation to colored peoples today. Washington is the capital of our nation and one of the great centers of the Allied war effort toward the achievement of the Four Freedoms. To a south-bound Negro citizen told at Washington to change into a seg-regated coach the Four Freedoms have a hollow sound, like distant lies not meant to be the truth.

The train crosses the Potomac into Virginia, and from there on throughout the South life for the Negro, by state law and custom, is a hamburger in a sack without a plate, water, napkin, or stool—but at the same price as the whites pay—to be eaten apart from the others without shelter. The Negro can do little about this because the law is against him, he has no vote, the police are brutal, and the citizens think such caste-democracy is as it should be.

For his seat in the half-coach of the crowded Jim Crow car, a colored man must pay the same fare as those who ride in the nice air-cooled coaches further back in the train, privileged to use the diner when they wish. For his hamburger in a sack served without courtesy the Southern Negro must pay taxes but refrain from going to the polls, and must patriotically accept conscription to work, fight, and perhaps die to regain or maintain freedom for people in Europe or Australia when he himself hasn't got it at home. Therefore, to his ears most of the war speeches about freedom on the radio sound perfectly foolish, unreal, high-flown, and false. To many Southern whites, too, this grand talk so nobly delivered, so poorly executed, must seem like play-acting.

Liberals and persons of good will, North and South, including, no doubt, our President himself, are puzzled as to what on earth to do about the South—the poll-tax South, the Jim Crow South—that so shamelessly gives the lie to Democracy. With the brazen frankness of Hitler's *Mein Kampf*, Dixie speaks through Talmadge, Rankin, Dixon, Arnall, and Mark Ethridge.

In a public speech in Birmingham, Mr. Ethridge says: "All the armies of the world, both of the United States and the Axis, could not force upon the South an abandonment of racial segregation." Governor Dixon of Alabama refused a government war contract offered Alabama State Prison because it contained an anti-discrimination clause which in his eyes was an "attempt to abolish segregation of races in the South." He said: "We will not place ourselves in a position to be attacked by those who seek to foster their own pet social reforms." In other words, Alabama will not reform. It is as bull-headed as England in India, and its governor is not ashamed to say so.

As proof of Southern intolerance, almost daily the press reports some new occurrence of physical brutality against Negroes. Former Governor Talmadge was "too busy" to investigate when Roland Hayes and his wife were thrown into jail, and the great tenor beaten, on complaint of a shoe salesman over a dispute as to what seat in his shop a Negro should occupy when buying shoes. Nor did the governor of Mississippi bother when Hugh Gloster, professor of English at Morehouse College, riding as an inter-state passenger, was illegally ejected from a train in his state, beaten, arrested, and fined because, being in an overcrowded Jim Crow coach, he asked for a seat in an adjacent car which contained only two white passengers.

Legally, the Jim Crow laws do not apply to inter-state travellers, but the FBI has not yet gotten around to enforcing that

Supreme Court ruling. En route from San Francisco to Oklahoma City, Fred Wright, a county probation officer of color, was beaten and forced into the Texas Jim Crow coach on a transcontinental train by order of the conductor in defiance of federal law. A seventy-six-year-old clergyman, Dr. Jackson of Hartford, Connecticut, going South to attend the National Baptist Convention, was set upon by white passengers for merely passing through a white coach on the way to his own seat. There have been many similar attacks upon colored soldiers in uniform on public carriers. One such attack resulted in death for the soldier, dragged from a bus and killed by civilian police. Every day now, Negro soldiers from the North, returning home on furlough from Southern camps, report incident after incident of humiliating travel treatment below the Mason-Dixon line.

It seems obvious that the South does not yet know what this war is all about. As answer Number One to the question, "What shall we do about the South?" I would suggest an immediate and intensive government-directed program of pro-democratic education, to be put into the schools of the South from the first grades of the grammar schools to the universities. As part of the war effort, this is urgently needed. The Spanish Loyalist Government had trench schools for its soldiers and night schools for civilians even in Madrid under siege. America is not under siege yet. We still have time (but not too much) to teach our people what we are fighting for, and to begin to apply those teachings to race relations at home. You see, it would be too bad for an emissary of color from one of the Latin American countries, say Cuba or Brazil, to arrive at Miami Airport and board a train for Washington, only to get beaten up and thrown off by white Southerners who do not realize how many colored allies we have —nor how badly we need them—and that it is inconsiderate and rude to beat colored people, anyway.

Because transportation in the South is so symbolic of America's whole racial problem, the Number Two thing for us to do is study a way out of the Jim Crow car dilemma at once. Would a system of first, second, and third class coaches help? In Europe, formerly, if one did not wish to ride with peasants and tradespeople, one could always pay a little more and solve that problem by having a first class compartment almost entirely to oneself. Most Negroes can hardly afford parlor car seats. Why not abolish Jim Crow entirely and let the whites who wish to do so, ride in coaches where few Negroes have the funds to be? In any case, our Chinese, Latin American, and Russian allies are not going to think much of our democratic pronunciamentos as long as we keep compulsory Jim Crow cars on Southern rails.

Since most people learn a little through education, albeit slowly, as Number Three, I would suggest that the government draft all the leading Negro intellectuals, sociologists, writers, and concert singers from Alain Locke of Oxford and W. E. B. Du Bois of Harvard to Dorothy Maynor and Paul Robeson of Carnegie Hall and send them into the South to appear before white audiences, carrying messages of culture and democracy, thus off-setting the old stereotypes of the Southern mind and the Hollywood movie, and explaining to the people without dialect what the war aims are about. With each, send on tour a liberal white Southerner like Paul Green, Erskine Caldwell, Pearl Buck, Lillian Smith, or William Seabrook. And, of course, include soldiers to protect them from the fascist-minded among us.

Number Four, as to the Army—draftees are in sore need of education on how to behave toward darker peoples. Just as a set of government suggestions has been issued to our soldiers on how to act in England, so a similar set should be given them on how to act in Alabama, Georgia, Texas, Asia, Mexico, and Brazil— wherever there are colored peoples. Not only printed words should be given them, but intensive training in the reasons for being decent to everybody. Classes in democracy and the war aims should be set up in every training camp in America and every unit of our military forces abroad. These forces should be armed with understanding as well as armament, prepared for friendship as well as killing.

I go on the premise that most Southerners are potentially reasonable people, but that they simply do not know nowadays what they are doing to America, or how badly their racial attitudes look toward the rest of the civilized world. I know their politicians, their schools, and the Hollywood movies have done their best to uphold prevailing reactionary viewpoints. Heretofore, nobody in America except a few radicals, liberals, and a handful of true religionists have cared much about either the Negroes or the South. Their sincere efforts to effect a change have been but a drop in a muddy bucket. Basically, the South needs universal suffrage, economic stabilization, a balanced diet, and vitamins for children. But until those things are achieved, on a lesser front to ameliorate—not solve—the Negro problem (and to keep Southern prejudice from contaminating all of America) a few mild but helpful steps might be taken.

It might be pointed out to the South that the old bugaboo of sex and social equality doesn't mean a thing. Nobody as a rule sleeps with or eats with or dances with or marries anybody else except by mutual consent. Millions of people of various races in New York, Chicago, and Seattle go to the same polls and vote without ever co-habiting together. Why does the South think it would be otherwise with Negroes were they permitted to vote there? Or to have a decent education? Or to sit on a stool in a public place and eat a hamburger? Why they think simple civil rights would force a Southerner's daughter to marry a Negro in spite of herself, I have never been able to understand. It must be due to some lack of instruction somewhere in their schooling.

A government sponsored educational program of racial decency could, furthermore, point out to its students that co-operation in labor would be to the advantage of all—rather than to the disadvantage of anyone, white or black. It could show quite clearly that a million unused colored hands barred out of war industries might mean a million weapons lacking in the hands of our soldiers on some foreign front—therefore a million extra deaths—including Southern white boys needlessly dying under Axis fire—because Governor Dixon of Alabama and others of like mentality need a little education. It might also be pointed out that when peace comes and the Southerners go to the peace table, if they take there with them the traditional Dixie racial attitudes, there is no possible way for them to aid in forming any peace that will last. China, India, Brazil, Free French Africa, Soviet Asia and the whole Middle East will not believe a word they say.

Peace only to breed other wars is a sorry peace indeed, and one that we must plan now to avoid. Not only in order to win the war then, but to create peace along decent lines, we had best start *now* to educate the South—and all America—in racial decency. That education cannot be left to well-meaning but numerically weak civilian organizations. The government itself should take over—and vigorously. After all, Washington is the place where the conductor comes through every southbound train and tells colored people to change to the Jim Crow car ahead.

That car, in these days and times, has no business being "ahead" any longer. War's freedom train can hardly trail along with glory behind a Jim Crow coach. No matter how streamlined the other cars may be, that coach endangers all humanity's hopes for a peaceful tomorrow. The wheels of the Jim Crow car are about to come off and the walls are going to burst wide open. The wreckage of Democracy is likely to pile up behind that Jim Crow car, unless America learns that it is to its own self-interest to stop dealing with colored peoples in so antiquated a fashion. I do not like to see my land, America, remain provincial and unrealistic in its attitudes toward color. I hope the men and women of good will here of both races will find ways of changing conditions for the better.

Certainly it is not the Negro who is going to wreck our Democracy. (What we want is more of it, not less.) But Democracy is going to wreck itself if it continues to approach closer and closer to fascist methods in its dealings with Negro citizens—for such methods of oppression spread, affecting other whites, Jews, the foreign born, labor, Mexicans, Catholics, citizens of Oriental ancestry—and, in due time, they boomerang right back at the oppressor. Furthermore, American Negroes are now Democracy's current test for its dealings with the colored peoples of the whole world of whom there are many, many millions —*too many* to be kept indefinitely in the position of passengers in Jim Crow cars.

COUNT US IN

By STERLING A. BROWN

A YOUNG EUROPEAN scholar, back from a swift trip through the South, picked up from my desk a copy of Hal Steed's *Georgia: Unfinished State*. A passage on the last page confused him. It read: "I would not say that the Anglo-Saxon is superior to other races, but that this race makes up nearly one hundred per cent of the population of the South augurs well for unity— unity in political beliefs, in religion, in social problems." [1] The European was amazed at the figure—nearly one hundred per cent Anglo-Saxon. "But I saw so many Negroes there," he said.

I could have mentioned other oddities in the enumerating of the Negro, from the adoption of the Constitution when a Negro slave counted as three fifths of a man, to the present when a Negro is counted as a unit, a fraction, or a zero, according to the purpose of the counter. Instead I assured him that the evidence of his eyes could be trusted: the gatherings at one side of the depot to see the train go through, the hordes in the ramshackly slums of the cities, the crammed Jim Crow waiting rooms and coaches. Negroes were there all right. Even the publicists who excluded Negroes as part of the population would admit that they were there. Too much so, some might say ruefully, pointing out the large numbers of Negroes as the cause of the poverty and back- wardness of the South, apologizing for the belt of swarming cabins engirdling the cities, hoping that the stranger might soften his verdict on the town until the business section around the

[1] Hal Steed, *Georgia: Unfinished State* (New York, 1942), p. 336.

depot slowly came into view. Too numerous, therefore Negroes had to be kept in their places, the argument might run. Such spokesmen would have a glib reply to reconcile the statistics of "nearly one hundred per cent Anglo-Saxon" with the patent reality: "Oh, that's easy to understand. By population we mean the people that count."

I knew that longer study of the South would convince the visitor that in certain respects Negroes definitely counted. He might learn how it was that one scholar called them "the central theme of southern history" running constantly through the record of the section. It would be easy for him to see how the presence of Negroes was chiefly responsible for the political "solidifying" of a region, so far from solid in many other respects. Fear of Negroes' voting had been the primary cause for a poll-tax peculiar to the region, resulting in the disfranchisement of ten millions of American citizens, half again as many whites as Negroes. This disfranchisement, he might learn, exerts more than a sectional influence, since it has been estimated that one poll-tax vote is worth more than five votes in states with no poll-tax. Many poll-tax Congressmen seem to have a permanent tenure on their seats in Congress, and their resulting seniority gives them a power disproportionate to the number of people who voted them into office, to say the least. The European might learn that the Federal ballot for soldiers was most forcefully opposed by those who feared that Negro soldiers might vote; that Federal aid to education was defeated because the race issue was raised; that the "G.I. Bill of Rights" providing unemployment insurance for returning soldiers was jeopardized because of what the Senator in charge of the bill calls the "hatred of certain Congressmen for the colored portion of our armed forces." He might learn how a program of social reform—the Farm Security Administration—though it aided Southern whites as much as Negroes, was in danger of being scuttled by those who feared it meant that the Negro would "get out of his place."

Just how the Negro counted might be clarified should the visitor read Lillian Smith's "Two Men and a Bargain: A Parable of the Solid South," in which the rich white man says to the poor white man:

There's two big jobs down here that need doing: Somebody's got to tend to the living and somebody's got to tend to the nigger. Now, I've learned a few things about making a living you're too no-count to learn (else you'd be making money same way I make it): things about jobs and credit, prices, hours, wages, votes and so on. But one thing you can learn easy, any white man can, is how to handle the black man. Suppose now you take over the thing you can do and let me take over the thing I can do. What I mean is, you boss the nigger, and I'll boss the money. [2]

The visitor would thus learn that the Negro counted, and still counts in this "Anglo-Saxon" section. But he would learn also what the Southern spokesmen mean by "people that count."

Negroes have lived too long with this paradox, as with so many others, to be confused by it; they understand the reality behind it. They have been counted out for so long a time.

"Sure, the Negro is all out for the war," my friend the sociologist told me. "He's 72 per cent all out for it." Some might consider this estimate to be cynicism, others optimism. The general conclusion is hardly to be disputed: that for all of its high promise, this war has not summoned 100 per cent of the Negro's enthusiasm and energies.

Before attacking this apathy as short-sighted, it might be wise to look for its causes. They are unfortunately too ready at hand to require much searching. On a six months' stay in the deep South of wartime I saw my fill of them; even casual observations in a border city and on trips to the North have heaped the measure to overflowing.

Documentation of the refusal to count the Negro in the war effort is hardly needed. Discrimination in industry was so flagrant, North and South, East and West, that Executive Order 8802 was issued to ban discrimination in wartime industrial jobs, and the President's Committee on Fair Employment Practices was set up to investigate cases of alleged discrimination. While Negro employment was definitely aided, progress has not been in a straight line. All sorts of obstacles have been in the way: Con-

[2] Lillian Smith, "Two Men and a Bargain," *South Today*, VII (Spring, 1943), 6.

gressmen and pressure groups continue to snipe and blast at the Committee; the governor of a Southern state openly violated the Executive Order; the railroads have defiantly challenged a show-down. The integration of Negroes into industry has been op-posed even with violence; strikes have been called because Negro workers were upgraded; and one of the causes of the Detroit riot is said to be the influx of Negro workers. In spite of welcome gains, Negroes are far from convinced that fullest use is being made of Negro manpower, North or South.

A powerful symbol to the Negro of his "not belonging" was the refusal of the Red Cross to accept Negro donors to the blood bank. Against the medical authorities who stated that there was no such thing as Negro blood, that blood from the veins of whites and Negroes could not be told apart, the Red Cross sided offi-cially with Congressman Rankin, who saw, in the proposal that Negroes too might contribute much needed blood, a communist plot to "mongrelize America": "They wanted to pump Negro or Japanese blood into the veins of our wounded white boys re-gardless of the dire effect it might have on their children." The establishment of a segregated blood bank—needless, complicated and irrational—did not help matters much. Nor did the fact, pub-licized by the recent Spingarn Award, that one of the most im-portant men in the successful establishment of the blood bank was Dr. Charles Drew, a Negro.

In the armed forces, advances have certainly been made over World War I. Drafted to their full quota, Negroes are supposed to be serving in all branches of the Army. Only recently it was reported that Negro paratroopers in Atlanta proved to white paratroopers that they really belonged to the dare-devil's branch. Except in training for pursuit piloting, Negro officers are trained along with white. There are more Negro officers than in the last war, several officers of the rank of colonel and one brigadier general. Negro airmen are now being trained as bombardiers and navigators. Negro squadrons have seen action in the hot fighting in the Mediterranean theatre, and have been highly commended by military authorities. The long-closed ranks of the Marine Corps are now open, and Marine officers praised Negro Marines as "good Marines," to be used everywhere and exactly as other

Marines. In the Navy, Negroes have finally been admitted to other capacities than messboys. Some are to serve as seamen on patrol boats and destroyer escorts. The first ensigns have been commissioned. The record of the Coast Guard toward Negroes has been a good one, and the Merchant Marine, with its Negro officers and mixed crews, is looked upon as an achievement in democracy.

Advances have been made, but the Negro was so far behind in opportunity that he does not let his glance linger on the gains; he looks ahead along the road to full participation. This is good Americanism rather than ingratitude. The gains are not unmixed: there still seem to be, for instance, a ceiling on Negro officers and an opposition to having white officers serve under Negro officers. Negroes are dubious about the large number of Negro troops in the service and non-combat units; when the famous Tenth Cavalry, a source of historic pride, was assigned to service duties, Negroes were disturbed in spite of the assurance that military necessity required the transfer. And the Negro still looks askance at the Navy.

In the South I met on every hand the sense of not belonging. On a bus near Baton Rouge, conversation had hardly started with my seat-mate, a little fellow who looked like a black Frenchman, when he offered me a sure way of staying out of the army: I was to roll a piece of "actican" (Octagon) soap in a pellet of bread and eat it just before the physical examination. He himself knew it would work, he said in his patois. He didn't have nothing against the Germans or Japs, neither one, but he did know some enemies over here. I found the same embittered spirit in a young Negro lieutenant who wanted to get overseas, anywhere, where he could find an enemy *to shoot at*. At the Negro section of an air base, segregated from the rest by a marker reading Beale Street, I found the men not proud of belonging to the Air Corps, but disgruntled at the type of menial labor they were called on to perform. I talked with a well-educated young Negro corporal, who had felt that some meaning might be given to his work in the Army when he learned that he was to be sent to an "area and language" school, but who on the eve of going was told that the school had suddenly been closed to Negroes. I talked with Negro pilots, who in the long hours of the day were learning the intricacies of high-powered P-40's, reading the involved instrument boards, soaring into the "wild blue yonder," with their lives and planes dependent on split-second judgments, developing the aggressiveness and self-reliance necessary for combat pilots. At night, these men were forbidden by curfew to be seen in the downtown section of Tuskegee. This kind of thing, and so much else, rankled.

With a few honorable exceptions, newspapers, radio programs, and motion pictures (omitting of course, Negro newspapers and newsreels for Negro theatres only) have done little to convince Negro soldiers of belonging. Some Northern periodicals, *PM* outstandingly, may publicize Negro military service. But in practically all Southern newspapers, the daily row on row of native sons with the armed forces never showed a dark face. I should have known better, perhaps, than to look for one: pictures of Negroes in these papers were traditionally confined to those of prizefighters or recently deceased ex-slaves. In the North the practice is little better. In a Northern railroad station, a picture, "blown up" by marvelous photographic technique, showed departing soldiers what they were fighting for: a sea of American faces looking out, anxiously, proudly. All were white. An observer saw a contingent of Negro troops entraining; they gave the eye-catching picture a swift glance, and then snapped their heads away, almost as if by command. He wondered, he told me, what thoughts coursed through their minds.

"The Negro Soldier" is a first-class picture, wisely aimed at offsetting some of this indifference and ignorance concerning one-tenth of our armed forces. But only when the picture reaches American white people will Negroes believe its real service to be achieved.

The situation that I found in the South was not solely that of whites refusing to count Negroes in, and of Negroes sensing that they did not and could not belong. It would be inaccurate to omit the friendliness that undoubtedly exists in the South between many whites and many Negroes. Though exaggerated by sentimentalists into a mystical cult of mutual affection instead of a human attachment, certain Southern whites have for a long time protected "their Negroes" and have cherished them with a fondness that has been gratefully received. But, as is frequently pointed out, this has generally been on a basis of master and underling. It has been affection rather than friendship, patronage returned by gratefulness, not the meeting of friends on a plane of mutual respect. It has been Santa Claus and the child. In certain phases—in the courts for instance—when a white man protects *his* Negro regardless of innocence or guilt, the relationship is dangerous. Kindness can kill as well as cruelty, and it can never take the place of genuine respect. Those who boast of the affection between the races below the Mason-Dixon line must be brought up sharp when they realize that one of the worst insults to a Southern white is to be called "nigger-lover," and one of the worst to a Negro is to be called "white-folks nigger."

Genuine respect between whites and Negroes can be found in the South, though to a smaller degree than paternalistic affection and dependent gratefulness. It would be serious omission to fail to recognize undoubted services rendered by many white people, not in the spirit of "Christmas gift," but at the price of social ostracism, loss of preferment, and even physical violence. Sheriffs have braved mobs to protect their prisoners; women have leagued against lynching; preachers, editors, professional men, scholars and authors have spoken and acted against flagrant abuses; trade union organizers have risked life and limb in efforts to establish industrial democracy. Many people, less dramatically, have been generous and courageous in treating Negroes in the spirit of brotherhood. People like Frank Graham, Arthur Raper, Thomas Sancton, Lillian Smith, and Paula Snelling, to name a conspicuous few, are warrants that there are white Southerners who believe that a New South of justice is attainable, or at the least, worth fighting for.

These exceptions must be noted. Yet what I found most apparent among Southern Negroes—civilians and military men, upper and lower class, conservatives and radicals—was a sense of not belonging, and protest, sometimes not loud but always deeply felt. It is a mistake to believe that this protest in the South is instigated by Negroes from the North, or other "furriners," as Eugene Talmadge called them. I found a large degree of mili-

tancy in Negroes who were Southern born and bred, some of
whom have never been out of the South. I talked with sharecroppers, union organizers, preachers, schoolteachers, newspaper-
men and bankers who spoke with bitter desperation and daring.
Clinton Clark, certainly among the sturdiest fighters, was born
in one of the back country parishes of Louisiana; when he was
arrested for organizing in a parish nearby, the planters refused
to believe him a native of the section. The protest I heard ranged
from the quietly spoken aside, through twisted humor and
sarcasm, to stridency. Time and time again I heard the anecdote,
which spread like a folk tale, of the new sort of hero—the Negro
soldier who having taken all he could stand, shed his coat, faced
his persecutors and said: "If I've got to die for democracy, I
might as well die for some of it right here and now." Some of
the protest, undoubtedly, is chip-on-the-shoulder aggression, like
that of the Negro woman who in a jammed bus lumbering
through the Louisiana night, suddenly raised her voice, seem-
ingly apropos of nothing, to say: "I had my Texas jack with me,
and I told that white man I would cut him as long as I could see
him."

At Columbus, Georgia, buses marked "K.O. for Tokyo" roared
past Negro soldiers, who had to wait for special buses to take
them to Fort Benning. It was not only the boys from Harlem or
Jersey who griped. The Negro train passengers who, standing
in the aisle, wise-cracked at the flushed conductor seated in his
"office" in the Jim Crow coach, and then belabored the Negro
porter for being a good man Friday, were not Northerners. It
was not a Northern waiter who told the Negro sitting in the
diner after lavish and ostentatious service: "Man, I was afraid
you weren't coming back here." They were not Northern Negroes who repeated the refrain, whether called for or not, "That
ain't no way to win the war."

I found this protest natural, since the Southern Negro is where
the grip is tightest and the bite goes deepest and most often. The
legend of Negro docility was always exaggerated. The novelists
and poets, "befo' de war," wrote soothingly of contented slaves,
but many of their readers lived in dread of insurrections, and
applauded the politicians who, fuming about the loss of their

property via the Underground Railroad, sought anxiously to put teeth into the fugitive slave bill, and to set up a code of *verbotens* to prevent slave uprisings. Printers, whose presses busily ran off stories of docile Mose and Dinah, kept handy the stereotype of a Negro with a bundle on a stick, loping towards free land. The image of docility was cherished as a dream, but the hard actuality of furtiveness, truculence, rebelliousness and desperation gave other images to the nightmares. The praises of old massa that white men wrote in "'Negro" speech and "Negro" melody ring falsely when set beside "I been rebuked and I been scorned," "Go Down Moses, tell old Pharaoh, let my people go," and "I thank God, I'm free at last."

"When a man's got a gun in your face, ain't much to do but take low or die," a sharecropper in Macon County told Charles S. Johnson. In that setting he was talking sense, not docility. Southern Negroes too often have seen the gun in their faces; but many, all along, have asserted their manhood as far as they were able, walking as close to the danger line as they could and still survive. Some edged over, some were dragged over, and some found the line a shifting one; many of these last paid the penalty. This has been true through the long years, and now, when fine-sounding talk of freedom and democracy comes to them from the newspapers and sermons, tales swapped around the cracker-barrels of country stores, letters from their boys in camps, and speeches over the radio, Negroes begin putting in stronger, though still modest claims. Talk about freedom did not reveal a new discovery; true freedom was something they had long been hankering for. I do not believe that they were so naïve that they expected full values for all of the promissory notes. Freedom was a hard-bought thing, their tradition warned them; the great day of "jubilo" had been followed by gloomy days; but the talk sounded good and right, and perhaps a little more freedom *was* on its way. Through the radios—many of them the battery sets which fill needs in small shacks once filled only by phonographs and guitars—booming voices told them of the plans for a new world. Over the air-waves came the spark, lighting and nursing small fires of hope; the glow and the warmth were good in the darkness. "One of the worst things making for all this trouble," a Mississippi planter told me, with frank honesty, "is the radio. Those people up in Washington don't know what they're doing down here. They ought to shut up talking so much."

Evidence of the Negro's not belonging is readier at hand in the South. But the North is by no means blameless in its race relations. According to an alleged folk anecdote a Negro said he would prefer to be in a race riot in Detroit than in a camp meeting in Georgia. And orators repeatedly urge, "Come North, young man," as the only solution. Nevertheless, the folklore that the North is a refuge, a haven, has met up with the hard facts of unemployment, discrimination and tension. Paradise Valley, Detroit is as badly misnamed as Ideal, Georgia. The mobs that wrecked that Negro section of Detroit showed a crazed lust for bloodshed and destruction that was no Southern monopoly. Harlem has been fondly spoken of as a Mecca for Negroes; but the rioting Negroes who smashed the windows and looted the stores reveal that Negroes have found causes there for desperation and fury. In Northern cities that cradled abolitionism, Negroes are to be found cramped in ghettos, still denied a chance to earn decent livelihoods, to make use of their training, to develop into full men and women.

Though convinced that the Negro is "thoroughly Jim Crowed all over the North—considering Jim Crow in its deepest aspects," Thomas Sancton writes:

> And yet it is true that the main body of the race problem lies within the boundaries of the Southern states, because some three-fourths of America's 13,000,000 Negroes live there.... The Negro is oppressed in many ways in the North, and certainly economically, but the long anti-slavery tradition has at least given him some basic civil and social rights which the white South continues to deny him and would like to deny him forever. [3]

Since the problem of the Negro in America is of national scope, steps to integrate the Negro ·into American democracy must be taken everywhere. Nevertheless, it remains true that the gravest denial of democracy and the greatest opposition to it are

[3] Thomas Sancton, "The South Needs Help," *Common Ground*, III (Winter, 1943), 12.

in the South. It goes without saying that what happens to the Negro in the South has great bearing on what participation the Negro will attain in American democracy. If a Negro is allowed only second or third class citizenship in Tupelo, Mississippi, his Harlem brother's citizenship is less than first class. And if America has more than one class of citizenship, it is less than a first class democracy.

NO TRESPASSING

What are the chances that freedom is really on its way; that the Negro may finally be "counted in"? Some signs are none too propitious. For instance, Negro soldiers are indoctrinated to believe that they are to fight for the four freedoms, but what they run up against daily is confusing, rather than reassuring. Fraternization between Negro soldiers and white soldiers is largely discouraged; it seems to be considered un-American for soldiers of different color, though fighting for the same cause, to be brothers-in-arms. A bulletin from headquarters may attack the subversiveness of race-hostility, but part of the bulletin will warn Negro soldiers that dissatisfaction with Jim Crow is tantamount to subversiveness. Democracy to many seems to be symbolized by this message, printed under a large red "V" on a bus in Charleston, South Carolina:

Victory Demands Your Co-operation

If the peoples of this country's races do not pull together, Victory is lost. We, therefore, respectfully direct your attention to the laws and customs of the state in regard to segregation. Your cooperation in carrying them out will make the war shorter and Victory sooner. Avoid friction. Be patriotic. White passengers will be seated from front to rear; colored passengers from rear to front.

Looking about them, especially in the South but also in the North, Negroes see convincing proof of these implications: that patriotism means satisfaction with the *status quo ante* Pearl Harbor, that co-operation really does not mean pulling together but rather the Negro's acceptance of the subservient role; that otherwise friction threatens.

A current anecdote tells of a white officer who, seeing a Negro officer eating in the diner, exclaimed: "I'd rather see Hitler win the war than for niggers to get out of their place like that!" Negroes do not believe the attitude to be exceptional.

With all of the commendable efforts of the Army to improve the morale of Negro troops and to investigate and iron out the difficulties, Negro soldiers still find too many violations of democracy, ranging from petty irritations to rank injustices. Negroes may lose precious hours of leave because they can find no place to ride on the buses. Negro officers may find a studied refusal on the part of white soldiers to salute. Negro soldiers may be manhandled, cursed, and even killed by civilian officers of the law. Living the rough, exacting life on maneuvers, driving a jeep, manning a tank or machine gun, servicing or flying a fighter plane, the Negro soldier is expected to be a man doing a man-size job. In contact with civilian life, however, the Negro soldier is expected to be something else again.

There are signs elsewhere that do not reassure. That Negroes were given jobs at a steel plant "that have always been filled by white men," that Negro veterans of World War I were filing legal action "to force the American Legion in Alabama to charter Negro posts," that Tuskegee officials were demanding that pistols be restored to Negro military police in Tuskegee—these frightened and angered Horace Wilkinson of Bessemer, Alabama into urging the foundation of a "League to Maintain White Supremacy." He was shocked at the impertinence of the Fair Employment Practices Committee in coming to Birmingham and recording proof that Southern industrialists and labor unions discriminated against Negro labor and thereby hampered the war effort. Mr. Wilkinson's efforts have reached some success; the "League to Maintain White Supremacy" has been set up. A race-baiting sheet, *The Alabama Sun*, is being published. The first issue has a picture of Mrs. Roosevelt greeting a Negro Red Cross Worker, back from service in England, with the caption "Mrs. Roosevelt Greets Another Nigger."

Mr. Wilkinson is playing an old game, of course, and is a member of a large squad. Mrs. Roosevelt, because of her genuine and gracious democracy, has long been the target of abuse in the

South. Years ago, in order to aid the election of Eugene Talmadge, the *Georgia Woman's World* published a picture of the
first lady escorted by two Negro cadet officers on her visit to a
Negro university. Recent rumormongering has built up a folklore
of mythical Eleanor Clubs, dedicated to getting Negro women
out of the kitchens, and white women into them. The smear
campaign was indecently climaxed when a Mississippi editor,
hardly concealing his satisfaction at the Detroit riots, blamed
Mrs. Roosevelt for the massacre. The editorial impressed Representative Boykin of Alabama so favorably that he had it inserted in
The Congressional Record. It closed:

> In Detroit, a city noted for the growing impudence and in
> solence of the Negro population, an attempt was made to put
> your preachments into practice...Blood on your hands,
> Mrs. Roosevelt, and the damned spots won't wash out,
> either. [4]

According to a Gallup Poll, many white Southerners believe
that the Negro has been made "unruly and unmanageable" because "large scale reforms have been undertaken too swiftly." [5]
Writing from his winter home in Florida, Roger Babson lectured
his friends—"the several millions of colored people"—about their
"lazy, wasteful, saucy moods." White workers may "strike when
they shouldn't, but they are not lazy nor do they throw away
money."

In all likelihood "sauciness," rather than laziness or wastefulness, is the chief cause of the present wide race-baiting. Any
symbol of the Negro's getting out of "his place"—a lieutenant's
shoulder bars, or even a buck private's uniform; a Negro worker
at a machine, or a Negro girl at a typewriter, or a cook's throwing
up her job—these can be as unbearable as an impudent retort, or
a quarrel on a bus, or a fight.

The demagogues have had and are having a field day. Running
for re-election as Governor in 1942 against strong opposition,
Eugene Talmadge of Georgia preached race-prejudice from
Rabun Gap to Tybee's shining light. He ordered his state con-

---

[4] *The Congressional Record,* June 28, 1943.
[5] George Gallup, "The Gallup Poll," *The Washington Post,* August 28,
1943.

stabulary to be vigilant against Northern Negroes and other "furriners" and warned Southern womanhood to arm. His opponent
was not above race-baiting himself; it seemed that he had to do it
to win. In neighboring states in the Deep South the demagogues
may have been less spectacular, but they were busy. Results were
soon forthcoming. Three Negroes, two of them boys, were
lynched within a week in Mississippi. Negroes were beaten and
thrown off buses and trains in all sections of the South. Crises
have followed close on crises. A riot stopped work in a Mobile
shipyard because Negroes were upgraded; a pogrom laid waste
the Negro section of Beaumont, Texas, because of a rape charge,
later discredited; and murder ran wild in Detroit.

Any concessions to Negroes—any guaranteeing of democratic
rights—set the demagogues off full steam. Sometimes they cry
"wolf," as in the instance of the voluminous report of the Office
of Education which, among other recommendations, urged cooperation between Negro and white colleges "in the interest of
national welfare." Congressman Brooks of Louisiana equated this
co-operation to "forcible co-mingling of students of the two
races in the South...unthinkable...leading to the producing of
a mongrel race in the United States."

When two anthropologists published a pamphlet, *The Races
of Mankind*, to give wide circulation to the scientific proof of the
brotherhood of man, and to help bring it about that "victory in
this war will be in the name, not of one race or another, but of
the universal Human Race," Congressman May of Kentucky was
enraged. He was especially irked to read that Northern Negroes
scored higher on the A.E.F. Intelligence Test than Southern
whites (of his native state, for instance), although the authors
advised that the statistics meant only that "Negroes with better
luck after they were born, got higher scores than whites with less
luck." As Chairman of the House Military Affairs Committee,
Congressman May decided that these scientific facts had "no
place in the Army program," and promised to keep his eyes open
lest the soldiers be contaminated with such doctrine. The pamphlets went to an Army warehouse.

Coincidental with the fight waged by the National Association
for the Advancement of Colored People to equalize teachers'

salaries in South Carolina, the South Carolina House of Representatives resolved:

> We reaffirm our belief in and our allegiance to establish white supremacy as now prevailing in the South and we solemnly pledge our lives and our sacred honor to maintaining it. Insofar as racial relations are concerned, we firmly and unequivocally demand that henceforth the damned agitators of the North leave the South alone. [6]

Shortly after the Negro teachers of South Carolina won the fight to equalize salaries, a Charleston judge stated that many Negroes "would be better off carrying a load of fertilizer rather than a bunch of school books.... I am going to break up some of this education."

The perennial demagogues of Mississippi, Senator Bilbo and Representative Rankin, hold the limelight. Senator Bilbo recently held up for the admiration of his constituents his old scheme for deporting Negroes to Africa. One of the first steps he planned as chairman of the Senate Committee for the District of Columbia was clearing Negroes out of the alleys of Washington. "I want them to get into the habit of moving so as to be ready for my movement to West Africa." Until the day of that migration, Senator Bilbo promises alley dwellers of Washington that they can find places to stay in the basements of city homes, and on farms in neighboring states, where the need for cooks and farm hands is acute. Senator Bilbo also threatens to repeat his record-making filibuster against the repeal of the poll tax.

Representative Rankin also stays busy: attacking the President's Committee on Fair Employment Practices as subversive of democracy, since white and Negro sailors in the National Maritime Union are assigned to the same ship; threatening with lynching "that gang of communistic Jews and Negroes that... tried to storm the House restaurants, and went around arm in arm with each other"; [7] attacking the Federal ballot for soldiers; and raging at every specter of "social equality."

Both Senator Bilbo and Congressman Rankin, as so many other

[6] *The Washington Post*, March 7, 1944.
[7] *The Congressional Record*, July 1, 1943.

demagogues, protest that they act in the interests of the Negro. Senator Bilbo says, "I am the best friend the Negro has." And Representative Rankin blames "communistic Jews" for causing "the deaths of many good Negroes who never would have got into trouble if they had been left alone."

So run the warnings from the demagogues. But it is not only among the demagogues and their Gestapos—the frontier thugs, the state constabularies, the goon squads and the lynchers—that violent aversion to change is found. Many of the intellectuals speak lines that sound like Talmadge and Rankin. A decade ago, *The American Review*, now defunct, published their ideas. Donald Davidson viewed with dire misgivings "a general maneuver, the object of which is apparently to set the Negro up as an equal, or at least more than a subordinate member of society. The second, or unavowed, program was the new form of abolitionism, again proposing to emancipate the Negro from the handicap of race, color, and previous condition of servitude." [8] Mr. Davidson considered this program (he was talking chiefly of a program of ownership of small farms by Negroes) to be "unattainable as long as the South remains the South," and its sponsors he called ruthless. The only possible solution, he thought, is "to define a place for the American Negro as special as that which they [the American people] defined for the American Indian." Allen Tate, condemning the reformers "who are anxious to have Negroes sit by them on street cars," wrote:

> I argue it this way: the white race seems determined to rule the Negro race in its midst; I belong to the white race; therefore I intend to support the white rule. Lynching is a symptom of weak, inefficient rule; but you can't destroy lynching by *fiat* or social agitation; lynching will disappear when the white race is satisfied that its supremacy will not be questioned in social crises. [9]

Tempting the Negro to question this supremacy, he believes, is irresponsible behavior.

[8] Donald Davidson, "A Sociologist in Eden," *The American Review*, VIII (December, 1936), 200 ff.

[9] Allen Tate, "A View of the Whole South," *ibid.*, II (February, 1934), 424.

Frank Owsley called the agitation to free the Scottsboro boys the "third crusade." [10] More important to him than the defendants' innocence or guilt was the fact that some Negroes were going to get hurt: "The outside interference with the relationship of the whites and blacks in the South can result in nothing but organizations like the Ku Klux Klan and in violent retaliation against the Negroes—themselves often innocent."

It is to be expected that the die-hards should interpret Negro aspirations to democracy as incendiarism. But there are Southern liberals who do the same. Some congressmen, noted for their support of New Deal reforms, have been recently forced into race-baiting, in order to prove that they are not "nigger-lovers." Some of the liberals protest with David Cohn that they view the position of the American Negro with "a sore heart, a troubled conscience, and a deep compassion." A few of these have shown genuine sympathy with the Negro's progress. Nevertheless, by and large, they are defeatists. Mark Ethridge, one of the leaders of Southern white liberals, stated flatly: "There is no power in the world—not even in all the mechanized armies of the earth, Allied and Axis—which could now force the Southern white people to the abandonment of the principle of social segregation." [11]

Since the Negro hardly would count upon the armies of the Axis as friends in any case, the prophecy is all the more direful. Mr. Ethridge warns that "cruel disillusionment, bearing the germs of strife and perhaps tragedy" will result from exacting the abolition of social segregation as the price of participation in the war. It is inaccurate to say that the Negroes were exacting this: Negroes at the time of Mr. Ethridge's prophecy were in all likelihood participating as fully as they were allowed to participate.

It is the gravity of the fear, however, rather than the accurate description of its cause, that concerns us here. Howard Odum also sees the net results of outside agitation in the affairs of the

[10] Frank L. Owsley, "Scottsboro: The Third Crusade," *ibid.*, I (Summer, 1933), 285.

[11] John Temple Graves, *The Fighting South* (New York, 1943), p. 125 f.

South to be "tragedy of the highest order, tragedy of the Greek, as it were, because it was the innocent Negro who suffered." [12] Virginius Dabney sees the two races edging nearer and nearer "to the precipice," if the Negro continues his demands.

David Cohn echoes Mr. Ethridge. As so many Southern intellectuals do, he finds comfort in William Graham Sumner's adage that you cannot change the mores of a people by law. Segregation is "the most deep-seated and pervasive of the Southern mores"; Negroes and whites who would break it down by Federal fiat had therefore better beware. "I have no doubt," Mr. Cohn writes, "that in such an event every Southern white man would spring to arms and the country would be swept by Civil war." Patience, good will, and wisdom (wisdom meaning acceptance of segregation without protest) are needful, otherwise the question will be delivered out of the hands of decent whites and Negroes "into the talons of demagogues, fascists, and the Klu Kluxers, to the irreparable harm of the Negro." [13]

It is significant that Southern spokesmen, reactionaries and liberals alike, are exercised over the harm that may come to Negroes. Watch out, the warning goes, or *Negroes* will get hurt. This is an old refrain; over a century ago the first proslavery novelist threatened, when Garrison's blasts were sounding off from Boston, that the "mischievous interference of abolitionists would involve the negro in the rigor which it provokes." And the latest demagogue expresses this threat and this tenderness.

The whites and Negroes who hope for a democratic solution to the problem must learn that the problem is insoluble, warns Mr. Cohn: "It is at bottom a blood or sexual question." Southern whites are determined that "no white in their legal jurisdiction shall marry a Negro" and "white women shall not have physical relations with Negro men except, when discovered, upon pain of death or banishment inflicted upon one or both parties to the act." [14] And John Temple Graves takes his stand on two bedrock

---

[12] Howard W. Odum, *Race and Rumors of Race* (Chapel Hill, 1943), p. 155.

[13] David L. Cohn, "How the South Feels," *The Atlantic Monthly,* CLXXIII (January, 1944), 50 f.

[14] *Ibid.,* p. 49.

"facts": "The unshakable belief of southern whites that the problem was peculiarly their own and that attempts to force settlement from outside were hateful and incompetent. The absolute determination that the blood of the two races should not be confused and a mulatto population emerge." [15]

Negroes have long recognized this as the hub of the argument opposing change in their status. A chief recruiting slogan for the Ku Klux Klan of Reconstruction, when Negroes were "getting out of their place" by voting, buying farms and homes, and attending schools, was that Southern white womanhood must be protected. "The closer the Negro got to the ballot-box, the more he looked like a rapist," is the quip of a Negro who has studied the period closely. Thomas Nelson Page wrote that the barbarities of Reconstruction were based upon "the determination to put an end to the ravishing of their women by an inferior race, or by any race, no matter what the consequence." [16] Though a later Southern student, W. J. Cash, has estimated that "the chance [of the Southern white woman's being violated by a Negro] was much less... than the chance that she would be struck by lightning," [17] it is Page rather than Cash whose opinions are most followed. Political campaigns still seem to be waged not so much to get into office as to protect women. In his last campaign, Eugene Talmadge reported "an unusual number of assault cases and attempts to assault white ladies" (though newspaper reporters could not find them), and he denounced the Rosenwald Fund, noted for its benefactions to the South, as being determined to make a "mulatto South." Senator Ellender, in one of his attacks on an anti-lynching bill, revealed the train of thought of so many filibusters when he promised that if the bill should pass, he would propose three amendments all prohibiting intermarriage. If mobs were forbidden by Federal law to lynch Negroes, white people were at least not going to be allowed to marry Negroes. Instances of such reasoning make up a sorry tale.

For all of their protesting of decency and good will, the intel-

[15] Graves, *op. cit.*, p. 239.

[16] Thomas Nelson Page, *The Negro: the Southerner's Problem* (New York, 1904), p. 100.

[17] W. J. Cash, *The Mind of the South* (New York, 1941), p. 115.

lectuals do not talk very differently from Gerald L. K. Smith, a spellbinder generally considered to be of the native fascist variety. The Reverend Smith inherited one of Huey Long's mantles; he is certain that he knows what people want or at least that he can rouse them into wanting what he wants. Immediately after the Detroit riot, the Reverend Smith wrote in *The Cross and the Flag* that most white people would not agree to any of the following: intermarriage of blacks and whites; mixture of blacks and whites in hotels, restaurants; "intimate relationships" between blacks and whites in the school system; "wholesale mixture of blacks and whites in residential sections"; "promiscuous mixture" of blacks and whites in street cars and on trains, "especially when black men are permitted to sit down and crowd in close to white women and vice versa." The Reverend Smith added generously, "I have every reason to believe black women resent being crowded by white men." Mixture in factories was also offensive, "especially when black men are mixed with white women closely in daily work."

It is true that the Reverend Smith is no longer tilling Southern fields, but he learned his demagoguery in the South, and many of his audience were transplanted Southerners. It is also undeniable that his words struck responsive chords in many Northerners. But he expresses a cardinal tenet of the Southern creed that social mixture must be forbidden, or else as John Temple Graves puts it, "a mulatto population will emerge."

Negroes know well that that horse has been out of the stable too long a time for the lock to be put on the door now. Even the race purists must realize the large amount of mixture in the American Negro, that hybrid of African, Indian and Caucasian stock. And though, as the anthropologist Montague Cobb says, the Caucasian component is "the most apparent and the least documented," race purists must realize how the Negro got that way.

Fears that lowering the barriers of segregation will lower the level of civilization are often expressed. If these fears are not liars, one consequence might be that civilization in such Southern cities as Atlanta, Birmingham, Memphis, and Vicksburg will decline to the level of that in unsegregated Boston, New York,

Iowa City, and Seattle. According to these fears, intermarriage will result when Negroes and whites eat in the same restaurants or in a diner without a little green curtain; when they stop in the same hotels, and ride the same street cars and buses without wooden screens, or other separating devices. Negroes laugh at the suggestion that crowded buses and street cars and cafeterias are marriage bureaus. They know that intermarriage is not widespread in the states where there are no segregation laws and no laws forbidding intermarriage. They believe with great reason that there is more illicit sexual relationship between the races in the states whose laws forbid intermarriage than there are mixed marriages elsewhere.

Intermarriage is hardly a goal that Negroes are contending for openly or yearning for secretly. It is certainly not a mental preoccupation with them and scarcely a matter of special concern. Nevertheless, they do not want laws on the statute books branding them as outcasts. They do not want governmental sanction of caste, however long they have seen it hardened about them. They know how prophetic were the words of the anguished heroine of George Washington Cable's story of the last century: "A lie, Père Jerome! Separate! No! They do not want to keep us [white men: colored women] separate: no, no! But they *do* want to keep us despised!"

It is likely of course that friendships will develop where Negroes and whites meet on a basis of respect and where people can be drawn together by kindred interests. It is likely that some of these friendships might ripen into love and marriage. That certainly should be left as a private matter, the affair of the persons involved, as it is now in most civilized lands. An individual's choice of a mate should hardly be considered as a chief cause of the downfall of western, or American, or even Southern civilization. A more grievous cause for alarm, a more dangerous omen of ruin, is the contempt for personality based on skin color and hair texture. Negroes laugh a bit ruefully at the dread that one-tenth of a nation's population will corner the marital market of the nine-tenths. They know to what a degree in the past the opposite has prevailed, though the market could not with accuracy be termed marital. They could scarcely consider laws banning intermarriage to be protective of their own women. And they do not share the Southern white man's fear that the white women of the South are so weak and easily misled that they cannot be trusted to select their own husbands. They agree instead with the numerous white women of the South who have publicly stated that they do not need lynching or special legislation to protect them.

The black herring of intermarriage has been dragged too often across the trail to justice. "Would you want your sister to marry a nigger?" is still the question that is supposed to stun any white man who sponsors rights for Negroes. It stirs Negroes to ironic laughter, although on all levels they recognize the white man's fear of intermarriage as deep-seated. From the jokes of the people —of Negroes talking to Negroes, where "Miss Annie's" name is changed to "Miss Rope" or "Miss Hemp"—to the satire of the publicists, this awareness is to be found. A Negro editor, fighting a covenant restricting housing, was asked point blank: "Do you believe in intermarriage?" to stop his guns of logic and facts. Some Negro public speakers, faced with the question, dodge behind statements like "Well, I'm married already myself." Some take refuge in Kipling's line, "Never the twain shall meet," without sharing Kipling's assurance or hope. The twain have met and the twain will meet. But Negroes are not convinced thereby that they must give up their struggle to share in American democracy.

Though David Cohn warns that irony and reason cannot answer what he calls "blood-thinking," the "biological" fear of "a chocolate-colored American people," Negroes wonder if that fear is as real among Southerners as the determination to keep the Negro in his place economically. Certain Southern liberals have stated their willingness for Negroes to have the rights of voting, good schools, sanitation, paved and lighted streets, justice in the courts, and equitable employment. But Negroes wonder if the possibilities of these—merely these without intermarriage—do not stir great and widespread fears, real instead of spectral. They wonder if the smokescreen of intermarriage is not raised to frighten Southerners from conceding any of these rights, which are fraught with more danger to privilege and exploitation. Some

Negroes wonder if maintaining a cheap labor reservoir is not as important a motive as preventing Negroes from crowding whites on buses and proposing marriage to them. Pointing to a group of poor whites and poor Negroes, a planter said to Ira Reid and Arthur Raper: "As long as these whites keep those Negroes humble, we'll keep them both poor." [18]

Many Negroes are sardonic about the oddities of segregation. The white patron, who is willing to eat soup prepared in the kitchen by black hands and served by a black waiter who may get his thumb in it, but who nearly faints when he discovers a Negro eating at another table in the same restaurant; a man's fulsome worship of the black nurse in whose lap he was rocked to sleep, and his horror at sitting next to a black man on a street car (it might be the nurse's son); the preservation of white supremacy on a diner by a little green curtain, or on a street car by a screen or a rope, in a Jim Crow coach by a chalk line beyond which the overflow from the white coach may not roll, in a government office by setting a Negro's desk cater-cornered, slightly off the line of the other desks; these afford ribald amusement. They do not make sense; they do not add to respect for the rationality of Southern whites. Such instances are recognized as sprouting from deep roots, certainly; but other superstitions have been uprooted. Maybe these can be.

Some Negroes, of course, realize that a logic does lie behind the apparent oddities. This is the time-hallowed logic of dividing and ruling—the playing off of underprivileged whites against Negroes to prevent a real democratic union—a practice that has paid the oligarchs well. Northern industrialists in the South have done their full share of capitalizing on race hostility, exciting it by talk of Negroes "getting out of their places." Some Negroes, therefore, see segregation as more than a superstition; but they are convinced that it can, and must be uprooted.

Negroes are not contending for wholesale entree into drawing rooms. They see no contradiction in democracy that people shall select their own friends, cliques, husbands, and wives. They do see as contradictory that false fears of social intermingling should

[18] Arthur Raper and Ira De A. Reid, *Sharecroppers All* (Chapel Hill, 1941), p. 78.

be raised to jeopardize honest aspirations to full citizenship. What segregationists denounce as "wanting to be with white folks," Negroes think of as participating in the duties and enjoying the privileges of democracy. This means being with white folks, undoubtedly, since whites have nearly monopolized these duties and privileges. But it means being with them in fields and factories, in the armed forces, at the voting booths, in schools and colleges, in all the areas of service to democracy.

COUNT US IN

Negroes want to be counted in. They want to belong. They want what other men have wanted deeply enough to fight and suffer for it. They want democracy. Wanting it so much, they disregard more and more the warnings: "This is not the time." "The time isn't ripe." "Take your time, take your time." Nearly a hundred years ago, in desperation at the plight of the slaves, Herman Melville wrote, "Time must befriend these thralls." And in crucial moments since, time has been pointed to as the solvent. Patience, urges David Cohn, rule out the emotional and irrational and then the burden will rest "upon the whites to do for the Negro what they have not done at all, or only in part." But the Negro has difficulty in finding the guaranties of this hope that so many Negro and white spokesmen have promised to him. Southern Negroes are not of one mind with Southern whites that "outside interference is hateful and incompetent." They do not see democracy as a commodity to be quarantined at the Potomac and Ohio Rivers; as a sort of a Japanese beetle to be hunted for in the luggage before travelers are allowed to go on. Negroes are glad whenever democratic ideas circulate through the South, whether by means of liberal weeklies, *PM*, the· speeches of labor organizers, pamphlets, sermons, radio forums, books, Negro newspapers and magazines, or letters from the boys in service. They know, of course, that if democracy is to be achieved in the South, where it is least found, the greatest work must be done by Southerners, whites and Negroes together. But they welcome whatever help they can get from any sources.

And they know, furthermore, that the agencies working for

democracy are not necessarily "outside agitators." The National Association for the Advancement of Colored People may have its headquarters in New York, but, as its name suggests, it is a *national* association. Many of its leaders are Southerners by birth and training. Many of its courageous workers are living in the South. The Negro teachers who risk their jobs and even worse in the struggle for equalization of salaries are Southern born and bred. Negro journalists in the deep South generally speak out uncompromisingly for justice. Southern Negroes have not needed Northern agitators to stir up dissatisfaction with discrimination and abuse. As pointed out earlier, they have learned the hard way, and the lessons have sunk in deeply.

They have heard the threats. Against their democratic aspirations they see a concerted line-up: college professors as well as hoodlums; congressmen as well as vigilantes; Rotarians as well as manual laborers; cotton planters as well as cotton hands. Negroes expect that some of them are going to get hurt before they get what they want. This is no new experience for them; they have been getting hurt in this country since 1619. But getting hurt in a stand-up struggle for justice is one thing; getting hurt merely because of the color of your skin, while lying down, is quite another.

On trips through the South, I have talked with several who had been hurt. With Roland Hayes, for example, shortly after he had been savagely beaten by the policemen of Rome, Georgia. With Hugh Gloster, a young college professor, who had been thrown off a train in Tupelo, Mississippi, because he asked the conductor to let Negroes who were standing in the aisles of the Jim Crow coach overflow into a white coach, only partly filled. With Clinton Clark, who had been beaten, arrested, jailed and threatened with the rope time and time again for organizing the cane-cutters and cotton hands of Louisiana into a union. Roland Hayes talked broodingly; Hugh Gloster, sardonically; Clinton Clark, stoically, without any surprise: "You try to organize people to get out of slavery, may as well expect the big planters and their boys—the sheriffs and deputies—to get tough." But all of these, and others who told me their stories of abuse, knew the shock of the sudden oath, the blow, the murderous look in the eye.

They had been hurt, no doubt of that. But it is unlikely that they, or many other Negroes, merely because of the violence, will become reconciled to what caused it. Many Negroes are still going to protest rough language to their wives, as Roland Hayes did; or unfair travel accommodations, as Hugh Gloster did; or exploitation in the cane and cotton fields, as Clinton Clark did. "Get out and stay out of this parish," the jailer in Natchitoches told Clark. "I'll be back," said Clark, "I'll have a stronger organization behind me the next time."

Some of the victims do not forget the lessons that the rubber hose, the fist, the long black hours in the smelly cell fix so deeply. But from as many other victims comes this: "And if I had it to do all over, I'd do the same thing again."

Negroes who profess faith, whether real or not, in passive waiting for decent whites to take up their burden, are losing that faith. Negroes who feared that asking for democracy would lead to some Negroes' getting hurt, are losing that fear. But losing the passive faith is not defeatism, and losing the fear is not bravado.

There are many Negroes who are not convinced, as some forlorn liberals are, that democracy is a doomed hope in the South. They see heart-warming signs. They see the opponents of the poll tax gathering strength. The filibusters may rant so long or maneuver so craftily that the repeal may not pass this year, but the struggle against the poll tax will continue. Negroes applaud the Supreme Court decisions outlawing the white primary as a private club's election. They see the FEPC holding on, a symbol of the hope to abolish discrimination in industry, though challenged on many sides, flouted occasionally, and hard beset. They hear native white South Carolinians disclaim the "white supremacy" resolution of their House of Representatives in humiliation "because it is white people who have thus held up the state to scorn.... The only white supremacy which is worthy of the name is that which exists because of virtue, not power." White supremacy is not the issue, they say, but that Negroes should serve on juries, that they should be allowed representation on boards which administer affairs involving Negro citizens and their property; that Negro policemen should be provided in

Negro residential districts; that the disfranchisement of all Negroes in South Carolina cannot endure indefinitely; these are some of the pressing issues. Negroes are aware of the importance of such words from representative citizens, neither interracialists nor "radicals," in Cotton Ed Smith's bailiwick.

Of course, many Negroes keep their fingers crossed. They expected Congressman Rankin's blast at the Supreme Court vote, which ran true to form: "I see that the parlor pinks in the Department of Justice are already starting to harass the Southern states as a result of the blunder of the Supreme Court. The Negroes of the South are having their hope of peace and harmony with their white neighbors destroyed by these pinks." Canny through long experience with the politicos, Negroes realize that the road from outlawing white primaries and the poll tax to widespread voting may be long and rocky. "Let 'em try it," said the *Jackson Daily News;* "There are other ways of preserving southern tradition," the *Birmingham Post* said; "We will maintain white supremacy, let the chips fall where they may," said the Governor of South Carolina.

It may be a long and rocky road. But it is the right road. Some Negroes may remain lethargic about their rights and duties as citizens. Some Negroes may get hurt; some may be timorous; the overpraised "harmony" may go off-key. As a sign that they are being "counted in" Negroes see several Southern editors applauding the decision. One called it "a much-needed political safety valve" instead of a threat. Virginius Dabney writes that Tennessee, Kentucky, North Carolina, and Virginia, all of them without the white primary, have never seen white supremacy endangered. More significantly, he writes: "No society...is truly democratic...which shuts out anywhere from a quarter to a half of its people from all part in the choice of the officials under whom they must live and work."

Another cheering signpost, indicating that some mileage has been covered on the long journey, is the work of certain Southern white liberals. Virginius Dabney performed a historic act in advocating the abolition of Jim Crow on Virginia street cars and buses. It is true that he had to surrender his proposal; though numerous white Virginians applauded it, Mr. Dabney became convinced that the time was not right. But it was a first step that may count, and the proof that Virginia white opinion was not unanimous for Jim Crow is worth recording. Hoping that Negro leadership will rest in Atlanta (not so coincidentally Walter White's native city) rather than in New York, Mr. Dabney realizes that steps toward democracy must be taken *in the South*. This realization is quite as honest as his fear of trouble.

Southern white liberals deplore the demands of outsiders, and then come out themselves for many of the same reforms. The Atlanta Conference of representative white Southerners praised the Southern Negro Conference at Durham for frankness and courage. Among so much else the Atlanta Conference conclusions stated: "No Southerner can logically dispute the fact that the Negro, as an American citizen, is entitled to his civil rights and economic opportunities"; and "we agree...that it is 'unfortunate that the simple efforts to correct obvious social and economic injustices continue, with such considerable popular support, to be interpreted as the predatory ambition of irresponsible Negroes to invade the privacy of family life....' We agree also that 'it is a wicked notion that the struggle by the Negro for citizenship is a struggle against the best interest of the nation.'"[19]

Negroes look with hope to the continuing conference, composed of several Southern Negro leaders who met in Durham and Southern whites who met in Atlanta. The conference is "to convenant together for better co-operation, more positive and specific action, and for enduring ways and means for carrying out the recommendations." They have reason for confidence in the two co-chairmen, Guy Johnson of the University of North Carolina and Ira Reid of Atlanta University. Many Negroes deplore the isolation of the problem as a Southern regional affair, but they want the results that such a conference may achieve. They notice the stress on good manners and good will and on the absence of "any suggestion of threat and ultimatum," and may wonder just how these terms are defined; but they suspect that this forward step would not have been taken without the activity of organizations like the N.A.A.C.P. "We want those

[19] Odum, *op. cit.*, p. 199.

fellows to keep the heat on," a quiet Southern Negro preacher said to me.

On the national scene, wherever significant work is done to integrate the Negro into the war effort: in industry, in agriculture, in community planning, in the armed services, Negroes are cheered, and their morale rises accordingly. Sometimes discounted as drops in the bucket, these instances of integration might also be considered leaks in the levee, straws in the wind, or as the signposts I have frequently called them. If signposts, Negroes know that the longer, perhaps rougher journey lies ahead. They are therefore not in the mood for stopping, for laying over, for slowing up, or for detouring. And they do not want to be mere passengers, a sort of super-cargo, hitch-hikers being given a lift, guests being sped along. They want to do some of the map-reading and some of the driving. Thomas Sancton, a white Southerner who recognizes this truth, writes: "The real liberal knows that the Negro is never going to win any right he doesn't win for himself, by his own organization, courage, and articulation." [20]

The sticking point in the co-operation of Negro and Southern white liberals is segregation. The Atlanta Conference stepped gingerly about it: "We do not attempt to make here anything like a complete reply to the questions raised.... The only justification offered for [segregation] laws ... is that they are intended to minister to the welfare and integrity of both races." [21]

However segregation may be rationalized, it is essentially the denial of belonging. I believe that Negroes want segregation abolished. I realize that here, as so often elsewhere, it is presumptuous to talk of what *the* Negro wants. I understand that Negroes differ in their viewpoints toward segregation: the half-hand on a back county farm, the lost people on Arkansas plantations, the stevedore on Savannah docks, the coal miner in Birmingham, the cook-waitress-nurse in Charleston, the man-on-the-street in Waco, Los Angeles, New York, Boston, the government workers, the newspaper editors, the professional men, the spokesmen for pressure groups—all see segregation from different angles.

[20] Sancton, *op. cit.*, p. 15.
[21] Odum, *op. cit.*, p. 197.

An illiterate couple on Red River may differ greatly in attitude from their children on River Rouge. On the part of many there has been a long accommodation to segregation; but I believe that satisfaction with it has always been short.

An old railroad man in Birmingham, directing me to the FEPC hearings in the Federal Building, told me that whites and Negroes entered the court room by the same door (there was only one), but that they did not sit together. "No," he said. "They sits separate; whites on one side, the colored on the yother." Then he added, "And that's the way I'd ruther have it, too, ef'n I had my druthers. Of course I don't believe in scorning nobody, but——" He might have had memories of whites and Negroes "mixing socially," where the gains had all fallen to the whites, or where insult or violence had followed. But he knew, in spite of his "druthers," that segregation and scorn were bedfellows.

During Mr. Talmadge's campaign against the co-education of the races, one Georgia Negro college president gave white folks the assurance that "Negroes didn't want to attend the University of Georgia; all they wanted was a little school of their own." I found a young Negro Army doctor who sharply opposed the setting up of mixed military units, especially a mixed hospital. Only in an all Negro hospital, according to his experience, could a Negro physician function to the best of his ability, realize his full development, and be free from insult. He was nevertheless violently opposed to Jim Crow in transportation and public services.

I heard varying defenses of segregation, but I still did not find many supporters of it, even in the South. Of the many who had gained from it in safety, comfort, wealth and prestige, I found some who were candid enough to admit that in segregated schools, churches, lodges, banks, and businesses, they had risen higher than they might have risen in competition with whites. Many were fighting to improve their side of the bi-racial fence, to equalize teachers' salaries, to obtain buses for students, and for similar ends. But the fighting was not to buttress bi-racialism, but to make the most of a bad thing, to lessen the inferiority that segregation always seemed to mean. The young flyers at the seg-regated Tuskegee base trained rigorously to become first-rate fighting men, to prove that Negroes should be piloting planes; but their most fervent admirers, however proud of their achievement, would not say that they would have made a poorer record at an unsegregated base. And they would not deny that there were indignities at the segregated base.

A sign in Atlanta read: "This line marks the separation of the races which were [*sic*] mutually agreed to by both." My friend, certainly no hot-head but long "accommodated," interpreted it: "Mutual agreement. You know: a man puts his gun in your ribs and you put your pocketbook in his hands."

When the conference in Durham excluded Northern Negroes, many white Southerners (and Negroes, for that matter) were led to expect a conservative set of principles. As Benjamin Mays, an important member of the conference, states: "They were Negroes the whites of the South knew. They were not radicals. They were Negroes the South says it believes in and can trust." Yet the Durham charter went on record as fundamentally opposed to segregation, and Walter White considered the recommendations to be almost identical in language and spirit with those of the N.A.A.C.P. and the March-on-Washington movement.

A chief difference between Southern and Northern Negro spokesmen is not that one group defends and the other condemns segregation, but that Southern leaders, in daily contact with it, see it as deeply rooted; Northern leaders, not seeing it to be so widespread and knowing that occasionally it can be ripped out, do not see the long, sturdy tentacles. The dangers are that Southern Negroes will believe it ineradicable and that Northern Negroes will believe it can be easily uprooted by speeches and governmental decree.

At Negro mass meetings in the North, demands that racial segregation should be abolished, "that the Negro and the white must be placed on a plane of absolute political and social equality," have been roundly applauded. It is doubtful if even the orators themselves envisaged that their demands would be immediately or even soon forthcoming. Delegates from the South knew that on the return trip home, at St. Louis or Cincinnati or

Washington, they would be herded into the inferior Jim Crow coach; that if they wished to travel by bus they would be lucky even to get on, into the rear seats; that once home, Jim Crow would be all about them wherever they turned. Even Northern delegates knew where Jim Crow had caught hold in their communities.

Negroes know that more than stirring speeches will be needed to remove Jim Crow. But they also know another thing, on all levels and in all callings—whether an illiterate sharecropper comparing the one-room ramshackly school for his children with the brick consolidated school for the white children, or a college president who knows, in spite of the new brick buildings, how unequal a proportion of state funds has come to his school—Negroes recognize that Jim Crow, even under such high-sounding names as "bi-racial parallelism," means inferiority for Negroes. And most American whites know this too, and that is the way that many prefer it. As the beginning of one kind of wisdom, Negroes recognize that the phrase "equal but separate accommodations" is a myth. They have known Jim Crow a long time, and they know Jim Crow means scorn and not belonging.

What Negroes applauded from their orators, many recognized as a vision, the vision of a good thing. Though a dream, and difficult of achieving, it still was not wild and illogical. It made more sense than the reality: that in the world's leading democracy, democratic rights were withheld from one man out of every ten, not because he had forefeited his right to them, but because his skin was darker and his hair of a different texture from those of the other nine. The reality was that in a war against an enemy whose greatest crimes are based on spurious race thinking, this democracy indulged in injustice based on race thinking just as spurious.

This war is the Negro's war as much as it is anybody's. If the Axis were victorious, Negroes would be forced from the present second-class citizenship to slavery. Hitler's contempt for Negroes as apes and his sadistic treatment of Jews and all the conquered peoples, and Japan's brown Aryanism, similarly ruthless and arrogant, offer far less hope than America's system of democracy, bumbling though it may be, but still offering opportunity for protest and change. Even at the cost of the preservation of the *status quo*, this is still the Negro's war.

These are truisms. But they do not incite high morale. Indeed, they are somewhat like telling a man with a toothache that he should consider himself fortunate, since he might have a broken back. True, but his tooth still aches, and he wants something done for it.

This is even more the Negro's war, if it is truly a people's war, a war of liberation, aimed at establishing the Four Freedoms, ushering in the century of the common man, as the fine slogans have it. The Negro could do well with the Four Freedoms, especially the Freedoms from want and fear, for these two Freedoms have long been strangers to him. This is all the more the Negro's war if, as Michael Straight hopes, the peace will "guarantee to all of its citizens the right to constructive work at fair wages; to good low-cost housing; to minimum standards of nutrition, clothing, and medical care; to full opportunities for training and adult education; to real social security."

There is more cleverness than wisdom in the remark of John Temple Graves that asking for complete democracy at home is as logical as saying "that because America's house was on fire America must take the occasion for renovating the kitchen or putting Venetian blinds in the parlor." The trouble with the house is more serious than that; it really has much to do with the foundations. Wendell Willkie warns that:

> We cannot fight the forces and ideas of imperialism abroad and maintain any form of imperialism at home...We must mean freedom for others as well as ourselves, and we must mean freedom for everyone inside our frontiers as well as outside.[22]

Pearl Buck points out:

> Our democracy does not allow for the present division between a white ruler race and a subject colored race. If the United States is to include subject and ruler peoples, then let us be honest about it and change the Constitution and

[22] Wendell Willkie, *One World* (New York, 1943), p. 190 ff.

make it plain that Negroes cannot share the privileges of the white people. True, we would then be totalitarian rather than democratic.[23]

Daily reports of the violations of democracy crowd upon the Negro, breeding cynicism. Nevertheless, while denouncing them, he does so in the framework of democracy. He continually relies on America's professions of democracy as having some validity; he has not yet descended to the hopeless view that America prefers totalitarianism.

As has been so often stated: If America is to indoctrinate the rest of the world with democracy, it is logical to expect that the American Negro will share it at home. It may take a long time, but segregation must be abolished before there will be true democracy at home. True democracy will mean the right and opportunity to win respect for human worth. It can have no truck with Nazi concepts of race-supremacy, with Nazi contempt for people because of race. Democracy will mean equal pay for equal labor, equal employment opportunities, opportunities to learn and use technical skills and to advance according to mastery of them, and the right to join and participate fully in trade unions. The tentative beginning made by FEPC must be developed. Democracy will mean equal educational opportunities, equalized salaries for teachers, equalized facilities in the schools. The spread of the segregated system of education must be checked and eventually abolished as wasteful and unjust. Democracy will mean that the Federal Government will go on record against mob violence, for, in spite of the decline in lynching, threats of mob-violence are still powerfully coercive. Democracy will mean the discouraging of police brutality, will mean justice in the courts rather than patronizing clemency or cruel intolerance. Negroes will serve on the police force, at the lawyers' bar, in the jury docks, and on the judges' bench. Democracy will mean the franchise, with elimination of the poll tax and the subterfuges and intimidations that keep qualified Negroes from the polls. It will mean training Negroes to fulfill the duties of free citizens. Democracy will mean the strengthening and

[23] Pearl Buck, *American Unity and Asia* (New York, 1942), p. 15.

extension of the social legislation begun by the New Deal in such agencies as the Farm Security Administration and the Federal Housing Authority; and the opportunity not only to share in the benefits of such agencies but also in their planning and operation. Democracy will mean the opportunity to qualify for service in the armed forces in all its branches; the opportunity for whites and Negroes to fight side by side in mixed commands. Democracy will mean simply the opportunities for all Americans to share to the full extent of their capacities in the defense of America in war and the development of America in peace.

This is not much to ask for, since it is essentially what America guarantees to every white citizen. Only when viewed from the angle that these opportunities are to be extended to Negro citizens, does the list seem staggering, outrageous to some, foolishly idealistic and unattainable to many.

I think that most Negroes are not so optimistic that they foresee the overnight arrival of these opportunities. No group should know better that perfectly functioning democracy in the United States has always been a hope, rather than an actuality. Even in those sections where one undemocratic practice—legal segregation—has been missing, democracy—to whites as well as to Negroes—has not been simon-pure. The poverty of the South would be oppressive on both whites and Negroes even if segregation laws were stricken from the books, and discrimination from the practices, tomorrow. The Negro's plight in the South will be lightened substantially only when the plight of the poor white is enlightened; when these cannot be pitted against each other in contempt and hatred; when genuine democracy replaces the fictitious (and fictitious not only in the matter of race relations). Nevertheless, however Herculean the task, Negroes are not so defeatist that they think democracy to be unattainable. They are good Americans in nothing more than in their faith that "democracy *can* happen here." Worth fighting for in Europe, it is worth working for here. But since time does not stand still, all America—black and white—had better start to work for it. President Roosevelt, speaking of the Four Freedoms, has said: "Magna Carta, the Declaration of Independence, the Constitution of the United States, the Emancipation Proclamation and every other milestone in human progress—all were ideals which seemed impossible of attainment—yet they were attained." [24]

Negroes should not want fundamental rights of citizenship donated to them as largesse, and should not consider them as barter for loyalty, or service. American whites should not consider Negroes as beneficiaries, being accorded gifts that to men of different complexion are rights. Nor should they think of Negroes as passive objects of humanitarianism, since Negroes can really be allies in a common struggle for democracy. Even after Hitler and Tojo are defeated, democracy is going to need all of its strength to solve grave problems. The strength of the Negro will be as much needed and as useful in the coming economic and political crises as it is needed and should be useful now.

I believe that many Negroes realize this, and wish to be allowed to share in the sacrifice and travail and danger necessary to attain genuine democracy. Wendell Willkie's world trip excited him with "fresh proof of the enormous power within human beings to change their environment, to fight for freedom with an instinctive awakened confidence that with freedom they can achieve anything." [25] In times of frustration, Negroes would do well to recognize that power, and to understand that it fights on their side.

Negroes know they have allies. There are the numerous colored peoples of the world, the millions of yellow, brown, and black men in China, India, the Philippines, Malaysia, Africa, South America, the Caribbean, all over the globe, where hope for democracy is stirring a mighty ferment. Almost all are concerned with their own perplexities, but they agree in their fight against color prejudice. The success of the Soviet Union in destroying race prejudice gives hope and courage. And there are other allies abroad, in the smaller as well as the larger, the conquered as well as the unconquered nations, who are tied, not by a common urge to abolish race prejudice, but by the determination to be free. And in America there are allies too. It does not seem over-optimistic to believe them on the increase, although still

[24] Franklin D. Roosevelt, "The Four Freedoms," in Clayton Wheat, ed., *The Democratic Tradition in America* (Boston, 1943), p. 291.
[25] Willkie, *op. cit.*, p. 163.

outnumbered by the indifferent or the hostile. Negroes must join with these American allies, in the North and in the South, in a truly interracial program, or better, a democratic program. The minority must work with the men of good will in the majority. Negroes recognize their allies here without difficulty, and their affection for them runs strong and deep.

Americans, Negroes and whites, may believe that to achieve full democracy is arduous. It may well take a slow pull for a long haul. But it can no longer be postponed. American dreams have been realized before this, however difficult they seemed to the faint-hearted and sceptical. Americans, Negro and white, have mustered the doggedness and courage and intelligence needed. I have confidence in my own people that they will help achieve and preserve democracy, and will prove worthy of sharing it. But we must be counted in.

WHO'S WHO

Mary McLeod Bethune was born in Mayesville, South Carolina, on July 10, 1875. She was educated at Scotia College, North Carolina, 1888-1895, and at Moody Bible Institute, Chicago, 1895-1897. She is the recipient of many honorary degrees, including an A. M. from South Carolina State College and from Wilberforce University and an LL. D. from Howard, Atlanta, and Lincoln universities. She taught school in South Carolina, at Haines Institute in Augusta, Georgia, and in Palatka, Florida. In 1904 she started a school in Daytona Beach, Florida, which was merged in 1923 with Cookman Institute of Jacksonville to become Bethune-Cookman College. Mrs. Bethune served as President until 1942. She was also founder and first President of the Southeastern Federation of Colored Women; President of the National Association of Colored Women; Founder and President of the National Council of Colored Women. She is also on the board of many other national organizations. From 1936 to 1943 she was Director of the Division of Negro Work of the National Youth Administration. At the present time Mrs. Bethune is devoting her time to the National Council of Negro Women, which she founded in 1937. In 1935 she was awarded the Spingarn Medal and in 1936 the Francis A. Drexel Award, both for distinguished service to her race. In 1932 Ida M. Tarbell included her among the fifty greatest women in American history. In 1942 she was given the Thomas Jefferson award by the Southern Conference for Human Welfare.

Sterling A. Brown was born in Washington, D. C., May 1, 1901. Educated in the Washington schools, Williams College (A. B., Phi Beta Kappa, 1922) and Harvard University (A. M., 1923), he has taught at Virginia Seminary (Lynchburg), Fisk University, Lincoln University (Missouri), as visiting lecturer at Atlanta University and at New York University, and at Howard University where he is now Professor of English. From 1936 to 1939 he served as Editor on Negro Affairs for the Federal Writers' Project; in 1939 he was a staff member of the Carnegie-Myrdal Study of the Negro. He was a Guggenheim Fellow 1937-1938. He has contributed poetry, reviews, and essays to numerous publications. His books are *Southern Road* (1932), *The Negro in American Fiction* (1938), *Negro Poetry and Drama* (1938), and *The Negro Caravan* (1941) which he edited in collaboration with Arthur P. Davis and Ulysses G. Lee. He is now completing work on *A Negro Looks at the South.*

William Edward Burghardt Du Bois was born in Great Barrington, Massachusetts, on February 23, 1868. He was graduated A. B., Fisk University, 1888; A. B., 1890, A. M., 1891, and Ph. D., 1895, Harvard University. He also studied at the University of Berlin. From 1896 to 1910 Dr. Du Bois was Professor of Economics and History at Atlanta University, where he edited the *Atlanta University Studies*, 1897-1911. He was Director of Publicity of the National Association for the Advancement of Colored People, which developed out of the Niagara Movement of which he was one of the founders in 1905, and Editor-in-Chief of the *Crisis*, the official organ of the Association, from 1910 to 1932. He returned to Atlanta University and served as Professor of Sociology during 1932-1944. Dr. Du Bois, who was Spingarn Medalist in 1920, was the founder of the Pan-African Congress which met in Paris, 1919; in London, Brussels, and Paris, 1921; in London and Libson, 1923; in New York, 1927. In 1924 he was appointed Envoy Extraordinary and Minister Plenipotentiary to Liberia on the occasion of the inauguration of the President. In addition to contributions to the leading magazines, Dr. Du Bois has written *Suppression of the African Slave Trade* (1896); *The Philadelphia Negro* (1899); *The Souls of Black Folk* (1903); *John Brown* (1909); *Quest of the Silver Fleece* (1911); *The Negro* (1915); *Darkwater* (1920); *The Gift of Black Folk* (1924); *Dark Princess* (1927); *Black Reconstruction* (1935); *Black Folk: Then and Now* (1939); *Dusk of Dawn* (1940). He was, 1940-1944, editor of *Phylon, The Atlanta University Review of Race and Culture*, which he founded.

Gordon Blaine Hancock was born on June 23, 1884, at Ninety-Six, South Carolina. He received his A. B. at Benedict College, 1911, and a B. D. in 1912. He studied at Colgate University, 1918-1920, and took A. B., B. D., and A. M. degrees at Harvard University in 1919, 1920, and 1921, respectively. He has also studied at Cambridge and Oxford universities, and has traveled widely in Europe and the Near East. Benedict conferred a D. D. upon him in 1925. He served as Principal, Seneca Institute, South Carolina, from 1911 to 1918. Since 1921 he has been Professor of Economics and Sociology at Virginia Union University, Richmond. He has contributed articles to the *Journal of Social Forces* and other periodicals. Dr. Hancock was one of the founders of the movement that resulted in the establishment of the Southern Regional Council, Inc.

Leslie Pinckney Hill was born on May 14, 1880, in Lynchburg, Virginia. He was graduated from Harvard University A. B. (Phi Beta Kappa), 1903, and A. M., 1904. He taught at Tuskegee Institute from 1904 to 1907, and was Principal of Manassas Industrial Institute (Virginia) from 1907 to 1913. In 1913 he became Principal of the Institute for Colored Youth and its President when its name was changed to State Teachers College, Cheyney, Pennsylvania. Lincoln University conferred the degree of Litt. D. upon him in 1929 and Morgan an LL. D. in 1939. He is the founder and President of the Pennsylvania State Negro Council; a member of the Committee of National Council of Student Christian Associations of Work among Negro Colleges; of the National Y. M. C. A. Committee of Colored Work; of the Peace Section of the American Friends Service Committee; and of many other boards and committees. Dr. Hill has contributed articles to a number of educational magazines and is the author of the lyric poems, *The Wings of Oppression* (1927); a dramatic history, *Toussaint L'Ouverture* (1928); an idyl, *Marc Anders* (1933), and occasional poems.

Langston Hughes was born in Joplin, Missouri, on February 1, 1902. He was educated in the grammar schools of Topeka and Lawrence, Kansas, and Central High School, Cleveland. He studied one year at Columbia and was graduated from Lincoln University in 1929. His alma mater conferred upon him the degree of Litt. D. in 1943. He is a member of The Authors' Guild, the Dramatists' Guild, ASCAP, the Advisory Council of the Writers' War Board, the Music War Committee, and the board of the magazine *Common Ground*. Mr. Hughes has contributed to the *Saturday Evening Post, Survey Graphic, Esquire, New Yorker, Nation, New Republic, Crisis, Opportunity, Theatre Arts, Poetry,* and *Common Ground*. He wrote in collaboration with Clarence Muse the scenario for "Way Down South." His play, "Mulatto," ran for a year at the Vanderbilt Theatre, New York. "Don't You Want to be Free?" gave 135 performances at the Harlem Suitcase Theatre. His historical pageant, "For This We Fight," was presented at Madison Square Garden, June 7, 1943. His works, all published by Knopf, are *The Weary Blues, The Dream Keeper, Shakespeare in Harlem, The Ways of White Folks, Not Without Laughter* and his autobiography, *The Big Sea*.

Rayford Whittingham Logan was born in Washington, D. C., January 7, 1897. He was graduated from Williams College, A. B. (Phi Beta Kappa) in 1917; from Harvard University, A. M., 1932, and Ph. D. (history), 1936. He served as a first lieutenant in the A. E. F. in World War I. After studying and traveling in Europe until 1924 he taught history and modern languages at Virginia Union University, 1925-1930; history at Atlanta University, 1933-1938. Since 1938 he has been Professor of History at Howard University where he was also Acting Dean of the Graduate School from September, 1942, to January, 1944. He has contributed articles and reviews to the *Nation, Hispanic American Historical Review, Phylon, Inter-American Quarterly, World Tomorrow* and other journals and is the author of *The Diplomatic Relations of the United States with Haiti, 1776-1891* and of *The Operation of the Mandate System in Africa, with an Introduction on the Problem of the Mandates in the Post-War*

World. He has also edited *The Attitude of the Southern White Press toward Negro Suffrage, 1932-1940.* He is *Commandeur* of the Haitian National Order of Honor and Merit.

Frederick Douglass Patterson was born in Washington, D. C., October 10, 1901. He received the degree of D. V. M. from Iowa State College in 1923; M. S. from Iowa State College in 1927; Ph. D. from Cornell University, 1932. He has been awarded an LL. D. by Virginia State College; D. Humanities, Wilberforce University; and D. Sc., Lincoln University. He is a trustee of Tuskegee Institute, Fisk University, Hampton Institute, Booker T. Washington Agricultural and Industrial Institute of Liberia, Palmer Memorial College and Bethune-Cookman College. He taught at Virginia State College and Tuskegee and since 1935 has been President of Tuskegee. Dr. Patterson is a member of the Southern Education Foundation, the Executive Board of the National Urban League, the Southern Conference for Human Welfare, President Roosevelt's Commission on Farm Tenancy, the Southern Regional Council, and other boards. He is also serving as a Special Assistant to the Secretary of Agriculture. President Patterson has contributed articles to a number of journals.

Asa Philip Randolph was born in Crescent City, Florida, on April 15, 1889. He completed a high school course at Cookman Institute, Jacksonville, and studied political science and economics at the College of the City of New York. He worked as a waiter, elevator operator, and porter in New York City. In 1915 he and Mr. Chandler Owen launched *The Messenger,* "the only radical Negro magazine in America." Because of his militant opposition to World War I he was arrested but released after a few days. He became an Instructor in the Rand School of Social Science, New York, and in 1921 ran as the Socialist candidate for Secretary of State in New York. In 1917 he had organized a union of elevator operators in New York City and in August, 1925, he began the organization of the Brotherhood of Pullman Porters. *The Messenger* became its official publication. In 1934, after a long contest with the Pullman Company, the porters were brought within the scope of the amended Railway Labor Act. In 1937 he signed a contract with the Pullman Company for the porters. He served as President of the National Negro Congress, 1939-1940. As Chairman of the National Committee for March on Washington, he directed the negotiations that resulted in the President's Executive Order 8802 against racial discrimination in war industries. Howard University conferred upon him the degree of Litt. D. in 1941. Mr. Randolph has contributed articles to many publications. At the present time he is President of the Brotherhood of Pullman Porters, AFL, and of the National March on Washington Movement.

George S. Schuyler was born in Providence, Rhode Island, on February 25, 1895. He has contributed articles to the *American Mercury, American Spectator, Common Ground, Crisis, Globe, Nation, New Masses, Opportunity*, and *Spirit of Missions*. He also writes a column and editorials for the *Pittsburgh Courier.* Mr. Schuyler has written *Black No More* (1931) and *Slaves Today* (1931). At the present time he is Associate Editor of the *Pittsburgh Courier* and of *The African.*

Willard S. Townsend was born in Cincinnati, Ohio, December 4, 1895. He was graduated from Walnut Hills High School of that city in 1912. After serving in the army during World War I, he was commissioned a lieutenant in the Ohio National Guard. He took pre-medical work at the University of Toronto and received a degree in chemistry after two years of further study at the Royal Academy of Science. He has been awarded an LL.D. by Wilberforce University. After teaching for a brief period in a Texas high school, he worked as a Red Cap in Chicago. Four years later, 1936, he was elected Vice President of the Chicago local, which had just been organized into a federal local of the AFL. The following year Mr. Townsend was elected President of the independent International Brotherhood of Red Caps, which in 1940 changed its name to the United Transport Service Employees of America. This organization, which has jurisdiction over many other railway service employees, affiliated with the CIO in 1942. Mr. Townsend is a member of the General

Executive Board of the CIO; Secretary of the CIO Committee to Abolish Race Discrimination; a member of the Board of Directors of the National Urban League, of the Mayor's Committee on Race Relations (Chicago), and of many other local and national boards and committees.

Charles H. Wesley was born December 2, 1891, in Louisville, Kentucky. He received his bachelor's degree from Fisk University in 1911; his master's degree from Yale University in 1913; and his doctor's degree (history) from Harvard University in 1925. During 1930-1931 he was a Guggenheim Fellow in London. From 1913 to 1942 he served as Instructor, Assistant Professor, Associate Professor, Professor and Head of the Department of History at Howard University. From 1938 to 1942 he was also Dean of the Graduate School. Since September, 1942, he has been President of Wilberforce University, Wilberforce, Ohio. Dr. Wesley served in the Army Y. M. C. A. during World War I, and was a Pastor and Presiding Elder in the A. M. E. Church from 1918 to 1938. He is a Trustee of Fisk University and a member of many local and national boards and committees. Dr. Wesley has contributed articles and reviews to many scholarly journals and is the author of *Negro Labor in the United States, 1850-1925* (1927); *The History of Alpha Phi Alpha* (four editions, 1930, 1934, 1939, 1942); *Richard Allen* (1935); *The Collapse of the Confederacy* (1938); and a *Manual of Research and Thesis for Graduate Students* (1941).

Doxey A. Wilkerson was born in Excelsior Springs, Missouri, April 24, 1905. He attended the public schools of Kansas City, Missouri, and completed his high school work in Kansas City, Kansas. He was graduated from the University of Kansas, A. B., 1926, and A. M., 1927. After teaching English and Education at Virginia State College, he served on the faculty of Howard University from 1935 to 1943. For a year he was Education Specialist with the OPA, a position which he resigned on June 15, 1943, to join the Communist Party and become its educational director for Maryland and the District of Columbia. He was National

Vice-President of the American Federation of Teachers from 1937 to 1940 and later an active member of the United Federal Workers of America, CIO. In 1943 he was elected Vice-President of the International Labor Defense. He is now Executive Editor of *People's Voice* and a member of the National Committee of the newly organized Communist Political Association. Mr. Wilkerson has contributed articles to many journals, is the author of *Special Problems of Negro Education* (1939), and contributed a chapter to J. S. Roucek's *Sociological Foundations of Education* (1941).

Roy Wilkins was born August 30, 1901, in St. Louis, Missouri. He received the degree of A. B. from the University of Minnesota in 1923, majoring in journalism and sociology. From 1923 to 1931 he was Managing Editor of the *Kansas City Call*. Since 1931 he has been Assistant Secretary of the National Association for the Advancement of Colored People and since 1934 has also served as Editor of the *Crisis*, the official organ of the organization. Mr. Wilkins has contributed articles to *Magazine Digest*, the (M. E.) *Methodist Social Service Bulletin* and to many other publications.